Knowledge, Power, and Discipline

Contradictions

Edited by Craig Calhoun, Social Science Research Council

Volume 19 Pier Carlo Bontempelli, *Knowledge, Power, and Discipline: German Studies and National Identity*

Volume 18 Elizabeth Jelin, *State Repression and the Labors of Memory*

Volume 17 Gil Eyal, *The Origins of Postcommunist Elites: From Prague Spring to the Breakup of Czechoslovakia*

Volume 16 Alan Milchman and Alan Rosenberg, editors, *Foucault and Heidegger: Critical Encounters*

Volume 15 Michael D. Kennedy, *Cultural Formations of Postcommunism: Emancipation, Transition, Nation, and War*

Volume 14 Michèle H. Richman, *Sacred Revolutions: Durkheim and the Collège de Sociologie*

Volume 13 Pierre-André Taguieff, *The Force of Prejudice: On Racism and Its Doubles*

Volume 12 Krishan Kumar, *1989: Revolutionary Ideas and Ideals*

Volume 11 Timothy Mitchell, editor, *Questions of Modernity*

Volume 10 Giovanni Arrighi and Beverly J. Silver, *Chaos and Governance in the Modern World System*

Volume 9 François Dosse, *History of Structuralism, Volume 2: The Sign Sets, 1967–Present*

Volume 8 François Dosse, *History of Structuralism, Volume 1: The Rising Sign, 1945–1966*

Volume 7 Patricia Hill Collins, *Fighting Words: Black Women and the Search for Justice*

Volume 6 Craig Calhoun and John McGowan, editors, *Hannah Arendt and the Meaning of Politics*

Volume 5 Gérard Noiriel, *The French Melting Pot: Immigration, Citizenship, and National Identity*

Volume 4 John C. Torpey, *Intellectuals, Socialism, and Dissent: The East German Opposition and Its Legacy*

Volume 3 T. M. S. Evens, *Two Kinds of Rationality: Kibbutz, Democracy, and Generational Conflict*

Volume 2 Micheline R. Ishay, *Internationalism and Its Betrayal*

Volume 1 Johan Heilbron, *The Rise of Social Theory*

Knowledge, Power, and Discipline

German Studies and National Identity

Pier Carlo Bontempelli

Translated by Gabriele Poole

Contradictions, Volume 19

University of Minnesota Press
Minneapolis
London

Originally published as *Storia della germanistica: Dispositivi e istituzioni di un sistema disciplinare* (Rome: Artemide Edizioni, 2000). Copyright 2000 Artemide Edizioni, Rome, Italy.

Published by the University of Minnesota Press
111 Third Avenue South, Suite 290
Minneapolis, MN 55401-2520
http://www.upress.umn.edu

Library of Congress Cataloging-in-Publication Data

Bontempelli, Pier Carlo.
[Storia della germanistica. English]
Knowledge, power, and discipline : German studies and national identity / Pier Carlo Bontempelli ; translated by Gabriele Poole.
p. cm. — (Contradictions ; v. 19)
Includes bibliographical references and index.
ISBN 0-8166-4111-0 (alk. paper) — ISBN 0-8166-4112-9 (pbk. : alk. paper)
1. Germany—Civilization—Study and teaching—Italy—History.
2. National characteristics, German. I. Title. II. Contradictions (Minneapolis, Minn.) ; 19.
DD61 .B633 2003
943'.007'2—dc22

2003014231

Printed in the United States of America on acid-free paper

12 11 10 09 08 07 06 05 04 10 9 8 7 6 5 4 3 2 1

In that Empire, the craft of Cartography attained such Perfection that the Map of a Single province covered the space of an entire City, and the Map of the Empire itself an entire Province. In the course of Time, these Extensive maps were found somehow wanting, and so the College of Cartographers evolved a Map of the Empire that was of the same Scale as the Empire and that coincided with it point for point. Less attentive to the Study of Cartography, succeeding Generations came to judge a map of such Magnitude cumbersome, and, not without Irreverence, they abandoned it to the Rigours of sun and Rain.

Jorge Luis Borges, "Of Exactitude in Science,"
in *A Universal History of Infamy*

Captain Jonathan
Found a pelican
On an island in the Far East.

In the morning
Jonathan's pelican
Laid an egg all round and white.

Out of the egg
Came another pelican
That resembled the first a lot.

In its turn
The second pelican
Laid another round white egg.

And predictably
One more pelican
Came out and laid one more white egg.

This story could go on forever
Unless someone makes an omelet.

Robert Desnos, "The Pelican,"
in *Chantefleurs, Chantefables*

Contents

Acknowledgments

Acknowledgments might provide the object for an interesting study of the relations of domination that preside over the conduct of those who have just completed a scholarly work. Even in such an apparently "neutral" situation, they tend to express, with varying degrees of awareness, a strategy of self-legitimation: gratitude as an opportunity for evoking illustrious names as witness to one's filiation to great masters and to one's belonging to a lineage or a school.

Since my object in this book is to describe the relation of power and knowledge, I certainly cannot afford to neglect the heterogeneous forces and motivations interacting in the field of acknowledgments. Hence, my embarrassment in acknowledging my actual debts and expressing my very real gratitude to a number of scholars, friends, and scholar friends, lest my acknowledgments be read as either self-interested or perfunctory.

Having thus declared my ambivalence, I wish to thank, in no particular order, all the friends who have variously helped me while I was writing this book, and I shall leave to each the task of recollecting the motives (sometimes remote) for my mentioning them: Gerd Simon, Vanda Perretta, Alfonso Berardinelli, Simona Gasparetti, Ute Lipka, Andrea Landolfi, Klaus-Dieter Goll, Gabriele Poole, Carlo Martinez, and Sonia Di Loreto.

This book was first published in Italian as *Storia della germanistica: Dispositivi e istituzioni di un sistema disciplinare* (Rome: Artemide Edizioni, 2000). I thank my Italian publisher, Vincenzo Innocenti Furina, for believing in this project from the beginning and for granting permission to republish it in English. The introduction has been written expressly for this English edition, and other parts of the book have been slightly revised and updated.

I thank Cesare Casarino for his perceptive reading of the Italian version of my book. His insight detected even those meanings and intentions that had not been explicitly spelled out, and his comments and suggestions have been crucial for this English edition.

I thank Jack Zipes not just for his generous assessment of this work, which he has encouraged and helped in countless ways at every stage of its publication, but even more for the rare gift he has liberally offered, the friendship of a committed scholar and a generous human being.

Finally, I wish to thank Donatella Izzo for originally providing the theoretical framework that helped me construct my own vantage point for viewing German Studies—and for more reasons, both personal and professional, than I can really be expected to explain here.

Introduction

The Metamorphoses of Domination and the Subject of German Studies

The purpose of this book is to analyze German Studies as a disciplinary system. Accordingly, this is not a historical account of representative authors, currents, and methods, but a critical history addressing the institutional and exclusionary practices that have constituted and established German Studies as a discipline. As should be clear from my title, the theoretical framework of my study has been provided by the works of Michel Foucault and Pierre Bourdieu, whose critical insights have helped me define my object and offered the conceptual tools for my investigation and interpretation of the history and development of German Studies.

Having thus briefly stated the scope and object of my work, let me now outline in more detail the discursive context that frames it, the questions that it addresses, and the circumstances—both personal and historical—that have produced it. In other words, let me justify the need, not at all to be taken for granted, for yet another book on German Studies.

Indeed, the question of German Studies as a discipline is by no means a new one. In the fields of both research and teaching, it has undergone severe criticism and self-criticism for the past three decades or more. The defeat of the Third Reich and the related downfall of its educational system and its apparatus for the production and circulation of culture might well have engendered a generalized process of self-analysis and self-criticism on the part of German Studies—a discipline whose nationalistic values and assumptions had been fully compatible, and in many cases complicitous, with National Socialist cultural politics. Such a process was in fact begun by a few scholars in 1945; but soon the Cold War and the rise of two different German states embodying two conflicting political and ideological systems put an end to all efforts toward reform and critical revision and reinstated the existing values and structures, bracketing National Socialism as merely an accidental episode in the history of German Studies. The issue of a critical reexamination of German Studies and its complicities with the Nazi regime was raised again in 1966 at the Munich Congress, and the critical process gained new momentum in 1968, when the student movement radically questioned all forms of knowledge and all institutions entrusted with its production and reproduction, viewing them as inherently complicitous with power and domination in the bourgeois capitalist system. My own project is in some ways a belated fruit of that political moment and of its subversive thrust toward unmasking the relations between knowledge and power—a task that the theoretical works of Foucault and Bourdieu (themselves, as is well known, closely connected to the 1968 movement) undoubtedly performed with greater sophistication over the years that followed.

Even the sweeping political and ideological critique produced by the 1968 movement, as I shall argue later, failed to affect the disciplinary structure of German Studies. However, 1968 was certainly in many ways a turning point in the history of the discipline. In the years that followed, under the favorable new national and international political circumstances, a reformist approach to the whole question of academia prevailed. A new, more socially heterogeneous student body went to universities in unprecedented numbers; new disciplines and methodological approaches enriched and renovated German culture at large; new and valuable work was produced on noncanonical authors, themes, and fields hitherto neglected by orthodox German Studies. As a result of these critical efforts, new texts and sources have been made available on German literature and culture, as well as on German Studies itself. Archives and specialized institutions have been established, such as the Arbeitsstelle für die Erforschung der Geschichte der Germanistik (the Workplace for the Research of the History of German Studies, established in 1972) and the Marbacher Arbeitskreis für Geschichte der Germanistik (the Marbach Circle of Work for the History of German Studies, established in 1989), which have collected a wealth of documents and letters invaluable for a reconstruction of the history of the discipline. The fall of the Berlin Wall in 1989 gave further impetus to this process of historical reconstruction and analysis, both by unifying the energies and efforts of Eastern and Western German scholars and by opening a large number of state archives, previously inaccessible for political or security reasons and containing valuable documents and information about ministries, universities, academies, secret services, and other relevant institutions involved in the cultural policies of the various successive German states.

The 1990s saw the publication of a number of important and wide-ranging works on German Studies, the fruit of two decades of self-reflective efforts: Klaus Weimar's *Geschichte der deutschen Literaturwissenschaft bis zum Ende des neunzehnten Jahrhunderts* (1989); *Wissenschaftsgeschichte der Germanistik im 19. Jahrhundert,* edited by Jürgen Fohrmann and Wilhelm Voßkamp (1994); Jost Hermand's *Geschichte der Germanistik* (1994), particularly valuable in that it militantly addresses present perspectives and methodological controversies; and *Wissenschaftsgeschichte der Germanistik in Porträts,* edited by Christoph König, Hans-Harald Müller, and Werner Röcke (2000).[1] To these more general works might be added countless monographs focused on various themes and specific moments in the history of German Studies, such as the links between individual career performances and the institutional conditions that to some extent determine them; competition and conflict between scientific schools; corporate resistance to external cultural situations; and the relations between the discipline, on the one hand, and the political agencies or aims of states, parties, and social groups, on the other. These new investigations of German Studies as an organized discipline and of its relationship with the outside world are doubtless fruitful since, as Jürgen Fohrmann has noted, they allow German Studies to go beyond critiquing the mere ideology of German Studies and to frame that critique within a new theoretical context of its organizational, productive, and functional aspects.[2] This approach makes possible new investigations that are based on methodological tools taken from a variety of fields and explore a wider range of issues beyond the traditional boundaries of the discipline, as witness the monumental *Wissenschaftsgeschichte der Germanistik im 19. Jahrhundert* (1994), edited by Fohrmann in collaboration with Wilhelm Voßkamp.

Why, then, have I written this book, when so many original and important contributions have recently been produced on the history of German Studies? I shall try to answer this question by framing it in the twofold context of German Studies and of my own development as a Germanist.

In 1991, Peter Uwe Hohendahl, an astute critic of the history of German Studies, remarked that in spite of the intense production of new discourses in German Studies, a prohibition (or perhaps a decision) still seemed to be operating, demanding "the exclusion of the question of power (in Foucault's sense)" and the neglect of an analytical investigation of "the relation between knowledge and power."[3] After a decade, the issue raised by Hohendahl still seems to be largely evaded by German Studies, with only a few exceptions; or, rather, the question of the relation between knowledge and power may be said to be haunting the field of the discipline as a powerful but repressed ghost. This book is first and foremost an attempt to address that question, and I shall now try to situate it more precisely by outlining the historical contingencies and political urgencies that dictated my choice of both subject and method of inquiry.

While German Studies as an institution was responding to larger historical events, my own individual path to disciplinary self-reflection was decisively affected by minor, but to me very significant, microhistorical events. The fall of the Berlin Wall in 1989 had prompted me to reflect on the great potentialities that the new situation offered for the development and expansion of a particular individual freedom like the academic freedom of teaching and researching once teachers and researchers were no longer burdened by the limits and conditionings created by the harsh rivalry and competition between the two German states. The peaceful reunification of Germany, meant to create freedom for all, seemed, however, to be producing paradoxical consequences precisely in the field that I was professionally more interested in, the field of university teaching and research. Freedom, after having triumphed on the political and historical plane, seemed to be advancing with difficulty on the terrain of the production and reproduction of academic knowledge. As is well known, the reunification of Germany also meant the unification of its two distinct university systems. This process involved the creation of committees of professors from former West Germany charged with evaluating the scientific qualifications of their colleagues from former East Germany in order to make decisions about the possibility of rehiring them to work at the new unified German universities.[4] Perhaps there was no other legal way to achieve the integration of the faculties of the two states. Probably if the reverse had been true and West Germany had been annexed to East Germany, committees would also have been formed in order to produce equally arbitrary evaluations. What struck me, however, was the idea that in the face of such an epoch-making event as the German reunification one should resort to a procedure of exclusion or legitimation to reinstate academics to their corporation. A multitude of scholars and thinkers, particularly in the humanities, had to undergo an "evaluation" *(Evaluierung)* in order to keep their posts.[5] It was as if, for instance, all the members of the Collège de France or a group of French thinkers like Foucault, Bourdieu, Lacan, Derrida, Lyotard, Nora, Fumaroli, Augé, and so on, had had to be assessed by other colleagues in order not to be dismissed because of some dramatic new development in the political situation of their country.

The symbolic complexity of that act, where power and knowledge seemed to be inextricably intertwined, first led me to meditate on the arbitrary character of the values and procedures adopted under such circumstances. A personal episode may further illustrate my point. Shortly after the reunification, I attended a conference in Germany, where I found myself sitting between two prominent figures in German Studies: one was from West Germany and was a member of an evaluation committee; the other was from East Germany and was being evaluated by the committee on which the former sat. At the time I was not aware of this; I came to know about it only a few months later. But even then, during the conference sessions and in between, during informal lunches, dinners, and conversations, a relation of power and subordination was manifest between the two scholars, equally eminent until a few months before; and their mutual attitude made it impossible to doubt which was the judger and which the judged. It was an exemplary situation of symbolic violence where one individual had been socially legitimated to exert power over another according to utterly arbitrary parameters. In other words, the criteria on which the respective positions of judger and judged were based were not those traditionally paraded by German Studies—classicism, Goethe, Schiller, Mann, Brecht, and whatever other subjects have made up its history. Until a few months before, no one could have demonstrated the superiority of one scholar over the other on "objective" and "scientific" grounds; their respective positions at that time were based exclusively on a power relation. Let me add that in this particular case there was a "happy ending": having passed the evaluation, the scholar from East Germany has been reinstated to his former rank of equality with his judge. But that episode revealed to me the operation of symbolic violence and domination and the arbitrary character of power, even when legitimately exerted. I was also struck by another element of the situation: the fact that the modern state, while retaining an unprecedented power over most aspects of contemporary life, when it came to intervening in the reproduction of knowledge had to defer to the independent power of the academic body and to its prerogatives. One of those prerogatives was that of co-opting its members according to criteria for which it was accountable only to the scientific community itself, in this case, that of assessing the degree of compatibility of scholars and scientists from East Germany with the scientific community of unified Germany. The two scholars whom I encountered were, then, emblematic characters in an allegory of academic power, as it were, representing orthodoxy's control over the production of discourses and the processes of legitimation necessary to speak authoritatively within the institution. Those processes—apparently, merely "technical" and limited to a particular emergency in national life—were in fact violently arbitrary and were an integral part of the academic institution. Two hundred years of disciplinary history—with all its accompanying sacred, necessary, and everlasting values—were thus condensed into a symbolic triumph of the arbitrariness of power. This realization led me to reflect on the history and present situation of my own discipline, German Studies, and to focus my attention on the interweaving of knowledge and power that has constituted it.

From this new perspective, all existing histories of German Studies seemed to share a common characteristic. Even those works that address the institutional and material conditions of the discipline have been produced from inside the institution, taking for granted its unspoken assumptions. They are based, in other words, on what might be called a methodological pluralism, partly because some of them are collective and therefore internally articulated works, but much more because they share the basic assumption that the history of German Studies is itself its own object. In this view, German Studies keeps thinking itself in different terms; it keeps "interpreting" itself, that is, regarding itself as the coherent development of an original disciplinary core that has been enlarged and enriched along the way. The underlying unity of the discipline allows it to keep its inherent identity even while adopting new perspectives and dealing with heteronomous themes. However complex and varied their reconstruction, the point of view these works adopt is still the point of view of the discipline itself, and the process they describe is a linear one. From a point of origin that I would term, in Foucault's words, a "site of truth" *(lieu de la verité),* the order of things and of concepts unfolds according to an immanent teleology.[6] From this spotless, self-mirroring original identity, a devotion to truth and methodological rigor is engendered that in turn produces knowledge and unconditional love for orthodoxy (that is, the original core of knowledge, to be scrupulously kept and reproduced by the adepts). This historical foundation grounds a seamless reality that admits of no ruptures or lateral dashes, but only of different interpretations of the same essence.

What was needed, then, was a bit of lateral thinking, which would create a new vantage point. In my case, this was provided by Foucault's concept of genealogy, as expressed in his well-known essay "Nietzsche, Genealogy, History." In Foucault's view, genealogy is opposed to continuity, metaphysical laws, and general essences; it eschews the search for depth and describes the past in order to critique the teleological construction of history and of histories. It warns us against historical truths: they are ideas devoid of essence, efforts to bestow unity on one's representations of the world. Even interpretation—a key word for anyone who studies humanities in the modern age—leads to no deeper understanding of deeper meanings. Interpretations do not lie in the essence of things; they have been created and imposed from the outside, and hence, they have a necessary relation with history and with the operation of power: "If interpretation were the slow exposure of a meaning hidden in an origin, then only metaphysics could interpret the development of humanity. But if interpretation is the violent or surreptitious appropriation of a system of rules, which in itself has no essential meaning, in order to impose a direction, to bend it to a new will, to force its participation in a different game, and to subject it to secondary rules, then the development of humanity is a series of interpretations" (151–52).

Genealogy records and reveals the history of these interpretations. Rules, norms, paradigms, scientific objectivity, systems, and universals all reside in a space or, in Pierre Bourdieu's terms, in a field of forces determined not by essences but by social relations and practices. The genealogist's task is revealing "the various systems of subjection: not the anticipatory power of meaning, but the hazardous play of dominations" (148). Where others have seen progress, seriousness, and necessity, the genealogist sees power relations and the play of domination. This perspective implies focusing on the operation of arbitrariness and domination present everywhere in human life and history and congealed into rituals that impose rules and obligations, establish and administer proper procedures, and discipline and punish conduct in every field of life as well as—what interests me here—in the field of knowledge and its production.

Foucault, then, helped me reconceive the discourses and cultural practices that were the object of my work as a closely knitted network of power and knowledge, a field crisscrossed by the partially autonomous trajectories of individual and group responses. This enabled me to overcome my epistemological impasse by adopting a finally subjective, rather than allegedly objective, perspective on the social processes that had in the first place defined me as a scholar within the specific field of German Studies. By positing myself as a subject aware of his own subjection, I could finally refuse to subject myself to it, at least to some degree and within the limits of my own subjectivity. Simultaneously, I was also aware that the way out of the hermeneutic boundaries of German Studies could not lie in replacing one truth with another or in disengaging truth from power, since the two were in principle indistinguishable. What one could do, though, was take as a starting point the analysis of the modes of production of orthodox knowledge and investigate the ways in which that knowledge was always already involved with power in a variety of forms from the very beginning: in the case of German Studies, from the foundation of Berlin University in Prussia in 1810.

As a result of this perspective "from below," that is, from the vantage point of a consciously subjected subject, the focus of my inquiry shifted from the representative authors, the main currents and methods, the unveiling of essential truths of German Studies, to the development of the mechanisms and procedures that legitimized German Studies as a discipline at the beginning of the nineteenth century. The conceptual tools for my investigation were provided by Foucault's analytics of power in its manifold articulations: his critique of history and philology; his analysis of discursive formations and "discourse societies" as closed, self-referential communities validating utterances in terms of coherence with their internal norms rather than truth value; his inquiry into the places and ways whereby disciplinary power is enacted in the modern age; his introduction of the notion of *"dispositif"* (apparatus), that is, a set of coherent discursive *and* material practices that organize both social reality in its actual operation and the ways it is understood and represented. Without this theoretical scaffolding, which I illustrate as I unfold my argument in the chapters that follow, my project would have been very different, or rather it would never have been completed at all.

Along with Foucault's theoretical work, the work of another lately deceased French thinker has had a decisive impact on my project. The sociological work of Pierre Bourdieu has provided me with both the general framework and the specific terminology I needed to conceptualize and analyze a complex social institution such as the modern university, its practices, and its manifold articulations with the outside world. Bourdieu's studies on the institutional establishment and operation of power in general, and academic power in particular, have helped me dissect and analyze the constitutive acts and documents of German Studies and its gradual consolidation; his analysis of the self-reproduction mechanisms of the university as an institution and of the characters of professorial power as a social and cultural practice, along with the related notions of "habitus," "cultural arbitrary," "symbolic violence," *"illusio,"* "heritage," and "cultural capital," all play a cardinal role in the unfolding of my argument. Indeed, as will be seen in the individual chapters, they constitute the very terrain where my argument unfolds.

As the inevitable result of the theoretical framework I have adopted, my work does not aim at producing a correct historical reconstruction and interpretation of the history of German Studies from a purportedly neutral and objective point of view. Neither is it my object to offer some interpretations as intrinsically more valuable than others: the very process of interpretation pretends to appropriate and employ a set of rules, submitting them to an individual will and strategy, and thus to unveil the truth. Rather, I have tried to record the emergence of individual interpretations in their contingency and then their conversion into ideal significances and absolute truths. My interest lies in reconstructing the social practices, the interplay of power and knowledge, that has produced a specific disciplinary technology endowed with specific original characters. It has been pointed out to me that this is an unusual and unsuitable object for a history of German Studies. So let me state again explicitly, as I did at the beginning, that it has never been my intention to write a history of German Studies. Rather, I have attempted to investigate the operation of a disciplinary system—in Foucault's sense of the expression—that has confronted all sorts of historical crises and faced severe criticism and self-criticism, but still has managed to keep its apparatus virtually unscathed. Self-criticism, however honest and uncompromising it may be, can hardly touch a corporation that, like a veritable "discourse society," has repeatedly closed ranks in defense of the existing state of things. Even the present trend toward self-reflection in German Studies, when regarded in the light of historicism rather than genealogy, can be presented as the final achievement in the universal progress of historical reason. And the huge projects of historical self-reconstruction that have characterized German Studies in the past few years have been produced, with few exceptions, from an inside and institutionally hallowed perspective; their method has been the careful accumulation of an ever-increasing amount of minute detail and information whose overall effect is one of self-complacent monumentalization.

This is hardly surprising if one regards this phenomenon as one episode in a lasting chain of patrilineal identifications and hereditary successions that have constituted the caste of Germanists as such. Viewing oneself as the worthy and legitimate representative of a corporation is precisely the result of relations of domination and disciplining practices that lastingly impress norms and values, along with rights and obligations, on the disciplined subject. Whoever adopts the reassuring point of view inscribed in the identity thus acquired is ipso facto heir to a cultural patrimony and draws legitimacy and consecration from it; simultaneously, though, he is inevitably bound to stay within the limits of a historicist and teleological perspective. Accepting a genealogical perspective, on the other hand, implies a priori renouncing the effort to demonstrate the progressive, objective, and "serious" character of the discipline's history, highlighting instead its arbitrary quality, its procedures of domination and submission, and the power-knowledge compound on which the notion of "serious" science is founded.

Accordingly, my account is aimed not at retrospectively justifying the rightness and inevitability of the discipline's development, but, quite the reverse, at foregrounding the mechanisms of choice and domination operating at every turn in its history. My argument is based on the pragmatic acts and the official and unofficial documents that produced and accompanied the institutional establishment of the discipline, then secured its status by firmly grounding it in a set of fixed principles while providing it with a definite trajectory and direction. These ensured the survival of German Studies and its capacity for cultural reproduction, but also proved effective in blocking all alternative paths for its development.

The "evaluation" of the East German scholar I mentioned earlier was, in this sense, nothing but another link in the continuity of disciplinary history. The right and duty to independently train and select scholars, thus reproducing its principles through the generations and ensuring the orthodoxy of individual statements, has been an integral part of German Studies since it was first established as an institution. The main foundational act establishing German Studies as a system was the creation and consistent adoption of what Foucault calls a "disciplinary apparatus," that is, a coherent system of heterogeneous practices, both discursive and material: scientific statements, institutions, rules of behavior, regulations concerning the use of space, laws, philosophical propositions, moral norms, material rewards, and so on. These diverse actions and regulations operate as a single apparatus and constitute, organize, and rule subjects along the lines of a power-knowledge system. In the case of German Studies, as I have tried to show, these include the philological statute of the discipline (a direct filiation from classical philology), defining the correct hierarchical and patrilineal modes for the transmission of knowledge; the respecting of a number of moral norms that collectively define the philological ethos and ensure the separateness, distinction, and perpetuation of the caste; and disciplinary power as exercised through practices of training, selection, normalization, hierarchization, and centralization, resulting in the subject's enduring acquisition of a habitus (a habit, a frame of mind, an attitude, and a role) capable of perpetuating the original identity of the discipline through the generations. This institutional foundation, which elevated a few sanctioned forms of knowledge to axiomatic status, became in turn the basis for a normalization of the contents of knowledge through the operation of a process of systematic discarding and removal of falsity and nonknowledge, that is, the knowledge of laymen and amateurs, those who, outside the corporation, are by that very fact not entitled to speak.

This relentless sifting process—to some extent paradoxical in one of the human sciences, by definition endowed with an uncertain epistemological status—is a peculiar feature of German Studies: other academic disciplines, such as Romance Languages or English Literature, though they share other features with German Studies, have undergone quite different evolutions. This is due to the different functions they performed in the national pedagogic system, where—for reasons that I will try to make clear—German Studies played a decisive role from the outset, and consequently to the different relation other academic disciplines had with modern power and its technologies. In the field of German Studies a veritable "discourse police" was operating, controlling statements and their enunciation and acting at all levels of the scholarly community from the very inception of its institutional existence. This effective way of sorting out statements and excluding nonconforming ones has secured for the discipline a remarkable capacity for self-reproduction in a virtually endless perpetuation of its statute, paradigms, and canon, since the corporation has been solely in charge of selecting and rearing the new disciples.

The continuity of the discipline through the succeeding generations and historical events, then, has been guaranteed by the existence of a system of beliefs shared by all its disciples. This might be termed, in Bourdieu's words, a "cultural arbitrary," a notion defining a cluster of shared norms, functions, and values that are represented and reproduced as objective truths and employed by and in the interest of a dominant class or group. Having identified the main features of the cultural arbitrary of German Studies, as just outlined, I have focused on the disciplinary technologies employed to inculcate it, that is, on the procedures that create the lasting habitus of the professor, establish a close connection between philology and ethics (philology as a lifestyle), determine the norms regulating the training and cooptation of younger scholars, valorize cultural heritage, and foster its accumulation as cultural capital. No form of compulsion is more effective than the symbolic one: the symbolic violence of pedagogical action, as Bourdieu argues and as I have tried to show, is more lasting than any other action (e.g., political violence or the repressive violence of a state) because, as long as it can operate independently, it keeps producing and reproducing its own reproducers and the conditions for its own reproduction. This explains the survival of the apparatus and values of German Studies virtually intact even through dramatic historical junctures such as two world wars and the creation and fall of different regimes.

Having thus outlined the methodological framework of my work and the theoretical and political questions it addresses, I shall now briefly sketch the organization of its argument. The nine chapters of this book present some crucial stages in the definition of the disciplinary identity of German Studies, starting in 1810, when the University of Berlin was established. Throughout the book I focus on exemplary situations and turning points and highlight the basic unity and continuity of the discipline both in its underlying assumptions and in its disciplinary technologies. Chapter 1 examines the emergence of German Studies from classical philology and the ensuing creation of its habitus, modeled on the assimilation of national philology to classical philology. While this has often been presented as a necessary and inevitable development, I emphasize the alternative options confronting German Studies at its birth: founding its identity on a liberal political commitment to the emerging German nation or grounding its legitimacy in the academic domain by modeling it on the philological "science" of classical antiquity as propounded by Karl Lachmann and his school. The first option was represented by Jacob Grimm's "wild" philology, which refused to establish a hierarchy within linguistic acts and consequently refused (as Foucault would in his *Archaeology of Knowledge*) to specify, classify, and catalog linguistic utterances and the human beings who produce them; the second and finally prevailing option, represented by Karl Lachmann, was bent, on the contrary, on selecting, discarding, ordering, and normalizing—control procedures that turned out to be ultimately more compatible with the academic system. The notion of German Studies endorsed by Lachmann and, through him, by the mainstream of the discipline revolves around a "tame" and taming philology: that is, a philology capable of performing an essential pedagogical function in the education and disciplining of the younger generations. Philology is thereby conceived, in initiatory, sacred, and patrilineal terms, as based on the direct transmission of unquestionable knowledge from an undisputed master to his pupils and later successors legitimized by the master—a notion that is both embodied and sanctified in the academic professional community. This master-pupil relation is cloaked in a thick Oedipal haze that envelops all the places and spheres where the disciplining process is enacted, from the university classroom to the other forms and modes of professional communication: journals, reviews, letters, obituaries, and posthumous celebrations.

Chapter 2 focuses on a different path, which was proposed by the scholar Georg Gottfried Gervinus as a viable alternative to the philological option and the related apparatus that was being constituted around it. Gervinus, who was a professional historian, saw national literature as the strategic battleground between different perspectives of social and political development for the German nation. In his view, the issue of national literature was the pivot on which the construction of a liberal German state turned. Following the defeat of the ideas of 1848, however, a different notion of national literature prevailed. Both Theodor Wilhelm Danzel and Wilhelm Dilthey promoted an idea of literature as no longer committed to any public, political, or oppositional interests, but yearning to define itself as a relatively autonomous spiritual sphere—a world of aristocratic distinction whose exemplary icon is the detached, unchallenged, and supreme figure of Goethe.

Chapter 3 examines Wilhelm Scherer's role in accomplishing the process of institutional validation of German Studies within academia. When he made a stand in favor of the Prussian unification of Germany (which took place in 1871), Scherer forged an important alliance between philology and political power. Within this context he devised his "scientific" method, thus defined by analogy with the method of the natural sciences, in order to outline an "ethical system of national values" to which German society might refer. The positivist method of Scherer and of his followers, based on the strict philological procedures inherited from the previous generation, made a major contribution to the editing and publication of German national literature, whose different texts were valued in all their diversity as belonging to a single tradition and as parts of an organic whole. Scherer was also the first to promote and accomplish the academic legitimization of contemporary literature, which—due to its antifeudal and liberal contents—had been formerly deemed unsuitable for the classroom, that is, for the disciplining of future generations.

Chapter 4 deals with Wilhelm Dilthey's *Geistesgeschichte* (intellectual history), the defining feature of German Studies in the years between 1890 and 1933. The starting point of this new development was Dilthey's clear-cut distinction between the natural sciences and the "sciences of the spirit," more popularly known as intellectual history. The critical and interpretive trend originating from this distinction, *Geistesgeschichte* (whose most significant contributions were produced between approximately 1910 and 1933) centered upon a definition of the mind, spirit, or intellect as essentially unconnected to social and historical reality. Some of its representatives, such as Gundolf, propounded a kind of "aesthetic fundamentalism" whereby the *Bildungsbürgertum* (the educated middle class) was endeavoring to create for itself an autonomous conceptual and aesthetic space separate from and opposed to the public sphere. This occasionally brought *Geistesgeschichte* into conflict with the philological orientation of the discipline and produced antagonism and dissension among different schools and trends. During the period of the Weimar Republic, the self-regulation mechanisms of the corporation, enforcing the conformity of individual statements to the normative apparatus of academic German Studies, were at their most active: exclusionary procedures affected all those individuals—Walter Benjamin among them—who were deemed incompatible with the discipline's paradigmatic values for political, ideological, or racial reasons.

The selection and control of statements enacted by the corporation's "discourse police" were so effective that, as I argue in chapter 5, the National Socialist Party found German Studies perfectly aligned with its outlook. There was no outcry, and no public stand was made against Hitler by Germanists: indeed, mass concurrence with the new regime was immediately taken for granted. After a while, however, the self-referential mechanisms preserving the disciplinary autonomy of German Studies—lasting and enduring ones, thanks to the firm, patient pedagogical action that had instilled them—collided with political power when the latter tried to exert an influence on the corporation's reproduction. Aware that its survival depended on its control over self-reproduction, the corporation put up a stubborn resistance on this issue and effectively managed to override Hitler. Even the German SS (Schutzstaffeln), in a report produced for internal use by their Security Service, explicitly mentioned the difficulties encountered in dealing with a corporation whose members were prepared to declare their loyalty to the regime and to repeat every one of its slogans, but refused to modify their professorial habitus and to give up their caste privileges.

The disciplinary habitus and its culturally "arbitrary" quality, whose capacity for endurance had overcome even Nazi power, allowed Germanists to bracket Nazism after 1945 and go back to work as if nothing had happened. Chapter 6 examines the unfolding continuity of the discipline in the postwar years. Its whole apparatus—from the statutory rule of philology to the hierarchical organization of seminars, from methods to canon—was carried over from the Weimar age into the postwar period, frequently featuring the same actors and scripts. In this chapter I investigate a few case studies in order to highlight the contradictions inherent in the denazification process from 1945 to the present, among these the Schneider/Schwerte scandal that exploded in the spring of 1995, fifty years after the end of World War II. I also analyze some short-lived student journals published in the immediate postwar period, along with their proposals for a reform of German Studies, which specifically questioned the professorial habitus and the embattled defense of the traditional values of the discipline. When regarded from outside the boundaries of the discipline, German professors were generally credited with no potential for self-correction or capacity to reform the university system.

Chapter 7 deals with the discipline's turning points in the 1960s. The first was the Munich Conference in 1966, where a substantial part of the establishment of German Studies expressed a determination to confront the past, to update the discipline, and to open it to the contributions of other fields of knowledge (structural linguistics, sociology, Marxism). A much more radical attack was launched in 1967 and 1968 by students and prospective scholars who had not yet achieved the rank of professor through the process of *Habilitation,* an arduous process that results in the acquisition of a postdoctorate degree that is necessary if one wants to become a full professor. This generation's critique, I argue, was subversive in its contents, in its methods, and above all in its unprecedented willingness to question the very principle of academic power, that is, the procedures whereby professors were selected and recruited. No longer sharing the *illusio,* as Bourdieu terms it—that is, the fundamental uncritical conviction of playing a game whose stakes were universally acceptable—they challenged the alleged neutrality of the academic operation system. Along with the issue of discipline reorganization, they also raised the question of the German literary canon, congealed for decades and immutably revolving around the unquestionable greatness of Goethe's and Schiller's classicism. This heritage, equally endorsed by the mandarins of both German states, was now rejected in a conscious and overt refusal to "inherit" from the previous generations.

Chapter 8 confronts later developments in the discipline as regards both contents and methods. Following 1968 a renovation process was started: new authors, literary trends, and literary forms were increasingly accepted, and the very notion of literature was transformed and enlarged as a result. In the critical field as well, new critical tendencies were legitimized in both West and East Germany: tendencies toward Marxism in its different forms, structuralism, women's studies, deconstruction, *Sozialgeschichte* (social history), and an interest in the new critical subjectivities made visible by the events of 1968. These, however, did not affect the discipline as an institutional structure, leaving in place both the power and the authority of the professors and the procedures for their training, selection, and reproduction. When the Berlin Wall fell in 1989, the apparatuses of German Studies in the two states became one. As I have already mentioned, this unification involved further forms of corporative discourse control on the former faculty of East German universities and academies, but it also allowed some barriers to break down and empowered new, syncretic, and innovative research directions.

In the present historical and political situation, German Studies is confronted with a dilemma whose terms I try to outline in my final chapter. On the one hand, the philological statute is still powerful in the discipline, and its patrilineal pattern, based on the transmission of power-knowledge from a founding father of the discipline to his legitimate inheritors, is still in full sway. On the other hand, the scope of German Studies has now been enlarged to embrace a wider sphere, including everything that can be relevant to a *Kulturwissenschaft,* that is, to Cultural Studies. This new German Studies addresses all forms of human communication in history, and thus redraws the boundaries of the discipline, overcoming the restrictive notion of "literary sciences." But for the past three decades, ever since these issues were first raised, all such perspectives have been clashing against a disciplinary structure whose resistance to change creates a veritable epistemological impasse. The present recruiting system, based on the hiring of dutiful pupils enrolled in the succession list and submissively waiting for their turn to be co-opted, effectively avoids conflict; candidates for *Habilitation* are not willing to take risks that might jeopardize their professional careers, and therefore take shelter in the elaboration of a repetitive form of knowledge that proceeds by accumulation and leads to scholasticism. As one critic has written, lack of originality is not a flaw in the *Habilitation* process; rather, it is its true aim. Anyone attempting to open up new directions for German Studies has to confront the fact that the discipline, with its rigid institutional structure and rules, is at present in a state of epistemological impasse and will be able to overcome it only by eliminating its causes. This, however, would imply questioning its present apparatus, as well as its values, canon, and paradigms—a difficult task, since it is exactly in that apparatus that the legitimacy of German Studies and the habitus of its representatives are grounded.

This brief outline of my argument and of the individual characters, episodes, and periods that I analyze may have conveyed the impression that my approach to German Studies is quasi-deterministic in its recurrent emphasis on the continuity of the discipline from its original foundational core. Nothing could be further from my actual convictions. The continuity I am trying to highlight is not genetic but (in Foucault's sense) genealogical: it arises from the material conditions of the production and reproduction of knowledge in the field under examination. After all, from 1800 to the present day, few academic generations have succeeded one another: at some universities there have been no more than six or seven "generations" of professors. This makes for very close ties connecting all members along each line of descent. The values and principles constituting the "cultural arbitrary" can be most effectively reproduced when deemed worthy of reproduction and directly handed over from one generation to another, as is the case with German Studies. Moreover, another element fostering stability and continuity is operating between consecutive generations: the selection procedure, established by the founding fathers and steadily carried out for decades. Today's office-holders have been consecrated by their predecessors, and they must consecrate them in their turn, since it is owing to their predecessors that they have acquired their status, legitimacy, and institutional power. Denying their forefathers' merits would amount to lessening their own degree of legitimacy in filling their posts. In this hereditary chain, no link can afford to question the nobility of the previous one. This also applies to the issue of heritage: one's cultural inheritance is inevitably assessed as valuable, since the amount of cultural capital that the inheritor will be able to spend depends on that initial assessment. This property will then be in turn passed on to the inheritor's aptest pupils. The self-referential logic of this system creates a vicious circle: a fixed patrimony of qualities, values, and paradigms is passed on from generation to generation and is legitimized anew at each successive stage, carefully avoiding contamination from all knowledge that is unsanctioned by the disciplinary hierarchies, from novelty, and from amateurish insight—in other words, from nonknowledge.

This situation, as I hope I have made clear, is not just ideological but involves the material and legal exercise of academic power: my reading of German Studies and its *dispositif* is constantly intertwined with the history of the university as the institution presiding over the production and reproduction of knowledge, both in Germany and elsewhere. It is no coincidence that the only rupture in the history of the discipline originated from outside it and took place as a result of public events in the years 1967 and 1968, when the student movement broke the chain of "anticipatory identification," as Bourdieu terms it, with a preordained career goal by refusing to undergo the process whereby the habitus was instilled and rejecting the inheritance that it was bound to convey. For the first time, however briefly, a generation of students and young scholars declared that they no longer shared any *illusio* and questioned both the rules and the stakes of the game. The response of German Studies to this new subversive situation in academia and in society at large, however, has been on the whole confined to an exquisitely ideological plane, and consequently wide of the mark of actual structural change. On the one hand, the institution now insists on methodological pluralism and on the need for rereading and revision of all German-language authors, intent on reconciling the new paradigms with the revalidation of the cultural tradition in different terms, as is the case with new critical readings of Goethe. This has also involved an opening up of the canon (urged from outside the corporation rather than from within), which has, nevertheless, done little to modify the general interpretative framework of German literary history. On the other hand, the academic field is now infiltrated by minority currents that do not identify with the disciplinary paradigms and propound (prudently, since they wish to change the rules from inside the game) a reform of the recruitment process, which is still—as it was in Lachmann's days—completely controlled by those who have best interiorized the habitus of the professorial caste. Thus conceived, German Studies has no chance to reform itself: in its epistemic standstill, it will either entropically implode or survive as a closed and self-referential "discourse society," or rather as a collection of different "discourse societies," organized as individual monads.

It would be difficult to propose solutions to this impasse or predict its developments, and I am certainly not going to do so. Since my work is an analysis of the social practices constituting German Studies, it can engage only the forms and manifestations of its concrete realizations. There are, however, some signs and indications of potential developments that might reward inquiry within a few years. As I have mentioned, other fields of study in Germany have had a different development, not because of a more stable epistemological foundation, but because they have been less crucial to the national pedagogical system and less involved in the exercise of institutional power.[7] They seem to be less obsessed by the need for a strict control over the production of statements and more prepared to accept forms of nonorthodox and nonsubjected knowledge; in other words, having a less rigid statute, they are more willing to accept innovation. If German Studies were to melt into a wider comparative and cultural field, it would probably be able to provide interesting solutions to its present crises, to mobilize new forces, and to explode the fundamentally teleological structure of the discipline. Otherwise, the world of German Studies runs the risk of surviving in much the same way as does a wildlife sanctuary.

The creation of a new identity for German Studies, however, would imply abandoning some defining characters—first among these, the notion of national philology and the related apparatus—that the corporation as a whole cannot probably afford to give up as yet. A hybridization of the contents and statute of the discipline is not likely in the short run, even though much is being done to bring it about. An important role in the cross-fertilization of themes, approaches, and contents of the discipline has been played by the German Studies of the United States; another important role is probably going to be played by the German Studies of Eastern European countries. The reason I am singling out these two fields of forces is that, in different contexts and for different reasons, they paradoxically converge in posing a challenge to the German Studies of German-speaking countries.

Over the past few years American German Studies has displayed a remarkable theoretical, political, and economic ability to confront German German Studies on an equal footing, stimulating the production of new discourses and starting important collaboration projects.[8] However, it is now undergoing a crisis: the number of its students is rapidly decreasing for a number of different reasons, and in an academic system based (unlike the German one) on private institutions and free-market competition, it runs the risk of losing positions and funds.[9] Furthermore, as Jost Hermand has noted, "Ever since 1989, that is, the fall of the Eastern bloc and of the Berlin Wall and the end of the direct confrontation with the U.S.S.R., Germany has become a comparatively unimportant country for the United States."[10] Unified Germany is no longer strategic to the United States: having gained victory in the Cold War and defeated the Soviet bloc, the United States no longer needs such a political outpost. Even on the cultural plane, Germany is no longer the boundary separating the Free World from communism; its great culture of music, poetry, and philosophy need no longer be upheld as the common heritage of the West and the antitotalitarian bulwark of liberty. This change in the geopolitical world situation might paradoxically entail a diminishment of American German Studies, in terms of both power and prestige, as compared with German German Studies, and thus the loss for the latter of an important dialectical pole of dialogue and confrontation—a loss all the more harmful, in my opinion, in that German German Studies badly needs in its critical and theoretical elaboration the constant test and stimulus of reliable partners, on a footing of equality, and therefore unaffected by psychological and economic subjection.

The German Studies of another area that is likely to play an important role in the future development of German Studies in Germany is in many ways pointed in an opposite direction. The German Studies of Central Europe (that is, all Eastern European countries lying between the Baltic Sea and Romania, excluding Russia) is closely linked to the general apparatus of national philology as constantly emphasized and upheld through all economic transformations and political upheavals from the nineteenth century to this day.[11] In the last decade or so, when the countries of Central Europe have witnessed the nearly complete collapse of their economic and political structures, and hence of their research potentialities, they have looked to German German Studies as a guarantee of professional seriousness, philological rigor, and capacity for producing order. The German Federal Republic has responded to their expectations with resolute policies of economic development and cultural and political penetration. The use of German as a lingua franca that would compete with English and replace Russian is a hypothesis that many intellectuals and academics from Eastern Europe regard with favor. Meanwhile, cultural agreements and common research projects are increasing every day. For the Germanists of Eastern Europe they are sometimes the only opportunities for international research and qualification. A Mitteleuropäischer Germanistenverband (Central European Association of German Studies) has been established, excluding Russia from membership, and several important projects are under way, such as the writing of a history of Central European literature, an encyclopedia of the most important cultural terms relating to the idea of Central Europe, and so on.[12] This collaboration might entail—and anyone who deals with the relation and interplay of power and knowledge should not omit this aspect—an asymmetrical power relation between two partners that are formally on an equal footing but actually in a relation of economic subordination that frequently carries neocolonial overtones. One should also remember that the habitus in turn inculcated and acquired by the scholars of Eastern Europe both during the Austro-Hungarian Empire and more recently during the Soviet domination was not so different from the canonical one of German Germanists: hierarchy, subjection, scientific rigor embraced as a lifestyle, formal submission to political power, and faithful reproduction of the corporation, its canons, and its norms. As a result, the faculties of Eastern European universities frequently share lasting traits that are perfectly compatible with the philological apparatus of German German Studies. Indeed, one might argue that their habitus is sometimes displayed in even more pristine and unsophisticated ways, because the forms have not been critically challenged thus far. There is even a recurring tendency to extol the traditional "greatness" of German culture, with laudatory accents that are difficult to understand if one does not keep in mind that German culture represents in that area a considerable cultural capital in which one may still wish to invest. In a field of forces such as those found in Eastern and Southeastern Europe, the patrimony of "German culture," however reduced in degree, can be invoked as a potential bulwark against the penetration of American culture, which is represented there (and indeed, frequently presents itself) in utterly negative terms.[13] The encounter between the present German Studies of Germany and the German Studies of Eastern Europe is bound to create an interesting interplay of knowledge and power (both economic and political), habitus and research expectations, cautious management of inherited capital and innovation, individual directions and the field of forces within which all the above elements operate. The genealogist's task will be, then, that of investigating the manifestation of power relations in particular events, historical moments, and a network of minute relations that fall beyond the historian's ken.

One

The Origins of Modern German Studies

The term *Germanistik* (German Studies) is usually applied to the "*Wissenschaft von deutscher Sprache und Literatur*" (the science of German language and literature), which in turn branches out to various specialized areas and subareas.[1] Starting in 1810, when the first chair of German Studies was established in the newly created University of Berlin and assigned to Friedrich von der Hagen, the discipline developed according to a two-pronged system: on the one hand, the study of the German language and literature of the Middle Ages; on the other, in what was originally an inferior position, the study of literature from the sixteenth century to the present day. Today the most common system is a triadic one, thanks to the addition of *Germanistische Linguistik* (German linguistics). In some universities, other related disciplines can be found: Scandinavian Studies, Didactics of Language and Literature, German as a Foreign Language, General Literature, and Comparative Literature. The current system, however, is only the end result of a process begun in that bygone 1810, a long and complex process that has been almost inextricably interwoven with the history of Germany at large. It is my intention to trace the steps of this process in order to explore the origin of a number of issues that are crucial to the discipline.

German Studies, Law, and National Identity

The birth of German Studies must be seen in the context of the early efforts by the liberal middle class to foster a sense of national identity. These efforts began in the aftermath of Prussia's defeat at the hands of Napoleon's army in 1806, which meant the imposition of a humiliating peace treaty and the end of the Holy Roman Empire of the German Nation. Within the German middle class a debate developed, often marked by different and polemically opposed political perspectives, which focused on a number of issues, such as the concept of nationhood, the future of a national state, and the most suitable ways to achieve the unity and liberty of the German fatherland. But Germany's particular political situation—the feudal fragmentation of the land; the lack of unified political institutions; the attitude of local governments, which were fundamentally antiliberal and hostile to the idea of a single German nation—prevented these aspirations from leading to the creation of a parliament and of a liberal and democratic constitution. Nevertheless, the debate on the historical, linguistic, cultural, and juridical identity of the German nation continued among scholars of German Studies.

Before we proceed, it will be useful to pause a second and consider what the term *Germanistik* actually meant at the time. One of the most interesting definitions is found in Wolfgang Menzel's *Die deutsche Literatur* (1828). Menzel (whom Ludwig Börne, the incisive journalist, called a "French-eater" for his hostility toward that people[2]) wrote:

> In contrast with science, the new party makes conscience a principle, and, in contrast with the isolation of caste, it makes the republican public opinion its form of law. . . . We should call this party the party of Germanists, in contrast with the party of Romanists. Because the Germanists elevate the conscience to a principle of law and public opinion to a form of law, they tend toward democracy. They consider judging a legal case something natural and common to all men. It is not an aristocracy of the learned that must judge but the common people. And thus the people, too, feel authorized to judge, and the force of juridical power coincides with popular sovereignty. Democracy cannot be based on the will of an individual. . . . Monarchy cannot be based on the will of many. . . . Therefore, Roman law must necessarily lead to the autocracy, German law necessarily to the republic. . . . Juridical questions are, therefore, political ones. The discussion on the principle of law and on the form of law coincides precisely with the discussion on the principle of the state and on its form.[3]

By elaborating the distinction between Roman and German law, Menzel clearly outlined his position on a question that was hotly debated during those years: the necessity to adapt law to changing historical conditions. In Restoration Germany, jurists had to take on the responsibility of reorganizing the German legal system on principles opposed to those of Roman law, the dominant tradition in Germany since the fourteenth century.[4] Thus *Germanistik* ("the new party") was for Menzel the expression of German law as opposed to Roman law, two different legal views that imply opposite views of the world: on the one hand, the progressive and democratic triad of liberalism, Protestantism, and German law, on the other the reactionary movement rearing its three ugly heads: enslavement, Catholicism, and Roman law. It is significant that Menzel mentioned a "new party" capable of expressing the political interests of the nation. At this particular moment in the history of Germany (a country without suffrage whose territory was parceled into thirty-nine states, all governed along more or less feudal lines), German Studies seemed to Menzel a movement or party endowed with great political import and capable of playing a crucial role in the project of national unification.

Jacob Grimm and the First Two Congresses of Germanists

The best proof of the wide-ranging involvement in politics of German Studies as a discipline is found in the proceedings of the first two congresses of German Studies, held in Frankfurt in 1846 and Lübeck in 1847. As a premise and also to clarify the terminology employed, we may begin by noting that in the letters of invitation Germanists were described as experts "who dedicate themselves to the study of German law, German history and language."[5] Invitations to the first congress were drawn up by scholars of the above-mentioned disciplines: six jurists, six historians (among them Ernst Moritz Arndt, Friedrich Christoph Dahlmann, Georg Gottfried Gervinus, and Leopold Ranke), and six philologists (among whom were Jacob and Wilhelm Grimm, Karl Lachmann, Moriz Haupt, and Ludwig Uhland). Historians of literature were not invited as such: Gervinus and Uhland, authors of important histories of literature, were invited for their other areas of expertise, since both *Literaturwissenschaft* (the science of literature) and *Literaturgeschichtsschreibung* (literary historiography) were excluded from German Studies, for reasons I will deal with later on.[6] Though the purpose of the "*deutsche Wissenschaft*" (German science), as German Studies was called, was to reconstruct the juridical and cultural identity of the nation, the discipline did not take on the debate on modern national literature that had already begun.[7]

German Studies presented itself as the "science" whose task was to weave the web of national identity out of the many strands already spun in the past from the soul of the German people. There has recently been extended debate on whether this project actually had a political import.[8] To bolster the thesis of the nonpolitical origin of German Studies, critics often make use of the following passage from the speech delivered by Jacob Grimm at the first conference of which he was president: "As for the actual politics, it is outside the scope of our meetings, where nothing can be decided about that."[9]

The passage does seem unequivocal; but if one continues reading, it becomes evident that Grimm's speech invites different conclusions: "As for the actual politics, it is outside the scope of our meetings, where nothing can be decided about that, while, on the contrary, it will be natural and inevitable, in the fields of history, law and language, to deal in scientific rigor with questions bordering on the political. To remain within narrow borders in the current historical moment, lively and passionate, would be below the dignity of individual members and even more of an assembly, whose participants are used to look in all directions and speak freely without having to carefully weigh their words."[10]

Grimm was clearly aware of the necessity to keep a low profile as regards politics: the Congress of German Studies was not a national parliament, and it would have been unrealistic and even ridiculous for it to pursue immediate political goals. Nevertheless, the political significance of the event was clear to the organizers. The 1846 Congress of German Studies was the first to include Germanists from all the states of the *Bund*. The choice of the city (Frankfurt) and of the place (the *Kaisersaal* of the *Römer*) was also symbolic of the participants' hopes for national unity.[11] And there is no doubt that public opinion, too, was aware of the genuine political import of the meeting, as witnessed by the words of an acute observer, Karl August Varnhagen von Ense: "The assembly of Germanists in Frankfurt am Main is truly a special event. German scholars—the greatest among them—are publicly discussing the question of the Schleswig-Holstein in contrast with the King of Denmark! Metternich will be tearing his hair out. The thing happened on its own, and the moderation of Grimm and Pertz, who excluded all political questions, wanting to leave room only for scientific ones, could not prevent the assembly from turning into a political demonstration."[12]

Furthermore, if one examines the agenda of the first congress, one sees that all of the issues discussed had more or less immediate political implications (as was also the case with the following year's conference in Lübeck).[13] In Frankfurt, the three plenary sessions were on the problem of the Schleswig-Holstein, the relations between Roman and German law, and the plans for a German dictionary. There was a definite awareness that German Studies, with its three areas (law, history, and the study of language), could play a central role in a project aimed at establishing the liberty, unity, and identity of Germany. This was already evident in Grimm's above-mentioned keynote address, which, in the light of the historical moment and of its implicit and explicit political import, positioned itself at the heart of a national and revolutionary middle-class project centered on the juridical, linguistic, and cultural identity of the German people.

The election of Jacob Grimm as president of the assembly, after his nomination by Uhland, also implied an increased emphasis on language, an area that, up to then, had held second place to law. Grimm's position was legitimated in the eyes of the participants by his legal studies with the highly regarded Professor Friedrich Carl von Savigny and his constant attention to the relation between poetry and law in the national spirit.[14] Indeed, Grimm was one of the few who could fully represent all three disciplines of German Studies: he was a philologist; he had a legal background; and in his work he had always shown a genius for combining different elements taken from history, law, and language in his study of the German tradition. He was also the one capable of developing a project that, while based on language, was not strictly philological or scientific, nor did it intend to be.

Let us consider Grimm's perspective in more detail. The common and vital thread binding the three disciplines of German Studies, said Grimm, is the German language; it is the precondition of any study of history, law, and philology (meaning here simply the study of language). But language is not a neutral instrument of communication; it has a higher function since, in the absence of a national state, it defines the identity of a people ("a people is the quintessence of the men who speak the same language").[15] Precisely for this reason, language cannot be left to the cold, dissecting hands of science. The apparent contradiction of Grimm's position is significant: if his emphasis on the notion and the role of the German language and his effort to protect it from overzealous and detached analysis do not sound particularly scientific or philological, it is because Grimm, through his passionate defense of language, wished to shift the focus from a scientific perspective (a neutral objective perspective, where one never takes sides) to a political one: he wanted to remind his public, as he was to state repeatedly on later occasions, that in the special situation of Germany, where literary and linguistic unity was in marked contrast with political and institutional *Zerrissenheit,* or fragmentation, philology could not be dissociated from patriotism and the aspiration to national unification. German Studies is the "deutsche Wissenschaft" because its object of inquiry is the German language in its totality, admitting of no exception or exclusion; its agents are German scholars; and its goals are pursued in the interest of the German people and nation.[16] The notion of philology, as the study of language that Grimm continuously and explicitly referred to, thus took on special connotations. It was conceived as the "science" (though with the above-mentioned reservations) that defines, documents, and studies a supreme value, language, which offers the only concrete, actual, realistic possibility of rallying a nation together. In Grimm's writings the concept of language became the focus of the national, antifeudal interests of the middle class, which were expressed in the Assembly of the Germanists. Philology, in turn, became the crucial tool in the definition of national identity, which it preserves and evokes, functioning as memory and exhortation, constantly oscillating between the mythologizing celebration of the past and the pedagogical drive.

Grimm's keynote address focused on the importance of the study of language within a larger project that is not limited to the legal, historical, and philological context, but includes a political dimension, with the achievement of national unity as its telos. This shows once more how ambiguous and contradictory is the notion "science," which is constantly and obsessively invoked in German Studies. It is no coincidence that in his second address at the Frankfurt conference, entitled "Über den Wert der ungenauen Wissenschaften" (On the value of inexact sciences), Grimm, anticipating Wilhelm Dilthey's distinction between *Naturwissenschaften* (natural sciences) and *Geisteswissenschaften* (human sciences), was careful to outline the respective domains and specific qualities of exact and inexact sciences: "Exact sciences extend their domain to the whole earth and can be used by foreign scholars, but they have no hold on our hearts."[17] History, philology, and even poetry are "inexact" sciences, but, because they flourish in the warm and safe soil of the motherland, they are closer to the heart of the people than exact sciences which, using their cold, alien language, scrutinize plants, animals, and nature in general for the sole purpose of classifying them within a given system. Grimm sees a conflict between what is *"fremd,"* "exact," hostile, enemy, foreign, and what is familiar, friendly, "national," "inexact," within the context of his ongoing dialectic between national and foreign—*"du propre et de l'étranger,"* as Wyss writes—though he does not claim the two poles to be completely irreconcilable.[18] Poetry, language, and law, the privileged witnesses of past culture, have a strong, lively connection to the culture and history of a people, whereas the abstract philosophical method (French Enlightenment, Roman law, modern universal science) seems coldly incapable of grasping a domain where the language of free men is spoken.

Indeed, Grimm's entire work can be read from a patriotic perspective: from the edition of Hartmann von Aue's *Der arme Heinrich* (1815), prepared with his brother Wilhelm, prefaced by a decidedly anti-Napoleonic interpretation of the short novel, to his *Geschichte der deutschen Sprache* (1848), up to the *Deutsches Wörterbuch*—which Grimm meant as a "Hausbuch" (a household reference text) like the Bible—Grimm was constantly striving to unify and liberate the patriotic energies of his country.[19] On the other hand, in his works one would look in vain for nationalistic or racist representations of the German nation as superior to other nations: even his anti-French and anti-Enlightenment polemic was primarily directed against a general method of interpreting reality that, in Grimm's view, ends up by dissecting, dividing, and ultimately destroying all manifestations of national identity. This explains the antinormative and antipedantic character of his work, which, precisely for these reasons, was judged to be confused and unruly by those among his colleagues who adopted a more rigidly philological perspective.[20] Grimm's relentless activity, while devoted to an object seemingly open to nothing but a scientific and philological approach, was in fact aimed at an archaeological reconstruction of national culture in view of a present task: his commitment as a scholar was to the past, but to the past as a means for directing and liberating the present. He was as interested in the general political development of the nation as in the study of questions of pure grammar and lexicography.

Grimm never aimed at fulfilling the role of the strict master equipped with strong normalizing shears. It is important to bear in mind, however, the unusual and marginal nature of his position within the corporation of philologists: the nature of his work, the unruly character of his philology, the absence of a proper method, and especially his inability to create an actual school made him a completely atypical representative of the discipline of which he is paradoxically considered to be one of the founding fathers. As Wilhelm Scherer acutely observed, Grimm "had above all else the luck of not becoming a true authority in the scientific field."[21] Scherer acknowledged and appreciated Grimm's originality. Elsewhere—as, for example, in Moriz Haupt's necrologium—we find instead an emphasis on his methodological unreliability.[22] The question at stake was, in fact, the role of philology, whether it should arm itself with "knife and file" or rather indiscriminately preserve all that is handed down by tradition.[23] Grimm himself, in his speech on the death of Karl Lachmann, had confronted the position of the deceased and taken his stand vis-à-vis Lachmann in an explicit and determined fashion. Thus when Haupt, a representative of the Lachmann school, in turn criticized Grimm in his eulogy, he was only obeying his conditioning as a scholar and defending the methodological orthodoxy of his school's founding father. By defending his teacher and his school, Haupt was defending himself, since it was faithfulness to a school that enabled a philologist to construct and establish his identity as scholar; to question the school's validity was tantamount to questioning his own curriculum.

Georg Waitz's commemorative speech, on the other hand, was entirely different. This difference was no accident: while usually the deliverer of a speech belongs to the same discipline as the deceased, Weitz was a historian and had no need to align himself with either Grimm or his adversaries for reasons of academic orthodoxy. He was therefore able to produce a perceptive description of Grimm in which he managed to bring out both sides of the coin, emphasizing the great passion and popularity of this politicized German scholar while acknowledging certain methodological weaknesses in his philology. Grimm's figure is thus historicized and appreciated for its distinctive characteristic: the capability of acting at once as Germanist, philologist, and politician, addressing both the German people at large and the professional world to which he belonged.[24]

Grimm's death represented the end of a trend in philology, a discipline that from that point on would be dominated by Lachmann and his school.[25] The above-mentioned congresses of German Studies were themselves in fact the final result of a process—an end rather than a beginning. At those congresses, intellectual debates and research still seemed part of the effort by an intellectual elite to establish some kind of collective identity (the *Volk,* the language, the nation), the Archimedean fulcrum that would allow them to reverse the humiliating fragmentation of their fatherland. The failure of the parliamentary experience of 1848—in which many of the Germanists of Frankfurt and Lübeck played a major role, demanding among other things the establishment of a German constituent parliament—also entailed the failure of German Studies as a unified political and cultural project.[26] The subsequent division of German Studies into separate disciplines (law, history, philology), while responding to objective practical difficulties (the undeniable increase in specialization within the various disciplines made their common management very difficult), ended up by relegating philology to an isolated position, largely self-referential, and mostly bent on defending the status of philology as a separate academic community. In Frankfurt and Lübeck the emphasis had not been on critical editions, literary history, or aesthetics, but on the importance of not separating philology from its historical and political context and from the general interests of the nation. After 1848 and Grimm's death in 1863, this was no longer the case.

The Birth of the University Teaching of German Language and Literature

The two conferences of German Studies were the culmination and the end of a project that had begun many years before, at the beginning of the nineteenth century. To continue my exploration it is necessary to go back to those early years, focusing this time on the institutional development of philology (or *Germanistik*). And it is necessary to start once more from the privileged object of inquiry of philology, namely language.

The emphasis on the language question must be seen in the context of the marginal position of the German language within Germany up to the end of the eighteenth century. Only in the latter half of the eighteenth century did teachers begin to use German in schools, and only with the reform of the Prussian university system—implemented by Wilhelm von Humboldt in 1810 in an effort to achieve an anti-Napoleonic modernization—did the German language become the object of scholarly studies at the university level. Sciences began to be taught in German and no longer in Latin: Grimm passionately defended the use of the mother tongue in his *Antrittsrede* (opening speech) at Göttingen university on 13 October 1830.[27] German language and literature itself acquired a new importance and became the object of a specific university discipline. The first chair was set up at the University of Berlin in 1810 and assigned to Friedrich Heinrich von der Hagen at his own request. As mentioned earlier, this reform was part of the rediscovery of a German literary tradition in the context of the nationalist, anti-Napoleonic movement.[28] Significantly, von der Hagen was a jurist who in 1807 had published a new edition of the *Nibelungenlied* in which he had emphasized the aspects he thought could most contribute to the national cause and the fight against Napoleon. Therefore, his interpretation of the *Nibelungenlied* had obvious political overtones, which were largely instrumental in determining the subsequent reception of the work. For von der Hagen the bitterness of the current political situation could be assuaged through the perusal of works showing the indomitable German spirit prevailing over countless difficulties to regain liberty and nature. The publication of the *Nibelungenlied* was meant to reawaken love for the German language and literary tradition: "So it is that today in Germany, in the midst of devastating storms, the love for the language and for the works of our glorious ancestors is well and alive as if one is seeking in the past and in poetry what is sadly lost in the present. But it is precisely this desire, which bears witness to the enduring unquenchable German character, which is above any servitude to foreigners and sooner or later breaks free of the bonds, and thus becomes meaningful and rediscovers its innate nature and its liberty. . . . No other song can thus move and captivate, regenerate and support, a patriotic heart."[29]

Let me draw attention once again to the fact that the use of the national language to foster a knowledge and appreciation of the monuments of the national literary tradition in an institution as important as the university of the capital of Prussia was an entirely new and outstanding aggregating factor for the German nation as a whole. For the first time the unity of teaching, research, and the spread of knowledge over the national territory was ensured by the use of a common language and a set of common objects of reverence and inquiry. The notion of a cultural and geographical community grounded on language as a prefiguration of the political unity of the nation was a central tenet during the years of the anti-Napoleonic coalitions and was to remain a feature of the newly established German philology. The institutional birth of the discipline of German Language and Literature was therefore completely in line with the spirit of Prussian anti-Napoleonic university reform and must be seen as another step toward national unity.

On the other hand, since the process of rediscovery and celebration of the German past in relation to the issue of national identity was charged with so much political and ideological significance, it could not help giving rise to contrasts, considering that in 1815 the politics of the Holy Alliance was based on antiliberal criteria and dominated by dynastic and feudal interests that went against the national aspirations of the European peoples. German fledgling patriotism, while useful against Napoleon, had to be kept in check and, in some cases, directly repressed, since its effervescent revolutionary drive threatened to upset the political organization of the fragile feudal states.[30] We have seen how the rediscovery and promotion of the German past was instrumental in establishing a sense of the German nation as an independent historical entity, an active player and collective subject in history. The forces that were suspicious of the development of the German people's sense of national affiliation exploited these feelings in their fight against Napoleon, but then did their best to hinder and boycott the development of the German nation as an independent entity legitimized solely by popular will. Thus the nation and its identity became the controversial focus of all political and economic interests, as well as of the debate on culture and national education.

At its early official congresses, as we have seen, German Studies adopted a highly militant stance, striving for the development of political awareness among the middle class and in the nation as a whole. The situation of German philology in universities was substantially different, being the product of a complex dialectic between the pre-1848 ideological and political climate and the more narrow confines of the academic world. Two issues especially deserve our attention: the way German philology was established as a spin-off from *Altertumswissenschaft* (the study of classical antiquity corresponding to classical philology) and the steps that led to the gradual institutionalization of German philology and to the controversial acceptance of modern literature and the study of the same as *Literaturwissenschaft* (the science of literature), *Literaturgeschichte* (the history of literature), and *Literaturgeschichtsschreibung* (literary historiography): that is, in Foucauldian terms, the discourse of literature.

Philology and Classic Philology

German philology, as the linguistic study of the documents of the German past, was gradually accepted in academia as part of the movement toward national independence. Starting in the 1840s, it became established in universities as *Altdeutsche Philologie* (Medieval German Philology); the full acceptance of modern literature (and associated discourses), however, came about only in the 1870s, with the birth of the Second Reich. Following that event, a change occurred in the interpretative paradigms applied to contemporary literature, which legitimized its existence and allowed it to be wholly subsumed within the corpus of values on which the national educational system was based.[31] What, then, were the characteristics, the interpretative models, the disciplinary canons, and so on, that needed to be assimilated in order to provide academic and scientific dignity to the branch of philology that studied the language and, to some extent, the literature of the past? What did the study of the German language need in order to achieve the same status as, say, philosophy or the study of classical antiquity? What strategies were chosen, and how was this result achieved? In what follows I have tried to outline the various phases of this initial period, which was crucial for the future of the discipline.

In the early stages, the German community of philologists was characterized by very loose ties, as was typical of pre-nineteenth-century groups of men of letters. Then came the period of "*disziplinäre Gemeinschaft*," that is, the community seen as a meeting ground for various types of specialists: philologists, literary historians, librarians, high school teachers, and experts in aesthetics, philosophy, and so on.[32] In the final and decisive period, this disciplinary community transformed itself into a purely academic community; this process involved only philologists, who gave rise to a rigid, often instrumental opposition between the professional academic community of philologists and all others (amateurs and nonacademics).

Turning the *Wissenschaft von deutscher Sprache und Literatur* into an academic profession (split into two "containers," the philology of the past and, after 1870, modern philology) required—as for any academically institutionalized discipline—establishing a system of communication, promotion, and control and selection of knowledge based on an efficient network of specialized journals. At the same time, the discipline of philology, like any other respectable discipline, gradually established codes of behavior, rituals, procedures of exclusion—in short, the norms necessary for the production of scientific discourse or, rather, for its disciplinary discourse to be accepted as scientific. This process of the codification of procedures and canonization of contents was carried out following the model of a closed, almost impenetrable disciplinary community whose members were privileged by birth and position and whose ranking was the highest possible in a German university, that is, classical philologists.[33]

At the time, classical philology had a hegemonic role in universities and lyceums not only in terms of teaching hours, but also, and more important, because it stood as an institutional and social model. It was by all standards the leading discipline, having bested worthwhile opponents such as philosophy and history. It presented itself as the science of the text, hermeneutics, theory of understanding and interpretation; in other words, as a discipline capable of achieving unity and universality through the appropriation of a number of specific contents and procedures. Philology was one discipline and was related to all objects using the same method and in the same spirit: philological science "is not meant for amateurs and well-meaning friends, since there is only one philology," as Karl Müllenhof wrote.[34] It aspired to a totalizing vision of the whole, believing itself capable of reconstructing from the smallest detail that the philologist's eye unerringly apprehends an entire cultural system based on the detail whose relevance the philologist has recognized and highlighted. For this reason it considered itself superior, as a textual science, to subjective literary criticism, to the purely theoretical speculations of aesthetics, and to literary historiography. The dualism of detail and synthesis, of particularity and universality, did not represent an irreconcilable opposition for the philologist: the instruments of the science of the text allowed the philologist to identify the object of his operations by examining all the variants; then, as a hermeneutic specialist, he could grasp the truth of the text through a sophisticated interpretative game that related each individual element to the whole. The philological method was considered applicable to all sectors of antiquity: language and literature, mythology and economy, law and philosophy, history of religion and ethnology. In short, classical philology aspired to the totalizing and all-encompassing status of the "science of antiquity."[35]

This view of philology, however, did not work so well for modern philology. The complexity of modern civilization made the notion of a "science of modernity" absurd, since it logically required the existence of separate specialized disciplines or, at the very least, of a number of subsectors, something that went against the all-encompassing ambitions of philologists. This difficulty was compounded by other characteristics of classical philology. First, there was the apparently banal fact that classical philology was closely associated with the study of a foreign language.[36] Its role was to clarify what needed to be clarified in the original text through the study of the language in which it was written. This required a regular and intense course of disciplinary study based on seminars carried out in universities, with exercises and verification, enabling professors to transmit to students the rules, contents, norm, and canon of the discipline directly and efficiently—a process that had an obvious socializing and pedagogic effect. The problem was that while the classical method was applicable to Medieval German, which could be treated as a foreign language, it faltered when it came to modern German literature, which students had little or no difficulty understanding. So much the better, one might have thought. Instead German philology pursued an aristocratic and exclusive strategy, turning what was accessible into an obscure object of investigation by insisting on the use of an esoteric professional language as a prerequisite for scientific legitimacy. Canonical texts were rendered foreign and difficult by eliminating any explicative apparatus in order to simulate in some way the difficulties presented by classical texts. The message conveyed was that only through an intense moral commitment could a novice become worthy of being granted access to philological studies: study, personal sacrifice, and the acquisition of the professional jargon under the control of strict teachers were necessary to enter this aristocratic circle, the caste of philologists mentioned by Jacob Grimm. Like any aristocracy, the community of philologists spent a lot of its energies in forcing its members "to accept the sacrifices that are implied by privilege, or by the acquisition of durable dispositions which are a condition for the preservation of privilege."[37] The dominant party, the party of the institution, had to found, establish, invent, through a formal act of *institutio,* a form of education that would ensure enduring models of behavior, with deeply rooted and unalterable mental habits and attitudes. Ascetic practices and initiation rites are all the more effective and long-lasting in their results, and capable of ensuring the loyalty of adepts, if they are strict and excruciating. The rites also have the function of discouraging adepts from recrossing the line—the holy border—artificially established by the institution, in other words, to discourage desertion, transgression, and the return to nature. In Bourdieu's words, "The universally adopted strategy for effectively denouncing the temptation to demean oneself is to naturalize difference, to turn it into a second nature through inculcation and incorporation in the form of the habitus."[38] Offering or accepting an identity means acquiring a competence that also entails a number of duties. It means doing only what is in one's acquired nature without transgressing or crossing the line. It means acting according to one's definition and assigned function. Those who are able to endure all the initiation rites (learning dead languages, enduring prolonged isolation and various ascetic practices) are then accepted as full members of the caste and are entitled to perform their function within university and society with "all social titles of credit and credence—of *credentials.*"[39]

Among the most prestigious institutional functions of classical philologists was that of examining and selecting those who wished to teach in classical lyceums.[40] This was the only type of high school that allowed access to the university, and within classical lyceums Latin and Greek played a dominant role: this created a network that connected classical philologists, lyceum teachers, and students from the lower classes who wished to rise on the social scale by attending a gymnasium and a university or, more commonly, higher-class students who wished to reinstate their right to belong to a privileged group.[41]

Karl Lachmann and the Foundation of the Discipline of German Studies

The close connection during the early years of German philology between the latter and the *Altertumswissenschaft* is clearly exemplified by Karl Lachmann. While Grimm was the representative of an unruly philology, deeply sensitive to the voice of nature in all its nuances, Lachmann was the great normalizer. In Martianus Capella's allegory, old "Grammatica" has an ivory box containing a knife and a file with which it corrects children's mistakes. The image suits Lachmann perfectly. His goal was to set down the rules governing the recovery, restoration, and interpretation of classical texts, rules that he then applied also to Medieval German texts and then to modern ones (Lachmann was the author of the critical edition of Lessing's works). Lachmann was responsible for the so-called *Philologisierung* (philologizing) of German Studies, which had a lasting influence on the discipline.[42] Let us consider some of its methodological aspects. Lachmann's method is characterized by a highly discretionary approach to texts, legitimated by his scientific authority and academic power.[43] In some cases (as, for example, that of the *Nibelungenlied*) he went so far as to decide on an entirely subjective basis what was the right meter in which epic poems should be presented.[44] In the case of modern authors (Lessing), Lachmann chose to give absolute precedence to the *"letzter Hand"* edition (the last edition supervised by the author). Variants in previous editions had little or no value, and the final version (approved by the author) was the definitive and authoritative one.[45] Equally totalizing and rigid, as well as highly arbitrary, was Lachmann's approach to ancient and medieval texts. Lachmann had no qualms about excising, adapting, and ordering the many manifestations of ancient German poetry for the purpose of recovering noble and elevated authors, perfectly restored and cleansed of the signs of time.[46]

The normalizing violence of Lachmann's philology was denounced by the man who, in my view, was his greatest opponent, the one who had proposed an alternative path for philology, namely, Jacob Grimm. His attack came in a very special presentation—the eulogy for Lachmann's funeral, delivered on 3 July 1851—when Grimm once more refused to comply with the code of behavior of the corporation, thus showing how crucial the issue was to his mind. Grimm so urgently felt the need to restate and defend his position that he broke the usual bounds of the eulogy genre.[47] According to his acute definition, "One can divide all philologists who have achieved significant results into two categories: those who deal with words for the love of things and those who deal with things for the love of words."[48] Lachmann "was a philologist who dealt with things for the love of words," whereas

Grimm identified with the category of those who "deal with words for the love of things." Grimm went on to meticulously outline the difference between Lachmann's approach and his own: Lachmann's effort to achieve the "right" word at all costs; his tendency to cut out, reduce, and erase and to impose arbitrary meters on all texts; his wish to recast the primitive epos in aesthetically perfect forms by means of an operation of artificial embellishment that smoothed over irregularities and disguised all contradictions, thus cutting it off from the uninterrupted poetic flow of the national spirit: all this seemed to Grimm to go counter to his own view of philology.[49] What was at stake here was no less than the fundamental criteria and definition of philology. Lachmann was the main representative of a *"domestizierte Philologie,"* a domesticized and domesticizing philology, and Grimm could not help but bring out their irreducible difference.[50]

Lachmann's philology, as well as his personal traits, marked the extension of the fundamental disciplinary principles of the *Altertumswissenschaft* to German philology.[51] This transformation within German Studies is extremely instructive, since the constitutive rules that it brought about remained dominant for a long time and to a large extent still are. I have already referred to the disciplinary characteristics of classical philology and to the transformation of German philology from a somewhat amateurish community of enthusiasts into a disciplinary one. It is through Lachmann that the notion of a disciplinary community became decisive, and in the light of this transformation it is worth spending a few words on this subject. As Foucault writes: "In the course of the eighteenth century, knowledge was slowly reduced to a set of disciplines; that is, all knowledge was internally organized as a discipline endowed, within its field, with the criteria for selection that enable the rejection of what is false, of nonknowledge; with forms of homogenization and normalization of contents; with forms of hierarchization; and finally with an inherent, centralized system revolving around an implicit axiomatization."[52]

This transformation of different kinds of knowledge into disciplines had been carried out in France by the new university of the Napoleonic period and in Prussia by the reformed university. In both types of university, philosophy was no longer the link and communication channel between kinds of knowledge. This brought about a situation like the one described by Foucault, where the selection of knowledge takes place through a form of legal and de facto monopoly: "All knowledge that has not come into existence, that has not taken shape, within this institutional field whose boundaries are indefinite, but which includes the university and all official research institutions, all knowledge that falls outside these boundaries, all wild and untamed knowledge, all knowledge from elsewhere, is automatically, immediately, a priori disqualified if not outright excluded."[53] Foucault also explains the evolution of dogmatism in the course of the transition from the old type of knowledge to the new disciplinary knowledge of the nineteenth century. Previously there was a control over the content of utterances—an ecclesiastic and religious form of knowledge control that required great effort, since it entailed studying, passing sentence, and, if necessary, banning specific statements or ideas. With the growth of disciplines, control was changed from repressive to regulatory: the problem was no longer the content of the utterance but the regularity of its enunciation, that is, who said it, whether he had the correct qualifications and disciplinary role, and whether the utterance was in line with the discursive rules of the discipline. This process certainly meant freeing discourse from anachronistic, ineffective, and troublesome forms of censorship, but at the same time it brought about a more rigorous and thorough control, wielded from within rather than from outside: "One might say that the shift is from a censorship of utterances to a discipline of enunciation or, rather, from orthodoxy to something that I would like to call 'orthology,' a form of control that is now wielded from within the discipline."[54]

In the light of these brief considerations, the crucial importance of Lachmann's role in creating and firmly establishing the discipline is clear. Along with his methodological differences from Grimm, we should bear in mind his specific contribution to the success of the philological school of which he was the founder. The founding of a method or a school, that is, the presence of a homologated doctrinal group, ensures that a certain scientific and disciplinary discourse will be propagated along with the knowledge and the power it entails. Lachmann, as the founder and main exponent of a method, was the true father of philology as a discipline. His role is evident also in his fierce, clear-headed determination to control the forms through which the discipline expressed itself and opened itself onto the external world, seeking new outlets and establishing a new type of relation between disciplinary knowledge and power. Lachmann edited only works clearly belonging to the category *"hohe Literatur"* (high literature), in contrast, once again, with Grimm, who saw texts as the testimony of a popular, collective culture that the philologist should refrain from manipulating.[55] Lachmann saw philology as centering instead upon the texts, which must be "*sauber*" (clean), and on the author, who must also be freed of the dust and impurities of time. It is unquestionable that Lachmann succeeded in freeing philology from a mild, unruly state of nature, submitting it to a disciplinary process and thus turning it into a true discipline. The birth of a disciplinary technology necessarily entails the elimination of all knowledge that is anarchical and untamed and of the figure of the amateur. Lachmann, who was a professor of classical philology and then also, simultaneously, of German philology at Berlin, was able, thanks to his experience and position, to accomplish the "philologizing" of German Studies as an offshoot of classical philology. But the transformation of German Studies into a full university discipline also meant its demise as a cultural and political project of national interest.

Lachmann's role was crucial in at least three ways. First, in establishing the criterion for the circulation of texts: a text is published only if noteworthy, and then only in an esoteric form that is incomprehensible to the uninitiated. Second, in promoting the establishment of university seminars of German Studies based on the model of those existing in classical philology. Finally, in creating a work ethos involving the sacrifice of everything (and demanding the same of his pupils), an apparatus necessary to ensure disciplinary control and repression.[56]

With Lachmann the competence in and responsibility for the control of utterances was transferred from the people and the nation to the professional experts of the discipline. The target of philological publications was the philological community. Any effort to ensure a broader circulation for literary works was in contrast with the secluded, *intra muros* character of the discipline. Those who refused to comply with this rule were automatically considered to be "unzünftig," that is, "outside the corporation," and their statements automatically fell beyond the corporation's disciplinary and theoretical horizon.[57] Lachmann's philology worked—in an exemplary fashion, I might add—according to Foucault's view of a discipline as "a principle of control over the production of discourse," a veritable discursive police.[58] Under the control of Lachmann and of Moriz Haupt, his pupil and heir of the Berlin chair, German philology became a disciplinary community bent on preserving and protecting their method and statements, making them circulate "in a closed space, distributing them only according to strict rules, and without the holders being dispossessed by this distribution."[59] Indeed, the community had characteristics that associated it to the archaic "society of discourse" cited by Foucault, made up of groups of rhapsodians, storytellers who possessed the knowledge of ancient poetry, which they preserved and prevented from circulating outside the group except in controlled forms: through study an individual could become a member of the group and have access to the secret texts, which could be recited but not otherwise circulated. The number of rhapsodians was limited, and they were the only ones allowed to circulate the knowledge and pass it on to other adepts.[60] Certainly the process of *Philologisierung* of German Studies cannot be directly equated with this archaic model; however, there are strong analogies that allow one to understand, for example, the extent to which the sharp distinction between holy and profane knowledge—"the claims of all groups of specialists seeking to secure a monopoly of knowledge or sacred practice by constituting others as profane"—was a constitutive one to philology even during the early stages of its institutionalization.[61]

In Foucault's terms, then, Lachmann was the one who carried out the disciplinary normalization of philological discourse, subjecting it to and protecting it through the corporation. In his defense of the discipline he displayed a willful determination to prosecute anyone who went against its rules. Rather than focusing on scientific status, he emphasized the issue of moral integrity, a somewhat paradoxical strategy considering the scientific status to which philology aspired. The validity of the ritual was made to depend on the moral value of its officiant.[62]

In focusing on the moral integrity of the philologist, Lachmann acted as a specialist who, unable to legitimize his success and validate his knowledge within the framework of his system and its intrinsic qualities, resorts to anathema, intimidation, and moral condemnation in order to account for his hegemony by circumfusing it with a halo of moral superiority. Yet the tendency to insist on moral superiority in order to disqualify outsiders is in fact characteristic of scientific systems. Lachmann was exemplary in this respect. He correlated the status of his discipline with his own personal integrity and seriousness, the ground for his normative system and codified statements, and accused his adversaries of lacking the same. This philological ethos is summarized by Franz Schultz in reference to the founding fathers Lachmann, Haupt, and later Karl Müllenhof and Gustav Roethe—and with the latter we are already in the twentieth century: "Philological *ethos:* a reserved and responsible attitude, faithfulness to details, devotion to the insignificant, moderate way of life, dislike for subjective trivialities and for pure impressions, renunciation in all things, idiosyncrasy for the 'journalistic' and the 'feuilleton,' proud self-limitation."[63] Thus the ethos entailed an ascetic lifestyle, absorption in the text, and specific forms of communicating research results. In no way should a philologist make his results accessible, removing his work from the exclusive control of the mandarins.[64] In support of his arguments and academic and institutional positions, Lachmann used an aggressive strategy based on aristocratic arrogance, contempt, and harsh attacks, whose purpose was to delegitimize all purported amateurs and nonserious scholars who dared question his method or contents.

In 1822, for example, Lachmann passed the following judgment on Franz Josef Mone's edition of *Otnit:* "Mone's work is a discouraging example of what in 1821 people have the courage of calling edition, criticism and learned interpretation. In this field we do not perceive a great number of worthy masters, who by pure example could bring home those who have wandered astray. It is therefore the duty of the rightful to correct excesses. . . . Any benign indulgence would be here undutiful since our man has already shown that it is wasted on him without any result."[65]

No different was the treatment reserved to August Zeune, to whom Lachmann attributed "the superficial efforts of an amateur," a "great deal of arbitrariness," "the most blatant mistakes." His overall judgment was the following: "There is still a need to warn our younger friends in our discipline against such frivolities, from which only a serious scientific attitude and honest toil can save us."[66]

Lachmann's self-asserted pastoral right to drive his pupils back into the fold was based on his claim to having furnished the university discipline of philology with an objective and verifiable basis, thanks to mental discipline, precision, and total and unconditioned commitment (almost, we might say, a mystical union between philologist and philology). Love for truth, ascetic self-discipline, and absolute precision, as well as the ability—derived from training—to transcend himself toward higher functions: these virtues gave Lachmann the right and the duty to judge, condemn, and exclude those who lacked them.

Reestablishing the truth about a text was an operation that required firm moral qualities and strength of character as well as a stern scientific method (and anyone who lacked the first two could never hope to learn the third). From the heights of his moral and scientific superiority, Lachmann proceeded against all amateurs and "self-taught" scholars (the polemic in Lachmann and then in Müllenhof against amateurs and self-taught scholars is explicit and almost obsessive) in order to achieve total control of the disciplinary community of philologists.[67] But Lachmann achieved another extremely significant result as well: he succeeded in getting rid of any interest in the history of literature and the contexts in which it was produced as foreign to the scientific discourse of philology, thus separating serious philology from literary historiography and any debate on modern and contemporary literature, which were dismissed as amateurish, popularizing, and journalistic activities.[68] The elimination of the discourse on literature was the price paid by philology to achieve its full legitimization as a university discipline.

The Birth of German Studies Seminars

Another important factor in the institutional consolidation of German Studies was the development of university seminars, the first of which was established in Rostock in 1858.[69] This development is proof of the growing integration of the discipline into the university system and marks the end of the heroic phase of the foundation and the start-up of a new one. Philology gradually emancipated itself from *Altertumswissenschaft* and acquired new institutional functions as regards both socialization and cultural control (in lyceums, for example, where German gradually acquired the same standing as Latin and Greek, expanding both in terms of teaching hours and number of teachers).[70] This progress could be accomplished only by emulating the successful paradigmatic model, that is, the seminar of classical philology. The creation of German Studies seminars went on until 1894 (Münster was the last) and involved all German-speaking countries as well as those where, for political and colonial reasons, the presence of such seminars was deemed useful. That was the case with Strasbourg, for instance, where a seminar of German Studies was established in 1873—two years after the war that forced France to hand over the city to Prussia—and eventually became, thanks also to the charismatic presence of Wilhelm Scherer, one of the most prestigious.[71]

The creation of seminars had a great influence on the future development of German philology. It was a prestigious achievement that allowed the discipline to engage independently in the recruiting of new scholars and in didactic and research activities—in other words, to independently manage its own disciplinary processes. The seminar structure was different from that of the past: students needed to be accepted by the director of the seminar, who was a full professor endowed with absolute power, one who "enacted a monarchic principle, an aristocratic power over the entire study and research apparatus."[72] The students were divided into small groups and trained to work scientifically, using the texts and the materials provided by the library of the seminar *(Handbibliothek)*. Control over learning and method was constant, detailed, and far-reaching. Disciplinary knowledge was no longer acquired solely by listening, studying, and memorizing the teachers' lessons, but through constant daily activities (seminars were usually open twelve hours a day, with a break between noon and 2 P.M.). The philosophy of the seminar was to encourage more than a purely passive reception on the student's part, stimulating independent scholarly work. This goal was also pursued by granting scholarships to the best or eldest students, who were able to tutor the younger students through methodological exercises and overcome their natural passivity by setting a good example. This extraordinary cultural revolution was summarized with characteristic clarity by Wilhelm Scherer in a memo to Minister of Culture Von Gossler:

> Library-endowed seminars, where those who have been accepted by the director can work undisturbed from morning to evening and lessons supervised by the directors also take place, offer the same advantages in historical and philological sciences that they offer in natural sciences. Students are directly provided with study materials. There is absolutely no scientific research in the field of philology or history that can be carried out with one or two books. We university professors must train our students in scientific research: they can carry on their scientific study on their own with the help of the lessons. And research methods are learned only when one engages in independent work under the supervision of the teacher. To carry out research, however, it is necessary to have unrestricted, immediate and simultaneous access to numerous books. Simply to check previous observations and opinions on the object of research, it is often necessary to examine a great number of citations. For the grounds of research must not be second-hand, it must always be obtained directly from the sources.[73]

Scherer insisted on another methodological principle that was particularly dear to his heart: "There is a great difference whether the director simply provides the correct answer or the student finds it through his own efforts in the presence of the director."[74]

The birth and spread of philology seminars was part of a general process of modernization and rationalization of the German university and society. More specifically, seminars were the places where practices and systems of practices developed whose goal was to increase "disciplinary power." Disciplinary power, according to Foucault, has a fundamental goal: that of using "a mechanics of power" to produce human beings that can be treated as "subjected and practised bodies, 'docile' bodies."[75] This is achieved by moving from pure repression to "authority." The previous world of anonymous sanction that denied responsibility and eliminated guilt, the abstract and faceless power system, is replaced by the prestige of acknowledged authority, which legitimately judges "without weapons, without instruments of constraint, with observation and language only."[76]

Following Foucault's interpretative categories, the seminars were responsible for creating a new educational system: a system of pedagogical philology that rejected violent and arbitrary coercive instruments, developing instead a disciplinary technology in order to increase the usefulness and docility of the body and the mind. For the primary educational goal was not, as one would assume, the accumulation and expansion of knowledge; rather, it was the development of the correct attitude and behavior in the pupil—a sort of philological habitus, a second nature achieved through daily ascesis. In Foucault's terms, through such a process the human body becomes inscribed within a power system where its usefulness is in direct proportion to its docility. A new coercive policy is born based on a calculated manipulation of the body, of its gestures and behaviors. The discipline constructs submissive and trained bodies, that is, "docile bodies." The resulting body is stronger in economic and productive terms, but it is dissociated: on the one hand there is the habit, the capacity that the discipline seeks to increase; on the other, there is all its energy that must be controlled, "disciplined," that is, subdued and trained. In light of the above, certain remarks by Julius Zacher at the 1867 Assembly of German Philologists, referring to the brilliant victories of Prussia over Denmark and Austria, are especially significant: "How then were these great and speedy victories achieved? The true reason is nothing other than the rigorous and thorough Prussian disciplining, methodologically sound, yet not pedantic but energetic, action. Rigorous disciplining, correct and energetically applied method: this is also the secret thanks to which Prussia has established the foundation of the unification of Germany. And it is the same formula through which Grimm and Lachmann have achieved the foundation of German philology."[77]

The process of disciplining and socialization can be achieved only through method. Method is what distinguishes amateurs from the true philologist, the one trained according to the norms and mechanisms of the *Zunft* (which means "corporation" but also "sect"). Method means formal training, development of self-control techniques and subordination practices, all the necessary prerequisites of both Prussian military virtues and philological capabilities.

In 1937 Julius Petersen wrote about his promotion from extraordinary to ordinary member of Gustav Roethe's seminar in Berlin, and the ritual he described was part of the same pedagogical strategy. It consisted in engaging in "educationally very useful gloss-writing,"[78] a humble and rather uncreative activity, yet ideal for teaching young candidates the socializing significance of the ritual and the border that the ritual establishes. Full acceptance within the seminar community is dependent on the ritual and therefore sacred acknowledgment of the borders that one must not cross, of the difference between being inside and being outside. Outside, in the domain of transgression, are the others: laymen, profanes, amateurs.

Apparent exceptions confirm the rule. Scherer's case is often cited. During his Berlin years Scherer devoted himself to modern literature and literary criticism, inspiring a new generation of naturalist writers; wrote a very popular history of literature; and contributed articles to newspapers.[79] Such behavior was unthinkable for other philologists, even though by the 1880s modern literature had also been canonized and was no longer an object of distrust.[80] Yet I would argue that this was in fact an example of what Bourdieu calls "strategies of condescension": one of the privileges of "consecration"—and Scherer was certainly thus consecrated—consists "in the fact that, by conferring an undeniable and indelible essence on the individuals consecrated, such consecration authorizes transgressions that would otherwise be forbidden. The person who is sure of his cultural identity can play with the rules of the cultural game."[81] Transgression, for the ordained, only reinforces the boundary: it is "the privilege of privileges, that which consists of taking liberties with his privileges."[82] So long as one keeps in mind that *"quod licet Iovi non licet bovi,"* that what is fit for Jupiter is not fit for oxen.

The development of the seminar had further implications: its rigid and authoritarian, yet not obviously repressive, model seemed to actualize one of the myths of modern Western culture: the possibility of replacing pure and arbitrary repression within the patriarchal framework by creating an "asylum constituted in the family mode."[83] The prestige and authority of the director, teacher, and founder of the discipline (who, incidentally, was often single, as if married to science, as in the case of Jacob Grimm and Lachmann) recalls that of the bourgeois father whose virtues he displays.[84] The teacher-father encourages, helps, controls, and his punishment is imparted only through his gaze or words. Through his authority, power, and prestige he determines the rhythm of the pupil's growth and his eventual position. The pupil finds himself within a simulacrum of the family—indeed, an institutional parody of the same. This grotesque "family" functions as a safe haven based on symbols, rituals, and mechanisms, which protects the pupil from the influence and dynamics of society, but at the same time alienates him from the external world and creates in him a deeply ingrained psychological dependency.[85]

The director of the seminar wields a lot of power, bestowed on him by the state and legitimated by the prestige of authority and superior reason, on which his authority is apparently based. But he also has more practical powers (Bourdieu speaks of "clients," a transparent allusion to the ancient Roman *clientes* who sought favors from their rich and powerful patrons), since he decides the destiny within the professional community of each one of his pupils.[86] This kind of power (a veritable apparatus in Foucault's sense, and one still very common in modern academic communities) is what lies behind statutes, paradigms, canons, that is, all that is necessary to the functioning and survival of university disciplines. Those who are in a dominant position are dependent on the consensus that allows the institution to exist, while those who are dominated must go along with the official discourse and knowledge, and cannot unite as an independent group because this would call into question "the categories of perception of the social order, which, being the product of that order, inclined them to recognize that order and thus submit to it."[87] One could paraphrase this by an ecclesiastical Latin motto: *"Extra ecclesiam, nulla salus"* (Outside the church, there is no salvation).

Efforts toward Disciplinary Self-awareness

Lachmann's organization of German Studies did not go completely unchallenged by other philologists. In time, the first generational changes began. Those who inherited chairs by right of primogeniture faced a twofold legitimation problem: they had to prove, on the one hand, that their masters' choices were justified (including the choice of themselves as successors) and, on the other hand, that they were capable of reaching the same level as their masters in order to further the development of the discipline.[88] The principle "Better to err according to the method than to find truth by chance" emphasized the socializing and pedagogical function of the method, which required disciplinary self-control, namely, the elimination of all that was new and different and the rejection of all forms of experimentalism.[89] Lachmann's biographer wrote: "He achieved this result through hard and methodic discipline. . . . Lachmann demanded clarity above all things, awareness of the limits of one's knowledge. Any effort to guess, to conjecture, to formulate hypotheses on half-known facts disgusted him. When necessary, he had no problems admitting his ignorance, acknowledging a mistake, learning something from one of the members of the seminary. But idle talk, impertinence, intellectual arrogance were harshly dismissed by him as superficial and insecure forms of knowledge. 'Such young men,' he said, 'must be cut down.'"[90]

The fact that German Studies lacked an academic tradition caused it, paradoxically, to emphasize its disciplinary mechanisms and rituals more than other disciplines in order to furnish itself with solid institutional foundations. In fact, the "statute" of German Studies established by founding fathers Lachmann and Moriz Haupt has endured to the present day and is largely still operative.[91] Indeed, it is amazing to note the discipline's capability to go unscathed through historical catastrophes, social upheavals, revolutions, dictatorships, military defeats, the division of Germany, and so on—in other words, its utter resilience and impermeability to external pressures. Obviously the ability of German Studies to perpetuate itself is largely dependent on the co-optation system and the passing on of academic chairs "from father to son" or from master to pupil (the most obedient, docile, and academically disciplined among pupils), following the law of primogeniture.[92] It would be interesting, in this regard, to reconstruct the genealogy of university chairs from their origins to the present day.

Some of the most interesting results of the training of philologists according to the Lachmann-Haupt system are found in obituaries and biographies. One finds countless publications celebrating the image of Lachmann as founding father. This applies also to Grimm, but to a much lesser degree, since Grimm was never, as noted earlier, a true authority or master. Lachmann was presented as the incarnation of the philological ethos to which everything had to be sacrificed (including truth, as we have seen). There is a complete absence in these writings of any critical examination of the discipline, which was replaced by a desire to celebrate, establish, even codify the abilities of the master without ever seriously examining his philological achievements. The scenario was completely fixed and evidenced the utter epistemological rigidity of the discipline, deriving from the absolute subservience of pupil to master. The pupil defined his identity by reinforcing and celebrating that of his master. Those who wished to partake in the scientific discourse of the discipline had to ensure that their statements complied with the rules of the order, the only ones that might have allowed them to be declared true. There was no need for direct repression or censorship, since the dominated (the pupils) willingly subjected themselves to the dominant discourse: to question it would have been tantamount to questioning the institution and their own participation in it, that is, denying their own identity, besides having to face the charge of heresy and consequent excommunication. The effectiveness of the co-optation process is shown by the fact that the latter sanction, while theoretically possible, rarely needed to be applied.[93]

While Lachmann's philology left practically no room for autonomous work, Grimm offered, to a limited extent, the possibility to "energize the philological *ethos,*" integrating new subjects into the interdisciplinary debate.[94] Yet even in this case nobody could hope to discuss the discipline without referring to the spirit, the ethos, and the writings of a canonized figure. Thus the appeal to the truth and moral superiority of one's master (whether Lachmann or Grimm) ended up replacing scientific debate and the examination of evidence: moral superiority is what guarantees the truthfulness of a proposition.

Pfeiffer contra Haupt

An example of the obstacles faced by philology along the path set by Lachmann in its early days is the clash between the Berlin school, headed by Lachmann and Haupt, and the Vienna school, headed by Pfeiffer and Bartsch. Rather than outlining in detail the struggle between these two groups, I am interested in verifying the degree of disciplinary self-awareness of the participants as regards the situation of apparently satisfied *autopoiesis* in which philology found itself. I shall examine a specific case, comparing the programs of the two journals *Zeitschrift für deutsches Altertum* (established in 1841 with Haupt as director) and *Germania* (established in 1856 by Franz Pfeiffer after having collaborated with Haupt's journal).

Haupt is arguably the most pure example of mimetic submission to one's master, a true clone of Lachmann. His works are characterized by an absolute dogmatic and reverential adherence to Lachmann, whom he assisted on his deathbed until the end.[95] From this perspective, Scherer's judgment of Haupt, undoubtedly not dictated by a prejudice against him, acquires involuntary ironic overtones: "For philology it was an incalculable advantage that Lachmann, in a sense, manifested himself twice, that such a similar nature resurrected in Haupt, such a kindred personality, who found total satisfaction in appropriating the method of his friend, perpetuating it and transferring it into his writings and his teachings."[96]

Haupt wished to consolidate philology on an entirely dogmatic and closed basis: the journal he founded was to function as the highly specialized institutional seat of professional communication within the corporation. The premise of the first issue summarizes Haupt's general program for philology. In the first place, he wrote, it is necessary to curb the excessive desire to investigate the ancient past: "The hundreds of tombs we have discovered have told us almost nothing about the ancient times whose language is now lost."[97] Indiscriminate archeological efforts must be replaced by a selective reconstruction of the monuments of the past. Haupt personally took responsibility for deciding what deserved to be published: "I will personally make sure that only what is truly noteworthy is published here."[98] He proceeded to explain the method through which documents were to be presented. He rejected the accusation that all German philologists wrote as if for a secret society, defending instead the philologist's right to "rub off the rust that covers old works of art."[99] The philologist was to provide the reader with a readable text, since not all readers have the time to engage in the necessary "cleaning" of the work (*Sauberkeit* and *sauberer Text* were key words for Lachmann and his school). The study of literary history *(Literaturgeschichte)* was allowed only as an "analytical examination of details," but was to be performed carefully, since it implies a reflection on a more general context and constitutes the "ultimate goal of these efforts."[100] Finally, Haupt programmatically refused to let the journal be a place where philology and philological work were debated by deciding not to offer any reviews. What would normally be preserved in reviews might be communicated "in the form of additions and corrections," as Haupt wrote, skirting this crucial issue in a cursory and apparently neutral fashion.[101]

This editorial enterprise was no doubt complex, but I would draw attention to two specific features. In the first place, Haupt refused to let the journal be an instrument of communication and interaction between various schools or between the various positions inside and outside the discipline. As Jan-Dirk Müller notes, theoretical-methodological issues as well as institutional ones (i.e., who wrote, why he was chosen, how he did it, what he intended to demonstrate) were completely ignored.[102] The procedure through which one arrived at the final "clean" page that was presented to the reader of the *Zeitschrift* was never outlined and never made public. Second, the development of philology was based on purely quantitative criteria. At the time, the number of documents was increasing dramatically. Libraries and archives were continuously gathering, ordering, and producing new texts. Lachmann and Haupt's disciplinary approach, which was to remain dominant, was one of addition and subtraction: each new text, each new datum was added to the previous collection or, when necessary, replaced the older datum that was cast off. Yet the general context in which the datum was produced and the criteria on the basis of which it was selected were never discussed. Who would decide what was to survive? What were the philological alternatives to the decision taken? What were the rules according to which a given text was chosen? How could a layman orient himself in the labyrinth of philology? The answers to these questions provided by the Lachmann school relied ultimately on the moral superiority of the master and the total and unconditioned dedication of the adept to science (i.e., to the discursive society to which he belonged). The readings of each successive master were justified solely on the basis of the preestablished monopoly over truth that the latter possessed.

It is worthwhile to keep in mind that Haupt was also a brave patriot. He struggled for the German cause, was tried for high treason in 1848, then lost the Leipzig chair and returned to the University of Berlin only in 1853, to replace Lachmann. His political biography might appear in contrast with his curriculum as an academic philologist.[103] In fact, since the discipline had already established its domain, its rules, paradigms, and control mechanisms, Haupt's divergent attitudes (liberal-patriotic in politics, aristocratic and elitarian within academia) had their roots in the contrast between different domains, identities, and worldviews. What interests me is Haupt's role within the institution, the fact that he was authorized to speak within the institution as its "legitimate" representative, that is, as Bourdieu writes, "an agent capable of acting on the social world through words," being equipped with "the signs and the insignia aimed at underlining the fact that he is not acting in his own name and under his own authority."[104] Haupt's symbolical use of power was perfectly consistent with the general mechanisms that regulate the administration of power within a given discursive society. His philological decisions were legitimated by the group because they were acknowledged as true and authorized propositions speaking the language of institutional authority. Haupt's was the *fatum* (investiture, nomination) of the pupil-heir: "The self-respecting heir will behave like an heir and, according to Marx's expression, will be inherited by the heritage: that is, invested in the things and appropriated by the things which he has himself appropriated," as Bourdieu writes.[105]

This, then, was the situation of philology during the phase of its institutional and academic consolidation. The highly esoteric character of the Berlin school and the negative consequences of this attitude on the future of the discipline were even then noted by many. In fact, there were many interdisciplinary conflicts about the issues I have examined so far.[106] What strikes one among other things is the systematic use of insults on both sides, as well as the nature of the insults bandied: these extended from more predictable ones (philological incompetence ultimately due to lack of character or morals) to more fancy ones, such as accusations of cowardice (e.g., for having dared kick "Lachmann the lion" only when he was dead) and even allusions to sexual impotence.[107] By resorting to insults, a chosen individual who speaks on behalf of the whole group symbolically expels the transgressor from the social group or forces him to submit to common rules of conduct. In this case, however, the insults did not achieve their purpose. The reason is that both groups were in a position to claim their right to symbolic authority, that is, the socially acknowledged authority to impose the worldview and rules of the discipline. Both groups could appeal to philological virtues, to the authority of the founding fathers (Grimm on one side, Lachmann on the other), and so on. And these appeals took the place of any serious debate on the role and future of philology. Such a debate was in fact impossible given the characteristics of the discipline: a power structure based on the homologation and co-optation of adepts, and therefore lacking any self-critical capability.

It is interesting to see, however, how the opponents of the "Clique," as Pfeiffer called the Berlin school, sought to establish an alternative to the disciplinary orthodoxy of the same.[108] As in the case of the *Zeitschrift für deutsches Altertum,* one way to examine the issue is to take a look at the program of the journal *Germania.* This journal was founded in 1856 by Franz Pfeiffer, full professor in Vienna, and opponent of the "Berliner Schule." What was the practical difference between Pfeiffer's philological work and Lachmann's? It is easier to compare the two, because in 1864 Pfeiffer published an edition of the works of Walther von der Vogelweide that was explicitly and polemically in contrast to a similar edition published by Lachmann in 1827.[109] Pfeiffer's goal was to produce a philologically and scientifically accurate edition, yet one that was accessible to the larger public. To achieve this goal, he strove to provide the public with all the information necessary to understand the text. The edition was therefore accompanied by information on the author, on the meter adopted, on the literary context, and on literary genres and by explanations of the more obscure passages and words. The result was significantly different from that of Lachmann's edition, where all we were given was a brief premise and the notes were limited to the text and its philological history.

Pfeiffer presented himself, on the one hand, as a rigorous philologist critical of all efforts to modernize the text and, on the other hand, as one who insisted on the importance of communicating the results of the scientific work to the outside world.[110] Pfeiffer spoke of the necessity to expand the horizons of philologists: "It is therefore German antiquity as a whole, German life in all its forms, that must become the object of our research."[111] Consequently his journal was open to language (in Grimm's broader acceptation) and literature (while the journal did express some reservations on literature, it also stated that it could not be excluded in advance). The program called for information, notes, and reviews. The goal was to increase the quantity and quality of communication within the discipline, but also to stimulate interest in philological studies among the more general public. It is here that Pfeiffer launched his attack on the Berlin school: "The spirit and the method through which things have been handled," he wrote, had had the effect of restricting "the circle of those interested in shared research" rather than expanding it.[112] Pfeiffer proceeded to outline the current condition of philology with remarkable lucidity: "One cannot deny that in the field of German philology, as in no other field of learning, the absolute power of authorities and the prestige of the school have reached a level where it no longer serves as stimulus but as a hindrance, and has become incompatible with free research and the unimpeded search for truth."[113] It is true that Pfeiffer, too, resorted to arguments based on moral superiority: "For this clique, science and truth have no value. All that counts is their fame and prestige. To maintain this power, no means is too low or too mean. . . . But who can doubt on which side lie spiritual liveliness and progress and on which side negligence, laziness and stagnation?"[114] Yet while both opponents resorted to a rhetoric of moral superiority and philological ethos, Pfeiffer did express a view of the discipline that was not narrowly conservative and self-referential, but strove instead to expand its horizons, its methods, and its language in order to stimulate or recover the interest of the larger public.

In regard to the Lachmann school, Pfeiffer left little room for compromise: "This system of belief must be destroyed, otherwise there shall never be any progress."[115] Pfeiffer was convinced that German philology had gotten itself to a dead end. And indeed it was dominated by the reproductive logic of disciplinary knowledge, whose goal is to preserve the essential element on which the group is based: the adherence to a consolidated and arbitrary cultural principle, a form of "primordial *illusio* without which there would be no stakes to play for, nor even any game."[116] The possibilities of reforming such a system are practically nil: the institution has been consolidated by generations of pupils turned masters who are "the ultimate product of the dialectic of acclaim and recognition which drew into the heart of the system those most inclined and able to reproduce it without distortion."[117] From this perspective the constant and, indeed, obsessive insistence on philological gravity and ethos can be seen as the expression of a suspicion and resentment, of an "aversion to ideas and to a free and critical spirit," an obstinate resistance to innovation and invention.[118] This attitude, however, is not a degeneration of the academic system, but, on the contrary, represents the most effective, celebrated, and undisputed instrument of academic and institutional consolidation. The epistemological dead end at which philology found itself was dramatically evident to Pfeiffer: the "primordial illusion" of the correct philological decision, and the consequent fear of mistakes and ensuing moral sanction, had transformed the original discipline into a power structure, in which members establish relations that are increasingly opaque and removed from their original goals (the search for truth through science).[119] It is significant that much of the debate among schools centered on the conduct of philologists. The term *conduct,* in fact, fully expresses the specificity of power relations: *conduct* refers both to guiding the behavior of others and to behaving in certain ways within a given sphere of choices. As Foucault has written, "The exercise of power consists in guiding the possibility of conduct and putting in order the possible outcome."[120]

The problem of philology, as I have sought to demonstrate, cannot be separated from a discussion of power as rule, as an instrument for guiding the conduct of individuals and groups within a given domain. Ruling means structuring the field of possibilities available for the actions and options of individuals; the latter, however, are still fundamentally free, since the alternative would be literal enslavement. Philology, as established by Lachmann and Haupt, appears as an institutionalized power system which, in addressing the complex dialectics of freedom and submission, uses all its authority, its apparatus, its procedures to affirm the prevalence of the latter over the former.

Two

Under the Aegis of Goethe: Liberal Historiography from Gervinus to Dilthey

The philological paradigm embraced by institutional *Germanistik* was by no means the only available option: an alternative path existed that, however, proved less viable under the circumstances due to political implications that could not easily be accepted at that point in German history. This alternative path was provided by the liberal historiographers' attempt to connect the study of national literature with the overall development of the German national identity in a liberal sense. The most significant instance of this attempt was Gervinus's effort to shape liberal historiography as a veritable "oppositional science" vis-à-vis both the general political situation of the pre-1848 era and the ways German Studies had been institutionally established as a university discipline.[1]

Literary History as an Oppositional Science

The label *oppositional science* aims at emphasizing the features and functions of the study of national literature within the liberal historiography of *Vormärz*.[2] While German Studies was in the process of establishing itself as an institution rigidly based on philological concerns—and, as we have seen, the prevalence of the philological paradigm ruled out the possibility of dealing with political and ideological issues—the mid-1830s witnessed the emergence of something that might be termed "the discourse of *Literaturgeschichte.*"[3] In ways and forms that were utterly unrelated to and independent of the world of academe, a strong demand began to emerge for a scientific literary history that would take into account national literature, and particularly recent national literature, as a vehicle for the circulation of antifeudal ideas and principles. The German literary tradition—from Lessing to Goethe—had articulated in its representations a complex dialectical analysis of the world that was, or was read as, in direct opposition to the dominant classes. In the *Vormärz* all political groups, both conservative and progressive, wished to use *Nationalliteratur* as the ground of a political conflict and as a way to present, defend, and circulate their political positions.

This view of the aims and functions of literature had as its referent the emerging bourgeois public sphere—in all its nuances, from reactionary to conservative to liberal to democratic—rather than the university, where the philological paradigm reigned unchallenged. It had virtually no relation to the academic world until the moment when the university as an institution was finally able to assimilate and neutralize the political interpretation of national literature. That happened only when, after the revolution of 1848 had failed, German liberalism underwent an acute crisis that led it, after 1866, to a realistic acceptance of the Prussian way to national unity. That acceptance created the preliminary conditions for a philo-Prussian revision of *Nationalliteratur* that enabled it to enter the university classroom along with philology—a development made possible by the prestige and credentials of a personality like Wilhelm Scherer.

The Gervinus Model

Georg Gottfried Gervinus (1805–71) was a professional historian. He was one of the seven professors of Göttingen who were forced to leave the city in a hurry after refusing to abandon their constitutional rights and to pledge total allegiance to an autocratic king. As a historian he took part in the first two congresses of German Studies presided over by Jacob Grimm, and in 1848 he joined the Frankfurt parliament as one of the foremost representatives of constitutional liberalism. His historical work had led him to advocate a change in the principles on which German society was based: from feudal and conservative to liberal and monarchical-constitutional. While these profound institutional transformations were the ultimate goal of liberal opposition, there was little consensus on *how* to bring them about: the French Revolution was seen at times as a model, at times as a nightmare. Nevertheless, there was a common feeling that the liberty and unity of the German nation were soon to be achieved.

The fact that national literature, notwithstanding the political insignificance of Germany, had been able to produce authors, works, and literary schools of worldwide fame seemed proof of the capacity of the German people to achieve great results in the intellectual and spiritual fields. The birth of a national state in which the middle class and the people as a whole could achieve liberty, progress, and spiritual emancipation seemed a natural and necessary extension of the success of its great national literature.

It is within this summarily described context that Gervinus's theoretical work must be viewed.[4] Gervinus represents arguably the most significant and consistent example of a historian who used his work to serve a political project aimed at transforming present reality. Significantly, his approach to national literature was a consequence of totally extraliterary events: Gervinus himself said that the event that spurred him to write a history of German literature was the July 1830 French Revolution and the corresponding intensification of reactionary politics in Austria and Prussia.[5] At a time when liberty seemed increasingly foreign to Germany, Gervinus felt the duty to show his nation its value, bringing to light the revolutionary potential of its extraordinary recent cultural, literary, and artistic period. In other words, Gervinus decided to open a new front in the war on reaction, focusing on literature and the question of national unity, two subjects dear to the hearts of all Germans and most likely to wake the middle class from its political slumber: "It seems to us to be high time that we made the nation understand at last its *present* value, that we gave it back its self-confidence that is now vacillating, that we bestowed on it, along with pride for its ancient past, an enthusiasm for the present moment and the most unshakeable courage for the future."[6]

With his *Geschichte der poetischen National-Literatur der Deutschen* (History of the poetical national literature of the Germans) Gervinus intended first of all to methodologically differentiate his work from other works of literary history. Contemporary literary histories took mostly the form of compilations and chronicles: they were lists of authors that obeyed a purely additive logic and made little effort to synthesize information, discuss the context, and interpret national literature by identifying its unifying factors. In other cases it was the critics' personal leanings that provided the criteria for the selection and discussion of specific works and authors at the expense of more general considerations of literary history. Like other historians of the *Vormärz,* Gervinus had as his goal to write a history that would not focus so much on specific texts or on events in the lives of given authors, but would seek to relate literature to the "spiritual life" of the nation and the people. The approach was to be consistent, unitary, and, most important, objective; the literary historian was to reject aesthetic subjectivism (the evaluation of works according to individual preferences) in favor of historical and political interpretation. Gervinus clearly stated the need to separate the history of literature from aesthetic judgment: "I have nothing to do with the aesthetic assessment of things, I am no poet and no literary critic."[7] Precisely because the history of literature was at the service of a pressing political project, it had to emancipate itself from aesthetics. Literary history thus became part of history and was separated from philosophy. Furthermore, Gervinus did not intend to write "for the compilers and the erudite scholars of this literature, . . . not for a special class of readers, but . . . for the nation," and consequently he purposefully excluded notes, since modern texts did not require philological clarification and bulky apparatuses risked making works less accessible to readers.[8] Clarity and accessibility were deemed necessary to differentiate his position from the esoteric stance of the academic "discursive society." Furthermore, Gervinus meant his history not to be used for philological inquiries on specific authors, works, or periods, but rather to be read in its entirety and understood in its overall thrust, since only thus would it reach the goals he had set for it.

Having established his methodological premises, Gervinus engaged in the task of defining an actual political education program for the middle class and the German nation. His *Geschichte der poetischen National-Literatur der Deutschen* had the moral intent to provide the middle class with a sense of its political and practical duties for the purpose of achieving a peaceful transition from feudal to bourgeois society. To this end, Gervinus began by searching in the most remote past for noteworthy examples of German literature and traced its history all the way to the anti-Napoleonic liberation wars, thus presenting the German middle class with a consistent historical model at once rooted in the past but also alive and relevant to the present.

His starting thesis was that German literature achieved its peak with Goethe and Schiller, with whom a unique cycle had gloriously come to an end. In fact, what is distinctive in Gervinus's interpretation is the notion that the golden age of philosophy, literature, and art had to be followed by the phase of political action, according to an internal necessity of historical development that could be termed the telos of the German nation. He presented the development of literature as a continuous, ceaseless movement toward progress and liberty guided by the "Zeitgeist."[9] The literary historian "must" understand the direction in which the "spirit of the age" is moving and anticipate its development, thus becoming part of it. He must be, in other words, "within the development" as one of its components, participating in the process of emancipation of the spirit. It is only when the spirit, in its evolution, achieves maximum self-expression within a given form (religion, art, philosophy) that it proceeds to embody itself in a new form.

One may easily guess the authors that most attracted Gervinus's interest: after Luther (the foremost and final embodiment of the spirit in religion), Gervinus extolled the *"Republikaners,"* those who, like Klopstock, constantly seek to relate poetry to religion and politics.[10] Among *"republikaner"* authors Gervinus cited Lessing, Forster (the republican par excellence), and, last but not least, Schiller. These he saw as the champions who best embodied a supreme principle, the principle of the *"vita activa,"* which becomes a value in itself. In Gervinus's history it is possible to discern a certain admiration for capitalistic virtues, such as the will to transform the world, discipline, reason, realism, a willingness to sacrifice. While feudal power is based on the force of tradition and theology, ruling "by God's will," he thought the middle class must necessarily construct, circulate, and gain consensus for its own tradition and specific habitus in order to achieve and legitimize a cultural hegemony as a step toward future political supremacy. This was, in short, Gervinus's theoretical framework.

On the basis of these theoretical and methodological premises Gervinus was able to produce a highly readable and intellectually outstanding history of literature where individual authors were always located in the context of more general trends. From this subordination of individual subjects and works to the necessities of the overall framework in Gervinus's work, a "mythical category" was born and consolidated that was to remain dominant in later decades, even in literary histories and interpretations much removed from Gervinus's liberalism: the "deutsche Klassik." The period from 1770 to 1830 was treated as an exemplary and unmatchable achievement, the moment of absolute perfection and completeness in art and literature. One may note that, on the contrary, neither Goethe nor Schiller nor the romantics considered their period the end of a phase or a peak in national literary development. It was only after the death of Goethe (1832) and Hegel (1833) that the idea began to circulate that "*the* great period" of literature, art, and philosophy in Germany had come to an end. This belief soon became general: Heine, too, for example, thought that an extraordinary age, "die Kunstperiode," had ended. He believed, however, that this could set the stage for a "modern literature" capable of addressing contemporary issues through new and adequate expressive forms. Heine did not proclaim the end of art, but he did believe in the impossibility of perpetuating within the new historical conditions the clear-cut separation between artistic sphere and historical reality that had been rigorously observed in Weimar classicism. In Heine's interpretation the autonomy of art, to which classicism owed its greatness, would lose all legitimation and become a conservative ideology if it was taken as a model for all ages. The literature of the new reality would instead have to be the result of a dialectical interaction between the transformations of the modern world and the means of artistic production. Heine went so far as to explicitly mention those who could serve as models for this new art, citing Jean Paul as an example of a modern author unburdened either by an exclusive concern with the past (as were the romantics) or by the shackles of classicism.[11] Heine did not criticize the romantics in the name of the Weimar pair (Goethe and Schiller), as Gervinus did, but looked for viable alternatives: in his essay "Concerning the History of Religion and Philosophy in Germany"[12] he proposed yet another model: Lessing, whom he saw as a synthesis between Protestant tradition, a form of progressive pantheism that translates into critical philosophy, and the more advanced manifestations of the bourgeois literary revolution of the eighteenth century. Lessing and Jean Paul are concrete examples of a different interpretation of art and philosophy and of the different functions they can take on. For Heine, too, the ultimate purpose of the great German spiritual revolutions was to obtain what the French had already achieved in 1789 and in 1830 with the July Revolution. But the history of the "German spirit" was not presented as a gradual, necessary, and fatal development free of any regression, detour, or rupture. Heine's judgments, while often brutal, sarcastic, and cruel, were always free from any dogmatic notion of "absolute spirit." Thus, notwithstanding his sharply polemical stance, his attitude was ultimately open, allowing for and indeed advocating the most diverse forms of artistic expression. This attitude was in contrast with those of other authors, such as Menzel or Börne, who, from opposite perspectives, in attacking Goethe for his apolitical stance seemed misled by a need to create and consolidate a cultural and literary tradition that might have been immediately exploited in political terms, and thus failed to take into account the specific nature of the work of art.

Gervinus's approach was completely different from Heine's. He started off with the assumption that a new and conclusive phase in the history of the spirit had been reached, which no longer drew its character from art or literature: "Competition in the artistic sphere is over; now we are to set ourselves a goal that no one here has ever reached; we shall see whether Apollo bestows on us once again in this the glory that he did not deny us elsewhere."[13]

In terms of artistic models, one may easily guess where Gervinus's preferences lay: he was for Schiller and against Goethe.[14] According to Gervinus, Schiller was constantly moved by the spirit of liberty, while Goethe was sensually immersed in the state of nature.[15] Schiller stood as a representative of stoicism, of the male element, activism, and the political will to fight against the feudal world, while Goethe stood for Epicurean and feminine passivity, for an apolitical, submissive, and contemplative stance vis-à-vis the world.[16] This interpretative framework explains Gervinus's belittling of works such as *Wilhelm Meister* and the second part of *Faust,* which he saw as "whims of old age" and even symptoms of senility.[17]

The two different approaches just outlined would appear to have excluded the possibility of any simultaneous canonization of both Schiller and Goethe. But Gervinus was responding to an extraliterary imperative—that of organizing literature in order to establish a great national tradition for a nation that was yet to be. From this perspective, the whole question of Weimar classicism (more specifically of the Goethe-Schiller collaboration from 1794 to 1805) can be interpreted and understood only within the context of the German tradition (other national literatures did not have to face the same problems) and of the effort by the various currents of German liberalism to establish a strong cultural identity that would legitimize it in the eyes of the people and consolidate its hegemony.[18] Gervinus was well aware of the differences between the two authors, yet it was imperative for him to present the decade of collaboration between the two as a successful synthesis of aesthetic, spiritual, and literary values and as a milestone in national history. The collaboration was the final achievement of the cultural tradition of the German nation, and Gervinus read the entire previous cultural history as preparation for this achievement. In Gervinus's evolutionary model Klopstock and Lessing preceded the Sturm und Drang, which led to the *Klassik,* which prevailed until, after Schiller's death and the poetical senility of Goethe, the romantics acquired ascendancy.[19] Each stage superseded the former following an internal necessity of the history of the spirit. The final result was the achievement of an organic totality of cultural, literary, and spiritual values from which the flower of politics was to be born. This interpretative paradigm erased otherwise important differences and allowed Gervinus to include in the canon all those who had contributed to the spiritual emancipation of national literature. This was true especially of "classic" authors, while other "minor" authors, as well as all those who for one reason or another did not fit the paradigm, were either ignored or made to adjust to it.

This interpretative paradigm, I repeat, had an immediate political function. But it also had, on a functional level, two immediate advantages: first, it presented the history of literature as a continuous and necessary evolution of the national spirit; second, it also made it possible to fit the romantics into the overall framework (through a shift in critical approach and in the means and criteria for incorporation, as Dilthey and Scherer were to do later on), without having to change the arrival point (the death of Goethe), since Goethe and the romantics had been active during the same years. Gervinus can also be credited with clearly and simply describing the history of German literature, making it accessible to a large number of readers. He described authors, works, and literary periods in their interactions, but, more important, examined them in order to selectively reconstruct the past and define a traditional corpus, that is, a canon that must be preserved for posterity. He also selected and assessed the authors and texts from the national literary heritage according to their productivity in and relevance to the political demands of his own age. This approach implies the rejection of normative aesthetics, since it is the evolution, the movement, the progress of history that determine the working framework of the historian. Gervinus's view of literary history, culminating in the Weimar synthesis of aesthetic, literary, artistic, and philosophical values, allowed the German middle class to narcissistically represent itself as the avant-garde of the "kingdom of the spirit" while waiting to enter other more earthly kingdoms. This was doubtless one reason for its lasting success: the idea that German literature had culminated in the Weimar period was to remain, with minor revisions, a central tenet of all the more important histories of literature of the nineteenth century—for example, those of Hettner (1870) and Scherer (1883).[20]

From Political Opposition to the Aesthetic Sphere

Gervinus's highly politicized stance was destined to draw some criticism. An alternative to Gervinus, both in methods and content, is represented by the figure of Theodor Wilhelm Danzel (1815–50).[21] Danzel, a philosopher and art historian as well as author of important studies on Goethe, Gottsched, and Lessing, chose to study the history of literature from an aesthetic-philosophical perspective rather than a historical-political one. In his essay *Über die Behandlung der Geschichte der neueren deutschen Literatur* (On the ways of handling the history of modern German literature, 1849) he developed an extended and in many ways convincing critique of Gervinus's historiography, following an approach that was later to be appropriated to some extent by Dilthey.[22] Danzel's work represents an explicit effort to delegitimize the militant historiography of the post-1848 period and stands out as a milestone in the transition from *Vormärz* to *Nachmärz* liberalism: from the militant phase of the liberal middle class, centered on the search for an antifeudal national conscience, to the conscious acceptance, in the wake of a series of undeniable difficulties and defeats, of a "reasonable" compromise with the new post-48 situation, a compromise strenuously opposed by Gervinus. Danzel's confrontation with Gervinus ranged from philosophical to ideological to political issues and is characterized by a number of insightful observations that deserve to be examined in detail.

Danzel's first criticism centered on the lack of objectivity in Gervinus's method. According to Danzel, Gervinus had introduced into historiography an "external perspective" (318) (i.e., the necessary manifestation of the spirit in the political events of the German nation), which was offered as a priori, thus undermining the objectivity and autonomy of historical research. Thus conceived, Danzel argued, historiography lacks a scientific basis. According to Danzel, Gervinus had used the history of national literature to identify, address, and resolve the political problems of the present day: his historiography was functional to effect the emancipation of the middle class and the restructuring of the state. Danzel did not deny the legitimacy of these political aspirations; however, he dismissed as an abstract and arbitrary notion the idea that the spirit of humanity or of the German nation had to be exclusively concerned with religion, art, or politics at any given period in time, as if constitutionally unable to find expression in a plurality of interests. Danzel criticized all efforts to establish a direct connection between the political needs of the present and the historical representation or reconstruction of the past (319). Danzel believed that Gervinus's desire to belong to the "spirit of the time" had led him to produce "tendentious" and arbitrary works that had the same "philological rigor" as a preacher's sermon (321).

Danzel then moved on to another issue of great importance. It made no sense, he argued, to obsessively insist on the specificity of the "*deutsche National-Literatur.*" German literature is part of a European and world literature: "The mutual exchange between different national literatures and the common ground where they are all rooted" (324) must lead historians to focus on the close connection and mutual influence of national histories, avoiding distortions and arbitrary distinctions.[23]

Danzel's remarks were no doubt convincing. Yet in context they served to "sterilize" literature and its history of all the "external" elements associated with the idea of national development that Gervinus had arbitrarily introduced. Danzel proposed a number of methodological alternatives. In the first place, he said it was necessary to go back to "pragmatic" analyses of works accomplished through closely focused, monographic studies. These would lay the ground for great historical syntheses, which should be produced only "at a distance of twenty or thirty years from the events" (323).[24] Danzel thought the history of literature must be brought back within the domain of aesthetics: "Literary history should be regarded as one kind of art history; its task will be that of reconstructing the metamorphoses of poetic production according to purely inherent criteria, without a glance either right or left" (326).[25]

By reinserting the history of literature within the "objective" domain of aesthetics, Danzel strove to eliminate the subjectivism inherent in Gervinus's political perspective. While this position prepared for and to some extent anticipated Wilhelm Scherer's positivism, it also reintroduced Leopold Ranke's historicist approach, which Gervinus had sought to overcome. Ranke had also argued for a strictly objective historiography.[26] His explicit goal had been to put a stop to the spread of liberal views in historiography (presenting history as the development toward progress and liberty) by anchoring historical research to pure facticity. Ranke, while not denying the existence of progress *(Fortschritt),* introduced an important scientific distinction: the progress of humanity is possible, he said, only as the extension of man's dominion over nature. Such a notion loses all its validity when applied to arts, poetry, science, or politics, because in these areas human action, while influenced by historical circumstances, is also in direct communication with God.[27] Ranke postulated a sharp distinction between the sciences that deal with nature and the production of material commodities and those that deal with poetry, art, philosophy, and the human sciences (sciences of the spirit), which are related to the divine. The historian's role is to search for and identify the divine element in historical events. Ranke's reliance on the divine as that which underlies all periods and events undermined the linear conception of progress that typifies liberal historiography. Gervinus's "external" point of view was to Ranke totally internal to history, because history and the divine idea are one and the same. Through *"intuitives Verstehen"* (intuitive understanding) God is found within specific events; historical research is thus freed from the liberal notion of progress as an independent and linear evolution.

What did Danzel do, then, in order to emancipate historiography from "external points of view"? What was his approach? Let us consider by way of example Danzel's essay *Über Goethes Spinozismus* (1843), a monograph whose goal was to go beyond philosophical or idealistic interpretations of literature.[28] While it is not possible to examine this work in detail, it is useful to consider the way Danzel presented the figure of Goethe and what this presentation can tell us about Danzel's method. Danzel depicted Goethe not as undergoing various artistic as well as personal phases, but as an almost unchanging figure.[29] Danzel strove above all to defend Goethe from accusations that he was resigned or indifferent to the great historical events of his time and lacked political commitment, which had been made by

Vormärz historians. His interpretation of Goethe's attitude was to remain canonical for most nineteenth- and twentieth-century criticism. For Danzel, Goethe was capable of rising above the contradictions of his time. He succeeded in achieving a form of "self-preservation of the individual" (53) that allowed him to contemplate his age from a transcendent, timeless perspective.[30]

According to Danzel, Goethe regarded the history of politics as nothing but "the ultimate goal of petty interests, finitude left to its brutish instincts." His response to the French Revolution and the spread of its principles in the world was "a struggle to keep a better Self."[31] His entire poetics can be read as an effort to rise to "a more elevated totality," going beyond human weaknesses and imperfections. Danzel believed that Goethe's *"Erhebung"* (elevation) is "also the method of knowledge." By rising to a superior level the poet gains "a calm contemplation of things in their timeless essence." And it is "genius" that allows the individual to rise "to the eternal within himself."[32] Through this act the individual does not understand a substance outside the self; rather he understands the eternal nature of his own internal content and its specific form.

The scope of Danzel's essay far exceeds the foregoing description, but this brief summary serves to highlight the features of a way of representing, interpreting, and assessing the figure of Goethe that was to leave an indelible mark on German Studies.[33] Danzel's Goethe is interested in human events only insofar as he perceives in them the unfolding of the eternal in its own self-awareness. Otherwise, he "rises" above them to an elevated sphere of aesthetic, artistic, and philosophical interests from which he looks down with detachment on petty political and historical events. The figure of Goethe thus takes on aristocratic, heroic, and geniuslike overtones that would be fully canonized through the historiography of the *Geistesgeschichte* (see Friedrich Gundolf's representative essay *Goethe,* 1916).

Danzel had started off, as we have seen, by criticizing the "point of view" in historiography. Gervinus had always admitted that his activity as a historian depended on the "spirit of the time." Danzel, on the other hand, aspired to objectivity (even though it could easily be argued that his system, too, was far from exempt from arbitrary statements and apologetic sophisms). My point, however, is not to seek to establish the scientific superiority of the one over the other. It is certainly more useful to accept the fact that we are confronted with two different notions of literature and of the relation of literature to politics and history. While Gervinus's approach was openly militant, Danzel's allegiances were more covert: he was a representative of a "high bourgeois" view of literature marked by strong aesthetic and philosophical overtones—a view that, after being filtered and canonized by Dilthey, was to remain dominant in German Studies throughout the twentieth century.[34] This shows that, already in the troubled decade between 1840 and 1850, the development of the bourgeois-liberal conscience was not univocal, but took a variety of different paths, exploring alternative solutions to its political and existential crisis. Gervinus considered the mercantile class the top example of the right way of life, an opinion consistent with the preeminence he accorded to the principle of the *"vita activa."*[35] He sought to point out for the middle class an ideal route leading to economic and political power, which, in his general theoretical scheme, belonged to that class by right. For Danzel, instead, the highest achievement of the spirit was not found in politics, but in an aesthetic world in which the relation between the individual (as genius) and the world is an "absolute vision" corresponding to Spinoza's *"cognitio reflexiva,"* which, as an idea of the idea, comprehends within itself both nature and spirit in total reflection.[36] Danzel's model, Goethe, achieved the self-reflection of the spirit through his genius: this is made possible by *"Entsagung"* (renunciation), as a precondition of *"Erhebung,"* and so on. This interpretation of Goethe's greatness, derived from categories such as vision, genius, renunciation, elevation, and indifference to politics, would later be extended to the literary critic and the historian (for example, by the group of authors, poets, critics, and Germanist followers of George), who were considered privileged mediators between "greatness" and the general public, precisely because to some extent they partook in the genius typified by Goethe.[37]

Dilthey and the Institutionalization of *Literaturwissenschaft*

While for Gervinus *Literaturwissenschaft* took on the character of an "oppositional science," or *Oppositionswissenschaft,* in Danzel it lost all its militant aspects. Starting with the 1850s, the interpretative paradigms used for the more recent national literature underwent a profound change: on the one hand, liberal historiography lost its prestige (in parallel with the loss of prestige of the public sphere to which it was addressed); on the other hand, there was a growing need even within academia to reinterpret recent literature on the basis of the new political framework and as an integral part of a general national education program. Philology was seen as the discipline that necessarily had to oversee this process: only through the authority and guarantee of the philological approach was an organic integration of modern literature into the academia seen as possible. It was by no means an accident that the task of ushering modern literature into the university was achieved by a great philologist like Scherer: it was the integrating capability of the philological apparatus and its paradigms, of which Scherer was an eminent representative, that gave the process scientific authority and prestige.[38] From this perspective, it is worth noting that until 1860 literary histories were written by nonspecialists (Gervinus was a historian; Danzel a philosopher, like Rudolf Haym; Robert Prutz was a journalist with a classical background; etc.).[39] They were also addressed to the general public rather than academics, because of the hostility of philology to modern national literature during its phase of institutionalization and disciplinary consolidation.[40]

The slow transformation of *Literaturwissenschaft* into a university discipline inside German Studies entailed, after 1848, a methodological, ideological, and political restructuring, which has often been interpreted as a "fall" from the principles of *Vormärz* liberal historiography to an unconditional surrender to the idea of the Second Reich.[41] While there is an undeniable relation between the evolution of German liberalism as the ideology of the German middle class and the evolution of literary historiography and German Studies in general, one must also keep in mind that during this period new interests and new methodological and organizational demands emerged within the discipline that cannot be dealt with simply in terms of ideological critique (which, however, remains of the utmost importance). The fact is that the defeat of 1848 called into question all the criteria on which literary historiography was based. It showed that political-practical problems could not be solved according to Gervinus's simplistic blueprint. The immediacy of political praxis gave way to other approaches based on the separation of the political and cultural spheres. A significant section of the German middle class saw the new post-48 order as a concrete possibility to establish the economic bases of the future national state and focused its energies on production. The *Zollverein* (Tax Association) of 1834 and the beginning of industrialization gave the capitalistic middle class the sensation of being on the verge of an irreversible process leading to economic success and national unity. The events of the years between 1860 and 1870 also brought about a number of significant changes: the victory of Prussia over Austria, the end of the *Deutscher Bund* and the exclusion of Austria from the *Deutsche Nation,* the solution of the *Verfassungskonflikt* (constitutional conflict) and the ensuing division in the liberal field, all of which caused a series of political, ideological, religious, cultural, and philosophical ruptures that German Studies could not help taking into account, especially in view of its new institutional role and function.[42] In other words: the creation of the national corpus, canon, and value system—both in literary and in extraliterary matters—could no longer be based on a liberal-bourgeois project of opposition to the status quo, but had to be reshaped by the urgent need to legitimize the current state of things and German-Prussian supremacy.

This happened both with Scherer and the positivist school and with Dilthey and the *geistesgeschichtliche Schule.* While Scherer sought to overcome the methodological crisis by combining philological rigor with an organic and positivist conception of literary history, adopting the method of the natural sciences as an objective safeguard against the philosophical "lucubrations" of *Vormärz* historiography, Dilthey went the opposite direction, sharply distinguishing between the methods of the "spiritual" and natural sciences. The ultimate goal, however, was the same. Both thinkers aimed at defining a corpus of national values: a "national ethical system," wrote Scherer, a system which, as Dilthey specified, should be active "at the heart of the political and material interests of the present moment."[43]

It fell to Wilhelm Dilthey (1834–1911) to resolve the controversy between Danzel and Gervinus. In Dilthey's work the decade from 1860 to 1870 was marked by the effort to address certain theoretical issues, an effort that took the form, after some initial uncertainties, of a clear-cut critique of liberal historiography and, specifically, of Gervinus's approach. These were the years of Dilthey's reflection on Scherer's positivist method, of his monograph on Schleiermacher and of the foundation of hermeneutics: years of intense labor and great creativity. These were also the years of his studies on the literature of Goethe's period, which significantly coincided with the rise of Prussia as the nucleus of the nascent *Reich* in the years between 1864 and 1866. The problem that Dilthey addressed, again in the context of a conservative shift in his personal development, was that of reconciling the core of national literature (Goethe and the "spirit" of Weimar) with the Prussian state as the nucleus of the future German state. For this reason Dilthey developed a general philosophical, cultural, and literary framework functional to the project of restructuring the *Bildung* of the nascent nation. In his essay "Literaturhistorische Arbeiten über das klassische Zeitalter unserer Dichtung" (1866) Dilthey discussed the critical approaches of liberal historiography (Gervinus, Hermann Hettner, Julian Schmidt).[44] His preferences lay with the histories of Hettner and Schmidt (he especially valued Schmidt's fifth edition of *Geschichte der deutschen Literatur seit Lessing's Tod,* in which after 1866 the author clearly distanced himself from *Vormärz* liberalism), while predictably it was Gervinus's history that came under attack. Dilthey criticized above all its moralistic approach: Gervinus had introduced an external moral judgment, or at any rate an external value system, into historical analysis, and this was totally at odds with Dilthey's notion of history: "The essence of history is the historical becoming itself, and if one wishes to call this essence a goal, then the goal of history is solely this historical becoming."[45]

During this period Dilthey laid the foundation of a veritable history of the *Goethezeit,* the "age of Goethe," through his essays on Novalis, Lessing, and Goethe, later gathered in the volume *Das Erlebnis und die Dichtung* (Inner experience and poetry, 1905).[46] However, it was in his *Antrittsvorlesung,* his "introductory lesson" at the University of Basel in 1867, that Dilthey outlined for the first time the key tenets of his interpretation of the age of Goethe. Let us briefly consider them. For Dilthey the period from 1770 to 1830 was characterized by a great harmony among man, nature, society, and state. A positive, ordered, harmonious *Weltanschauung* reigned, which tended to expand from the spiritual-literary sphere to the political-institutional one. Dilthey believed that internal contrasts within literature and culture are of secondary importance and had little impact on the great "spiritual movement" that took place in the period between Lessing's first work and the death of Goethe, Hegel, and Schleiermacher, a unitary, organic whole that proceeded "with a consistent and continuous motion." In contrast with what happened in Spain and Germany, the great literary creation of the German people was not the consequence of a "perfectly realized national spirit," since Germany was a "fragmented country."[47] The military might of Prussia, too, with the strong national feeling it created, produced a particular vision of society and state. The German middle class was excluded from political affairs, but found a way to develop its *Bildung* and fully express its internal world. The vital impulse of a spiritually mature nation, lacking an external outlet on account of the political situation, was channeled into literature. In Gervinus's interpretation this great spiritual movement was a necessary stepping stone toward the future politicization of the German middle class. Dilthey instead transformed—indeed, he hypostatized—a particularly fertile moment in the history of national literature associated with a highly undeveloped political condition into a positive, permanent trait of the German spirit. The great literature of the *Goethezeit* ended up representing, for Dilthey, the beginning of a movement that produced "a vision of life and the world . . . in which the German spirit [found] its fulfillment."[48] Thus a specifically German spiritual movement was identified, the "Deutsche Bewegung," derived from the Weimar *Klassik* and concomitant with the political events of 1866. In Dilthey's interpretation the concept of the *Vorklassik* (preclassical period) was used for the first time in relation to Lessing and the literary production of the period of Frederick II. A harmonious and positive worldview was seen as a distinctive quality of German-Prussian culture of the later half of the eighteenth century, in contrast with French Revolutionary culture. Dilthey's selection of canonical models was functional for his purposes. For example, he celebrated Lessing's poetic insight at the expense of his analytical, rational, critical, or discursive qualities.[49] All cultural movements, from the *Aufklärung* (Enlightenment) to the *Romantik* through the Sturm und Drang and the *Klassik,* were seen as necessary and therefore legitimate moments in the cultural development of the nation.

Dilthey, as noted earlier, conceived the history of literature in immediately didactic terms: it was a "personal education and spiritual distinction."[50] His interpretation of the age of Goethe had an explicit political and ideological import: it celebrated a view of the world and of life that rejected contrast or criticism.[51] This, in turn, promoted an ideal but historically specific notion of society as a political order in which conflicts are not institutionalized and the place in which conflicts are expressed and addressed in liberal democracy (the parliament) is discredited. Dilthey was evidently influenced by the polemics about the role of the parliament in Prussia during those years and fully accepted the solution of the *Verfassungskonflikt.* After German unity the critical function of literature had become a divisive and destructive element that was harmful to the *Bildung* of the nation, as witness the treatment reserved for Heine in certain 1878 comments, in which Dilthey called him a disruptive figure incapable of accepting national harmony.[52] Dilthey's *Antrittsvorlesung* established the need to eliminate the critical and "destructive" aspects of literature in favor of an affirmative and positive stance. The achievement of national unity under Prussian cultural hegemony represented a new "point of view" that allowed one to understand the past. The transformation of the function of the *Literaturwissenschaft* was thus also achieved: from the science of the opposition to the apology of the present.[53]

But the *Antrittsvorlesung* is also indicative of another tendency that was to leave its mark on German Studies and, indeed, on the literary criticism of European modernism in the following decades. This was the effort to establish a completely autonomous bourgeois aesthetic sphere. While the notion of the autonomy of the arts had played a significant role in the struggle for emancipation of the middle class in the late eighteenth century, Dilthey's effort (anticipated by Danzel) was to define an aesthetic domain that would be "exalted and distinguished" in regard to political, economic, or social factors, in which solely the *Bildungsbürgertum* (educated middle class), with its history and peculiarities, would have a place.[54] The figure of Goethe clearly reigned unchallenged there, both for Dilthey and for Danzel.[55]

Dilthey's later works, as well as those of a number of authors who fell under his influence, developed in the direction described, that is, toward the establishment of an elevated and autonomous cultural sphere that was to be protected from external contamination lest it lose its inherent essence. This meant also that it would have to be defended from any literary movement that was liable to introduce, even simply through representation, any factor that threatened to alter its intrinsic purity (see, for example, Dilthey's judgment of Heine or the opposition toward naturalism, guilty of having artistically represented contemporary social conflicts).

It is always risky to establish a direct connection between great historical events and the human sciences. But in the case of *Literaturwissenschaft* one may safely affirm that the achievement of national unity (in 1871, but in practice already in 1866) determined an extraordinary shift in its functions and, consequently, in its interpretative paradigms. The achievement of the national telos had two specific consequences in the human sciences: the first was the severing of the previously close tie between the Zeitgeist (with its humanistic, progressive, and liberal characteristics as defined by Gervinus) and the world of history, between national culture and material development, between the ideal motivations of scholars and the historical progress toward liberty. Once national unity was achieved, the notion of a "law inherent in historical development" became dangerous. It could be interpreted as implying the necessary transition from a bourgeois society to a socialist one, a notion that was obviously distasteful to the middle class.

Dilthey thus took on this role: ensuring the status quo of the nascent nation and guaranteeing its unity and social harmony. This was possible only if art and literature renounced their roles as defenders of the political liberty of the people and accepted their being "elevated" to a completely autonomous aesthetic sphere. As is often the case, this program was brought to its most extreme and often absurd consequences by the followers of Dilthey, as well as by the *Geistesgeschichte* of the 1920s and of the decades that followed.

Three

The Science of Literature and the Steam Engine: Wilhelm Scherer and the Positivist School

Wilhelm Scherer (1841–86) was the first professor of *Neuere deutsche Literatur* (modern German literature) to become a member of the Royal Science Academy of Berlin. This event marked the positive conclusion of the long march of German literature toward full acceptance within the academy. And it was by no means accidental that this conclusion was brought about by a charismatic Germanist like Scherer. The dominant philological school had little interest for contemporary literature and tended to dismiss as amateurish and nonscientific any effort to discuss it within an academic context. On the contrary, Scherer, a distinguished philologist and linguist, had an active interest in and sometimes a personal acquaintance with contemporary authors, as witnessed by his writings on Otto Ludwig, Gottfried Keller, Berthold Auerbach, and especially Gustav Freytag. His interest in post-Goethe literature was instrumental in the institutionalization of the interest in contemporary literature and in the modernization of philology and literary studies in the context of the new historical situation created by the establishment of the Second Reich. Scherer tried to respond to the new situation, starting from the premise that it was no longer possible to ignore the importance of the natural sciences, which were enjoying a moment of extraordinary development, and the great methodological and pragmatic potential implications of this development for the humanistic, hermeneutical, and historical sciences.

Scherer's Political Biography

Scherer was born in Austria in 1841 and died in Berlin in 1886 after having exercised an enormous influence on German culture as a full professor in Strasbourg (1872–77) and then in Berlin, the capital of the Reich. He grew up in the period in which Austria and Prussia were competing for hegemony over the movement for national unity. In 1859 in Vienna he organized, along with other students of the liberal movement, a commemoration of the centenary of the birth of Schiller, an author who was a symbol of liberty and therefore banned by Austrian authorities. The following year he moved to Berlin to study the "scientific method" under the guidance of Karl Müllenhof. In his Berlin period he met Herman Grimm, Wilhelm Dilthey, and the literary historian Julian Schmidt, of liberal leanings. Most important, however, was his close relationship with his teacher Müllenhof, who taught him the basics of philology. He returned to Vienna in 1862, where he had to deal with the hostility of colleagues and the generally oppressive climate. By then Austria seemed to him "no longer a state but merely a repressive apparatus."[1]

The general situation appeared unbearable also due to the negative influence of the Catholic Church, which Scherer saw as dead set against any change or progress. This climate had a direct influence on the general character of the Austrian middle class, which Scherer believed was capable only of "praying and acquiring, cultivating domestic and private virtues."[2] In contrast to this image of passivity and narrow-mindedness, Scherer invoked the active, enterprising, and innovative spirit of Protestant culture. He was convinced that only Prussia was capable of unifying Germany. While certainly concerned with the lack of democracy within Prussia, in the debate over "unity after liberty or liberty after unity" he opted for the second solution, even while voicing his hopes that sooner or later the "time to fight for rights and freedom" would come again.[3]

After the French-Prussian war, Scherer's position became impossible: Austrian authorities instituted disciplinary proceedings against him, which were suspended only after his appointment at the "Kaiser Wilhelm" University of Strasbourg in 1872. In 1877 Scherer was appointed in Berlin, where he taught till his death of a heart attack in 1886.

The most significant year in Scherer's biography was no doubt 1872, the year in which he accepted his teaching post in Strasbourg. The significance of this event was uniquely political: Strasbourg had been seized during the 1870 war by the Prussians, who had founded a German university for the purpose of unifying Alsace and Lorraine to the fatherland not solely "by the strength of German weapons" but also "by the strength of the German spirit."[4] The German spirit was thus completely subordinated to Bismarck's *Realpolitik*. German liberalism had already undergone its conservative metamorphosis, turning into a nationalist political movement and putting on hold its original libertarian objectives. Unable to achieve direct political power, the German middle class supported the Bismarck regime, obtaining in return the protection necessary for its full economic development. Thus an exclusive focus on the development of production replaced the demand for liberal democracy and an increase in the parliament's powers. The state directed the economy from above, defending the interests of agrarians, industry owners, and state bureaucracy, and it obtained in return political and ideological support against external and internal enemies (as in the case of the Kulturkampf and the *Sozialistengesetz,* the law against Socialists passed in 1878). As a result, liberalism was increasingly discarded by the bourgeoisie in both the political and the economic fields, and Bismarck's unprincipled and authoritarian policy, in the wake of its political successes, came to be regarded as the only realistic political route. The idea of a strategy of development and modernization based on ideological and social elements different from the ones that characterized U.S. or English capitalism was codified in the notion of Germany's special way to progress *(deutscher Sonderweg)*.

Within this context (the change in the function of the concept of nation and nationalism, the crisis and internal divisions of liberalism, the transformation of German capitalism in monopolistic capitalism, the founding of the German state on partly preindustrial and predemocratic bases and principles—a phenomenon that may be defined as the *Refeudalisierung*, of refeudalization, of German society), the founding of the University of Strasbourg symbolized the alliance between the national middle class and the nascent German expansionism. It marked the moment when the liberal opposition, which up to the electoral program of 25 January 1871 had made the demand for liberty on German soil a central issue, basically renounced its political and cultural heritage and began a collaboration with Bismarck in the name of the realistic acceptance of the status quo. German philology thus became an effective instrument for the elaboration of German-Prussian ideology and the legitimization of imperial power. Scherer, the former liberal turned liberal nationalist, accepted being one of the "pioneers of the German spirit" within the newly conquered territories.[5] He explicitly spoke of his work in Alsace-Lorraine as "work of colonization."[6] His role also emerged clearly in a letter of 18 June 1875, from the Bismarck Chancellery to the minister responsible for the universities. In the letter Bismarck expressed his desire to let Scherer teach in Strasbourg for two or three more years on account of the good work he had done there within as well as outside academic confines, work to which he attributed "a particular significance from the political point of view as well."[7]

Redefining the Functions and Goals of Philology

Having summarized the distinctive nature of Scherer's political and academic socialization process, let us now consider his response to the challenge posed by the exact sciences.[8] Scherer's first goal was to get philology out of the impasse in which it found itself, reorganizing it as a unitary discipline that not only would include *Literaturwissenschaft* (conceived both as literary analysis and as literary history) but would function as an extended general field covering the study of society, culture, and man. Scherer's goal was to achieve a unitary knowledge based on linguistics, psychology, and culture. As one can see, his project was very ambitious and wide-ranging. It is hard to say how much he achieved. The undeniable merits of Scherer and his disciples have traditionally been acknowledged: detailed study of sources and the production of accurate critical editions (still valid to a certain extent), detailed biographies, exhaustive bibliographies, and so on.[9] To these I would add the importance Scherer gave to a systematic relationship with the natural sciences, which led him to elaborate a method for interpreting literary phenomena that in many ways anticipated the sociology of literature, using categories derived from political economy and paying attention to the material aspects of literary production. Consider, for example, Scherer's interest in the financial aspects of the production, circulation, and consumption of literary works and his study of the relation between the writer and the public and the influence of public taste on the planning of works of art. These were a number of working hypotheses—which remained largely unexplored due to Scherer's premature death—that might have proved useful for an examination of literary phenomena from a nonteleological, nonspiritual, and nonidealistic perspective, one that would take into account the roles of economic and social factors.[10] Let us examine in more detail Scherer's method and the way in which it was practically applied.

In dedicating to Karl Müllenhof his work *Zur Geschichte der deutschen Sprache* Scherer wrote: "That which everyone wishes for himself and, with a more restrained but more intense regard, for one's own and the general welfare, we wish and fight for to a much greater extent for that human society to which we are indebted for our best and highest possession and for our greatest blessing: that is, our nation."[11]

The function of German philology should therefore be to create a "national ethical system" and to determine "who we are and what our significance is."[12] In reviewing the cultural values of the German nation, Scherer designated the *Romantik* as the essential stage in Germany's national development and self-awareness, in opposition to the *Aufklärung,* which was associated with French thought (especially Rousseau and his abstract egalitarianism): "Against cosmopolitanism, nationality; against an artificial education, the power of nature; against centralization, independent powers; against the all-powerful state, individual freedom; against artificial ideals, the heights of history; against the search for novelty, respect for the old; against construction, development; against intellect and deduction, feeling and vision; against the mathematical, the organic form; against the abstract, sensible reality; against the mechanical, the living."[13] The values to which Scherer appealed in order to constitute a corpus of models of behavior and of national paradigms were all marked by this particular aspect that was to have a profound influence on German thought, namely, the idea of a difference between Western civilization (enlightened, democratic, and rational) and German *Kultur* (irrational, romantic, and organic), the latter based on biological nature and not on the historical-political development of human society. Scherer accused the Enlightenment of having—in the wake of the great scientific discoveries from the Renaissance to the eighteenth century—centralized state and culture and made them uniform, mechanizing and bureaucratizing the lives of individuals.[14]

It might seem strange for Scherer, who is considered a typical positivist thinker, to have made these accusations against the Enlightenment rationalist culture, but in fact Scherer's true enemies were the principles of 1789 and the results of democratic-bourgeois development. The more backward, prebourgeois aspects of Germany up to its unification under Prussia were "Germanized" by Scherer and celebrated as the expression of the true nature of the people: within the national ethical system, he thought, the values of the past serve to illustrate and justify the present in all its achievements.

In establishing a national identity Scherer highlighted the central role of romanticism, but methodologically his own critical approach was characterized by a rigid determinism that introduced into the historical sciences precisely the principle of causality from which he believed the mechanistic view of nature had developed: "The fundamental historical category is the law of causality."[15]

The contradiction between the celebration of romantic literature and the positivist-scientific method did not trouble Scherer, who sought to resolve it by attributing to his own determinism a religious, German, and Protestant character in opposition to the superstitious dogmatism of Austrian Catholicism: "We believe determinism, the democratic dogma of unfree will, this central category of Protestant doctrine, to be the cornerstone of any true notion of history."[16]

The problem that most concerned Scherer was how to bring the development of the "sciences of the spirit" to the same level as that of the natural sciences. Scherer was perfectly aware of the gulf that separated the two in Germany. He perceived that society was undergoing profound and irreversible transformations. The economic development of society, planned and controlled by the great banks and companies, was continuing at a rapid and apparently unstoppable pace. Scherer's concern was that of rethinking the function of the human sciences at a moment in history when they had fallen behind compared to the general development of knowledge and of its technological applications. The large-scale application of the discoveries of the natural sciences to production processes had come to be understood as a productive resource of central importance: since 1871, following the lead of the chemical industries, scientific research had often been funded by private capital and marked by a close relationship between theory and practical applications, as well as between private research and university institutions. This enthusiastic development of the natural sciences relegated humanities to the margins of the culture of the Reich and diminished their importance within the academy, insofar as they seemed void of any immediate practical value as compared with the dramatic development of production.

Scherer believed that the sciences of the spirit could find a solution to this impasse by discarding general philosophical questions, which he saw as metaphysical and obsolete, and adopting the modern scientific "method" as a safeguard against the "crazy" ideas of 1848. The norms of technical rationality, automatically applied to philological, historical, and hermeneutical sciences, could ensure a priori that they, too, would necessarily progress constantly and energetically: "The very same power that has made the railway and the telegraph, the very same power that has caused an unprecedented development in industry, improved the comfort of life, abbreviated wars, and in a word produced an extraordinary step forward in man's mastery over nature, that very same power controls as well our spiritual life: it makes a clean sweep of dogmas, it revolutionizes sciences, it puts its seal on poetry. The science of nature moves solemnly forward on the triumphal chariot to which we are all bound."[17]

In Scherer's view, the analogy between the sciences of the spirit and the experimental sciences, which is based on the fundamental unity of knowledge as process and procedure, can or should eliminate any subjective distortion in the application of the scientific method. The fragmenting of intellectual labor and the transformation of man into a cog of a much larger mechanism—which during those very years Nietzsche had stigmatized as one of the degenerations of philology and of culture in general—Scherer saw instead as a source of greater productivity.[18] He thought that the dissolution of the subject within a predetermined philological-interpretative structure, based on solid scientific premises and hence necessarily infallible, reduces the margin of error, as in natural sciences. The science that deals with literary texts can therefore be considered an actual "means of production . . . like a steam engine" and can be used as such.[19] Scherer believed that the division of labor, which had speeded the extraordinary progress of the natural and technical sciences, could not but also help the human sciences regain the lost ground in the new industrial society.

The Positivist Method and National Ideology

From a larger perspective, the continuous celebration of the scientific method served as an ideological cover for an economic, cultural, and political system that needed to extend its dominion to all aspects of society. The Reich was presented as a single organism: the relationship between society and individuals was defined on the basis of its analogy with the relationship between organisms and their individual organs. Social-economic development was consequently viewed (again through an analogy with natural evolution) as an astronomical, physical, or physiological phenomenon, that is, as subject to unchanging natural laws.

"*Impavidi progrediamur!*" (Let's bravely go on!) was the motto of Darwin's advocate in Germany, Ernst Haeckel: up to the 1890s, German culture (including Scherer) continued to conceive social-economic development as a seamless natural progression. Collective growth was the goal; subjectivity, like individual genetic deviations, was dysfunctional in relation to this goal. The period from 1870 to 1890 was marked—as noted by historian Helmut Böhme—by "harmony" as "a decisive force shaping development."[20]

As in the great positivist classics (Comte and Spencer), conflict was seen as a disruptive force. The organicist social model, by eliminating conflicts and radical breaks, sought to restore the social order that had been called into question by the French Revolution (see for example Saint Simon or, even better, the young Comte). The reestablishment of the previous social order was presented as a return to an organic society, that is, to "a society based on ties of mutual solidarity and on a firm hierarchy, legitimized by a system of beliefs shared by all members of the social body."[21] Positivist science, as a system of knowledge based on intrinsic and incontrovertible truth, provided the foundation and legitimation of the social order.

French positivism was at any rate associated with an independent political project of the middle class, opposed to both restoration and revolution: the effort to interpret modern society as industrial society was not an end in itself, but was tied, to some extent, to a political and social ideal. German positivism, instead—as a result of the weakness of the German middle class, which after 1848 had renounced any autonomous interpretation of national history and literature—was directly supportive of the status quo: the current social order was treated as the final natural, and therefore necessary, result of an organic national development. The Bonapartist system established by Bismarck was the achievement of the nation, conceived as a living organism: it was the duty of the individual (the subject, the organ) to harmonize with this development.

The specific role of German philology, or "*germanistische Literaturwissenschaft,*" then, was to research, reconstruct, and classify all the "objectivizations of the spirit of the nation," re-creating the national unity that was dispersed among myriad literary documents.[22] Works and authors had to be presented as exemplary stepping stones of the *Nationalliteratur,* whose ultimate goal was establishing a doctrine of national values and duties.

Scherer has been often criticized for an "overemphasis of the factual," his preeminent "emphasis everywhere . . . on completeness of description, discovery of sources, and embedding the accumulated data in biographical information."[23] The need, affirmed by positivist German Studies, for limited and closely focused research projects was, in fact, perfectly consistent with the ideological representation of society as organically structured in all its parts, nothing being left to chance.[24]

The achievements of the Scherer school, as already mentioned, were highly significant; critical editions as well as biographies were written with the patience, care, and objectivity of the scientist that sublimates individual reflection into method. Personal opinions were subsumed in the general method that ordered all elements with mechanic rigor and objectivity: biographical data, facts, sources, secondary and often insignificant aspects were collected, classified, and reconstructed in order to create an "imposing edifice of pure factuality."[25] The object of inquiry, genetically reconstructed according to Taine's deterministic formula, "race, milieu, moment," or, in Scherer's version, "*Ererbtes, Erlerntes, Erlebtes*" (the inherited, the learned, the experienced), was presented as an exemplary model and a link in the chain of the great cultural history of the nation.[26] The empirical and inductive character postulated by positivist German Studies was thus transformed into a normative one: the biographies of the great authors served to demonstrate "the unity of life and works" within the literary production of the author taken as paradigmatic (hence the great number of biographies, especially of Goethe).[27] The purpose was that of guaranteeing individuality and continuity within national literature, demonstrating the absolute organic relation of the individual models to the general evolution of the nation.

The History of German National Literature

The previously described project is clearly evident in the *Geschichte der deutschen Literatur,* published by Scherer in 1883.[28] Scherer presented

German literature as a living organism whose evolution had seamlessly extended from the early German tribes (in the second century B.C.) to the death of Goethe. Within this evolution Scherer identified a law of alternations and recurrences: German literature had peaked every six hundred years, and these peaks were followed by periods of decline, the whole resembling "three great waves, peak and hollow with a regular rhythm."[29] After the first peak in 600 A.D., and the second peak in 1200 A.D., the third and most recent flourishing of German literature had occurred around the year 1800: "Around the year 1800 Germany has its Goethe, its Schiller, and their companions and followers, poets and scholars, who gather within themselves, refine and bring into the national life the cultural influence of the French and English sources and of the ancient Germanic world. Again are the chants of the ancient heroes resurrected; the Nibelungen acquire great fame, and new poets elaborate that matter. The Grimm brothers become the leaders of a new science that proposes to rescue for the present age, with a careful and thoughtful hand, the works that have vanished in the shadows of antiquity."[30]

Thus the extraordinary poetic productivity of the period appears to be determined by a sort of immanent teleology. From the original virtues of the German people (faithfulness to their ideals, bravery, military prowess) already cited by Tacitus and Caesar, from the political talent of Frederick the Great up to the remarkable strategic qualities of Baron von Stein (the great reformer of Prussia), everything had concurred in the creation of a canonical corpus of national values and duties that should be used to guide future action.[31] Scherer ignored any dissonant voice in this harmonious symphony, any conflicting or discontinuous element in the history of national literature, or condemned it as dysfunctional in the overall organic framework (see, for example, Scherer's brutal attack on Hölderlin).[32] Scherer ended his history by interpreting even the conclusion of the second part of *Faust* as a call to action, where Goethe had symbolically expressed the German people's nostalgia for action. In Scherer's scheme, Goethe's death was followed by yet another period of decadence; as in the previous phases, however, the poetical peak was inevitably followed, as if out of biological necessity, by "a time of national expansion and economic development."[33]

Thus Scherer presented economic development as a distinctive characteristic of the current phase of national evolution, which individuals necessarily had to partake in. Scherer's history ends with a significant invitation to "act and work," with method and responsibility, to help the natural evolution of society, without questioning its mode of realization.[34] Scherer believed that Faust understood the need for action only after undergoing a series of vicissitudes; modern Germans, instead, had a chance to avoid wasting time and energy, setting their sails to the right winds from the start.[35]

One might object that the individual who sets the sails should be entitled to know and have a say about the direction his boat takes. But for Scherer this was not the case: he thought one must help one's nation achieve its destiny, moving according to the rhythm and direction determined by the laws of natural evolution. Human behavior, both individual and collective, should be evaluated not according to abstract moral norms (which Scherer called the remnants of a "metaphysical" mentality), but rather on the basis of their capacity to embrace, without petty reservations, the sense and purpose of national history.[36]

The Academic Legitimization of Literary History

Opinions of Scherer's work usually focus on his somewhat pedantic positivism. In fact, his personality was one of the more complex and interesting of the entire history of German Studies. He was not solely the foremost representative of the positivist method, but also the leading force in the reorganization of the discipline. I have already discussed his influence on the disciplinary process through the seminars, his political role in the Alsace-Lorraine region, his effort to bring the human sciences in line with the fast rhythm of development in the natural sciences. His charisma enabled him to transgress the official boundaries of the disciplinary corporation, something that others could not afford to do. He took a genuine interest in contemporary literature and devoted himself to its study without incurring the usual accusations of amateurism, journalism, lack of philological commitment, and so on. To a modern perspective, his motivations seem unexceptionable. Scherer's argument was as follows: Why should philology not study contemporary literature? Why should it ignore the positive results achieved even after the death of Goethe? Could not the new climate developed with the foundation of the Reich engender a new wave in literature and the arts? The German spirit—Scherer added—was reborn with that event. Why should philology not take it into account? Why should it remain tied to the past and reject in principle any interest in contemporary culture?[37]

Scherer exploited the privilege of transgression that his prestige afforded him by writing extensively and continuously for journals, using as a sort of preliminary theoretical justification his essay "Der junge Goethe als Journalist."[38] If the great Goethe could write as a journalist, it was conceivable that Scherer could, too. Thanks to this relentless activity, Scherer played a decisive role in restructuring the canon of German literature, opening it to post-Goethian authors. His sympathies, of course, went to those literary works that expressed in their form and content a reconcilement with the actual political situation. The model, as usual, was the harmonic classicism of Goethe and Schiller. Practically, in the new historical and political situation of Germany, this meant artistically reelaborating those experiences and events that were liable to reinforce the burgeoning national-liberal conscience of the German people. In other words, Scherer's goal was to combine the great Weimar classicism with the new culture of the Reich. Thus Scherer saw classicism as a stabilizing element in national politics, serving as a defense against past and present disruptive forces: this explains Scherer's harsh judgment not only on Hölderlin, but also on the German naturalists, notwithstanding his own influence on them.[39] At the same time, however, the *Klassik* within Scherer's national-liberal political and conceptual framework was also to function as a moderate ideology counteracting the strong tendency within contemporary German culture to bolster nationalism through an indiscriminate and crude exaltation of its Germanic origins. As Scherer once said, polemicizing against Felix Dahn and Wagner: "Those Germans who have the aesthetic education of their people at heart are of the school of Greece. Their spiritual home is Athens, not the muddy depths of the Rhine."[40]

Thus Scherer distinguished between a legitimate feeling, "the Germans' national self-awareness," and the "arrogance" of German reactionary parties.[41] His attitude during the Berlin *Antisemitismus-Streit* of 1880 was consistent with his position. Against the development of anti-Semitism and the effort to eliminate any "foreign" influence on German culture—advocated and legitimized by many university professors, among them the historian Heinrich von Treitschke—Scherer signed with other liberals a strong petition, published in the 14 November 1880 issue of the *Nationalzeitung,* asking for an end to such attacks and propositions. What may seem an obvious stance nowadays was not so obvious at the time: Scherer was the only Berlin

Germanist who signed the petition; Dilthey, for example, sided with the anti-Semitists.[42] Because of his stand, as he explained in a letter to his friend and colleague Steinmeyer, Scherer lost his friendship with his teacher Müllenhof: "No guarantee can be provided against Müllenhof's unpleasant letters either to you or to any other mortal. A tough skin is the only possible safeguard. I no longer have the least influence on him. He was offended by my saying that preparing for new anti-Jewish persecutions is unworthy of the German nation. Ever since, I have been regarded as guilty of high treason against the holiest treasures of the German nation."[43] In this case, too, it is evident that Scherer's position enabled him to transgress and fearlessly risk isolation.

This description of Scherer and the role he played in the reorganization of German Studies would be incomplete if I omitted mentioning his contribution to the status and apparatus of the discipline. I have already discussed his role in organizing seminars and establishing their mode of functioning. Let us consider now in what way Scherer contributed to the formation of the habitus of Germanists. Once again I will use an important obituary—Dilthey's speech in memory of Scherer—to focus on a crucial point: the authoritarian relationship between master and pupil. In defining the relation between Jacob Grimm (master) and Scherer (pupil), Dilthey spoke of a "relation of *pietas*" corresponding to "a relation of unconditional faithfulness and dependence in the ancient German fashion."[44] *Pietas* and devotion, then, but in fact also subservience, adulation, and conformism. Indeed Scherer defined the German personality in unequivocal terms: "surrender, subordination, submissive reverence, modesty, faithfulness, firmness, and truthfulness."[45] Clearly these virtues were also essential in defining a "code of philological virtues."[46] In his description of Lachmann, for example, Scherer underlined the absolute impotence of the pupils compared to the omnipotence of the master who in a "proud and confident manner" pointed out and punished mistakes "without giving his reasons," that is, without explaining his corrections in detail and providing the metrical or interpretative alternatives. Scherer continued: "One fears him, even when one loves him. The younger generations of philologists can be awe-stricken in front of him, like a sinful grandson in front of the image of a severe and virtuous ancestor."[47] What Scherer was clearly and objectively outlining here was what could be termed the process of formation of authoritarian personalities through a series of techniques, foremost among them a sort of scientific-disciplinary superego that would arbitrarily decide and punish. What applied to Lachmann also applied to Scherer, notwithstanding all the other ways in which he dissociated himself from disciplinary orthodoxy.

Scherer redefined the role that the humanities seemed to have lost within contemporary German society, which was rapidly turning into a technologically advanced industrial society: grounding themselves in the scientific method, they would serve to hypostasize and reproduce social and ideological values, norms, and integration mechanisms. Scherer realized that within Bismarck's Germany—that is, within a social-economic system where science, technique, industry, and bureaucracy were increasingly interconnected and served as the basis for domination—the historical and philological sciences could also have a social impact by helping to culturally "synchronize" the nation, transmitting, to use the words of a later official speech, "not just a knowledge, but a know-how."[48] The problem was thus brutally but precisely expressed as a problem of power: by implementing and reproducing specific models of socialization and social integration, the specialists of the "*nationale Wissenschaft*" could induce a generalized attitude to domination and help the functioning of power. State and society (first with Bismarck and then with Wilhelm II) relied on German philology to shape teachers and students according to the dominant ideology codified in the "*deutsche Erziehung*" (German education).[49]

After 1890 Scherer's positivist method was increasingly questioned and rejected (though his pupils retained their solid positions thanks to the well-known law of academic continuity), but the national pedagogic and socializing function of German philology continued to be universally accepted. In 1912, during the constitutive congress of the Deutscher Germanisten-Verband (the Association of German Germanists), Friedrich Panzer sought to redefine the role of Latin in light of its loss of prestige as the language of choice within the academy and the lyceums. In his speech Panzer clearly outlined the role of philology and of humanities in general: "This Latin language," even though it was not immediately useful in military matters, represented "a suitable means to a strict spiritual upbringing . . . , roughly comparable to the practice of arms or parade-step as a means to achieve military discipline."[50]

Toward the end of the nineteenth century, Scherer's method seemed outdated: Dilthey had sharply contested the application of the methods of the natural sciences to other fields of knowledge. The human sciences had to be reorganized in the light of their structural differences from the natural sciences. For Dilthey the methodologies of the two sciences were in fact antithetical: he believed that the natural sciences determine general laws and identify regular constants, while the starting point of the human sciences must be the "subjektives Erlebnis," which the natural sciences do not take into account and subsume into their general laws. The role of the critic is "to relive" *(nacherleben)* the experience that engendered poetic creation through an intuitive and almost divinatory comprehension, and "to understand" *(verstehen)*—instead of "to explain" *(erklären),* as natural sciences do—the *Weltanschauung* those creations express and contain. From diverse interpretations of Dilthey's thought, through often unexpected and contradictory developments, descended the critical and philosophical school named *Geistesgeschichte,* a name that basically refers to "an absolute autonomy of the spiritual, which expresses itself within ahistorical and phenomenological typologies."[51] The scientific objectivity of Scherer's school was countered with the absolute subjectivity of the spiritual and of its perception as the only interpretative principle applicable to works of art: the opposition between the two schools could not be any sharper. Yet the contrast between the positivist school and the *Geistesgeschichte* remained limited to methodological disputes or to more specific contrasts revolving around teaching positions and the distribution of academic power, without ever questioning the goals and functions of German Studies and German philology or its disciplinary apparatus.

Four

Wilhelm Dilthey and *Geistesgeschichte*

Around 1900 the disciplinary consolidation of German Studies was accomplished. The progress of the discipline that followed the successes of the positivist school is undeniable: Scherer's replacement in Berlin by his student Erich Schmidt (1853–1913) ensured the continuity and controlled evolution of the ideology and apparatus of the discipline. Historically, Germany was in the process of becoming the world's second industrial power and the entire ideological, philosophical, literary, and artistic scene was undergoing a tumultuous process of transformation, characterized by a series of innovative movements and tendencies. German Studies, while maintaining its institutional structure, was increasingly concerned with its ability to stay in touch with current reality and grasp its full complexity, a task that seemed to require something more than the limited interpretative tools offered by the positivist school. Thus a new interpretative movement was born under the name *Geistesgeschichte*, or intellectual history.[1] The name stressed the belief in the autonomy of the spirit and of spiritual phenomena in history and the desire to transcend the narrow confines of the positivist system.

In this new method the analysis of details and specific elements was to be replaced by a higher scientific ideal capable of grasping the essence, the ultimate meaning, of an author, a work, a period, a style, a movement, or a structure. In order to achieve this, a new system and a new interpretative praxis had to be established based on categories utterly new and foreign to the positivist method. The *Geistesgeschichte* was the product of many heterogeneous elements, such as a particular interpretation of Nietzsche, Bergson's intuitionalism, Rickert's definition of cultural sciences, the crisis of exact sciences, and neo-Kantian philosophy. But the most important influence was that of Wilhelm Dilthey, the representative of a penetrating interpretation of national literature and of its canonical aspects, both on a general philosophical level and on a more specific critical and literary one.

Dilthey's Method

Dilthey (1833–1911) was convinced that positivism mutilated the spiritual world and strove to establish a clear-cut distinction between the humanities and the natural sciences. In his "Einleitung in die Geisteswissenschaften" (1883) he extensively attacked the ambition of the physical and mathematical sciences to extend their method to all fields of knowledge. Dilthey believed that the humanities could be established anew only on the basis of their ontological and structural difference from the natural sciences. He saw the methods of these two branches of knowledge as diametrically opposed: the natural sciences discover general laws and identify regularities within phenomena; the humanities, instead, must focus on the *"subjektives Erlebnis"* (subjective experience). The scientist studies objects situated in space and time through rational tools such as observation, measurement, and material experience, while the life of the spirit is accessible only through inner experience, which is achieved and communicated through an individual cognitive moment, an intuitive apprehension—the *Erlebnis*—through which reality is perceived in its most vital essence. The goal of the critic is to "relive" *(nacherleben)* the experience of poetical creation through an intuitive and almost divinatory experience. Personal experience and understanding *(verstehen),* acting in close and necessary relationship, are the cardinal categories of Dilthey's philosophical-hermeneutical system: inner subjective experience is the necessary precondition of understanding. It requires the total emotional participation of the interpreter and is necessarily unique, since each person relates in his or her own way to the world, to life, to what Dilthey, following Kant, called the *Weltanschauung.* Yet few, in practice, are actually endowed with the ability to understand: Dilthey goes so far as to define three types (the poet, the prophet, the saint) who are capable of going beyond the rational knowledge of the philosopher, being endowed with other superior faculties: intuition, enthusiasm, empathy. These faculties allow them to identify the essence of a Weltanschauung, to penetrate its deepest recesses, and to finally re-create it through their imagination *(Einbildunskraft).*

This theory of knowledge and interpretation was originally developed in philosophy—Dilthey was, first of all, a philosopher—and it had an extraordinary importance for German Studies in general and for the study of literature and literary phenomena more specifically. In the opinion of some historians, Dilthey was responsible for the greatest revolution in *Literaturwissenschaft.*[2] If one were to put in a nutshell what this change was, one could say that Dilthey once and for all shifted the focus of literary studies onto subjectivity, onto the possibility that critics could identify and interpret the essence and spiritual unity of cultural phenomena using faculties analogous to the ones of great poets. Through this radical shift in focus, from the materialist objectivism of positivist philology to spiritualist subjectivism, new and as yet unthought-of vistas were opened for the twentieth century.

Along with his more strictly philosophical works, which from the start had a strong and wide impact in different fields of knowledge, Dilthey republished in 1906 a collection of more specifically literary essays, written between 1865 and 1877, which met with great success and marked a turning point in literary historiography and in the interpretation of the period from 1770 to 1830. The great success of Ricarda Huch's essays on romanticism, *Blütezeit der Romantik* (1899) and *Ausbreitung und Verfall der Romantik* (1902), convinced Dilthey of the opportunity of collecting his essays on the same subject in one volume. To both these authors Lukács attributes the revival of romantic studies in the context of the antipositivist turn in late nineteenth-century German culture.[3] Dilthey's volume, titled *Das Erlebnis und die Dichtung,* includes essays on Lessing, Goethe, Novalis, and Hölderlin.[4] Applying his philosophical-interpretative categories to the literature of 1770–1830, Dilthey outlined what was basically a history of German literature from Lessing to the death of Goethe. His work was important, among other things, for focusing institutional attention on the figure of Novalis and emphasizing the importance of Hölderlin, who up to then had been largely set outside the dominant canon, placed alongside the great authors of the classic period. Dilthey's essay on Goethe, previously published in 1877 under the title "Goethe und die dichterische Phantasie" (Goethe and the poetical imagination), is particularly important as a cornerstone of Dilthey's interpretative method. He presented Goethe as the sublime embodiment of the poet who is capable of going as far as "the daemonic aspect of the superhuman."[5] This capability is independent of history, of the laws of time and space, and has made it possible for Goethe to undergo experiences that have exceeded in intensity and duration those allowed to normal human beings. It is the faculty of the great poet to give particular form and expression to the experiences he has lived in his deepest inner life through imagination. The poet's imagination, by virtue of the geniuslike quality of his mental structure, can draw upon the "depth of the soul"—since "the soul, the feeling is the vital foundation of all poetry"—recreating through the *Erlebnis* a "new liberty" and an ideal and higher "second world" where material interests arrive only as faint reverberations.[6]

Dilthey believed that Goethe expressed in his works, with serene contemplative perfection, his *Erlebnis,* which in turn reproduced his interior life in all its intensity. This creative process took place thanks to a string of favorable and exceptional circumstances that manifested themselves through him, from the *Einbildungskraft* (imaginative power) to the *Gemüt* (soul) to the *Stimmung* (internal atmosphere). All these elements play a crucial role not solely in the creation of a poetic work, but also in its understanding, since understanding the poetic work means grasping its internal atmosphere, its *Stimmung;* it means understanding the experience undergone by the poet and re-creating it. This entails an effort on the part of the reader and the critic that is in itself a creative as well as an intellectual act. Author and reader share a common medium: both find themselves in a region of the spirit, participating in an aesthetic pleasure independent of space and time. Poetry allows man to understand the absolute life, free of daily contingencies. It is the life of the spirit that speaks through poetry. If the human spirit speaks through writing, Dilthey continued, some sort of exegesis is needed, an interpretation of the written word that will make it possible to grasp the interiority hidden behind material signs: this technique of interpretation of the written signs of life, which is part of the "personal geniuslike virtuosity of the philologist," is elsewhere called interpretation or hermeneutics.[7] The interpretation of the written signs of human existence is thus called hermeneutics—an art that is reserved for the happy few, since it depends on a close harmony of author, work, and interpreter. In the hermeneutics of Dilthey and his followers, the work of art was attributed with a hidden esoteric meaning. Against rational analysis and the mechanical principle of causality, Dilthey insisted on the idea of a personal, intimate, and privileged encounter between text and critic. The latter must rely on intuition, on intuitive synthesis, to penetrate the internal universe of the poet through the means at his disposal: the text, the (auto)biography of the author, journals, and any other written document, which are subjected to psychological analysis.[8]

In defining the interpretative act Dilthey was also responding to the strong need for personal gratification and aristocratic distinction common in the *Bildungsbürgertum* of the Wilhelm and Weimar periods.[9] He presented the interpretative critical act as an ineffable moment of great intellectual discovery, since through the work of art and through its author we are able to understand, more than through any other experience, the life of the spirit, of which the work of art is the deepest and fullest expression. Hermeneutic critical activity is reserved to an elite that shares the psychological and spiritual premises of this deeper and higher reality, which, following Kant, could be defined as the noumenal reality. This elite thus shares the privileges of the "great poet" and, like the great Goethe, participates in the creation of a "new liberty" and a "second world," free of the burden of material interests.

Aside from these more esoteric aspects, Dilthey's work obtained an important result that had a lasting cultural influence, notwithstanding its abuses and later distortions: it liberated the humanities and culture from the constraints of positivism and assigned them to an autonomous sphere. In various cultural areas of the early twentieth century, from philosophy to religion, history, sociology, German and Romance studies, and the history of arts—the list could go on—Dilthey's views opened new perspectives and engendered new methodological approaches that were to revolutionize the world of the humanities.[10]

Rudolf Unger and the Self-criticism of Positivist Philology

Dilthey's views, as we shall see, were applied and developed in different ways. One author must be especially remembered for the consistency with which he faithfully developed Dilthey's approach and for being the first representative of academic German Studies to question the principles of philological positivism: Rudolf Unger (1876–1942). Unger fought to extend to the academic institution the changes that Dilthey had achieved on a philosophical level. Having written important monographs displaying remarkable theoretical penetration (a quality that was to become increasingly rare among Dilthey's followers), Unger began reflecting on the general state of the *Literaturwissenschaft* in the years of the antipositivist revolution.

In the essay "Philosophische Probleme in der neueren Literaturwissenschaft" (Philosophical problems in contemporary literary criticism, 1908) Unger responded to philology's continuing aspiration to a foundational methodological status within literary studies. Unger's attack was moderate in form but radical in content. His goal was to relativize the hitherto unquestioned absolute value of philology, suggesting other avenues and conquering new spaces and perspectives for the study of literature. To achieve this Unger retraced the history of philology from its founders, Lachmann and Haupt, who had introduced the "method of classic philology in German Studies," all the way to Scherer, who had transferred the same method to modern literature and literary history "in all its extension and rigor."[11] Unger acknowledged the essential role of the founding fathers in establishing a disciplinary status as a safeguard against amateurishness and "unprincipled arbitrariness" (1),[12] introducing the age of "*Wissenschaftlichkeit*" and of rigorous and meticulous research. Following a well-established rule of rhetoric, he conceded the merits of his enemy, that is, the application of scientific discourse to philology:

> Thus an effective organic connection was established and consolidated between the study of contemporary German literature, the science of the more ancient periods of German literature, and linguistics. There is no need to demonstrate that through this process a decisive progress was achieved. It must be added, though, that thanks to this connection with the older German Studies, long acknowledged as a legitimate science, the history of modern and contemporary literature was accepted also within those groups that up to then had more or less considered it as an amateurish pastime. Directly related to these transformations was the awarding of teaching posts in this discipline to experts in German Studies and no longer to philosophers, scholars of aesthetics, or art historians, as a secondary teaching post. In some cases, in fact, it had previously been decided not to provide this teaching at all. Specialist German Studies journals also increasingly published research on the literary developments of the modern age, a sector that soon succeeded in having its own journals. Thanks

> to these positive developments, amateurishness, previously prominent in this sector, seemed to be definitely eliminated. Furthermore, with the emphasis on the methodological perspectives of this recent science a series of new problems and challenges emerged, along with the means and methods to address them; this is witnessed by the feverish activity that immediately took place, particularly in fields such as textual criticism (Goethe, Schiller, Herder, Lessing, etc.), the genealogy of individual poems, the search for sources, motifs and types, as well as the relations between national literatures, biographical and bibliographical studies, history of theater, etc. A great source of vital force and fruitful stimuli was found, therefore, in this "philological" movement, as I would define Scherer's approach by analogy to the "psychological" one in philosophy, with which it shares the fundamental tendency toward empiricism (4).[13]

But, Unger continued, these achievements notwithstanding, one cannot help observing—here Unger's judgment became unsparing—that "the philological method has basically failed when applied to the greatest and most difficult problems of the study of literature" (5).[14] The defeat of the positivist school derived from the fundamental error on which it was based, namely the idea that the principle of causality applies to the humanities—a hypothesis that, Unger added, was generally acknowledged as a "mistake" (6).[15]

Unger proceeded to offer a long and detailed list of those cases in which philology had failed: the case of the "reciprocal clarification of arts" (6), the tendency—Unger spoke of a "hunt" (8), of a "sort of scientific sport" (7)—to search for motifs, echoes, themes that A might have inherited from B, that is, the obsessive search for the influence of one author over another (what today is aptly called the "hypertrophy of the search for influence"[16]). He believed that another of philology's mistakes was the notion that one can establish valid connections among authors, even those belonging to different cultures, on the basis of wholly mechanical and external analogies and comparisons. It is easy to perceive that this criticism was primarily directed against Scherer's efforts to create a science of comparisons, or a comparative science, based on presumed regularities traceable in the events of the literary field (by analogy with natural sciences), even between literatures of different nations.

Unger argued that historical disciplines should go back to studying "the specific traits of the individual," the "organically developed inner specificity" and not the "external manifestations and forms of being" (6).[17] When the scholar tries to grasp the complexity of the world, the philological obsession impedes all but superficial forms of knowledge: "The more one proceeded from elementary dealings with the text to more complex and profound questions, the more urgently one felt the need to escape from the segregated world of philology into psychology, aesthetics and other nonphilological fields of knowledge" (9).[18] Unger believed that the exclusive concentration on pure philology was what had allowed amateurs to flourish like weeds in the fields of "*Literaturwissenschaft*" and "*Literaturgeschichte,*" since the philological approach in its myopic obtuseness was no longer able to control the new plants growing in the field of knowledge (9).

Taking for granted that the certainties of positivism belonged to the past, how was it possible to overcome the methodological uncertainties of the humanities? For Unger the solution lay in philosophy: it was only through philosophy that a new and more profound understanding of history and literature would be reached. After all, a close relation between philosophy and literature—Unger continued—was part of the origin of the new national literature: it was late eighteenth-century German philosophy that had created the new "view of the world and of life" from which had descended a new sense of history and literature (10).[19] Unger invoked Herder as the founder of a monist and organic-evolutionist "Weltanschauung" and the Schlegel brothers as the first authors of a history of literature positioned halfway between literary criticism and philosophical interpretation (10). From the "organic" nature of the original connection between literature and philosophy in Germany had descended certain unavoidable consequences for Unger's time. First, he observed, "from the perspective of pure content," modern and contemporary German literature had a great number of issues and ideas in common with philosophy (13).[20] The individualism and subjectivism of modern man, born with the Renaissance and grown in the following centuries, had been fed by "*Weltanschauungskämpfen,*" conflicts about the general conception of life and the world (14). The literature that had derived from this was so complex that it could not be understood through a purely philological approach. In the case of modern writers there was a process of individualization and inner differentiation, witness of a profound inner development (expressed in letters, diaries, memoirs, autobiographies) that had increased in quantity and complexity as one approached the current age:

> The inner life of the individual as well as that of the community becomes more profound and complex. The conditions of spiritual influence, of spiritual reelaboration and of spiritual action become increasingly diversified and developed: this process is naturally more pronounced the more the personality is significant, extensive and geniuslike. Thus there is a multiplication, a growth in complexity and depth, that also affects the role of the science of literature, especially in its psychological approach. Today we need to go from book to man, to understand literature as the expression of the inner life and soul. The organic connection between the external and inner life and the associated literary expressions must be studied; the particularities and evolution of this internal life, the development of individual dispositions as well as immediate and mediated influences that these receive through education, the milieu, life, readings and the Zeitgeist, must be examined in detail. Only by penetrating these subjective and personal foundations of literary production will one be able to achieve a truly subtle and profound understanding of its fruits, namely literary works. For these works, in line with the wholly spiritual character of the modern age and in contrast with previous ones, usually have a marked individual character. Content and form appear in this case, meaning on the average, in a degree that is proportional to the importance of their creators, and in such a varied form, that the objective interest in the works as such is replaced by the question of them as subjective expressions of a specific instance and of an inner individual life and literary personality, of which these manifestations are the expression (16–17).[21]

At this point Unger confidently described the first step that he thought *Literaturwissenschaften* had to take to make up for the lost time: develop as part of *Kulturwissenschaften* (cultural sciences), the study and understanding of the psychology of individuals, societies, and peoples. Along with psychological criticism, Unger rediscovered aesthetic judgment and the philosophical analysis of the problems typical of literary history (18). He established the concept of "Literaturgeschichte als Problemgeschichte" (the history of literature as the history of problems), which is the title of a seminal 1924 publication.[22] The methodological basis that would make it possible to address these problems, according to Unger, was the science of "historical life." This would constitute the interpretative key to life in its uniqueness, vitality, and organicity. This historical-cultural science would allow scholars to understand *(verstehen)* the world of history and culture, because this world is the product of the human spirit, while it should ignore nature on account of its ontological diversity, as nature is "something foreign" to us (29).[23]

Thus Unger saw the possibility for a rebirth of German Studies on the basis of a *Kulturgeschichte* (as a variant of *Geistesgeschichte*), which was better suited to respond to the stimuli provided by the philosophy of life—in all its variants—of the end of the nineteenth century. Unger's theoretical arguments bore witness to the need to find a new Weltanschauung, a vantage point that would take *Literaturwissenschaft* out of the shallows of positivism and resituate it in a "*geschichtsphilosophisch,*" that is, wide-ranging, historical and philosophical perspective (23).

In the previously mentioned essay "Literaturgeschichte als Problemgeschichte" Unger offered a list of works that exemplified his notion of the *Geistesgeschichte:* his own monograph *Herder, Novalis und Kleist: Studien über die Entwicklung des Todesproblem im Denken und Dichten vom Sturm und Drang zur Romantik* (1922), Fritz Strich's book *Die Mythologie in der deutschen Literatur von Klopstock bis Richard Wagner* (1910), Ernst Cassirer's essays *Freiheit und Form* (1916) and *Idee und Gestalt* (1921), Herbert Cysarz's volume *Erfahrung und Idee: Probleme und Lebensformen in der deutschen Literatur von Hamann bis Hegel* (1921), Paul Kluckhohn's monograph *Die Auffassung der Liebe in der Literatur des 18. Jahrhunderts und in der deutsche Romantik* (1922), and Hermann August Korff's colossal study *Geist der Goethezeit: Versuch einer ideellen Entwicklung der klassisch-romantischen Literaturgeschichte* (the first volume of which came out in 1923). Unger was thinking of a *Geistesgeschichte* that aimed above all at reconstructing—using the wide array of sophisticated critical tools Unger himself adopted—questions, problems, and the associated Weltanschauung. Unger provided a list of these problems: destiny, the relation of liberty and necessity, the conflict between spirit and nature, sensuality and morals, religion and nature; and, last but not least, natural forms, that is, the basic problems of human life, such as love and death, which he thought must be examined without overlooking their cultural and social context.[24]

After Dilthey

While it is fairly easy to see the linearity with which Unger faithfully developed Dilthey's arguments, it is very difficult to offer a general survey of the various interpretations, applications, and developments of Dilthey's approach. Since the *Geistesgeschichte* was not structured institutionally as had been the positivist school, being more of a tendency or a general approach, Dilthey's work was reinterpreted with great freedom and had a variety of highly differentiated offshoots. If one were to attempt a classification of sorts, one might identify a first group of scholars who focused on the relation between poetry and Weltanschauung: among these, along with Unger himself and the authors mentioned by Unger as representatives of the *Problemgeschichte,* I would include Oskar Walzel (1864–1944), the author of many works but best known as the editor of a successful reedition of Scherer's *Geschichte der deutschen Literatur* and as the author of *Wechselseitige Erhellung der Künste* (1917). In the latter work Walzel developed Scherer's notion of the reciprocal clarification of different arts in the context of the *Geistesgeschichte.* Walzel's goal was to identify within the plurality of artistic works characterizing a given period or style the "essence of the spirit" *(das Wesen des Geistes)* that had engendered them all. Walzel believed that this essence permeates all arts, making it possible to move from one to the other, using the tools necessary to grasp its ever-changing manifestations, in order to better understand the common spiritual substance. This marked an obvious difference from Scherer's analogical-comparative method based on the principle that similar conditions should produce similar results in literature (as well as in the other arts). With his method Walzel strove for greater intensity and interpretative complexity addressing all the artistic procedures through which the spirit expresses itself. The *Handbuch der Literaturwissenschaft,* a history of world literature begun by Walzel in 1924, was methodologically based on the constant comparison of the development of national literatures with the contemporary evolution of the other art forms. Other important works, too, such as Richard Hamann and Jost Hermand's excellent *Deutsche Kultur und Kunst von der Gründerzeit bis zum Expressionismus* (1959 ff.), in which the authors successfully sought to represent the various periods in all their spiritual, literary, and artistic complexity, followed *mutatis mutandis* in Walzel's footsteps.

The Apotheosis of Genius: The Gundolf Case

Other followers of Dilthey, on the other hand, strongly emphasized the critical and interpretative category of the *Erlebnis.* Among these the foremost representative was Friedrich Gundolf (1880–1931).

Gundolf (who was Jewish and whose real name was Gundelfinger) was one of the most brilliant and interesting examples of application of the *Geistesgeschichte* to the *Literaturwissenschaft.* Gundolf was one of the closest collaborators of the poet George, who for a long time was the theoretical proponent of an esoteric and elitist notion of poetry that also had a number of broader political implications: George's general cultural framework for the various activities of his followers was the foundation of an imaginary Reich that was to be achieved through a regeneration of the German spirit. The latter had to acknowledge its true essence and find in itself the force for its regeneration. This process could be achieved by the poets, who, as poets, were the *"Künder der Größe,"* the founders of a new national greatness and of a new Reich. *"Ästhetischer Fundamentalismus"* (aesthetic fundamentalism)—as Stefan Breuer has aptly defined George's doctrine—was the general approach of the members of George's circle, such as Ernst Bertram, who further developed the mythical view of the poet and the notion of hero worship, endowed with political-religious connotations, in works such as *Nietzsche: Versuch einer Mythologie* (1918), and Max Kommerell, who wrote *Der Dichter als Führer in der deutschen Klassik* (1928).[25] Gundolf over time slowly detached himself from George following contrasts on a number of issues: Gundolf's "betrayal" of poetry (he had accepted the bourgeois profession of university teacher, which George considered antagonistic to his mission as poet) and his marriage, which his master considered yet another betrayal in regard to the close, and tendentiously homoerotic, ties of his exclusively masculine community.

Gundolf was certainly another faithful representative of Dilthey's approach, which he consistently applied in the context of George's notion of a general regeneration of life and the spirit. In 1911 (the year of Dilthey's death) Gundolf published his successful *Shakespeare und der deutsche Geist,* in which he traced Shakespeare's influence on German literature and spirit in the seventeenth and eighteenth centuries. With this work Gundolf—who had graduated in 1903 in Berlin, the heart of the philological establishment—went openly against all the philological rules that were dominant in the academic world. He ignored sources, facts, biographical information, past commentaries and studies, all of which he assumed that the reader was familiar with, and proceeded instead to focus on a brilliant interpretation of the great literary trends and spiritual conditions that had paved the way to Shakespeare's success in Germany. Gundolf's goal was to demonstrate that Shakespeare's influence went hand in hand with the increasing quality of German literature from the *Aufklärung* to classicism and romanticism. Shakespeare in Germany became in Gundolf's hands a key to the interpretation of literature from the seventeenth century to Goethe. With the latter, he thought, German literature had produced a final achievement, reaching the same level as Shakespeare's all-encompassing genius. While Gundolf's work met with great public and critical success, it was after his *Goethe* (1916) that Gundolf finally established himself as a Germanist and literary critic.

In his monograph on Goethe Gundolf developed his own method, centered on the category of *Erlebnis.* He distinguished between *Urerlebnis,* all that Goethe experienced on the level of the "religious, titanic or erotic," and *Bildungserlebnis,* the "experience of the primitive German world, of Shakespeare, of classical antiquity, of Italy, and of the East, and also his inner experience of German society."[26] The distinction was functional to his strategy centered on the celebration of three exemplary and heroic poets: Dante, Shakespeare, and Goethe. Thus Gundolf presented the latter as a geniuslike, titanic, and at times demonic figure *(Gestalt).* While in dealing with Shakespeare Gundolf had, in his own way, depicted a historical process, in the case of Goethe he fully adhered to the mythic view of the great personalities of history and literature that had been characteristic of George. In his concise but dense introduction to *Goethe* Gundolf left no doubt as to the scope and purpose of his study. It was aimed "at representing the figure of Goethe in its totality, the greatest unity in which the German spirit has embodied itself" (1).[27] He considered Goethe's biography (in the traditional sense, as a list of facts and dates) irrelevant to this purpose: for Gundolf there were only "*Erlebnis* and works" without any "before and after" (1).[28] For "the artist exists only insofar as he expresses himself through the work of art" (2).[29] This raised the question of whether it is useful or even possible to investigate the life of the great poet outside his art. Gundolf thought it is both illegitimate and impossible, since what we call "the life of a poet or, more recently, the inner experience, is already contained in his art, it is the very impulse and force that constitutes his work" (2).[30] Gundolf proceeded to clarify other important aspects of his critical approach:

> The man who lacks an artistic sense believes the artist, the poet to have the same inner experiences he has and to perceive them in the same way, perhaps with a touch more of adventure and eccentricity. In addition, a casual accident would have given him the ability to evidence these experiences in images, poems or musical pieces: the so-called talent. This is true indeed for the great majority of producers of images, poems and musical pieces. It is not true only for the true artist, the true poet, who appears every hundred years. This person has an inner experience that already pertains to a sphere and has a form that is entirely different from those of the man who has no artistic sense (in our world, therefore, it is different from any type of middle-class man), so that his experience and the expression of the same (the two are basically the same thing) can never be understood by the latter even when it shocks and takes hold of him thanks to its superior reality. One of the differences between poetry and literature is that the first is the expression of a reality of its own, independent from the finite world, while the second is a copy, a reproduction of a finite reality, no matter whether the copy is naturalist, romantic, or idealizing. Since the mediocre person only knows one reality, his own, every time he perceives the reality he believes it to be his own, even when it is a completely different reality. Thus it happens that he, to choose an example, considers Shakespeare a good describer of reality. This is the basis of the entire theory of art as imitation and of the more recent one of art as identification. Art is not the imitation of a life, nor is it an identification with another life, but a primary form of life, which therefore does not take its laws from religion, or morals, or science, or the state, and not even from other forms of life, primary or secondary. Precisely this is the authentic meaning of the expression *l'art pour l'art* (2).[31]

The method for understanding and interpreting is the *Erlebnis,* which cannot be communicated or divulged because—as Gundolf solemnly stated—it is "*Divination.*"[32]

With Gundolf the *Geistesgeschichte* reached a point of no return: he declared that the method cannot be taught and therefore submitted to critical evaluation. Gundolf's style, apodictic and inspired, like that of some high priest whose language admits no rebuttal—a language that was to become particularly fashionable in German conservative circles of the 1920s—fascinated and seduced an entire generation of students, though with a few notable exceptions. Of great interest, from this perspective, is the testimony of a student who attended Gundolf's lessons in Heidelberg, the great literary historian René Wellek, who in 1923, when he was twenty, finally gave up on German Studies, unable to tolerate, first, in Prague, a self-referential philological approach, and then, in Heidelberg, Gundolf's language and esoteric stance. Wellek writes:

> The year before I had entered the Czech University of Prague in order to study Germanic philology. I had soon been disillusioned by the training; I did not care for Gothic vocalism and consonantism, nor for the (anyhow largely fictional) biographies of dozens of *Minnesänger,* nor for the sources of Grillparzer's *Libussa,* nor even for the precise itinerary of the Nibelungen down the Danube to their doom. Gundolf's books—free of pedantry, dazzling for the boldness of their generalizations and the authoritative tone of their judgments—seemed to hold up a new hope for what literary history could be or could become. But somehow I was subtly repelled by what I had seen at Heidelberg. I could not but feel that the implied demand for complete allegiance and even abject subservience to a creed was foreign to my nature. I gave up the idea of studying under Gundolf and soon shifted in Prague from Germanic philology to English literature.[33]

Wellek's unambiguous reaction and his consequent abandoning of German Studies can help us understand, more than any theoretical analysis, the situation in which philology found itself while trying to overcome the limits of positivism. There is a tendency in the thinkers of the *Geistesgeschichte,* especially the Georgian ones, to reinstate old values and norms, to reestablish a worldview that seemed threatened by the transformations of German society and culture in the early twentieth century. But the response of sensitive scholars like Gundolf was—in the very form in which they chose to communicate their knowledge—a response that descended from the codes of behavior and values that had been imposed from above on the faithful students of the university, the followers that German universities had accurately selected, trained, and disciplined. If one then proceeds to analyze the ideology of Gundolf's *Goethe,* one sees that his approach and his posturing were in line with the celebration of the aristocratic genius and of his right to place himself well above the common man. Gundolf concentrated his interest exclusively on the truly great poet, the only one who has "a figure of his own and a work of his own" and "a destiny of his own," while "the common man has only qualities, opinions, occupations, and experiences that are determined by the outside and not produced from the inside. Similarly the common man is affected by casual facts and events, which he allows to condition and influence him" (4).[34] Goethe was thus once again transferred by his destiny to a higher world distinguished from that of common people.

Gundolf dissolved any individual dialectic in the category of the "sphere of forces" rather than in some sort of growth, of maturation; he saw Goethe's works as "yearly rings in a tree trunk," and not stations in a linear development (15).[35] As Wellek notes, in some passages the adulation reached absurdity, as, for example, when Gundolf called Goethe "mysterious Zeus" or when, shortly after evoking "his daemonic knowledge," Gundolf called *Conversations with Eckermann* a "Gospel, the voice of a saintly figure" (741, 746).[36] In general, Gundolf's critical discourse—if such it may be called—amounted to approaching the great poet "with the most pure and modest devotion" to celebrate his greatness (7).[37] Gundolf believed that Goethe was the only German to have realized the harmony of all his components far beyond and above the everyday vicissitudes of common men: "Goethe is the only German who has perfectly achieved that form of harmony; he is therefore our classic par excellence" (4).[38] For this reason his figure can be taken as a model by those who aspire to a harmonious order established by destiny to which, willy-nilly, also common men must submit themselves.

Gundolf's cultural and political project, following George's directives, tended toward a specific pedagogical goal: "The first duty and the first result of any education [is] to maintain veneration alive: a sense of the dignity and greatness of man."[39] He thus sought to reestablish, in the very midst of World War I, the myth of charismatic authority, using the figure of the poet to oppose the secularization of the world that his colleague in Heidelberg, Max Weber, was studying from a very different perspective. The history of literature, as interpreted by Gundolf (setting aside his unquestionable interpretative and analytical capabilities), was a firmament in which only a few extraordinary fixed stars shone, by which common men had to plot their courses. To reach great objectives, great models are necessary, guiding lights located on the level of the eternal, the ultrahuman, the myth, far off and unreachable, models who, nevertheless, represent through their thoughts and actions a charismatic guide at such times of crisis.

The Persistence of the Philological Statute

From what I have argued so far, one might get the impression that after 1910 the *Geistesgeschichte* movement exercised an unquestioned dominion over *Literaturwissenschaft.* In fact, this was not really the case. First, as previously noted, the movement was not homogeneous: it is therefore difficult to say exactly which scholars belonged to it, and in any case, within the movement there was room for different positions.[40] Second, although the *Geistesgeschichte,* with its critique of pure philology, was certainly the new and controversial element in the critical debate of the first three decades of the twentieth century, this does not mean that it promptly supplanted philology: in fact, as Rainer Kolk tells us, only 20 percent of the full professors of the 1930s could be ascribed to the *Geistesgeschichte* movement. Focusing on the more prestigious universities, Kolk names Korff in Leipzig, Unger in Göttingen, Gundolf in Heidelberg, Cysarz in Prague, Kluckhohn in Vienna and Tübingen.[41] This means that the great majority of Germanists stayed faithful to the older ideas and philological disciplinary statute.

Within this traditional group, along with the customary critical-editorial work (see August Sauer's editions of Grillparzer and Stifter), there was an effort to provide an answer in terms of method and content to the array of tendencies that go by the name *Geistesgeschichte.* It was especially pupils of Scherer and Schmidt, like Sauer (professor of German philology in Prague since 1886) and Josef Nadler, who made an effort to infuse new life into the positivist school that, while dominant within the institution, ran the risk of slowly losing its critical edge. For this purpose in 1894 Sauer founded the journal *Euphorion.* In presenting the first number, quoting a passage from one of Scherer's lessons titled "Wissenschaftliche Pflichten," Sauer referred once again to the "more humble duties" of the philologist (precision, application of the correct method, search for sources, and especially avoiding mistakes) to which more elevated ones should be added.[42] Among the latter was one of the essential duties of philology: that of holding a mirror up to the nation so that it could see its blemishes and malformations and cure them.[43] However, it was in his *"Rektoratsrede"* (dean's speech), titled "Literaturgeschichte und Volkskunde" (1907), that Sauer explicitly outlined his theoretical position. Quoting, as the occasion warranted, his mentor Scherer, Sauer invoked the need to overcome the difficulties of positivism by rewriting the history of national literature, highlighting and emphasizing "the actual national part of our literary history."[44] In a typical positivist gesture, faced with the difficulty of defining the object of inquiry (the German national character), Sauer limited the field to the character "of the individual ethnic lines, of the districts, of the provinces, of the regions," which were much easier to determine.[45] Sauer applied Taine's principle, "*race, moment et milieu,*" already reelaborated by Scherer in "*Erlebtes, Erlerntes und Ererbtes,*" in an utterly mechanical and biological fashion. His conclusion was that man must be considered a product of the "land" that generated him and that he carries the indelible marks of the "ethnic group" and family to which he belongs.[46] These "ethnic traits" constitute the deepest level of the personality onto which later influences from the social world (education and individual experiences) are added. Scholarly attention must be redirected to geographic, biographic, and ethnic data, and especially to the "blood mixture" in the poet, which has a decisive influence on his activities and on the quality of his work.[47]

Sauer's program was meant to emphasize the genuine "German essence" of the German people. The German essence was "simple, primitive and healthy" in contrast with the forces that threatened it: "hyperculture, aestheticism, speculation, artistic mannerism, playfulness, virtuosity"—in contrast, one might say, with the decadent germs of modern culture.[48] Sauer's dean's speech went much beyond the academic requirements of the occasion and was much more than an argument on the duties of philology and of literary history. The place where it was delivered (Prague) and its content made it, as Nadler correctly saw, "a program and comment on a much broader cultural project. The history of literature must not be a private affair of academic chairs but must become a pedagogical-cultural idea and a political-cultural guide."[49] Sauer's later work was similarly militant: from 1901 to 1918 he edited the Prague journal *Deutsche Arbeit: Monatsschrift für das geistige Leben der Deutschen in Böhmen,* in which he took a nationalist stance on the linguistic, cultural, and political conflict between the Czech majority and the German minority (60 percent of Czechs against 40 percent of Germans).[50] Sauer argued in favor of the German-speaking population, adopting in his interpretation of national literature an ethnocentric method that ended up dissolving its original object of inquiry, namely literature. If the work of art derived automatically from ethnic and regional features, the study of literature would end up being part of a general "*Volkskunde*" (the discipline that studies the people), which was to subsume all the disciplines that study the German people and culture in their various aspects.

Sauer's program and his view of literary history were developed by his student Josef Nadler (1884–1963), who ended his university career in Vienna, where he taught from 1932 to 1945. Nadler's major work was the colossal *Literaturgeschichte der deutschen Stämme und Landschaften* (the first volume came out in 1912, the second in 1913, the third and fourth before 1918; following editions, in 1938 and 1952, were extensively revised to bring them into line with the changes in the political situation). Nadler sought to create a national literary history starting from the people (an approach that made it possible for some critics to rediscover his work from a democratic perspective), rejecting the notion of national literary history common to Gervinus and liberal historians.[51] All the antifeudal, liberal or conservative, religious or secular contents (for previous literary history, as we have already seen, had been the expression and battleground of a wide array of different positions) were eliminated. What remained was a *Stammesliteraturgeschichte* ("ethnic literary history") in which values and canons are determined, in a mechanical and biologically deterministic fashion, by the race and ethnic group, "by soil and blood"[52]: "The economic problem is deeply connected to individual districts, to the soil, to its natural fruits and to the ethnic lines that have been nourished by their motherland. Literature and art, as an offshoot of economic forces, caused by the conditions and forms of material work, can be explained and interpreted in the place where man grew connected by a thousand ties to a specific land, and only in the totality of all the effects produced by the play of relationships between his motherland and lineage."[53]

Nadler's theory did away with individual characteristics and specific artistic manifestations, subsuming them in the superior category of "blood communities."[54] The latter he considered exemplary social organization models, eternalized in the sense that they were presented as the only possible form of society in Germany, a form in which any historical, social, or individual dialectic was ultimately dissolved. Other forms of organization, such as those present in modern society, characterized by conflict and dialectic, representation and mediation of material interests, he dismissed as foreign to the German community and people, of which Nadler stressed the fatal premodern status. Consistent with these premises, Nadler engaged in an operation of ethnic cleansing in national literature: he denounced foreign elements (French and Jewish in the first place) as enemies to the German people, responsible for introducing within the body of the nation germs that threatened its survival.[55] The next step was a laborious classification of German tribes according to their more or less recent and pronounced genetic affinities: Alemannians, Bavarians, Franks, and Swabians constituted the original group *(Altstämme),* to which later were added the Saxons, Silesians, and Brandenburgians, born of a fusion with Slavic peoples in the eastern regions of Germany *(Neustämme).* This distinction between ancient tribes and more recent ones influenced Nadler's interpretation of literature and the way he divided it into periods: while he ascribed Weimar classicism to the older tribes, he saw romanticism as a product of the more recent ones: "Romanticism is the crowning achievement of the Eastern-German colonization work, when the mixed blood slowly settled, and the Germanization of the soul followed the Germanization of the land and the blood. And if one turns his eyes to the most remote discernable horizon: romanticism was the adaptation of once Slavic people between Elba and Memel from eastern Rome to western Rome, from the Greek to the Latin essence, from the Orient to the Occident."[56]

Nadler believed that the history of romanticism was born "in the moment that new lines were born: it was the growth of the German blood in the Germanized people. . . . The East became German for the first time with romanticism."[57] He started by noting that the majority of the romantics came from the eastern regions of Germany, then proceeded to define early romanticism as a sort of belated and wonder-struck discovery of the Middle Ages by poets coming from lands that had been colonized only recently and therefore lacked a past and a tradition. From this encounter of the inexhaustible primal energy of the first romantic generation with the heritage accumulated in the old southern regions, the romantic movement was born. After this initial development, southwestern German authors discovered German national values and the need to return to the original values of the land and the people. As one can see, Nadler's method—I have summarily cited his treatment of romanticism as an example, but several other instances could be provided of the outcome of his tribal hypothesis—basically did away with independent literary creation as such, totally subsuming it in the racial, tribal, and genetic heritage of the nation.[58] Notwithstanding this, or perhaps for this very reason, Sauer's and Nadler's theses met with great success in the years after World War I, both inside and outside academia. This can be explained first by the prestige of both scholars: they were the legitimate heirs of Scherer and

Schmidt, that is, of the philological-positivist method, as well as prestigious representatives of the discipline in their own right. Second, Nadler's method—the importance given to ethnic groups, the defense of their purity, the assessment of literary contents on the basis of their ethnic origin—was a conciliatory and reassuring approach: it was still, all things considered, not openly racist, and it made it possible to reconcile deterministic positivism with the *Geistesgeschichte*'s tendency toward abstraction, conceptualization, generalization, and typology.

Between the Two Wars: German Studies and Germanization

Between 1910 and 1930, all the currents of German Studies had to face a series of challenges that were to leave their mark on the discipline for the following decades. World War I, the revolutionary attempts, the establishment of the Weimar Republic, and the advent of mass society, with its increasingly fractioned and irreconcilable political parties—all this gave rise to a general need to rediscover and reappropriate the German national cultural tradition. The academic world and the corporation of Germanists were no exception. As we have seen, it was no longer the liberal patriotic notion of Germany that was the focus of critical discourse on literature and national cultural identity as much as the notion of popular community, which radically excluded—on the basis of an assumed and arbitrary notion of national identity—the typical traits of Western civilization: parliamentary democracy, metropolitan and cosmopolitan intellectualism, liberalism, critical and discursive rationalism, and anything in art and literature that was perceived as a product of modern civilization. There emerged an aggressive and increasingly intolerant celebration of all those authors and literary movements in which, often with far-fetched distortions and grotesque ideological manipulations, the German nature was believed to express itself in its purest form. The German essence became the only interpretative paradigm that could lead to a positive judgment.

With a gradual shift in meaning, the spirit of the *Geistesgeschichte,* too, became increasingly identified with the German spirit, in parallel with the growing tensions between German imperialism and Western democracies. The first world conflict was, from this perspective, a turning point. As is well known, it was also a conflict between cultural ideas and values in which everybody and everything was enlisted. The French-English effort to exploit the alleged contradiction between Goethe's spiritual Germany and Prussian militarism, summarized in the formula "Weimar contra Potsdam," was unanimously countered by German academics—with Germanists in the front lines—by reaffirming the absolute identity of the German spirit and militarism: "Within the German army there is the same spirit of the German people because the two are the same thing and we too are part of it."[59]

Existing differences between the supporters of the *Geistesgeschichte* and the philological school were dissolved in a common corporate ideology whose goal was to transform literary history and the study of German language into a *Deutschwissenschaft,* a science that was to help reinforce "popular" and ethnic-national elements. The consequence was the basic ideological homogeneity of Germanists, which expressed itself in a hostility toward the novelties produced by the war and its aftermath. All Germanists, with practically no exceptions, took sides against the foreign body that was the Weimar Republic—a fact that is hardly surprising if one takes into account the power of control and the ability to produce homogenous discourses of such a rigidly structured disciplinary system. This occurred notwithstanding the efforts of the new democratic government to appease Germanists through the financing and granting of new chairs. An exemplary conflict developed in the Germanisches Seminar of the University of Berlin around the figure of its all-powerful director Gustav Roethe, who systematically rebuffed all the cautious efforts on the part of the Ministry of Culture to fill the chair that had been left vacant upon the death of Erich Schmidt in 1913. Through a series of vetoes, all in the name of the autonomy of the university, Roethe succeeded in preventing the chair from being filled until 1920, rejecting, among others, the prestigious candidacies of Unger and Gundolf, both tainted by their ties to the *Geistesgeschichte* and the latter a Jew, for good measure. Roethe also rejected the compromise offered by the ministry, that of filling the chair and simultaneously creating a new chair of *Neuere Literatur.*[60] In the end, Schmidt's student Julius Petersen (1878–1941) was nominated.

The period from 1919 to 1933, while liable to further internal periodizations, is marked as a whole by an organized opposition to the republic. In 1920 the Deutscher Germanistenverband (DGV) transformed itself into the Gesellschaft für Deutsche Bildung (GfDB), which sought to group all those who worked in German education for the purpose of contributing to the "renewal of the people and the motherland." The renewal was obviously meant to be antirepublican and to take the form of an identification with the highest values of the "German essence," as witnessed by the program presented in the first issue of the official paper of the GfDB, the *Zeitschrift für deutsche Bildung:*

> It is the education of the Germans to Germanicity, the rooting of the individual German soul in the soul of the German people. It is no longer today a question of educating man to live within a community, but rather of educating the German citizen to become the conscience of the German state. And the way to the education of a German conscience of the state is through the education of a German conscience of the people, and the education of a conscience of the people leads to the education of a German conscience of the motherland. Within the motherland lies the secret of all the original vital forces of the state and of the people. From the more circumscribed motherland to the German people and from the German people to the German state: this is the way that our young people must follow.[61]

Within this new situation, methodological disputes would vanish, dissolved in the great container of the *Deutschwissenschaft* or *Deutschkunde* (the science or knowledge of all that is German). In this context one may mention the speech given by Julius Petersen, which was particularly significant due to the occasion for its presentation—it was the opening speech for the foundation of the Gesellschaft für Deutsche Bildung on 30 September 1924—and the institutional importance of the speaker. Petersen appealed to all those who had helped reunify "the channels of the motherland . . . in a single great river" that had had its origins in the Grimm brothers, then flowed through Lachmann and Gervinus all the way to Scherer and Dilthey.[62] Petersen also mentioned more recent movements in the *Literaturwissenschaft:* the ethnologic approach (Nadler), the *Ideengeschichte* (Unger and Korff), and finally the school that focused more specifically on style (Strich). All these authors and methodologies, however, had merged in the great river of the *Deutschkunde.* In the period of great confusion that Germany was experiencing, "lost in the materialistic chaos," there was a way to salvation: transporting into the present Scherer's "national ethical system," "the duties of national education" invoked in the first congresses of Germanists in 1846.[63] Petersen's proposal was entirely based on the past, on values that had had a substantially different significance and function at the time they were originally upheld. He saw these values as the only solution to the present crisis: "Where can we, who are now guideless, find the force that may guide us but in the history of the fatherland and in bringing back to life the experiences of the great personalities of our past?"[64]

Petersen found the solutions to the general crisis of German society in words such as "self-knowledge," "self-awareness," "self-conscience," "self-education"; that is, only in oneself could there be salvation.[65] The idea of community that Petersen referred to was a sort of monadic model: between the monads he saw no dialectic exchange, and he saw their relative autonomy as preestablished (by God). The ideal society Petersen prefigured was dominated by the notion of the ego, both individual and collective, concentrated on its past and interiority, autocratic and sealed off from external influences: he saw the German essence as corresponding to a static and egocentric Weltanschauung, dangerously preoccupied with preserving its identity.

On the necessity of rediscovering and reassessing Germany's spiritual and ethnic roots the *Geistesgeschichte* and the positivist school were in perfect agreement, though the various ingredients were present in different quantities: from this agreement came a great number of works that sought to identify the periods and moments in literature that best represented the soul, the spirit, the character, the essence of the German people. Among these were the studies by Hans Much (*Vom Sinn der Gotik,* 1923), Oskar Walzel (*Vom Geistesleben alter und neuer Zeit,* 1922), and Richard Benz (*Blätter für deutsche Art und Kunst,* 1915–16), which celebrated the gothic element as typical of the German spirit in contrast to the romantic, and many works on the baroque period, foremost among them those of Herbert Cysarz (*Deutsche Barockdichtung: Renaissance. Barock. Rokoko,* 1924) and Emil Ermatinger (*Barock und Rokoko in der deutschen Dichtung,* 1926), in which the creative force of the baroque was presented as a spontaneous explosion of deep-seated northern sentiments in opposition to the static and superficial art of the Renaissance. But the period that had most lent itself to a celebration of national identity and of the introverted and metaphysical German spirit had been that of romanticism. Of particular importance was the long series of studies on romanticism by Julius Petersen himself, titled *Die Wesensbestimmung der deutschen Romantik* (1926). Petersen went so far as to claim that modern German Studies coincided with the study of romanticism.

The romantic movement, along with the gothic, the baroque, and the *Goethezeit,* benefited the most from the studies of the exponents of the *Geistesgeschichte* and of the Germanists of the 1920s in general. The romantic movement took a privileged place in the canon of those years because it was considered the most German of all literary movements for its capacity to emphasize categories such as spirit, soul, the unconscious, and interiority. Interiority especially was seen as essential to the *Deutsche Bewegung* (German movement), a concept elaborated by Dilthey and by Hermann Nohl to assert the refusal of German philosophy and literature to follow Western (French-English) culture, choosing instead a wholly German way based on a self-referential and apolitical form of interiority independent of social interactions.[66] An example of this view of interiority is found in the already mentioned essay by Petersen, "Literaturwissenschaft und Deutschkunde."

The prestigious journal *Deutsche Vierteljahrsschrift für Literaturwissenschaft und Geistesgeschichte* (founded in 1923 by Germanist Paul Kluckhohn and philosopher Emil Rothacker, soon to become the semiofficial journal of the *Geistesgeschichte* and still published today) was also prominent in the effort to identify and support what were believed to be the purest manifestations of the German spirit and soul. As one may easily imagine, in the context of the German Studies of the 1920s and 1930s, this meant above all selecting, excluding, and opposing foreign elements—an operation restricted, for the time being, to philosophy and literary history.

Five

German Studies in the Years of National Socialism

From what I have written so far, it is clear that the transition from the Weimar Republic to National Socialism was not particularly traumatic for German Studies: during the Weimar years the ground had been accurately laid and the entire official discipline had already been reoriented in its methods and contents toward goals that were perfectly compatible with the ideology of the National Socialists, who gained power in 1933. However, beyond this general affinity, the relation between the new regime and the university discipline of German Studies was more complex, varied, and, I might add, problematic than one might expect from what I have just said. Hitler stayed in power for twelve years, six of which were during wartime, when there was a general mobilization of all national energies toward specific duties and goals directly related to the war effort. German Studies did its bit—as we shall see, there was also a specific "wartime" German Studies—yet, especially in light of recently published documents, one must note that during those twelve years the degree of support the discipline gave to the regime varied.[1] More precisely, one can distinguish between militant positions consistent with the National Socialist strategy and Weltanschauung and other more qualified positions, which interacted, clashed, and negotiated with the former with varying degrees of tension and compromise in an effort to preserve the self-referential autonomy of the discipline.

Following a chronological order, I shall initially examine the transition from the Weimar Republic to National Socialism, then the relations and conflicts between the new regime and academic German Studies, finally focusing on the period extending from the outbreak of war to Germany's final defeat.

Farewell to Weimar

In German universities teachers and students alike reacted enthusiastically to Adolf Hitler's rise to power in 1933. The new Third Reich was, at this stage, a utopian model of state and social-economic organization that, precisely because of its still vague character, functioned as a powerful ideological magnet capable of attracting extraordinary energies within the academic world. The *deutsche Wissenschaft,* as we have seen, had already elaborated during the Weimar years a set of methods, paradigms, and contents that were preparatory to and consistent with the notion of a new Reich with a Führer at the helm. Furthermore, the structure of the academic world ensured its preselected and homogeneous character (on the basis of the previously mentioned co-optation principle and the rigid control over discourse exercised by the upper echelons). Access to academic life was regulated by a series of hurdles: the dissertation; the Habilitation, or qualifying examination for teaching; and finally the *Gutachten,* written evaluations of the candidate by academic or political authorities, needed for any university post.[2] Control was not exercised solely on scientific work but extended to the personal traits and private lives of those engaged in university careers: all the qualifications of those who aspired to the role of full professor had to be verified, since, after all, a full professor was ipso facto a *Beamte* (a state functionary for life).

It was not by chance that at the end of the nineteenth century (with the *Lex Arons,* purposefully conceived as an anti–Social Democratic tool) a procedure had been established requiring those who aspired to the post of full professor to undergo a series of evaluations by renowned professors acting as the trustees of the corporation and of the state, a procedure that included the previously mentioned *Gutachten.*[3] This system, which might be referred to as one of using "discursive police," worked perfectly, preventing those who lacked the necessary ideological, political, racial, and personal credentials from reaching the uppermost level in the academic institutions. There were only a few outsiders, such as Gundolf, and even in his case one must note that he never made it to full professor and that his work and personality (apart from his Jewish origins) were not particularly at odds with the dominant ideology of the corporation. Among the academic disciplines, German Studies was arguably the most efficient in applying this selection process, so much so that when Hitler assumed power in 1933 hardly any epuration was needed. As Georg Witkowski bitterly recounted, referring in the third person to his own Jewish origins and the circumcision that made it manifest: "The possibility of participating in the academic life was taken away from him, along with a part of his body, before he was eight days old."[4]

Thus academia—and especially German Studies, the most "German" of its disciplines—had already been oriented by its apparatus and selection mechanisms in a conservative, nationalist, and basically racist direction (having gradually replaced the founding notion of the centrality of language with that of race). Certainly one could make subtle distinctions between the biological view of race found in National Socialism and a more tolerant, cultural view of racial difference that saw Jews as the bearers of specific qualities that had a right to exist, though they could be a dangerous polluting factor for other cultures.[5] But in both camps the German essence, in all its variants, remained the central value, and the criterion for value judgments was the *Deutsch/Undeutsch* opposition.[6]

Nevertheless, within academia a certain "resistance" developed toward National Socialist policies: however, *resistance* must not be read as implying an actual opposition, but rather as a sort of implicit recalcitrance and jealous defense of the self-referential autonomy of academia, of its prerogatives and privileges. Misunderstandings and disagreements manifested themselves continuously between academia and the regime on this terrain. When National Socialism seized power, it immediately began its *Gleichschaltung* (aligning) policy, which called for the synchronization of national culture under a single political and ideological guide within a reasonable span. Within academia, the *Gleichschaltung* process reached its peak with the famous book-burning ceremonies of 1933, which took place at a number of universities with the participation of a great number of students as well as the support of most professors: indeed, some professors of German Studies even delivered official speeches for the occasion, including Gerhard Fricke in Göttingen, on 10 May 1933.[7] The purpose was to start anew with a clean slate, eliminating all impure (democratic, socialist, liberal, "Jewish" or generally *undeutsch*) elements typical of the intellectual world and of Western civilization. This initiation ceremony, whose purpose was purification and regeneration (the fire was intended to forge a new state, a new people, a new Germany) was generally approved of by the entire academic community, since the macabre ritual was seen as a means to reinforce the sense of belonging to a race and a national community. Yet these ceremonies and the whole *Gleichschaltung* process did not significantly alter the status of the discipline. Within German Studies everything went on more or less as before: the support granted, on the whole, to the new regime smoothly coexisted with the continuing belief that the sacred, unchallengeable autonomy of the discipline could at any rate be preserved.

The Characteristics of the National Socialist Regime

For their part, the National Socialists were concerned with providing stability to their regime. During the initial period of the regime, from 1933 to early 1935, they sought especially to reinforce and extend their dominion over the institutions responsible for educating the new generations. The new ideological framework was clear, consisting basically of a number of brutal variations on the theme of anti-Semitism.

With regard to this consolidation phase, one element especially must be stressed: the fact that National Socialism (especially in its early stages) was a still somewhat unstructured movement, coupled with the absolute dependence of the party in all its articulations on the person of Hitler. What might seem a problem—the lack of a well-defined program and of a well-organized structure to implement it—turned out, thanks to Hitler's brutal unscrupulousness and his total control over the movement/party machine, to be extraordinary assets for a new political organization, such as the Nationalsozialistische Deutsche Arbeiterpartei (NSDAP), that had no qualms about asserting its complete hegemony over the whole of German society. In the case of the institutions responsible for national education at various levels, from kindergarten to the university, there were many different and occasionally conflicting branches of the party, the movement, and the state charged with the task of controlling, supervising, and reorganizing on new foundations the educational contents and the production of cultural discourse, activities that were necessary for the forging of the new German essence. Their action, in other words, was not simply repressive: National Socialism did not function as a purely negative, destructive, irrational force, but actively stimulated and organized new initiatives and new projects necessary for the establishing of its Weltanschauung.[8]

The project of restructuring the cultural and educational sphere, however, was often hindered by the nature of the National Socialist power system, which was typically characterized by a complex and often confused overlapping and juxtaposition of party and state organs, special appointments, delegates of the Führer, and other institutional authorities. The system, which has been effectively defined as an "authoritarian anarchy," combined a monocratic leadership with polycratic executive structures, producing a sort of well-organized institutional chaos, in the sense that it was not the product of chance or bad organization, but rather of Hitler's open suspicion of any clearly codified government system regulated by explicit and objective rules.[9] Hitler preferred to maintain a number of competing power structures, often contradictory and ephemeral, in order to preserve his personal control over the system, willfully obscuring the boundaries between the role of the party and that of the state. As one can imagine, this situation frequently produced tensions, clashes, and mutual jealousies between different and overlapping party levels and branches, ministries, and Hitler's special appointees, all of which, in case of conflict, had the right to appeal to superior party organs or state institutions or to the Führer himself. The one fixed principle in this political and administrative whirlwind of juxtaposing and conflicting institutions and personalities was that Hitler had the last word.

The Dialectics of the "Aligning" Process in German Studies

Hitler's polycratic system soon found itself in a curiously ambivalent position in regard to German Studies. As sworn enemies of the Weimar Republic, the professors had paradoxically been given by its governments—in an effort to gain their support or at least moderate their opposition—a constant increase in funds and posts and an acknowledgment of their prominent role in national education. Their prestige, social reputation, and economic status were rather high, also because the republican state attributed great value to culture and respected its independence. Their support for National Socialism was not, therefore, an obvious choice. For some Germanists it was certainly sincere and unconditional; others only paid lip service to the Nazi cause for reasons of convenience, convinced as they were that National Socialism was to achieve its goals on a political and economic level, but it had to leave the university free to go on doing business as usual, largely ignoring the extra-academic world, once it had formally paid homage to the new rulers. Modifying the subjects, canons, and paradigms of academic work seemed quite unwarranted. This combination of a well-disposed attitude toward the new regime with the firm intention of preserving the traditional forms and activities of the discipline is well witnessed by a private letter sent by Karl Viëtor (who a few months later decided to emigrate on account of his Jewish wife) to Erich Rothacker. Viëtor admitted that in his case there was no real "compliance with party directives," though he was of course ready to loyally participate in a program explicitly geared toward reorganizing national culture on the basis of the notion of *deutsche Wissenschaft*.[10]

The reaction of Germanists to the new Reich was not, therefore, what National Socialist party ideologues really wanted: the corporate spirit prevailed over external affiliations with all its rituals, mental reservations, and self-perpetuation mechanisms. Once the 1933–35 consolidation period was over, National Socialism had to face a corporation that offered little opportunity for direct repression, since Germanists had officially adhered to the regime; had no Jewish, liberal, or left-wing members; and had practically never explicitly opposed the regime. Furthermore, the National Socialist control system—entrusted partly to party surveillance, partly to State supervision, and in both cases subdivided into central, semiperipheral, and peripheral branches—often produced different and contradictory results whose outcome was most often an impasse, since, at least on the more trivial issues, when different institutional subjects produced discordant recommendations, no action ended up being taken.

The case of Nadler is a good example. Diametrically opposed judgments of him were produced by different institutional subjects, partially suggesting his possible lack of reliability for National Socialism: while on the one hand the Vienna Gaupersonalamt, that is, the local National Socialist party center, wrote in 1939 that it had "no observation on a political level" on him, more or less in the same period the Nationalsozialistischer Deutscher Dozentenbund (NSD-Dozentenbund, the National Socialist German Professors Organization), described him as "intolerable . . . because for the party it is impossible to use people who are so clearly oriented toward a Catholic worldview."[11] Later, in August 1940, it was the Vienna Geheime Staatpolizei (Gestapo) that informed the president of the Reichsschrifttumskammer (Chamber of Writers of the Reich) that Nadler allowed his students to include in their syllabus authors who were banned as Jewish, and even assigned dissertations on Jewish or partly Jewish writers and poets.[12] In the meantime, however, a report of the Sicherheitdienst (Security Service) of the Schutzstaffeln (SS) was describing Nadler as a potential ally and a leading theorist on the alignment of *Literaturwissenschaft* with the racial ideology of National Socialism: "The collaboration between the study of races and German Studies is one of the most urgent problems of the two sciences. The efforts that both sides have made up to now are only a beginning and still partly unsatisfactory. In this context, it is important for German Studies to take into consideration the positions expressed by Prof. Josef Nadler, a literary historian at Vienna University, in his literary history based on ethnic differences."[13]

Possibly on account of these conflicting reports, Nadler ended up not being nominated corresponding member of the Preußische Akademie der Wissenschaften (Prussian Academy of Sciences). This partial setback in his career, however, made it possible for him to present himself in 1945 as a victim of the Nazi regime. There were certainly other cases of scholars whose careers were stopped or delayed by the opinion of one or the other of the organizations responsible for policing opinions, but the absence of any openly repressive action on the regime's part was in fact a consequence of the absence of any politically significant opposition within the academy.[14]

Nevertheless, the general situation within academia was not what the National Socialists had been planning on. The Germanists had symbolically adhered to Nazism on a general political and ideological plane, but were reluctant to actually reorganize the structure, contents, and methods of the discipline to align it to party directives. While the Nazi regime, as I have mentioned, lacked a coherent unitary line in regard to the university and German Studies in particular, it nevertheless reacted to this situation and set out to achieve a transformation of both the institutional form and the contents of German Studies. The first measure taken, which lasted almost until the outbreak of the war, was to freeze all transfers of full professors while in the meantime striving to promote to full professor and assign the chairs thus made vacant to more trustworthy scholars: Gerhard Fricke

(1933 Berlin, 1934 Kiel), Rudolf Fahrner (1934 Heidelberg), Karl Justus Obenauer (1935 Bonn), Franz Koch (1935 Berlin), Johannes Alt (1936 Würzburg), and Robert Stumpfl (1937 Heidelberg). This policy had the consequence of displeasing all the full professors who were teaching in peripheral posts and wished to transfer to more convenient ones. Furthermore, the creation of new full professors directly tied to the National Socialist regime was perceived by the corporation of Germanists as the intrusion of unqualified parvenus. Incidentally, after the fall of the Reich this policy made it possible for some Germanists to act the parts of the victimized members of a serious professional community who had sacrificed themselves in defending the independence and purity of the discipline (its "true discourse," in Foucault's terms) against the wave of ideological amateurs imposed by the Nazi Party for propaganda purposes foreign to the discipline's true mission. And given the difficulties that the National Socialist government faced in confronting the corporation of Germanists and the scanty results it achieved, there may well be some truth to this claim.

Even though it lacked an overall program for reform, National Socialism tried to reorganize the discipline on various levels—methodological, thematic, organizational, institutional, scientific—along its general lines; but while the documents produced by the various branches of the Nazi regime that dealt with the problem pointed out different impediments, they all agreed that *Germanistik* as a whole had fallen sadly behind in its process of alignment. It is interesting to consider, for example, the 1938 annual report of the Reichsstelle zur Förderung des deutschen Schrifttums (Reich Office for the Promotion of the German Language and Literature, also known as Amt Rosenberg). The report (probably written by Franz Koch, the Germanist who directed the pertinent section) reads:

> One must impartially and lucidly note that in the field of the humanities the National Socialist worldview is gaining or rather has gained ground quite slowly. Nor could it be otherwise, considering that in this field there has been a practically unhindered propagation of the most unilateral intellectualism, the most abstract spiritualism, along with an extreme fragmentation and disorder in methods and perspectives, as well as an open Alexandrinism, one might very well say, which has developed in an uncontrolled fashion. Another reason for the situation can be found in the fact that in scientific research the old generation is still dominant and the new one is slow in making progress in the field.[15]

Proposals for Disciplinary Reorganization from the Security Service of the SS

The concern of the National Socialist regime over the difficulty of reorganizing the humanities in accordance with party lines is confirmed by another extremely interesting document, published in its entirety only after the German reunification of 1989, which has led to the opening of many secret archives. It is a report on German Studies written in late 1938 by the powerful Sicherheitsdienst of the SS. The report was presumably prepared by Hans Rössner, the pupil and assistant of Karl Justus Obenauer in Bonn and a collaborator of the Security Service, who, on account of his background as a Germanist, was in charge of cultural and academic matters.[16] Written by a section of the Amt III, the office responsible for gathering information for the Ministry of Foreign Affairs, the report shows the importance attributed to aligning German Studies (generally conceived by this time as *deutsche Wissenschaft*) with National Socialist doctrine. The document is surprising for its frank analysis and penetrating judgments: because its purpose was to identify true enemies and its status was confidential, Rössner's report expressed opinions that in other contexts would have been considered undiplomatic or even defeatist. The report began by summarizing the duties that the National Socialist state attributed to German Studies and to literary studies in general:

> Within the framework of the ideological and political-cultural reorganization of the National Socialist state, all the sciences that deal with the history and essence of the German man and his cultural productions acquire greater significance and a vital importance. German Studies, too, as the discipline that studies the history and essence of the German language and literature, is given a decisive role that goes much beyond the boundaries of a specialist scientific activity. . . . It must provide a scientific interpretation of historical materials, reelaborating them for the purpose of using them from a political-cultural perspective. It must pay special attention to the foregrounding of fundamental German values within the tradition of the language and poetry of the German-Germanic people, in order for them to become a spiritual property of all the members of the community of the people, especially the so-called new academic generations, that is, especially the future body of German teachers (5).[17]

Two issues in the report seem central to me: first, the necessity of enlisting the scientific work produced by the discipline (the specific knowledge of the corporation) in the service of the cultural policy of the National Socialist state; second, the goal of establishing a new type of relationship with all social groups, in this case with the students destined to pursue university careers, which bears witness to the tendency of National Socialism to present itself as a political movement that promoted the renewal of society and the empowering of the new generation. In relation to these goals, the report continued: "We must acknowledge that today German Studies, as the science of the German-Germanic essence and humanity that has found in language its expression and representation, has still not fully understood the great role and chance that the National Socialist revolution is offering it. On the contrary, we must admit that precisely in the field of German Studies, of vital importance for our cultural policy, a scientific activity of liberal tendency is still dominant, in which a great number of enemy or at least conservative and liberal forces are active" (5).[18]

To address the problem, the report listed a number of priorities that can be summarized as follows: in the first place, there was a need to produce an accurate analysis of the current state of the Reich's university system in order to organize people, schools, and institutes around a common project that would promote German Studies' conforming to the letter, the spirit, and the ideology of National Socialism. This would require establishing the sort of "wide-ranging unitary strategy" that had been lost in the methodological chaos of the 1920s produced by the conflict between positivist philology, *Geistesgeschichte,* and what the report terms *"ästhetische Betrachtungsweise"* (aesthetic vision) (7, 8).[19] Esoteric or highly abstract interpretative models prevailed: Rössner was referring particularly to the militantly democratic literary criticism of the Weimar period and to its Jewish components.[20] This left little room for the more valuable work of critics and Germanists close to the National Socialist movement (Rössner cited Adolf Bartels), who were considered by other Germanists as "extravagant and semi-amateurs that are not to be taken seriously" and who, while active in literary historiography, were marginalized in academic German Studies, which was wholly absorbed in sterile and monotonous methodological disputes (9).[21] A negative example cited by Rössner was that of Julius Petersen, who, though a full professor at Berlin University, president of the Goethe-Gesellschaft, and "Literature pope," had done nothing to oppose these degenerative processes and the almost complete loss of "the pedagogical approach and the cultural and political mission of German Studies" (9).[22] In the last few decades, the discipline had sought its certainties elsewhere: in aesthetics, in the spirit, in religion, in philosophy. Thus it had lost—a central issue for all National Socialists—the capacity to hear the voice of contemporary poets and writers who had expressed positive and vital values, and for this reason had been constantly ignored or defamed during the Weimar years by literary critics who were all Jewish, democratic, and Bolshevik. The authors cited by Rössner were Kolbenheyer, Grimm, Strauss, Wilhelm Schäfer, Weinheber, Blunck, Carossa, and others. At least in terms of quantity, these authors certainly represented a conservative and reactionary counterpoint to what was seen as the veritable destruction of linguistic forms accomplished in some areas of literature and poetry during the Weimar years. For Rössner those authors were a defense against the "growing Bolshevik disruption of our German literary manifestations and of the expressive forms of the language" (9).[23]

The report proceeded to carefully, indeed almost cautiously, consider the problem of those professors it called liberal and considered hostile to National Socialism. According to Rössner, they had succeeded through a great number of manifestos, articles, and statements to gain a degree of political and ideological backing and continue working undisturbed. This tactic had been adopted by the majority of Germanists. Only a small group (Koch, Krummer, Obenauer, and others) was actually ready to engage in the new extensive strategic projects needed by National Socialism. The political goodwill of this minority, though, was hindered by objective difficulties: due to their militancy in the party, many young National Socialist scholars were unable to pass their qualifying exams and accede to academic posts (10). The situation was marred by compromises and petty tactics that made it difficult to find some sort of solution. Things were made worse by the professors' insistence on the liberal notion of academic liberty, which was dominant in almost all of the Reich's universities (with the exception of Bonn, Königsberg, and Kiel, which seemed more ready to collaborate with the new party directives) (15).

Scientific production within the discipline was also unsatisfactory, continued Rössner: existing journals of German Studies, while not openly against the regime, continued to work according to criteria that were "completely scientific in the strict sense" (57).[24] There was no National Socialist *Literaturwissenschaft* journal. The two existing ones

(*Zeitschrift für Deutschkunde* and *Zeitschrift für deutsche Bildung*) stupidly competed with one another, so that they both lacked a sufficient number of quality articles: it would be better to unify them. On the other hand, the *Zeitschrift für Literaturwissenschaft und Geistesgeschichte,* led by Rothacker and Kluckhohn, was limited by its continuing adherence to the methodology of the *Geistesgeschichte.*[25] *Dichtung und Volkstum* (previously *Euphorion*) was also not ideal: the presence of editor Hermann Pongs ensured that the journal remained the best in terms of scientific quality, yet the credentials of some of its collaborators were questionable. Also, the journal carried only theoretical and abstract articles. Rössner, however, recommended that the Reichserziehungsministerium (Reich's Ministry of Education) continue to finance it because it could be transformed into an excellent journal of German Studies aligned with National Socialism (57).

As for collective works, Rössner's report cited the great *Wörterbuch* (which, however, had been originally started by the Grimm brothers a long time ago) and the works published in the series "Deutsche Literatur," edited by Heinz Kindermann, a titanic achievement realized with the collaboration of many specialists.[26] The report, however, frankly noted that some of the volumes of the series, conceived as an exemplary demonstration of the capacities of the *deutsche Wissenschaft,* were lacking precisely from a philological standpoint, as the scientific-editorial work was *unsauber* (unclean) (61). Furthermore, Rössner noted, the publication of some of the texts was superfluous, since they were already available in other editions. In general, the criteria used for the subdivisions of the works were untenable. Therefore, Rössner concluded, the state's financing of the work should be suspended.

This was the *pars destruens* of the report. Rössner then proceeded to outline the "new duties of German Studies":

> Its educational and political-cultural use is not restricted to the academic world and to the area of scientific research, nor to the professional education of the new academic generations. It consists rather in correctly reelaborating the fundamental values of a new worldview starting from the linguistic tradition of the people, in order to make it again visible and the property of the entire community of the people. German Studies must furthermore produce a scientific and unquestionable account of the diffusion, the influence, and the efficacy of the German-Germanic heritage and of the way it

> is discernible in language and in poetry, in the European and extra-European cultural space, and in its national character, differently formed racially and politically (61).[27]

Rössner thought it necessary to restructure German Studies in such a way as to provide a "clean" scientific basis—he echoed almost obsessively Lachmann's concern with philological cleanness—for the history of the German man throughout the centuries and of his capacity to expand in all directions, but particularly toward the east, emphasizing all the "pure" and uncontaminated manifestations of the German people. To do this, a "science of the spirit" was no longer sufficient; there was a need instead to overcome the old university system, where philosophy was the hegemonic "queen of all disciplines," and to create a new one where German Studies (as *Deutschwissenschaft*), with its complementary and neighboring disciplines ("science of the people, of the German race and of its way of life, prehistory, history, history of art"), would play the leading role (62).[28] The disinterested wandering in the regions of the spirit, a residue of a belated idealistic philosophy, should be replaced by a new worldview expressed in the study of the German essence in all its manifestations, in line with the political-ideological goals of National Socialism inside and outside Germany.

After this general introduction, Rössner proposed a list of seventeen different areas of research for those scholars who were ready to subscribe to his project. I will summarize a few of them. The first area, he thought, had to be the product of a close collaboration between *Sprach und Literaturwissenschaft,* on the one hand, and *Rassenkunde* (study of race), on the other. Rössner deemed this collaboration urgent and crucial: no new German Studies capable of overcoming its present condition as "pure science of the spirit" would be possible if the focus on the study of the language and its written manifestations was not switched to the study of the ethnic-racial Germanic heritage, including that of all the historical, ethnic, psychological, and physiological components of all Germanic peoples (this is where the emphasis on Dutch and Scandinavian studies as an essential part of German Studies originated). As a positive methodological example, Rössner cited the historical-ethnic method used by Nadler in his *Literaturgeschichte,* which he saw as an important model in the National Socialist context. A second urgently needed related field of inquiry for the new German

Studies was the exact mapping of all the areas in which the Germanic people had settled in Europe, with special emphasis on those aspects related to their common origin that made them one. Rössner stressed the immediate cultural and political importance of the presence of German-speaking populations in establishing the future national borders to the west, east, and south (63).

Rössner believed that other areas of research should revolve around national literature. As his eighth point, Rössner suggested a confrontation with the elements that had produced an *Überfremdungen,* that is, a "hyperforeignization" or hybridization between the German heritage and such external hostile forces as the Christian religion (especially Catholicism) and Freemasonry. He gave special attention to the Jewish culture from two perspectives: in its relation to certain literary movements (the *Romantik* and the *Junges Deutschland* movements) and to the birth of modern journalism and as the breeding ground of a certain type of humanistic intellectual who in the Weimar period had developed into the hated type of militant, radical, and Bolshevik critic, destroyer of national values and language (7–9).

On a methodological level, Rössner's report then discussed what at that time appeared to be the main obstacle to the development of a National Socialist *Literaturwissenschaft:* the *Geistesgeschichte.* The latter current, Rössner insisted, was incompatible with the National Socialist worldview. Its place would have to be taken by a science of literature that would study poetry in its organic connections to the life of the people and to the great political events of the past and present. The history of literature should be, first of all, the political history of the German people and of its division along various ethnic lines throughout the centuries. This would entail a revision of the canons and paradigms used in the history of national literature: no longer an aesthetic museum for past works, the latter should become a discipline capable of responding to the new political responsibilities and cultural values of the nation and of the community of the people. The notion of the poet as an isolated genius detached from the world and history should also be abandoned. The poet should be exalted and legitimated only insofar as he related to the people and the state of which he was, and felt, an integral component (63–64). Rössner gave special importance to the examination of sources from all of Europe concerning the "German essence" as a whole. He also stressed the need to pay special attention to literary production in the German language by German communities residing in other states. The purpose of this would be to emphasize the linguistic and literary production of a larger German community identified on the basis of their common language, the embryo of the future Reich of all Germans (64).

Among the areas that should be developed in order to align German Studies with the new militant cultural policy, Rössner also mentioned studies of translation, both into and from German. His report attacked the complete absence of any central supervision in the decisions governing translation of foreign literary works that were thus brought into the Reich. The choices made were entirely up to private businesses concerned exclusively with commercial interests. A general coordination and planning of cultural exchanges, translations, and promotion of selected literary works of foreign countries would serve to increase knowledge of the psychology of other peoples and open new areas of research for German Studies outside the Reich (64).

This, then, was Rössner's analysis of the current situation and his list of proposals. But he added that the future did not look promising. While in the next four or five years many full professors would reach retirement age, this would not automatically solve the problem of the new academic generation. Since the number of students was falling, a cut in the number of teaching posts was predictable. Furthermore, while on the one hand it was possible to help selected young scholars improve their scientific qualifications through scholarships, research contracts, and so on, on the other hand there was no guarantee that in the end National Socialist candidates would prevail in academic competition. In German Studies, especially, the selection process continued to depend largely "on the personal wishes of the full professor"(65).[29] The only way to overcome this impasse was the traditional strategy of creating professors and controlling transfers. Rössner suggested controlling the selection of new professors in order to increase the number of those willing to work according to the lines suggested by the new regime. As an additional strategy, he proposed creating new posts and nominating a number of extraordinary professors more sensitive to their duties toward National Socialism and less subject to the hegemony of the academic structure (66). In order to do this, Rössner suggested eliminating chairs where possible (for example, in the many polytechnic institutes, where full professor posts could be easily replaced by untenured positions or transfers from sectors less decisive from a political-cultural standpoint), assigning the chairs thus made available to universities and institutes where it was necessary to counterbalance the existing academic power structure.[30] He also stressed the need for a centralized general restructuring of German Studies along the lines and toward the ends sketched in his report. He thought there was a risk, though, that such a plan might be formally approved by all academics, but in practice opposed by many, who would resist all forms of external intervention on the principle of academic liberty. Therefore—another interesting example of the caution with which the issue of German Studies had to be addressed by National Socialists—Rössner recommended finding a "healthy balance" between two exigencies: that of reorganizing German Studies in a National Socialist sense and that of respecting the autonomy of the university (66).[31] Rössner was well aware that any radical conflict with the corporation of Germanists had been foreclosed by the promptness with which the societies of Germanists, such as the Goethe-Gesellschaft, presided over by Julius Petersen, had already enacted an *"äussere Umschaltung"* (apparent alignment) with the directives of the new regime (68). The report explicitly mentioned the solicitude with which "precisely liberal Germanists had sought to gain political and ideological backing" through a profusion of manifestos and articles in support of the new regime, which had, nevertheless, had no counterpart in an inner transformation (10).[32]

The Conflict between Culture and Political Power

I have referred extensively to the Security Service report because, aside from the positions stated in it, it is surprisingly free of ideological rhetoric and full of stimulating elements. It would be difficult to find other official documents of the period that address the matter so knowledgeably and in such detail. Certainly not all National Socialist cultural institutions would have approved the document, but such heterogeneity, as we have seen, was a constitutive aspect of the regime. The strikingly original feature of the report, however, was that it went beyond the mere differences in methodological and thematic approaches that characterized the different branches of the National Socialist polycratic power system to express an awareness that the transformation of the discipline, which on the level of contents and institutional mechanisms had been already prefigured during the Weimar years, was in fact difficult to achieve insofar as it required aligning it to a general political project. What we see here was a conflict between a political project of direction and control and the values of culture, along with their means of reproduction through a separate, autonomous, and self-reproducing professional corporation. This was a situation that, following Bourdieu, we could term a clash between political power and the "cultural arbitrary."[33]

For Bourdieu the cultural arbitrary is the product of intense educational process through which, using symbolically violent imposition techniques, arbitrarily selected principles and values of the dominant group or class are reproduced and become, precisely, a cultural arbitrary. The interiorization of the principles of the acquired cultural arbitrary produces a habitus that has a lasting and indelible influence on the addressees of the pedagogical action. The habitus thus acquired and consolidated becomes "the equivalent, in the cultural order, of the transmission of genetic capital in the biological order" (32), transmitting information and practices that, in turn, will generate similar information and practices. The effective pedagogical action "demands and historically gives rise to the production of programming agents themselves identically programmed and of standardized conserving and transmitting instruments" (196). The process, as described by Bourdieu, has important consequences: "The length of time necessary for the advent of a systematic transformation of the transformative action is at least equal to the time required for serial production of transformed reproducers, i.e., agents capable of exerting a transformative action reproductive of the training they themselves have received" (196).

Any transformation of the pedagogical process is necessarily slow, the more so the more the pedagogical work has been effective, imprinting the cultural arbitrary in the students who, in turn, are charged with reproducing it. And the particular habitus of German Studies, as I have sought to show, perfectly performed its function, which was to imprint its arbitrary principles and produce durable practices that conformed to those principles. "All pedagogic action," writes Bourdieu, "is, objectively, symbolic violence insofar as it is the imposition of a cultural arbitrary by an arbitrary power" (5): education is "the imposition and inculcation of a cultural arbitrary by an arbitrary mode of imposition and inculcation" (6). This implies a rupture with all conceptions of pedagogic action as spontaneous or based on spontaneity, as in the case of the defeat of the "wild," untamed philology of the Grimm brothers and the victory of the rigid disciplining system of Lachmann and his followers. At the same time the pedagogic action, through various techniques and apparatuses, legitimates its action as objective truth. Such a disciplinary system lastingly reproduces its institutional conditions as well as the agents of reproduction: the body of professors. The latter, in turn, reproduce the institution that has produced them and through which they gain their economic and symbolic power. This implies a tendency to constant self-reproduction continuing throughout generations, a tendency that in the case of German Studies was established early on and became stronger and stronger in the face of generational changes and methodological disputes. Disciplinary self-reproduction has two further consequences: the discipline's monopoly over the agents charged with the reproduction of disciplinary knowledge and the independence of the reproductive mechanism from external events (which explains the belatedness with which the educational and academic system, entrusted to reproductive agents virtually impermeable to outer stimuli, tends to respond to any social and cultural evolution).

When read through Bourdieu's analytical categories, the conflict between German Studies and National Socialism becomes more comprehensible. The latter, as pure power, lacked the means to overcome the symbolic force of a pedagogical action that had been legitimated and inscribed over a long period of time, producing uniform ways of thinking, perceiving, evaluating. The National Socialists seemed, in fact, aware of the impossibility of winning this struggle without providing themselves with proper tools. Hence the importance attributed to the new pedagogical action: even though the traditional educational system was certainly not hostile to National Socialism, the party soon took on the task of pedagogical action and began founding its own schools and colleges for the purpose of producing, through totalitarian institutions, generations of students whose education would be aligned with party ideology.[34] Pedagogical action, for the reasons sketched earlier, seemed more capable of reproducing and perpetuating the cultural arbitrary than the political arbitrary. The latter could adopt more violent methods and specific and intense training programs, as the National Socialists actually did, but, as shown in the case of German Studies, it proved incapable of competing with the force of the cultural arbitrary and the lasting habitus it produced. The alternative was the physical elimination of its adversaries, but this was not easy even for the National Socialist regime, since Germanists could hardly be treated as enemies of the political establishment.

From this perspective, a significant section of the Security Service report was the one reserved to Petersen. One of the foremost representatives of nationalist German Studies and rabidly opposed to the liberal spirit of the Weimar Republic, Petersen had enthusiastically supported Hitler's rise to power.[35] Yet in the report he was included among the "liberals and reactionaries" and was attacked for the incapacity of the Goethe-Gesellschaft, which he directed, to respond to the new political and cultural requirements.[36] He was also accused of "liberal" management of the society and attacked for having done nothing to oppose Bolshevik tendencies among metropolitan intellectuals.[37] In fact, Petersen was very remote from any liberal view of the world or of culture; but for the National Socialist regime it was precisely his conception of the university, independent of his political positions, that was "liberal" and therefore represented an obstacle to the ideological alignment of German Studies. Indeed, if one considers the separation between political and cultural authority a liberal tenet, the definition of "liberal" does apply to Petersen. In the report the adjective was used as a derogatory term indicating an objective resistance on the part of the cultural institution, which in its will to affirm its complete independence was seen to pit its right to retain a monopoly over the reproduction of culture against the demands of the political system. The question was not Petersen's actual or alleged liberalism, but rather the academic institution as such, its structure and operation, its future and its ability to reproduce itself independent of great historical transformations such as the one that the National Socialist regime sought to achieve. The conflict was essentially one between the cultural arbitrary, controlled and reproduced by the university according to its institutional statute, and the political system that sought to introduce within it ideological discontinuities.

The Germanization of National Literature: *Germanistik* Goes to War

There was thus a basic institutional and disciplinary continuity in German Studies, notwithstanding its formal tribute to National Socialism. Hermand notes that many Germanists continued to offer the same lessons and seminars as in the previous period.[38] The publications of the years 1933–45 do not seem to have been significantly influenced by the new ideological climate: the change consisted mostly in an exasperation of the nationalist themes inherited from the German Studies of the Weimar period. German Studies continued to focus on its philological work, especially the revision of the canon of national literature. This revision was achieved in a rather simple way: the term *deutsch* was transformed from descriptive to normative, to a value judgment, and was equipped with a set of superlatives, prefixes, and antonyms.[39] The process allowed, of course, for variants and nuances, and *deutsch* can be seasoned with a variety of ingredients, ranging from heroic nationalism to daemonic individualism, from populist vitalism to tragic existentialism. Finally, *deutsch* stood for all that was heroic, irrational, intuitive, synthetic, metaphysical, noble, creative, vital, and aristocratic, in contrast with the racial degeneration and cultural decadence of the modern literature of other non-Germanic races.

Between 1933 and 1945 there was also an increased emphasis on the positive racial characteristics of Germanic mythological literature: Icelandic sagas, German myths, Celtic literature, medieval German literature.[40] The reinterpreted national canon extended from the medieval Meistersinger to the *Simplicissimus* to the Sturm und Drang (the movement inspired by that great "Germanic" playwright William Shakespeare) and ended with the celebration of the great authors of classicism and romanticism (though in the latter case critical judgments varied greatly).[41] The new literary history tended to exclude from the post-1850 canon all movements and authors classified as *undeutsch*. Naturalism, impressionism, expressionism, "*Neue Sachlichkeit*" (New Objectivity) were denied the status of literary movements and bearers of stylistic and thematic innovations, and national literature in general was interpreted as an irreconcilable conflict between legitimate German values and degenerate foreign influences that had been destructive of the national language and values. This was true of most histories of national literature of the period (e.g., the works of Hellmuth Langenbucher, Walther Linden, Heinz Kindermann, Franz Koch, Karl Justus Obenauer, Adolf Bartels, and Benno von Wiese), which usually ended with the celebration of contemporary German literature.[42] The emphasis on contemporary literature was evidence of the great rhetorical and propagandistic ability of the National Socialist regime to produce discourses, as well as cultural structures capable of adequately supporting them: contemporary literature was represented as the achievement of a high degree of congruence between the ideological and political project of National Socialism and literary expression.[43] This congruence, whose foundations had been laid by the nationalist and populist literature of the pre-Weimar period and the pro-war literature of the period following World War I, was manifest in a new wave of pro-Nazi writers who were particularly active in the fanatic celebration of the renaissance of the German people, such as Hans Grimm, Hans Johst, Erwin Guido Kolbenheyer, Hans Friedrich Blunck, Curt Langenbeck, and Will Vesper.

It is also significant for our analysis of this period that until the fall of the National Socialist regime in 1945 Germanists avoided meeting as a corporation in general professional conferences. This fact has been interpreted—to my mind, correctly—as a consequence of the desire to avoid an open conflict between the older hierarchy within the discipline and the new generations closer to National Socialism, who were often in a subordinate and marginal academic position but enjoyed the political support of the regime.[44] Even when new chairs were established, the representatives of the old system often succeeded in imposing their candidates by appealing to the *Führerprinzip* (the principle that the leader decided), since they had the majority in the organs that decided on the nominations and were able to prevail over the opinion of those who supported the candidates closer to the National Socialist Party. If a national conference had been held, the National Socialist regime would certainly have sought to influence the rules governing the corporation in order to foster generational turnover and hasten the alignment process. Furthermore, such a general assembly would have highlighted the differences in research and didactic methodologies within German Studies. Avoiding any change was for German Studies the best way to ensure that the "true discourse"—the serious, self-referential philological one—would remain dominant, contrary to any effort to enlist it for other purposes. Hitler and the new regime were to be allowed no more than a symbolic role as presenting purely nominal values within the discourse of German Studies.

As regards organization, it is important to note that in 1933 the Gesellschaft für Deutsche Bildung (the heir to the Germanistenverband) had officially adhered to the National Socialist Weltanschauung, and in 1935 had joined the Nationalsozialistischer Lehrerbund (National Socialist Teachers Association). From a purely formal point of view, the discipline's relations with the new ideology were ideal. On a practical level, however, the level of support of individuals within the discipline continued to range from that of dedicated National Socialists to generic sympathizers to pure opportunists bent on preserving their personal power and their status as holders of a "philological capital."[45]

The one success of National Socialism from this perspective was the official support German Studies gave to Hitler's attack on Poland in the autumn of 1939, which signaled the beginning of World War II. Like many professors of other disciplinary areas, Germanists declared their full support for the war, which they called a "war for the liberation of the German people," proclaiming it to be in some ways the crowning event of their studies:

> The present war is in a high degree not simply a military confrontation but also a conflict of spiritual and cultural principles that will determine the spiritual order of future Europe. Therefore, it is important for the German humanities to actively participate in this decisive historical moment, looking to the political and spiritual situation with a penetrating and wide-ranging gaze, preparing and highlighting the ideas on which it will be possible to build the new political and cultural Europe. In this decisive struggle for the German and European future, the humanities have their own and important role alongside the natural sciences, whose practical employment is immediately visible and already active on a large scale. When humanities aligns itself with the spiritual front of all the Germans, who want the war, it is fighting for its legitimation, which is still not to be taken for granted, and for its refoundation.[46]

Aside from the usual generic declarations expressing solidarity with and approval of the war, there was in this case an effort to develop a great common project. The project was presented in an assembly that was held in Weimar in May 1940 in the presence of the *Reichserziehungsminister* (minister of education for the Third Reich), Berhard Rust. Franz Koch, one of the Germanists closest to the National Socialist Party, presented the opening speech, entitled "Deutsche Dichtung als Kampffeld deutschen Glaubens" (German poetry as the battlefield of German thought). The decision was taken to create a great collective work in five volumes entitled *Von deutscher Art in Sprache und Dichtung* (About the German way in language and poetry). Koch and Gerhard Fricke (another militant National Socialist Germanist) directed the project with the collaboration of Klemens Lugowski.[47] The project was divided into nine thematic areas, each supervised by a specialist. Almost all the Germanists active at the time were involved in the project: Petersen, Nadler, Paul Kluckhohn, Fritz Martini, Benno von Wiese, Kurt May, Leo Weisberger, Karl Justus Obenauer, Heinz

Kindermann, Friedrich Maurer, Paul Böckmann, and Wolfdietrich Rasch. The purpose of the project was described by Koch in his foreword to the first volume: "The total war, as we see it, is not solely a military conflict but also a vast conflict of spiritual and cultural principles."[48] Thus German Studies, too, entered the war, aligning itself with the expansion plans of the German people on a European and world scale, as described by Heinz Otto Burger in the conclusion to his contribution to the last volume of the series: "With the National Socialist revolution and with the war, the German people have not only earned their right to be considered as equals by other European states: in fact, they are getting ready to conquer the whole continent."[49]

The "*Kriegseinsatz der Germanistik*" (military commitment of German Studies) was the last practical result of the collaboration between German Studies and the Nazi regime. In the winter of 1942, when Hitler's armies were stopped in Stalingrad, "wartime German Studies," too, began retreating. All great publications came to a halt for obvious reasons, such as the lack of paper and of personnel (many, like Lugowski, were sent to the Russian front) and the uncertainty over the future. In 1943 there was a general crisis in the journals of German Studies: the *Zeitschrift für Deutschkunde,* for example, gradually reduced the size of its monthly issues and finally ceased publication. By that time all efforts were dedicated to the final showdown.

Six

The Break in Political Continuity and the Continuity of the Disciplinary Apparatus, 1945–1968

In the spring of 1945, Hitler's armies were finally defeated and the Nazi regime came to an end. The country was occupied by the Allied Forces (the United States, the Soviet Union, Great Britain, and France) and divided into four zones of influence roughly corresponding to the territories occupied by their respective armies. From that moment on, all decisions in Germany had to go through the military commands of the Allies. No German individual or German institution could decide anything. There was undeniably a sharp break with the immediate past on political, administrative, and economic levels.

However, when we shift our focus from the general political context to the cultural and institutional situation in the universities, and specifically in German Studies, things look quite different. As had happened with the rise to power of National Socialism, maintaining the resistance of the cultural arbitrary, the continuity of the academic habitus, and the impermeability of the discipline as supreme values allowed German Studies to overcome the crisis without any particularly traumatic ruptures or changes. In this chapter I shall present a number of cases that basically confirm the thesis, already upheld by several other critics, that there was no real break with the past but, on the contrary, a fundamental continuity in the discipline's forms and contents, with a few inevitable but minor adjustments.[1] Only a few victims were sacrificed to the requirements of the historical moment so that the corporation as a whole could survive and go on reproducing itself and its own modes of reproduction.[2] At least until 1966, there was virtually no institutional effort to confront the galling issue of the recent past and the complicities of German Studies with National Socialism. Only in 1966, at the Congress of Munich, was there a marked effort, which was to remain famous in the history of the discipline, to begin reflecting on the relationship of the discipline with nationalism, first, and then with National Socialism.[3] In this case, too, however, in spite of the effort to finally address the issue of "German Studies and National Socialism," one must also note a tendency to evade the central issue, that is, the nature of the discipline as a whole, focusing only on the more superficial issue of the despicable behavior of individual Germanists during Nazism. I shall adopt Klaus Scherpe's metaphors in saying that Nazism had only added a few swastika-bearing flags to the façade of an impenetrable fortress. Removing those swastikas from the façade was right, but did not address the structural features of the edifice of German Studies, which had been erected on solid foundations long before Nazism.[4] It is significant that the most recurrent expressions in postwar German Studies are "renovate" and "restore" (used especially by Germanists who had been closer to the regime).[5] Both verbs imply the existence of a "sound" edifice that could still be comfortably inhabited and that had to be brought back to its original function without attempting any larger structural change. From this perspective, the criticism of German Studies voiced at the Munich Conference seems functional in terms of a modernization of the discipline to be achieved through a generational turnover rather than being a general critique of the discipline's status and premises.

A more general and penetrating critique was found, instead, in a number of student journals of the period from 1945 to 1949, where could be found many attacks on German Studies as an institutional discipline and on its authoritarian and hierarchical nature and structures. But these journals all ceased publication within a few years, and all these positions were basically abandoned during the so-called restoration period, from 1949 until the mid-1960s. Only after 1966 were they taken up again with renewed conviction and new theoretical tools by German students and intellectuals close to the left-wing "Ausserparlamentarische Opposition" (APO, extraparliamentary opposition). Therefore, I contend, the rupture within the history of the discipline did not occur at the end of the war, as one would expect, but in the years between 1966 and 1968, when the character of the discipline as a whole was questioned with enough force to bring it to a crisis.

The Resumption of Academic Activities in 1945

German universities recovered from the war with surprising speed. I am referring, of course, only to those located in the territories of the new Germany governed by the Allies and not to those universities, such as those at Strasbourg, Prague, and Königsberg, which were no longer on German soil. Two new universities were founded in the French sector (in Saarbrücken and in Mainz), while the Freie Universität was founded by the Americans in Berlin in 1948 as a Western response to the old University of Berlin (nowadays Humboldt-Universität), located in the eastern sector controlled by the Soviets. In general, all universities resumed activities within a few weeks, sometimes within a few days after the arrival of the Allies, thanks to the spontaneous action of committees of professors who immediately set about reorganizing the courses, which were successfully resumed in the winter semester of 1945–46.[6]

The situation of the universities was dramatic: most buildings had been vastly damaged and some destroyed.[7] Libraries had also been bombed: in some cases the books had been previously stored in safe places, but in other cases they had to be painstakingly dug out of the rubble. And in some instances, of course, they had been completely destroyed. Interlibrary loan was unthinkable. The great efficient organization of the German universities, already put to the test by the war years, was now facing its hardest struggle.

The material conditions of students, too, were especially difficult: cold and hunger were the dominant themes of the first months and years after the end of the war. Yet, notwithstanding all this, in 1945 there was an incredible increase in enrollment, beyond the existing *numerus clausus,* the official limit of the time. The new students were mostly very young, around eighteen, but had nevertheless almost all been at the front. There were also older students who had come back from battlefields and prison camps. Along with the veterans there was a rising number of female students. Interestingly, more students enrolled in the humanities than in the sciences. Some students of those years, later to become important figures in the process of self-examination of German Studies, in retrospect accounted for this choice by a need to find reference points (as well as escape from everyday reality) in a general study based on the values of classic humanism. Karl Otto Conrady, for example, wrote that he chose German Studies and Latin out of a desire to "retire, get out of the ranks, escape from the sufferings of the present, from misery, from the necessity to understand what had happened, to find refuge far away, in a separate world, supposedly apolitical, in the reign of interiority."[8]

The life of the students was also burdened by the obligation to help in cleaning up university buildings and in the reactivation of essential services. On the other hand, this mandatory labor helped some of them develop a sense of a student community—a new civil community that was an alternative to the military one of the past—as well as a belief, illusory as it turned out to be, in the future reform of the university system. If they had been asked to participate in cleanup of the university from rubble, why should they not be asked to participate in cleaning up its culture and organization? From this situation a series of explicit demands for a democratic reform of the university emerged, though one must stress here that these were advanced by a small minority of the students. The majority had only one wish: to go back to studying and forget what had happened. And this desire was complementary to that of their professors, who were anxious to resume working without engaging in dangerous digressions and annoying self-questioning.

Thus the universities had to start all over. But how? According to what mechanisms, paradigms, canons, values, models, and contents? How should the teaching be reorganized? What kind of knowledge had to be transmitted, and how? How was one to avoid mistakes such as the past complicity with or implicit support for National Socialism? The universities, with their values, with their unconditioned belief in the principle of authority and hierarchy, coupled with the defense of their separate and superior status, had in fact been excellent incubators for many of the principles of National Socialism. The horrible crimes committed in the name of those principles, and to some extent legitimized by the behavior of academia, should have led to an unforgiving self-examination by all members of the university community. Instead no answers were provided, and, even worse, the universities made sure the questions themselves were never asked, enacting a careful strategy of repression and concealment. Only a few intellectuals and scholars made the effort to critically analyze the postwar situation, starting with the psychological, social, and ideological factors that had led to the German people's massive support of National Socialism and to their inability to acknowledge their responsibility in later years.[9]

Attention was focused on the undoubtedly important task of denazifying and reeducating the German people. This, however, was mostly restricted to the purging of a number of former Nazis (on the basis, incidentally, of rather convoluted and arbitrary procedures), who served as scapegoats for all others. The majority of the German professors equated the forced retirement of a few former Nazis with the purification of the institutions, which they believed were now free to go on functioning as before, according to the same mechanisms, the same canons, the same values.

The Denazification Process and the Persistence of the Professorial Habitus

After the war, the Allies in Germany had to face the problem of those former Nazis who held posts in the state administration, including public education. With regard to the extent and effectiveness of the denazification process, the opinions are divergent. One may reasonably assume that a degree of purging was indeed enacted in all four sectors, according to different criteria and rules, given the different political and juridical systems of the Allies.[10] With the beginning of the Cold War, however, when Soviet communism became the main enemy, the Western powers opted for the notion of collective responsibility with regard to the crimes of Nazism, a criterion that had the political as well as the practical advantage of ridding them of the need to ascertain responsibility and punish individuals, at least in the minor cases. There was therefore a degree of indulgence toward a number of people who had been actively involved in the Nazi regime. After all, their Nazi past no longer posed a threat; indeed, in the new situation it served as a good anticommunist credential. Furthermore, out of a commendable desire to respect the rights of the accused, the procedures used against former Nazis were made particularly complex, requiring a number of different levels of investigation and prosecution. Though the four sectors adopted different procedures, in general the process was the following: in the first place, those suspected of providing support for the Nazi regime had to fill out a questionnaire detailing their past activities. Allied authorities then carried out a series of investigations—they had access to all the archives of the past regime, including the secret ones—on the basis of which the accused could be found guilty according to a five-level scale of responsibility, depending on their degree of support for or direct involvement in the Nazi regime. The accused had the right to appeal, which could lead to acquittal or to a change in level. In those cases where responsibility was particularly evident, the accused was suspended from his or her position while waiting for the final judgment.

This procedure was certainly reasonable, designed to ascertain responsibility while protecting the rights of the accused. In the case of public education, however, the general rules on denazification allowed an exception: the accused could retain his or her job until the final sentence if this was deemed necessary to the functioning of the university or school. The degree of necessity was determined by the head of the faculty, by the dean, or by a commission of academics. This naturally meant that many of the academics who had compromised themselves by supporting the Nazi regime were able to retain their jobs thanks to the help of their colleagues, former students, or classmates, who, being less (or less visibly) involved with Nazism, were in a position to decide. This allowed them to buy time until 1950, when, as a consequence of the Cold War and of the crucial role of the two politically opposed German states, the denazification process practically came to a halt and there was a more or less generalized rehabilitation.

To provide examples of the different ways the denazification process was implemented under different circumstances, I shall now examine the case of three Germanists—Franz Koch, Gerhard Fricke, and Clemens Lugowski—who had had major responsibilities with the *Von deutscher Art in Sprache und Dichtung* publication mentioned in the previous chapter, which, as was illustrated, was explicitly designed as an instrument by which the discipline of German Studies provided support to the ideology of the Nazi regime.

Little can be said of Clemens Lugowski, who died on the Russian front in 1942, but the cases of Koch and Fricke are in different ways representative.[11] Franz Koch had been a full professor in Berlin since 1936. After the war he found himself in the Soviet-administrated sector of the city and was immediately removed from his post by military authorities. He repeatedly tried to be readmitted to the university, arguing that his adherence to National Socialism could be attributed exclusively to his desire to continue serving science and culture instead of leaving "the field without a struggle to the amateurs of the party."[12] After a series of negotiations with a number of different institutional authorities (during which a number of other professors, among them Hans Pyritz, were fired), it became clear to Koch that his chances of being rehired in Berlin were slim.[13] Through the intercession of Dean Johannes Stroux he was able to carry on his research work at the Academy of Sciences, where he was paid by the hour. For a few years he continued his efforts to be rehired or to obtain a research contract, presenting various proposals and testimonies of colleagues bearing witness to his independence from the Nazi regime both as the head of his faculty and as a Germanist. In 1949 he was rehabilitated and moved to Austria. He later returned to Germany, to Tübingen, where he was able to continue his research work, though without teaching responsibilities. In 1960 the president of the council of ministers of Baden-Württemberg, Kurt Georg Kiesinger, a man with dubious credentials, nominated him full professor emeritus at the University of Tübingen. In 1962 the University of Vienna gave him a Ph.D. *honoris causa* for his scientific merits. He died in 1969 in Tübingen, and the letter of condolences that the dean of the university sent to his widow is an outstanding example of the inability of institutions to confront the Nazi past in any way.[14]

Gerhard Fricke (1901–80) was a pupil of Unger and, like Koch, one of the Germanists most actively involved in National Socialism, as well as a member of the party since 1933. His story is significant because Fricke was the only Germanist who publicly took a position in front of his students on his connections to the Nazi regime. Fricke had been "denazified" in 1948 and classified as a "sympathizer."[15] After a long quarantine period that lasted till 1957, which he spent in Istanbul organizing and directing a seminar of "*Deutsche Philologie*" at the local university for the Ministry of Foreign Affairs, Fricke returned to Germany, eventually becoming a full professor at the University of Köln.[16] In 1965, after a press campaign put pressure on him to take responsibility for his past (Fricke specifically mentioned *Die Zeit* magazine), Fricke spoke out in a lesson at the beginning of the summer semester, declaring himself responsible, though with a few extenuating circumstances, for adhering to National Socialism due to his attraction to its "undeniable positive impulses."[17] He said he had supported the Nazi movement out of a belief in the possibility of achieving a "new beginning . . . , a true future . . . , a community . . . , a significant service to the whole."[18] Immediately after this public confession Fricke applied for retirement, and the following year he became a professor emeritus. After that he abstained from participation in academic and institutional events or activities, limiting himself to scientific and editorial work.[19]

Other professors who were facing difficulties retaining their university posts solved the problem simply by moving from one occupied sector to another. This was the case of Hans Pyritz and the entire *Berliner Schule,* which transferred from the Soviet sector to Hamburg, controlled by the more tolerant British. This was possible thanks to the so-called Berliner connection, a group of former students of Petersen who were teaching in Hamburg and provided chairs for many of their former classmates who were facing problems elsewhere.[20] Many at the time viewed this simply as a brilliant move that allowed Western Germany to appropriate in full the representatives and the glorious tradition of the Berlin philological school.

In general, there were no mass purges. Only a few of the more visible exponents of Nazism within the discipline were given early retirement; a factor in their expulsion was that many of them had been disliked from the beginning by their more traditional colleagues. The scapegoat tactic was applied to the more compromised Germanists such as Walther Linden, Adolf Bartels, and Hellmut Langenbucher, who, apart from their Nazi sympathies, had strived to "popularize" German Studies, an activity that their colleagues had always deemed foreign to true scientific discourse.[21] These purges of marginal characters allowed the discipline as a whole to go on with its business with a clear conscience: no collective and individual critical self-examination was deemed necessary—even less a critical interrogation of the structure and contents of the discipline.

The Adventure of Schneider/Schwerte

An almost incredible example of the corporate spirit of German Studies and of the way it protected itself through discretion and isolation from the external world is the incredible story of Hans Ernst Schneider, aka Hans Schwerte. Schneider had been an SS official, a *Hauptsturmführer* with special assignments. As a student of German Studies, he had been assigned to a special SS office, the *Ahnenerbe* (Office of Ancestral Research), responsible for extending the political power of the SS to the cultural, spiritual, and ideological fields. One of the office's specific duties was identifying within the territories bordering Germany instances of the "space, spirit, action and heritage of the northern Indo-Germanic race" for the purpose of expanding German cultural hegemony over those territories.[22] In 1942 Schneider had been entrusted with a project called "*Germanischer Wissenschaftseinsatz*" (Use of Germanic Science) aimed at coordinating the activities of German Studies and related disciplines in a number of occupied territories (Holland, Norway, and Belgium) for the purpose of reinforcing the notion of a Germanocentric Europe. For this reason Schneider had had to reside for a long time in Holland, where he was particularly active and efficient in gaining the support of historical-philological disciplines, organizing and speaking at a great number of meetings and presentations.[23] In March 1945 he had become a collaborator of the *Sicherheitsdienst*. Officially, he had died on 25 April 1945 in the Battle of Berlin: he was declared dead following notification by his widow after being reported dead on the basis of the testimony of fellow soldier Hans Schwerte, who had allegedly assisted him in his last moments. But there had been no Hans Schwerte: Hans Schneider had simply assumed a (relatively) new name and managed to fool the authorities with this simple trick. Shortly thereafter, Hans Schneider, now Hans Schwerte, married his own widow.

"Schwerte" immediately resumed studying at Hamburg: he graduated, worked as an assistant at the University of Erlangen (under Heinz Otto Burger), and later passed his *Habilitation* with a dissertation entitled *Faust und das Faustische* (Stuttgart 1962). It seems impossible that none of the Germanists he came into contact with ever recognized him: many of them had collaborated with the very same institutions where Schneider/Schwerte had been active. But the esprit de corps of the discipline worked perfectly, and Schwerte was able to continue his career undisturbed. In 1964 he was nominated full professor at the University of Aachen. Some have speculated that his nomination—which from Jäger's description seems not to have followed the usual procedures—was influenced by a group of people tied in one way or another to the past regime.[24] In any case, Schwerte worked in Aachen until 1978, the year of his retirement. He was also twice elected dean, from 1970 to his retirement, as representative of a left-wing coalition that had won, thanks to the votes of students, administrative staff, lower-ranking teachers, and a minority of full professors. During his deanship some even went so far as to describe the "Aachen model" as the most progressive model of a university in the world.[25] Left-wing student representatives wrote at the end of Schwerte deanship: "Though . . . he often had to give in . . . to the pressure of professors, he always tried to address existing problems in a rational and objective fashion. He also strove to further . . . the interests of those groups that, up to then, at the expense of the university, had been insufficiently represented in collegial organs."[26]

Indeed Schwerte was a well-known intellectual of the social-liberal current and made an important contribution to the democratic transformation of German society: Habermas's expression "communicative reason," which he used to describe a method for solving controversies and attacking conservative positions, perfectly describes his approach.[27] It comes as no surprise that, upon Schwerte's retirement, Karl Otto Conrady edited a miscellany in his honor, *Literatur und Theater im Wilhelminischen Zeitalter* (Tübingen 1978), which was published with an introductory dedication by the Social Democrat minister for scientific research of North-Rhineland-Westphalia, Johannes Rau (currently president of the German Federal Republic)—an unusual act of homage by the institutions. Rau mentioned the excellent work done by Schwerte as a representative of the Ministry for Scientific Research and of the Ministry of the Interior, responsible for the cooperation of the universities of the North-Rhineland-Westphalia with the universities of Belgium and Holland. During his deanship Schwerte had shown a remarkable ability in establishing ties with universities and scientific institutions of neighboring countries (something for which his past work as an SS officer had well prepared him).

Seventeen years after his retirement, in 1995, Schwerte was exposed by a Dutch television network and confessed his past identity. The public reacted with violent indignation. His works and his entire past were closely examined in order to detect proof of his continuing adhesion to Nazi ideology, not a difficult critical task when done a posteriori on someone who had already been condemned on a political level.

Schneider thus became, in my opinion, yet another scapegoat. I certainly do not wish to deny his true and grave responsibility. He was not simply a scholar who had adhered to National Socialism (as had the majority of Germanists); he had directly participated in the cultural, political, administrative, and military organization of National Socialist dominion in the occupied territories. What is striking, however, is the reaction of the body of Germanists. At first the discipline's esprit de corps prevailed, protecting the member who had committed the crime, as if the university system were endowed with an independent legal statute. Even those who do not believe in the existence of a secret organization of former Nazis cannot avoid being struck by the fact that no one ever "recognized" Schneider, even though he remarried the same woman, took up the same job, and frequented the same academic institutions as he had in the past.[28] There must have been at least a few non-Nazis who recognized him, yet no one reported him. Corporate spirit, discretion, lack of communication with the outside, erasure of the past: the mechanisms that protected German academic culture in the twenty years after the end of the war worked perfectly in Schneider's case. Yet when the deceit was exposed from the outside, the corporation immediately and hypocritically applied the scapegoat strategy: the corporation of Germanists declared itself to have been completely taken in and reacted with indignation to this despicable trick (or series of tricks: there was talk of scholars who, favored by Dean Schwerte, had speedily risen in their careers on the wings of blackmail).[29] Once again the knee-jerk response of the corporation was to establish a binary opposition between simulators, amateurs, "true" Nazis, on the one hand, and the sound body of the discipline, on the other.

The unequivocal condemnation of National Socialism repeatedly voiced by German Studies in the fifty years since the end of the war is certainly the expression of a clear and uncompromising political and ideological position. This position, however, is often transformed into a rhetoric of indignation and condemnation that never goes beyond a conformist and comforting antifascism. When the mechanisms and status of the discipline and the network of personal histories behind it are at stake, everything becomes more complicated and muddled. The conditioned reflexes of the corporation, the mutual defense and self-defense, the need to prove the legitimacy of one's own co-optation by suspect or compromised masters, the willingness to sacrifice a few scapegoats in order to safeguard one's cultural capital and the prestige of the corporation, all come into play. And the sacrifice of the scapegoat erases the fact that the others, those who indignantly condemn him, are all links in the same hereditary chain.

The Return of the Exiled

The cases I have cited are proof enough, I think, that denazification was not pursued with particular energy within academia. A number of general political positions and measures were taken, but on a practical and institutional level the last word belonged to the collegiate institutional organs of the universities, who used it as we have seen.

Correspondingly, with regard to the issue of denazification, there was the problem of those who had been exiled by the Nazi regime. These people, of course, enjoyed the full solidarity of the occupying powers. In parallel with the denazification process, allied authorities assisted those who had been forced to emigrate for racial or political reasons in returning to Germany, believing that the construction of the new democratic Germany would benefit from the involvement of the people who had been cast out by the Nazi regime. But while the Allied powers quickly activated the laws and dispositions necessary to support the return to Germany of the exiles, the so-called reemigration process was boycotted by academia in many ways. Following the rules set down by the Allies, in order to be reintegrated within the universities the candidates had to apply for positions, and the universities had to declare that they had posts available and were amenable to evaluating the candidates. And here was the rub: the candidates often had been unable to pass their teaching qualification exams precisely because they had been forced to leave the country and live the difficult life of emigrants. If this was the case, a candidate could be reintegrated only following a favorable judgment of the faculty and in a rank established by the faculty. As one can imagine, university professors did not relish the notion of a return en masse of colleagues who had been previously banished or ostracized. The exiles would have embarrassed their more compromised colleagues, conflicts would have arisen, and they probably would not have been willing to go along with academia's hypocritical cover-up of its ties to the Nazi regime. For this reason almost all universities adopted very rigorous criteria, allowing candidates to be reintegrated only in the same, usually low-ranking, positions they had before their exile, thus discouraging many from returning. A good example of this method is the Berendsohn case.

Walter A. Berendsohn had been fired in 1933 and had escaped abroad. In 1945 he asked to be reintegrated at the University of Hamburg. His request was granted on the following terms:

> In your case the right to reintegration is acknowledged on the basis of your motivation. In the absence of legal grounds for other decisions, the reintegration will take place here in Hamburg at the same post previously occupied. The consequence of this would be that

> you would have to return and accept a post corresponding to the same one you had previously. You are kindly asked to inform us whether you accept this solution. In case of affirmative answer we will take all necessary actions to make the above post available. We assume that you are aware of the great existing material difficulties. Specifically, finding adequate lodgings for your family, even with the help of competent authorities, will entail great difficulty because of the increasing lack of housing.[30]

Berendsohn was thus allowed to return, but only in the same position he had held before the advent of National Socialism, that is, an untenured post, since at the time, although he had passed his teaching qualification exam in 1920, he had not held a chair. The law allowed candidates to appeal such decisions, but it is quite obvious how discouraging it was for exiles to contemplate returning to a homeland and a university where they would be treated as strangers. Berendsohn did appeal, however, and the dispute went on for years, during which he had to face many difficult as well as grotesque moments: he was initially asked to prove that he would have obtained a full professorship if National Socialism had not come into power in 1933, since not everyone necessarily becomes a full professor at a university. Then in 1956 the university sought to prove—using a report written by former Nazi Hans Pyritz—that Berendsohn lacked proper scientific qualifications, finally going so far as to state that "in the opinion of the faculty one may assume with a high degree of probability, bordering on certitude, that even without the change of 1933, with all its consequences, Prof. Berendsohn would never have obtained a chair (or have been nominated full professor)."[31]

Thus the only ones who could return as full professors to universities in the sectors occupied by the Western powers were those who had already been nominated before they were exiled, provided the faculties declared a position to be available and accepted the application. In the sector occupied by the Soviets, on the other hand, some Germanists who had not occupied tenured positions before 1933 were given professorships: this was the case, for example, of the great scholars Hans Mayer, Alfred Kantorowicz, and Albert Malte Wagner. In general, however, few Germanists actually decided to return to Germany.[32] Even those who were reintegrated into full teaching posts had to face moral as well as material difficulties. Richard Alewyn, for example, had taken Gundolf's post in Heidelberg. He had been fired in 1933 for racial reasons and rehired in 1948 at the University of Cologne. Alewyn publicly voiced his opinion on German Studies and its relationship to the Nazi past in 1949 during the ceremonies celebrating the bicentenary of Goethe's birth. During the ceremonies he gave a talk entitled "Goethe als Alibi," which contained a phrase that would become famous: "Zwischen uns und Weimar liegt Buchenwald" (Between us and Weimar lies Buchenwald). In his talk Alewyn publicly expressed his isolation within the corporation of Germanists and his unwillingness to join in the chorus that was celebrating the eternal values of German classic culture without having bothered to carry out any critical analysis of the recent past and of the reasons behind this suspiciously rapid and unconditioned return to the values of the "age of Goethe."[33] Alewyn's position was symptomatic of the cultural isolation of those who tried to question the topoi of the dominant national cultural and literary discourse.

The principle of university independence allowed those who had remained in Germany to continue to exercise their academic power, using legal quibbles to hinder the return of those who had been banished by the Nazi regime. In general, I think the various cases I have described are indication enough that the reeducation process, notwithstanding the sincere goodwill of all four Allies, at least in the initial phase, was carried out in a superficial, bureaucratic, and naïve fashion vis-à-vis the interlocutors—traditional Germanists—who had both the will and the skill to cover for their compromised colleagues, following their habitus and in accordance with the corporate esprit de corps of the discipline. Soon the reeducation process was degraded to a bit of paper shuffling, as if deeply ingrained political and ideological structures could be transformed through minor legal measures and questionnaires without reforming the university system as a whole and the identity of the various disciplines, foremost among them German Studies. Since within the universities power was mostly in the hands of the generation that had academically come of age in the years of National Socialism, from that side no renovation could be expected. The implicit understanding was that now that all that nuisance about National Socialism was over, German Studies could go back to its customary business.

Student Journals and the Debate over Philology

It would be incorrect and ungenerous not to mention, however, those few who did raise their voices asking for reform of the universities and of German Studies. These voices were mostly heard, as I already mentioned, in student journals, which drew attention to a set of issues crucial both in the universities and in German Studies. Foremost among these journals were the *Hamburger Akademische Rundschau* (1946–49) and the *Göttinger Universitäts-Zeitung* (1945–49, after October 1949 *Deutsche-Universitäts-Zeitung*). Both journals were published in the British sector and were marked by their special attention to the problems of university reform, democratic transformation of German society, and, most relevant to our perspective, the need for far-reaching revision of the contents, canons, and apparatus of German Studies.

The students and teachers who debated these issues in the journals were convinced that the construction of a democratic society—a process painfully under way in Germany, with different articulations in the four different sectors—could not be separated from the renovation of the university, which, however, kept celebrating itself as an illustrious example of continuity with the past and systematically perpetuated the old procedures and institutions as a way of repressing all forms of questioning and dissent. The *Göttinger Universitäts-Zeitung* soon stressed the impossibility of self-reform of the German university, publishing a report by a delegation of British professors who had toured the universities of the British sector and reached the following conclusion: "With the occupation by the Allies, new political, economic, and social forces have been liberated. At the same time, however, previous traditions, which Nazism had kept in check or completely repressed, are once again active. We believe it is our duty to stress with the utmost emphasis in this report our strong and unanimous perception that no lasting and far-reaching reform of the universities we visited is likely if the task is left solely to the initiative of the universities."[34]

The report went on to state that the full professors of the various universities were reorganizing the "professorial tyranny," resorting to academic liberty and the autonomy of faculty decisions.[35] It seemed a shame that the new historical moment should fail to bring about a re-education on the basis of values such as liberty, democracy, and critical independence of the new generation of students and young scholars, who instead were still being forced by the hiring co-optation system to adopt a "servile attitude."[36] The delegation concluded by sadly noticing the difficulty that émigrés were facing in being reintegrated due to German professors who, rather than hiring them, chose to remain understaffed and wait for the right moment to rehire those professors who had been suspended for their past ties to the Nazi regime. The general assessment of the reorganization of German universities in the report was therefore utterly negative: and it came from what was surely not a radically subversive source.

In the context of this general stagnation of German universities, student journals also specifically addressed the situation of German Studies. The pretext, so to speak, was an external intervention: Americans had fired thirty-three professors at the University of Munich in pursuit of the denazification policy. Many German newspapers had taken positions on the event, and *Göttinger Universitäts-Zeitung* also asked its readers to express their opinions. In the meantime, a related debate developed on the reintegration of emigrated scholars and on the "university-professor-student" theme.[37] The first person to publicly voice his opinion was Klaus Ziegler, a young Germanist recently returned from the Russian front. In an article titled "Gegenwärtigkeit," Ziegler, who was later to become a full professor at the University of Tübingen, discussed the role of the humanities in the current postwar situation, seeking to outline the guidelines for a renovation of German Studies. In the first place, Ziegler quietly but firmly stated, there was no future for the humanities in Germany outside a democratic political framework. And because German democracy was practically nonexistent, a far-reaching reeducation of the people was necessary, especially for the younger generation. In this context, the role of the "new" university would be decisive. But the field of the humanities in the German universities was generally marked by a dangerous tendency to return to the past. A form of education confined "with sober devotion and modesty" to "objective reality" was once again gaining ascendancy (2).[38] If German Studies and philology (Ziegler preferred the expression *Geisteswissenschaft,* which also included neighboring disciplines) were limited to a self-contained scientific approach that excluded any contact with general political issues, universities would finally lose their function and reason for existence. Therefore the universities must be reorganized based on a "synthesis of scientific objectivity and current living issues" (3).[39] Ziegler's argument became increasingly specific in its demands: first of all a "workers' university" had to be created, denazification intensified, and finally émigrés had to be reintegrated (3).[40] Up to this point, Ziegler's argument was still referring to a general cultural policy aimed at institutional reforms. But he went a step beyond general issues when he proceeded to argue that even these important, concrete acts would remain "in the sphere of the pure organization, of empty exteriority" if the main issue was not addressed: "The stakes are the usual ones: it is not a question of the forms that scientific activity takes, as much as that of the spirit that fills them, the professorial habitus" (3).[41] It was precisely this habitus that prevented even the more moderate reforms from being enacted. Without changing the habitus one could not hope to change the universities.

Ziegler also offered a set of practical suggestions aimed at achieving the synthesis described earlier between a scientific approach and a worldview that would also take into account current political issues. In the first place, there was a need to reeducate future educators, the new generation who were currently beginning their university careers. Ziegler advocated closer relationships between university students and high school teachers for the purpose of establishing personal ties with others and developing "one's inner vitality" (4).[42] Though this proposal may seem naïve, one must keep in mind that he was talking about young scholars, and this measure was meant as an alternative to the purely philological, ascetic, self-referential training they were currently receiving. In the second place, Ziegler called for expanding the criteria for the selection of candidates for future university posts, including on the evaluation committees the institutions (which he did not specifically list) and personalities characterized by a strong involvement in everyday life and current general issues (4). Finally, Ziegler addressed a controversial issue: he argued that in all fields of the humanities there were "amateurs" who had excellent scientific qualifications even though they were not academics. In some cases their close contact with everyday life would make them more useful to the discipline than many renowned specialists who pontificated ex cathedra. The universities, Ziegler concluded, should employ these external figures in more important roles than those currently assigned to them, thus achieving a synthesis between the abstract goals of the spirit and the concrete ones of everyday reality. In other words, Ziegler thought university teaching should go beyond the narrow limits of its self-referential specialization and move from an authoritarian-dogmatic model to a dialogic-discursive one.

A few months later, it was the turn of Swiss theologian Karl Barth, following a request of the editorial board of the *Göttinger Universitäts-Zeitung,* to take part in the debate with an article titled "Verlorene Generation?" (A lost generation?).[43] Barth's opinion was similar to the one of the British delegation. After having reminded readers that German university students had been indoctrinated by Nazi propaganda throughout their infancy and adolescence, he mentioned the contradictory and occasionally perverse effects of the denazification policy. But what appeared particularly desperate to him was the situation within the universities. There had been a few honorable exceptions, said Barth, but overall German professors had learned too little from the past and forgotten it too quickly to be of any help to their students. While most of them had not been true Nazis, they were all hopelessly nationalist, as had been the ones who sabotaged the Weimar Republic in the years from 1918 to 1933, setting it up for its fall to the Nazis and then hiding behind their roles as "decent people."[44] Barth outspokenly concluded: "It is a tragedy that many students are entrusted to the teaching, the education, and the model of this type of professor. In this school, they shall not become free men."[45]

The defense of the body of professors was taken up by Erich von Holst, a professor of natural sciences at the University of Heidelberg. To Barth's specific question "What were your eyes on in 1933?" Holst replied: "Like most of my colleagues and friends, I had my eyes on scientific research."[46] Holst's defense was entirely based on the celebration of the inner liberty that the German universities had managed to defend in the years of the dictatorship thanks to the very "type" of the apolitical professor criticized by Barth. Holst saw no need to modify anything in the education and habitus of German academics: he believed that what they were was exactly what guaranteed their ability to resist external pressures and reproduce the system. Barth's response was harsh: "I allow myself to consider it [this academic type], no matter what his personal qualities and scientific merits, one of the obstacles in the way of the present German students."[47]

Such criticism is evidence of the embittered situation in which German society and the German universities found themselves. German Studies specifically, because of its tradition and its function from its origins to 1945, had the most difficulty dealing with its heritage. As Ziegler's article shows, some critiques within German Studies were beginning to emerge in terms of both institutional organization and scientific approach; these critiques demanded a response. Kurt May—one of the signatories of the *Kriegseinsatz* of German Studies, the author of one of the sections of the previously mentioned *Von deutscher Art in Kunst und Dichtung,* and at the time a professor at Göttingen—undertook to provide such a response. His brief but dense article "Der künftige Germanist: Eigengesetzlichkeit deutscher Literaturwissenschaft" was one of the first explicit proposals regarding the postwar reorganization of the discipline by one of the protagonists of the preceding period. May began by empathically redefining the boundaries of the discipline: "Today, at the moment of its reconstruction, [the discipline] once again concentrates, after a limitless expansion that went on for years and has led it to become a stranger to itself, on the inner line of its essence, starting from its proper objects. Let lively objectivity be the keyword of its younger followers!"[48]

May then went on to trace the profile of the young Germanist: "He who wishes to prove himself more suited than others to the study of literature must be at least inclined toward that particular synthetic ability on which the interpretation of the work of art is based: the ability to sympathetically merge in a sort of mystic union with the contents of the life found in the works and shaped by the soul and the spirit" (2).[49]

Those who wanted to engage in the profession should have the ability to "interiorly relive experiences," to "reexperience themselves in the poetic experience," besides other general qualities such as "the ability to identify and a strong imagination" (2).[50] At the same time, May added, it was necessary to warn the new generations of the danger of abandoning oneself to "amateurish forms of self-expression" that would run the risk of making one lose the bearings necessary to one's study and also to one's life (2).[51] For the study of literature—here May was harking back to the notion of philological ethos—has a crucial educational value, it is "the interpretation of life" and must therefore be disciplined (2).[52] The final purpose of this disciplining was, then as in the past, the education of a "correct philologist," that is, a Germanist who would develop according to the guidelines set down by philology within a sealed-off unchangeable system: "Let every Germanist tread his field of studies with a firm belief in the imperishable ideal unity of the science of the history of German literature and of German language from the origins to the present day" (2).[53] German Studies could be reformed, according to May, by returning to its original independence and philological roots, renouncing any confrontation with the new reality born out of the ashes of Nazism and World War II. The idea that a new type of university student could be possible was completely foreign to May.

A reply to this proposal for restoration came from Joseph P. Stern, later a professor at University College in London and a member of the Göttingen Academy of Sciences, then a British student who was studying at May's university in Göttingen. Stern lucidly analyzed the situation within the German universities and German Studies especially, beginning from the "condition of intellectual inferiority" in which a student of German Studies found himself as a consequence of a system that was structured in a way that forced him to a complete "identification of the professor's idea of art with the idea of art in general."[54] He clearly and rapidly identified the central issue: "Either one identifies the contents of the professorial dogma, learns them, exhibits them at exams, and possibly transmits them to new generations, or else a catastrophe may occur capable of influencing an entire curriculum vitae."[55] The acceptance of the disciplinary system of values, demanded a priori as an "act of faith," had the function of preventing a dialectic articulation and modernization of the discipline, which continued to profess a sacred conception of knowledge. The independence of the discipline—the *"Eigengesetzlichkeit"* (autonomy) celebrated by May—was a pure form that served to suspend the constraints of the external world in order to affirm, as Bourdieu writes, "a new form of necessity or constraint."[56] For Bourdieu, the mechanisms for the reproduction of academic knowledge become ingrained in the mind in the form of acquired dispositions, which in turn become inscribed in the objective status of the scientific-disciplinary field in the form of institutions or procedures, which are made efficient and lasting through the symbolic violence exercised by the professorial arbitrary. Stern, in his own terms, described some of the same mechanisms that Bourdieu was later to analyze, and concluded that the student had no choice but to accept the conditions of professorial dogma or face academic failure.

There was a quick reaction to Stern's attack by May's students (the professor did not answer directly, probably because Stern ranked below him). As was predictable, all of them sided with their master.[57] Stern was accused of not understanding the "German way of studying and teaching," admirably exemplified by May.[58] Stern wrote again in response, noting the emotional and defensive character of the arguments brought forth by May's students.[59] He particularly criticized the assumption, repeatedly stated in the students' articles, whereby, at a moment of methodological confusion and great historical and political conflicts, they postulated the need for the independent self-referential status of German Studies. These petitions of principle were for Stern instrumental and were aimed precisely at legitimizing the dogmatic and autocratic attitude of German Germanists. Those voicing such arguments were incapable of understanding that what was at stake was no longer the status of the discipline, but rather civil and democratic conscience in general, which the student had to acquire as a citizen as well as a scholar: liberty from authoritarian dogmatism went hand in hand with liberty in research and with the expression of one's individuality. Stern's positions remained isolated: the students did all they could to legitimate their masters, by whom they were about to be legitimated in turn.

May's approach, based on serious philological method within the framework of the inherited status and apparatus of the discipline, was the winning strategy adopted by official German Studies in the postwar years. All efforts to carry out a critical discussion of the contents, the role, and the function of the discipline during the years of National Socialism (and the preceding decades) were successfully rebuked. The control apparatus of the discipline functioned perfectly, producing in all four occupied sectors a discipline that has been perceptively described as "a German Studies of concealment, silence, and disguise."[60]

The Restoration of Disciplinary Order

The dominant trait of postwar German Studies, as I have tried to show, was continuity, coupled with a strategy of concealment and repression that was, from today's vantage point, quite manifest. However, in spite of that a limited number of innovations did take place. These affected mostly the contents of the discipline, and they involved a moderate expansion of the canon in the search for new values to replace the no longer acceptable ones of *Volk,* race, and national community—in other words, the German essence in all its manifestations. On a methodological level, there was a renewed emphasis in the humanities on the notion of "*werkimmanente Interpretation*" (immanent textual interpretation), which was seen as a safeguard against any misleading involvement in politics. The methodological tenet of the free and disinterested interpretation of literature, which had already emerged in one current of the *Geistesgeschichte* in the 1920s, was now reinforced by the influence of the American New Criticism school.

In this return to an apolitical text-oriented approach, philology played a key role. The representatives of the *werkimmanente Interpretation* constantly and explicitly referred to the educational value of philology: the latter, with its emphasis on sacrifice, dedication, and asceticism, was a safe harbor for those who lost their way in the tempests of World War II. The almost priestly devotion to the written word (*"Dienst am Wort,"* service to the word, was a recurrent expression) was an extreme effort to preserve "eternal values" from the advance of the modern secularized world. The values that were more suitable to this goal were seen as the values of the West and individuality, which promptly replaced the German essence. In both cases, this allowed the discipline to maintain the canonical status of the German classics while annexing them to the overall context of Western literature, thus preserving Goethe and Schiller, Lessing and Hölderlin from any radical interpretative revision.

This stance was accompanied by the gradual canonization of modernist authors such as Hofmannsthal, authors who were deemed compatible with classicism because of their refinement and masterly complexity. In fact, the expression *"Klassiker der Moderne"* became one of the bywords of German Studies. Modernist authors were thought to be classic because they give classic form to a classic content (the values of "transcendental humanism," as Eagleton terms it).[61] This formalist aesthetic approach obviously devalued and marginalized literature based on different values, such as civil responsibility, a nonconsolatory attention to postwar reality (for example, *reportage* as a literary genre), or an effort to experiment with new forms.

The monetary reform of 1948, the creation of the two German states, and the beginning of the Cold War meant the suppression of a number of critical voices (such as the student journals mentioned earlier) and the beginning of the restoration policy of Adenauer's government (in place from 1949 to 1963). In the field of German Studies, the rehabilitation of some former Nazi professors further reinforced its conservative tendencies. As Theodor Adorno noted upon his return to Germany, the idea of a neutral culture and the emphasis on *Bildung* had the function of repressing the horror and obliterating individual responsibilities.[62] Cultural stagnation was accompanied, however, by a rather long period of political and economic progress in Federal

Germany, which lasted until the mid-1960s. In the meantime, East Germany moved on toward socialism. The creation of two German states led to the establishment of two different German Studies belonging to two opposing political, economic, and military blocks.

German Studies in West Germany

We may start by considering the teacher-student ratio in German Studies in the 1950s: eighty professors to five thousand students. The situation for students was optimal. Certainly they had to completely submit to the professors' authority, since as Hermand notes, after the rehabilitations had brought back and left unpunished almost all the full professors of the period before 1945, the latter's sense of omnipotence had grown, and they ruled their seminars as "kings."[63] But the low number of students—96 percent of whom came from middle- or lower-middle-class families—meant that at the end of their studies they would acquire a cultural capital that, however arbitrary it might be, would be respected by society and could immediately be put to use. All participants in the game acknowledged the value of the stakes, and this allowed the game to go on. This explains the apparent lack of contradictions in German Studies in the 1950s, when no significant conflicts or tensions emerged. In regard to the past, the dominant attitude was the tendency to deplore the sad destiny, the catastrophe that had struck Germany and its people without ever explicitly mentioning the Third Reich and its adepts. To overcome that crisis the best solution was the return to the eternal values of the West in all their variants: from the Christian ones to the humanistic secular ones. The methods that were to be adopted in pursuit of these values varied: a common denominator to most approaches could be the expression *Kunst der Interpretation,* the title of a famous work by Zurich Germanist Emil Staiger, published in 1955. The expression indicates a study of the work of art based on the identification of the interpreter with the creator, which serves to highlight the work's human and spiritual qualities without any reference to external elements. This approach clearly derives from the *Geistesgeschichte,* which has here undergone a "diet" of sorts to eliminate any dangerous involvement in history: any reference to the outside world was to be accurately avoided, even if it were simply a reference to the history of the spirit.[64] This explains why the theoretical framework of Germanists shifted from Dilthey to Heidegger (who resumed teaching in 1951 at the University of Freiburg) and Gadamer. On the basis of these new models, a hermeneutic emerged centered on the effort to identify within the work of art the eternal, the timeless, the human universal, the voice of Being, the original, and so on. Important examples of this tendency, which Hermand defines as humanistic-conservative with existential nuances, are the renowned works of Benno von Wiese (*Die deutsche Novelle von Goethe bis Kafka,* 1956–62, and *Das deutsche Drama vom Barock bis zur Gegenwart,* 1958).[65]

Another current can be associated with Wolfgang Kayser's *Das sprachliche Kunstwerk* (1948). From this original work a series of studies was engendered that focused on the literary nature of literature. The specific literary element, as Kayser saw it, corresponds to "structural forms" *(Bauformen),* such as rhythm, meter, style, verse, rhetorical figures, and all that serves to identify the characteristics of literary genres. To this current belong a number of studies on the "*Gattungsgeschichte*" (history of literary genres), foremost among these Paul Böckmann, *Formgeschichte der deutschen Dichtung* (1949), Eberhard Lämmert, *Bauformen des Erzählens* (1955), Käte Hamburger, *Die Logik der Dichtung* (1957), Volker Klotz, *Geschlossene und offene Form im Drama* (1960), and Franz K. Stenzel, *Typische Formen des Romans* (1964). The works of Peter Szondi (*Theorie des Moderne Dramas,* 1956) and Hugo Friedrich (*Struktur der modernen Lyrik,* 1956), while not directly associated with the *Gattungsgeschichte,* paid special attention to formal innovations in the genres they dealt with.

As one can see, there was an abundance of works that focused on the forms (or transformations occurring within given forms) of the great Western literature. It is not surprising, therefore, that there was a positive attitude toward foreign critical schools such as those of American New Criticism and Russian formalism. A particularly influential work in Germany as well as in Europe was, in fact, *Theory of Literature* (1942) by René Wellek, the already mentioned member of the Language Circle of Prague, and Austin Warren, one of the North American New Critics. The work, which has gone through numberless editions, describes the elements and approaches that are intrinsic to literature: the exclusive focus on the specific formal aspects of the work of art produced a formalist-stylistic critical evaluation that made it possible to include in the canon of classical literature all the modernist authors who had reached a high level of formal complexity and linguistic innovation. On the other hand, this interpretative grid excluded from the canon all the political and social aspects of avant-garde art. Expressionism is a case in point. Markus Gärtner has extensively and acutely examined the resistance of postwar German Studies, from 1945 to the mid-1960s, to accepting expressionist authors as suitable objects of "serious" scientific study. Expressionist poetry was the first to be gradually taken into consideration on account of its aesthetic and political compatibility with the dominant critical mode, while the more committed expressionism of theater, not to mention hybrid literary forms such as pamphlets and manifestos, was rejected for a longer period.[66]

With regard to twentieth-century authors, attention was focused on those who were judged to be more advanced in terms of form and formal innovation and more elevated on the aesthetic plane: among the poets, Trakl, Heym, Stadler, and Benn, representatives of the German-expressionist approach to modernity; among novelists, Kafka, who was interpreted in theological and eternalizing terms.[67] What was important was to avoid relating the works of art to the evolution of history or society in any way.

German Studies in East Germany

In the autumn of 1949, the German Democratic Republic was founded in the Soviet sector. The creation of two enemy Germanies belonging to two different economic and military alliances meant the creation of two separate German Studies organizations. But initially at least, their differences were minimal: here, too, changes were negligible, and the old organization went on basically intact. A spectacular case of continuity was that of Korff, who had become a professor at Leipzig in 1925.[68] Korff had started his *Geist der Goethezeit* in the 1920s during the Weimar Republic and terminated it in 1953, and it proved to be an outstanding example of disciplinary continuity: through the political upheavals and the advent of three different political systems the volumes of his massive study kept being published, one after the other. In some cases, though, émigrés such as Hans Mayer and others were helped to return and teach without having passed their qualifying examinations—which goes to show that this could be done without lowering the standards of teaching. In general, however, the situation was similar to that of West Germany: here, too, the resumption of academic activities was characterized by continuity, in terms both of individuals and of the contents and organization of the discipline.

German Studies in East Germany was well positioned in regard to the new political system: the specialists in the *Klassik* soon became its representatives, since the new republic longed to present itself as a *Kulturstaat* and needed experts that could present classic German literature as its rightful heritage. The professorial class of the newly established state was ready for the task and, on the whole, all too willing to oblige. Thus Weimar classicism was interpreted as the highest and most complete development of the German middle class in its progress toward emancipation and as an anticipation of the future liberation of all humanity. A linear path was established, stretching from Goethe and Schiller's bourgeois humanism—interpreted from an idealistic and transcendent perspective and with the addition of Lessing or Heine, according to the circumstances—all the way to socialist society, which was interpreted as the practical realization of the spirit of the *Klassik*. This was, in short, the official interpretation of literary history provided by eastern German Studies.[69]

Postwar studies by East Germanists can be read as revolving around three crucial issues: the question of heritage, the expansion of the literary canon on the basis of political and ideological considerations, and the problem of the method suitable to these two goals. While Hans Mayer proposed a study of literature more open to the historical, sociological, and material aspects of the work of art, his proposal was not taken up. It proved necessary, however, to subject the traditional classicist approach to a little touching up. The journal *Weimarer Beiträge* (founded in 1955) helped achieve this with a series of articles that reinterpreted the *Goethezeit* from a Marxist perspective, paying attention to revolutionary and historical-materialist elements. Yet the general interpretation of national literature remained centered on that crucial literary period on the basis of which later literature was judged and often disregarded.

Toward the end of the 1950s, a new phase in the reappropriation of the heritage developed: next to the emphasis on classicism (in all its aspects, and expanding the concept to include Heine and the *Junges Deutschland*), it became possible to overcome the limits of Lukács's critical realism, hitherto the prevalent critical doctrine, which excluded from the canon all literary works that did not critically reflect reality but emphasized instead the formal aspects (as for example in most expressionism) or an unmediated representation of reality, as in the case of naturalism. This change allowed the inclusion in the canon of authors who belonged to the left-wing tradition in German literature of the late nineteenth and twentieth century, from naturalists to the militant authors of the Weimar Republic. Thus at the end of the 1960s the East German canon had been extended in significant ways, including all those authors formerly deemed unworthy of belonging to it, such as Jacobins, authors of the *Vormärz,* naturalists, expressionists, working-class authors of the Weimar Republic, émigré writers, and contemporary ones. In the meantime a collective work was planned, the *Geschichte der deutschen Literatur von den Anfängen bis zur Gegenwart,* based on a Marxist perspective.[70] Its goal was to rewrite national literature from its origins to the current time, including the literature of the two different German states. The project was certainly interesting, but bogged down when it came to the two volumes on the contemporary literature of the two states. In both cases the work had to undergo continuous revisions due to changes in the political and ideological perspective of the editors and the authors, which delayed the work beyond any reasonable limit: the last volume on the literature of West Germany was published only in 1983.

Seven

The Dialectics of Rebellion: 1968 and Its Consequences

Toward the mid-1960s German society entered an entirely new phase. The traumatic postwar years were definitely over, unemployment was almost nonexistent, the reconstruction process was almost accomplished, and the people of the German Federal Republic were gradually coming to realize, with ill-concealed pride, that their country had become an economic superpower. The new society of affluence promised prosperity and happiness to all its members in the form of an unprecedented abundance of commodities. Many of those born during or after the war had had access to higher education, and, for the first time in German history, the universities were turning into universities of the masses. In politics, in 1966 a coalition of Christian Democrats (the Christliche Demokratische Union, or CDU, and the Christliche Soziale Union, or CSU) and Social Democrats (the Sozialdemokratische Partei Deutschlands, or SPD), representing almost the totality of the electorate, had come to power for the first time. The government included many outstanding politicians, among them Willy Brandt (as foreign minister), Franz Josef Strauß, Carlo Schmid, Herbert Wehner, and Kurt Georg Kiesinger (as president). In the face of this apparent political, social, and economic stability, however, a left-wing extraparliamentary opposition (Ausserparlamentarische Opposition, or APO), born of an alliance of the young socialists (Sozialisticher Deutscher

Studentenbund, or SDS) with other left-wing Marxist groups, began to develop, occupying the political space that had been left vacant by the traditional party, the SPD, which was now in power with the Christian Democrats. The only parliamentary opposition remaining was the small Freie Demokratische Partei (FDP, the Liberal-Democratic Party), which seemed incapable, in terms of both numbers and political capability, of playing this role effectively.

The construction of the Berlin Wall in 1961 had definitely done away with the tentative idea of free competition and mutual exchange between the models of organization embodied in the German Democratic Republic and the German Federal Republic. The Western type of society and the capitalist form of social-economic development were advocated as the sole legitimate option. In the face of these developments, the extraparliamentary opposition soon acquired a radical and militant profile; theoretical analyses of society were soon translated into concrete political action. The American intervention in Vietnam (1964) and the subsequent military escalation forced the German people to reflect on the legitimacy and ethics of a mode of production that affirmed its values through all means available, including military aggression. Soon, especially among university students, a movement developed in favor of the peoples who during those years were under the yoke, sometimes light and sometimes ferociously oppressive, of American imperialism and of other minor colonial powers. A turning point came in 1967, during a visit by Mohammed Reza Pahlavi, shah of Iran, one of the countries supported by Western powers as part of their Cold War strategy. Demonstrations were held against Pahlavi, who was accused of brutally repressing Iran's internal opposition, and a student, Benno Ohnesorg, was killed by the police. The incident engendered a radicalization of the political conflict that continued in the following years, demonstrating the opposition of many young Germans to the stagnation of the parliamentary political system.

For many, the overthrow of the present system they saw as necessary almost naturally required establishing ties with other revolutionary groups who were fighting throughout the world to free themselves of imperialist, colonialist, and, in the final analysis, capitalist oppression. From Vietnam to Cuba to Angola, the peoples of the Third World had emerged as the ideal political partners for the process of the liberation of Western society. A non-Western, noncapitalist country like China seemed to offer a great message of liberation to the young people of the Western world. Their leader, Mao Zedong, was inviting the young Chinese to rebel ("It is right to rebel"), to question all institutional political structures at the cry of "Bomb the headquarters." Whatever the current judgment on the Great Proletarian Cultural Revolution, whose origins historians tend to ascribe to a fierce power struggle inside the Chinese Communist Party, at the time it held an immense fascination for the young people of advanced capitalist societies for three main reasons: it made it possible to believe that communist regimes were open to radical changes in their bureaucratic-administrative systems when the lower classes demanded it, it made it possible to see the younger generations as a possible revolutionary political subject (as in China), and it morally legitimated the idea of rebelling against society and did away with the principle of authority.

For German students, the international situation was thus rife with invitations and theoretical motivations to rebel against the world order established by the two superpowers (the United States and the Soviet Union) and against those who, within West Germany, supported and perpetuated that order. The German university was naturally destined to be one of the first institutions to fall under attack as a quintessential example of oppressive self-reproducing power systems. And German Studies, which represented one of the vital sectors in the production and reproduction of culture, was particularly affected by this crisis.

The Nonhabilitated as Political Subject

The attack on the discipline of German Studies was the product of an entirely new situation, which had developed around the mid-1960s. As noted earlier, the rebellion and liberation struggles of the oppressed people of Third World countries carried a strong ideal significance. They also had a more immediate significance: the defeat of American imperialism at the hands of Vietnamese peasants was proof that power could indeed be a "paper tiger," that is, it was not invincible. It is difficult to fully grasp the symbolical impact on that generation of students of those peasants, or of Chinese students rebelling against those—deans, heads of faculty, professors—who managed academic power as had the mandarins of yore. The actions of these people caused the German students to embrace as an ethical principle the belief that historically stratified systems are not eternal and immutable, that it is possible and right to tear down the establishment. Within the university, this meant going against the apparatus, values and canons of the institution; it meant rejecting the basic rules of the academic game.

The demand for radical change within the university was related to a change within the social structure of teachers. The increase in the number of students had made it necessary to increase the number of lower-rank teachers (the so-called academic *Mittelbau*), such as untenured assistants, instructors, and so on. These subaltern figures were qualitatively different from other teachers. They had been hired in great numbers in order to teach the increasing number of students. They were entrusted with only what were deemed to be the less important courses and didactic activities, and they had no direct access to research funds (they could do research only under the supervision of a professor and on the subjects chosen by the professor). They had no *Habilitation;* that is, they had not passed the competitive qualifying examinations enabling a limited number of them to apply for tenured teaching posts.[1] Thus they constituted a sort of "academic proletariat," and for this reason they were often sympathetic with the demands of the students. Their attitude toward the institution varied between an anticipatory identification with the figure, the habitus, and the behavior of the "masters" (full professors) and the students' dislike for and critique of that type of figure. Practically speaking, the increased number of subaltern teachers meant that only a few of them could aspire to full professorship—formerly, the "natural" outcome of the apprentice years. Thus the old law according to which all respectful, loyal, docile pupils would be rewarded in due time was no longer valid. Many felt the attraction of the alternative: fighting, with the essential militant help of the students, for a new university that was no longer the expression of the structures of power but rather a site of critique and resistance to power and its institutions—a fight that was, in turn, part of a larger long-term revolutionary plan aimed at transforming capitalist society into a socialist one.

German Studies after the Munich Congress of 1966

German Studies was, as noted earlier, one of the disciplines most harshly criticized by students and assistants. In some cases the critique was so radical as to call into question the very existence of the discipline. This was the case, for example, of the critique made by the committee of the University of Frankfurt German Studies Seminar (renamed by the students "Walter-Benjamin-Institut"), which pronounced itself in favor of the elimination of German Studies as such in a document unequivocally titled "Schafft die Germanistik ab!" (Destroy German Studies!).[2] This position followed from an awareness of the impossibility of reforming the structure, the statute, the apparatus, the contents, and the training methods of a discipline that had developed along the lines I have sought to illustrate.

In the autumn of 1966, a few months before these direct attacks on the discipline, a Congress of German Germanists had been held in Munich. Simply establishing the agenda for the congress had given rise to a long series of contrasts and ensuing compromises.[3] A group of young professors (among them Karl Otto Conrady, Eberhard Lämmert, Peter Wapnewski, and Peter von Polenz) wanted to open a debate within the discipline on the past of German Studies and its relationship with National Socialism, also on account of recent widely influential press campaigns by leading national newspapers that had publicly discussed the issue, making it absurd for the discipline itself to continue evading it. After long negotiations the president of the Germanists, Benno von Wiese, inserted in the agenda the topic *Nationalismus in Germanistik und Literatur.* Some of the participants (Conrady, Lämmert, Killy, and von Polenz) gave harshly polemic papers against the political and ideological involvement of some representatives of the discipline with National Socialism, explicitly mentioning their names.[4] Against the possibility of repeating those mistakes and crimes, they advocated the opening of German Studies to the outside world. This meant increasing the discipline's exchange with other modern areas of knowledge (sociology, structural linguistics, Marxist historicism), which up to that time German Studies had disdainfully kept at bay. At the same time, the notion of a rigorously unitary discipline was questioned as possibly obsolete in the light of the pluralistic complexity of the modern world.

These younger scholars believed there was an urgent need to subdivide German Studies into new sectors, taking into account the distinction between the medieval world and the modern one, and also a need for a scientific study of the language from a synchronic perspective. But the most profoundly felt need was for a general liberalization and democratization of the discipline, in terms both of its contents and of its highly hierarchized disciplinary structure. The situation can briefly but correctly be described as the revolt against a generation of masters by a generation of pupils who, in Hermand's words, "suddenly awoke to a no longer acritical but critical conscience."[5] With the

Munich Congress a transformation of the discipline was set in motion that was referred to as a "*Paradigmawechsel,*" or paradigm shift, which led to a critical revisitation of canonical aspects of national literature and the discovery and legitimation of other aspects of German Studies that had been partly or entirely ignored, as we shall see later on.[6]

These, then, were the proposals of the reformist wing of German Studies. I would add that these transformations can be largely interpreted as an effort to modernize the discipline and adjust it to the increasingly differentiated and complex situation of the 1960s. But this reform plan aimed at integrating different and more "modern" methodologies within German Studies was promptly denounced as an excuse by those who advocated more radical change. In the words of one of the participants in a debate on the journal *Alternative* dedicated to the reform of German Studies: "What had survived after 1945, first in the form of evocative existential formulae, then in the aestheticizing interpretation immanent in the work, has nowadays become immune to any external attack thanks to the integration of apparently Marxist and sociological elements."[7]

It is true that at Munich a number of important developments took place on a methodological level. But this renewal seemed ultimately limited to replacing one generation of Germanists with another within the same disciplinary system. The generation of those habilitated during the Weimar Republic or during the years of National Socialism had been replaced by the following one, which, after all, had been habilitated by those same professors whose approach and disciplinary methods they were criticizing. It was the new generation that insisted on introducing the topic of *Nationalismus und Germanistik* into the Munich Congress agenda. Besides insisting on a critical and self-critical examination of the past and present status of the discipline, the new generation, in the light of the need for increasing specialization, also demanded that German Studies be made more efficient by giving up the fetish of unity and dividing the discipline into three sectors: *Neuere Literaturwissenschaft, Mediävistik,* and *Linguistik.* In fact, this new disciplinary organization was gradually implemented in the following decades and is still the one in use.

The Munich Congress of 1966 was thus a largely successful effort to reform the discipline from within; but precisely on account of its internal character, the reform did not question the structure and self-reproducing mechanisms of the discipline.[8] Those responsible for the reform were habilitated professors, that is, professors who had been qualified and granted the right to speak, through the selective process of *Habilitation,* by the upholders of the true disciplinary knowledge. In the papers given at the Munich Congress, the voice we hear is that of a generation that, notwithstanding its harsh critique of the academic power system, acknowledged the legitimacy of the latter and derived its own legitimacy from it.[9]

An entirely different type of protest developed after 1967, led by students and nonhabilitated professors, that is, the subjects who were *not* authorized to speak for and within the discipline. The choice of the Frankfurt students to rename their university after Walter Benjamin, to whom the German universities had denied habilitation, is significant in that sense.[10] Benjamin soon became the main reference for left-wing militant criticism, also, I think, on account of his established incompatibility with academic power. By using that name the Frankfurt students meant to signal their rejection of any compromise between their political and cultural project and the established disciplinary doctrine. As already mentioned, the title of the contribution of the Frankfurt students' movement to the discussion of the past, present, and future status of German Studies was itself unequivocal: "Schafft die Germanistik ab!"

The Strategy of Politicization and the End of the *Illusio*

Almost at the same time that proposals for the modernization and rationalization of German Studies were made at the Munich Congress, the students and subaltern university teachers had independently elaborated a series of considerations regarding the statute of the discipline. In July 1967, as the conclusion to a series of events centered around the theme "*Politisierung der Wissenschaften*" (the politicization of the sciences), a week of meetings, seminars, and plenary assemblies was organized at the Freie Universität of Berlin.[11] Three hundred students (out of a total of eighteen hundred), two professors (out of eight), and a dozen subaltern teachers participated in the final assembly. The event was particularly significant because of the special status of Berlin (still at the time under the direct control of the Allies), the role of the Freie Universität as an embodiment of and advertisement for Western democracy, and the political liveliness that had characterized Berlin students since 1964, when the first student demonstrations had been mounted for the purpose of attracting the attention of German public opinion and countering the influence of the mass media: radio, television, and newspapers. The student minority had often clashed with power in its various forms (at levels of the university, the town, and the state), which, behind its tolerant façade, had shown its determination to repress any dissent that manifested itself in nonritual forms.

The week of encounters on German Studies at the Freie Universität had been organized within the context of a strategy of demonstration as a moment of free, unprejudiced discussion on the development of a "critical university" rather than a university merely reproducing and reaffirming the established ideas and power systems.[12] The ideas and the documents that came out of those meetings represent the first effort to reform or transform the discipline from below. The professors who were present refused to speak, and that refusal was not without meaning. The meeting had been called by students who contested the absolute value of the institution and did not acknowledge the institutional role of the professors as invested ministers of the discipline who retained the right to speak the truth. The professors' speaking there would have meant renouncing their institutional right and role, as well as acknowledging ipso facto the legitimacy of the assembly.

Among the issues addressed in the documents produced in those meetings, some appear to me particularly innovative. The first is the emphasis on the *Selbstreproduktion des Faches,* that is, the self-reproducing and self-contained character of the discipline, which prevented any exchange between the discipline itself and the public sphere and any permeability by the discipline to demands for reform.[13] It was necessary to bring German Studies back to earth, turning it head over heels as Marx had done with philosophy. Even the celebrated notion of *Methoden-Toleranz* (methodological tolerance), which had developed after the closure of the early postwar period, was nothing—in the opinion of Helmut Lethen, one of the representatives of the Berlin student movement—but a last-ditch attempt to perpetuate the false conscience of German Studies, which was willing to compromise on the level of method, allowing a more liberal and tolerant interpretation of texts, in order to prevent any public debate, any external interference, and any change of its statute and social function.[14] For Lethen the way out of a situation where professors and the institution at large were permanently boycotting any effort to address the problems of the discipline was an explicit "*Politisierung der Germanistik*": "Politicizing German Studies means in the first place making the relations between professors, assistants and students democratic. The consequence of this democratization will be the participation of students in decisions regarding the organization of teaching, the division of funds, the assigning of chairs."[15]

This proposal was aimed at critically questioning the very foundations of the discipline, at reexamining the political and ideological history of the discipline along with its canons and contents. But the proposal went beyond a critique of ideology, insisting on the democratization of the institutional sphere and, specifically, of the relations between professors, assistants, and students. A new university and a new German Studies, as conceived by the Berlin students, could not be produced simply through goodwill and methodological tolerance (that is, on the level of ideas). It was necessary to reform the institution, to allow students and nonhabilitated teachers to participate in decisions regarding key aspects of university management by becoming members of the committees responsible for financing research and planning didactic activities, all the way up to what was and still is the key sector in the German university system: the bodies responsible for habilitations, new chairs, and the selection and hiring of new professors. For the Frankfurt students as well, the problem of power relations within academia was imperative: "The desolate condition of this discipline reproduces itself in its praxis, in its institutions. . . . Scientific positions are turned into the apodictic opinions of full professors, surrounded by gushing assistants and passive students ready to swallow anything. Any critique of the discipline that is not also a critique of its institutional organization is absorbed by authoritarian praxis, either in the form of the clownish license or as a contribution to methodological pluralism."[16]

The attitude of the Berlin students (and of their allies, the assistants) displayed entirely new features partly because it had been derived from an entirely new condition. Unlike their predecessors, these students no longer shared the *illusio* that is necessary to participate in the academic game. As Bourdieu writes: "At the basis of the functioning of all social fields, whether the literary field or that of power, there is the *illusio*, the investment in the game."[17] It is the collective belief in the game that is both the cause and the effect of the existence of the game and of its stakes. The belief in the game, the *illusio*, acknowledges the game and its usefulness, legitimizing its values and its rules. Thus there is an ultimate complicity even between adversaries who compete in the same field, having agreed to disagree on a common object whose value is recognized by both. What was radically new here was that the game itself was rejected. Similarly, the attitude toward the habitus of the professor was entirely different: the habitus—which is, as we have seen, one of the lasting conditions for the reproduction of the system—was denied its mystical, omnipotent, charismatic character by forcing those who "wore" it to enter a field where they were denied the insignia and paraphernalia of their accustomed institutional role. The traditional academic game, in which students won the right to replace the master in due course by dutifully accepting their subservient position and the rule of succession, was explicitly denounced and rejected by the new and old subaltern representatives of the academic system.

Those who have acquired the habitus, those who are habilitated or on the verge of habilitation, have a mentality that is perfectly adapted to the rules of the game and (apart from a few unlikely and extraordinary exceptions) cannot grasp how or why those rules should or could ever be rejected by others. They are part of the game, and even when they compete with one another they share a common understanding that the prize is worthwhile and that the rules of the game are to be respected. But this generation of students and assistants was different: they were not interested in the prize and did not intend to respect the rules. Their common subaltern condition and lack of perspective for the future destroyed the "chain of anticipated identifications" with the masters that is based on the certitude of the order of succession.[18] Lacking the certainty that they would gain the prize hitherto granted their predecessors, they questioned the validity of the competition. This sort of condition can be the starting point for a revolutionary process: the material impossibility of perpetuating the circle of expectation and fulfillment causes an important sector of the subaltern group to reject the competition as a whole and to stop legitimating its prescribed conditions. The ensuing conflict may have revolutionary outcomes in the given field, as new goals and rules are created that threaten the destruction of the present power structure.

This sort of choice requires new strategies and new instruments of legitimation and struggle. In the context of the complex strategy for the redefinition of the game, one tactic in which the Berlin students proved particularly apt was symbolic provocation, a tactic in which the spontaneous and instinctive acceptance of the traditional order was undermined through the adoption of unexpected behaviors that ran counter to the institutional ritual.[19] By occupying the spaces reserved for "serious" activities, by disrupting ritual and self-celebratory manifestations (lessons, conferences, administrative meetings), the students went against the norms that defined and limited the permissible use of time and produced "free" time, time in which everyone was entitled to vent one's opposition to the institutional structure, with a consciousness-raising effect. Obviously this violation of norms was transitory: a time of feast, a carnival. Yet precisely because it was used as part of a process aimed at disrupting the adversaries' plans, its effect was particularly subversive: it showed that the true discourse of the institution works only when it is acknowledged as such by all participants in the game, unmasking the inability of the establishment to deal with any modification of the institution and its rituals. At the 1968 Berlin Congress of Germanists (the first after Munich), for example, only eight papers out of fourteen managed to be delivered. Students demanded a preliminary debate on the wider significance of papers and attacked a number of them, which they considered irrelevant to the current political situation, for the express purpose of transforming an institutional academic event into a larger political one. This produced a clash between students and academic authorities, which resulted in occupations, demonstrations, and continuous provocations by students during the reading of official papers.[20]

The Perspectives of Disciplinary Reorganization

In 1967 and 1968 there was a tumultuous transformation of the modes of academic communication: students and assistants—following a model loosely based on the communist tradition in its various forms, from the Rosa Luxemburg brand of socialism to Marxist-Leninism, from Trotskyism to Maoism—founded a series of committees (Rote Zellen Germanistik, the Red Cells of German Studies, or Rotzeg) that adopted an entirely negative attitude toward the institution of German Studies, which they saw as an instrument of political and ideological oppression and control. Reconstructing the constellation of groups and their specific attitudes toward German Studies would be difficult and would indeed require specific research. In general, however, a common denominator was the rejection of the history of the discipline in all its components. The slogan "Politicize German Studies" was radically applied, producing a starkly political and ideological interpretation of German Studies and of its historical evolution. German Studies was totally rejected as a discipline historically subservient to political power and producer of subjects organic, initially, to the Prussian regime and then, in succession, to monopolist capitalism, Wilhelmian imperialism, Weimar conservatism, and finally National Socialism. Within this rigid interpretative scheme only Gervinus and Hettner were partially saved from damnation on account of their democratic stance.

There was also widespread consensus on the need for an institutional transformation of German Studies. More precisely, the goal was to intervene on certain crucial aspects of the organization of the university and of the distribution of power: the assignment of chairs, the habilitation system, and the allotment of funding. In general, this amounted to hindering the patrilineal mechanism of master-pupil succession. If this veritable pillar of professorial power were destroyed, the entire game would lose its ultimate prize and the discipline would find itself unable to reproduce. It was obvious to the students that the battle to create a new type of German Studies could be fought only on the terrain of power and institutional mechanisms, and that any generic demand for democracy that did not include a reformation of those mechanisms would achieve little. It was necessary to act on the apparatus that regulated the reproduction of the discipline and take the selection and habilitation power out of the hands of full professors.

Simply increasing the number of students and assistants in directive bodies whose goal was to maintain and reproduce the current system was not sufficient. Indeed, the mere presence of subaltern figures on decisional committees is in itself no guarantee of critical control over the institution or of modification of the existing power relations: as Bourdieu repeatedly points out, many students and assistants in fact have already interiorized the habitus and are endowed with a strong *conatus,* that is, the tendency or disposition to perpetuate the social order along with its power structure and privileges.[21] Indeed, the demand for reform of the university effected by allowing all components to elect their representatives in the governing bodies of the institution was a later development adopted after 1968, when European student movements were already on the wane and parties and trade unions in Germany, France, and Italy were trying, in different ways, to capitalize on the student rebellion and on the anxiety it had generated in the political and academic upper echelons. Eventually this resulted in the involvement of students, assistants, and nonteaching staff in the management of universities; there was an obsessive multiplication of commissions, committees, and supervising bodies that, however, never questioned the principle, reconfirmed in Germany by a sentence of the *Bundesverfassungsgericht* of 29 May 1973, that professors had to make up the majority in bodies making decisions on research, hiring, and the nomination of new professors.[22] This effectively put an end to the possibility of any substantial modification of the mechanisms governing the selection of members and the reproduction of the discipline.

A further issue raised in the debate on the reform of German Studies was the question of the methods and contents of the discipline, summarized in the "*Thesen zur deutschen Germanistik*" (Theses on German Studies in Germany) approved by the general assembly of Berlin students.[23] I find it significant that this particular aspect of reform was dealt with only after the other ones and with a certain degree of nonchalance. It was somehow taken for granted that the debate on the past and present ideology of the discipline and the reform of its institutional mechanisms would automatically entail a change in the focus and objects of its research. There was widespread agreement on the need to overcome the deficit of German research compared to foreign standards, a deficit that had been widely debated by the Germanists of liberal and reformist orientation during the Munich Congress.[24] Various theoretical approaches that had been neglected or even explicitly banned in official German Studies (Marxism in its various forms, psychoanalysis, sociology, linguistics, and structuralism) had to be included in the new study of literature, which was also to entail the study of the social-historical contexts in which literature is produced. Along with focusing on the new methodologies, the reformers insisted that attention should be given to areas that had been neglected or ignored in the past, such as certain aspects of the *Aufklärung*, minority literatures, working-class literature, political poetry, and literature of the exile. German Studies was also to revise its canons and paradigms in order to include, along with what was considered qualitatively superior literature, also "practical" literature (that of the mass media, of bureaucracy, of politics, of advertising) and popular literature (the so-called *Trivialliteratur*). These new needs, however, had to be addressed with a constant critical focus on the historical context and within the context of a heightened disciplinary self-awareness, since the discipline was a crucial site for the attribution of value and lack of value. Importance was also given to developing the study of the literature and culture of countries from all over the world, without any political preclusions.[25]

Renouncing the Heritage

These, then, were the *Thesen* of the assembly of Germanists at the University of Berlin, a set of "theses" that identified the contradictions of the discipline with sufficient precision and clarity. But there is another element of this assembly that needs to be demonstrated: the unusual way in which the subject of German literary and cultural heritage was dealt with. This subject has played a central role in the history of German Studies in the last fifty years, as in the case, for example, of the appropriation of the classical German heritage by German Democratic Republic. Yet at the Berlin assembly the subject was virtually ignored.

Indeed the fact that the issue was not raised, while remarkable in itself, is hardly surprising: in the context of that assembly the subject had little importance. To inherit means to acquire a patrimony by receiving and explicitly accepting it. By accepting the heritage the heir also accepts a series of duties and obligations, becoming part of a patrilineal axis (at least in Western Europe), taking the position of his predecessor, and committing himself to perpetuating it. In other words, there is what Bourdieu calls a *"reciprocal appropriation."*[26] The students of the movement of 1968, however, were characterized by an explicit rejection of the inheritance and refused to become part of "the order of succession,"[27] rejecting the mechanisms that regulated the inheritance of the discipline. Indeed the generation of 1968 is commonly referred to as a generation without fathers, or, as I would rather term it, a generation that rejected its natural fathers and adopted new references and role models. In any case, those students were firmly determined not to inherit in order not to be inherited, in turn, by a heritage they despised. They rejected the central principle of paternal authority, "the 'tendency to perpetuate in one's very being' the *social position* that inhabits the father."[28] To inherit also means to accept a destiny, a project, a *conatus* that is part and parcel of the inheritance. Those who accept the inheritance thus perpetuate the *conatus* and become docile instruments of its reproduction.[29] From this perspective one can understand the lack of interest in the question of heritage by the generation of 1968. One also understands the opposite attitude, that is, the *conatus* of the state, cultural apparatuses, universities, schools, academies, and religious institutions to preserve the heritage by establishing alliances with other power institutions in order to defend the status quo and its untroubled reproduction.

The rejection of the heritage, therefore, is a significant gesture and an act of consistency within the framework of an anti-institutional political action. The students' slogans, "Death to literature" and "Destroy German Studies"—setting aside the extremes of the following years, where the radicalization of political conflict engendered a spiral of terrorism-repression—expressed, in my view, their decision to reject the traditional patrimony and to refuse to become part of the patrilineal axis.

At the same time, the theoretical and political need to discover new cultural areas, literary movements, and noncanonical authors was part of a project aimed at developing new fields, going beyond the inherited tradition in order to emphasize what was in contrast with the institution and its instruments of production, reproduction, and administration.

Eight

After 1968: Transforming the Canon, Shifting the Paradigms

The period from 1968 to the mid-1970s was characterized by the production of critical and theoretical studies that marked a significant difference from the past. The study of literature and the debate on literary theory were now seen as integral parts of a general effort to transform society and the rules that govern its reproduction. Critics sought to apply to German Studies Karl Marx's XI thesis on Feuerbach—"Philosophers have only variously interpreted the world; the point, however, is to change it"—involving it in a general project of social change.[1] Germanists were forced to quickly update their theoretical tools. Critical approaches to literature and interpretative paradigms as well as the literary canon itself changed. Marxist thought became dominant, less in its immediately political implications than in its theoretical value as a historical-materialistic or materialistic-dialectic conception of human society and of its specific articulations as well as its overall development. The categories of Marxist thought, however, were combined with many other elements from other disciplines (sociology, political economy, psychoanalysis, linguistics) for the purpose of establishing an aesthetics and a theory of literature based on the materiality of historical processes while avoiding the mechanistic approach of orthodox Marxism, as found in the Soviet Union and East Germany. In rereading certain collective works published at the time, such as *Ansichten einer künftigen Germanistik* (1969) and *Neue Ansichten einer künftigen Germanistik* (1973), one perceives the passionate drive to rethink the profession of Germanist in the light of the new situation, questioning all existing tools and apparatuses in an unprejudiced critical light. This process of critical reexamination soon produced significant results in terms of the self-awareness of the discipline. In the first place I would mention those publications that first broke the taboo surrounding the question of the relation between writers, German Studies, and National Socialism: works like Ernst Loewy's *Literatur unterm Hakenkreuz* (1966) and Klaus Vondung's *Völkisch-nationale und nationalsozialistische Literaturtheorie* (1973).

In the meantime, a number of exemplary *topoi* that had been central to the history of German Studies were questioned precisely on account of their ideological function. Such was the case with Reinhold Grimm and Jost Hermand's *Klassik-Legende* (1972), whose critical import is evident even from the title. The study of classicism had always been considered essential to the training and formation of future Germanists: denouncing it as a "legend" amounted to demystifying one of the ideological (and consequently institutional) pillars of German Studies. It is worth noting that when the book was published both Grimm and Hermand—whose works have been crucial to the elaboration of new critical perspectives and the creation of a new canon in German Studies—had been living and working in the United States, at the University of Wisconsin, for a long time. Consequently, their perspective was substantially decentered with regard to the values and apparatus of the official discipline of German Studies in German-speaking countries, and openly critical of them. As Hermand himself points out in his memoirs, the very decision to organize a conference to foster a critical revision of German classicism amounted to provocatively challenging a veritable taboo. The reactions were vehement and came from a strangely motley coalition: former Nazis; Jewish Germans exiled to the United States (who saw "their" Goethe as a representative and guarantor of a kind of cosmopolitanism); East German Germanists, who regarded Goethe's and Schiller's humanism as the ideological foundation for the construction of socialism.[2]

The critical import of Grimm and Hermand's book was twofold. What they were criticizing was not simply a crucial aspect of the history of German ideology but also one of the highest levels in the hierarchy of academic values and corresponding academic interests. If one were to draw up an imaginary (or not-so-imaginary) classification of study fields, *Goethe-Philologie* and *Klassik* would come out on top. Applying Bourdieu's theory of cultural capital, one could say that the competence acquired by a scholar functions as accumulated capital and naturally tends to become institutionalized (cultural) capital. And no one is willing to spontaneously renounce the patrimony he or she has acquired over years of study and research. On the contrary, the scholar will strive to reproduce and increase it, following the law of accumulation. Transferring the interests of scholars to other less capitalizable fields is usually very difficult, since it entails a modification of the political and economic power structure within the institutionalized fields of the discipline.[3] During this period, however, conditions were favorable to a rediscovery of all those authors and genres that had previously been marginalized by mainstream German Studies: the protest movement was less strong and basically limited its demands to a revision of the methods and contents of German Studies, something that was ultimately acceptable even to conservative forces since it did not affect their disciplinary privileges.

From the early 1970s a number of works were published aimed at extending the critical debate to the "Jacobins," to the democratic authors of 1848, to naturalist writers, to the authors of the *Jahrhundertwende,* the expressionists, the writers of the Weimar Republic, and the exponents of *Exilliteratur.* Also, coherent with the demands of the students of 1968, in works such as Wolfgang Emmerich's *Proletarische Lebensläufe* (1974) the field of *Literaturwissenschaft* was extended to noncanonical genres: political and literary manifestos, reportage, autobiographies by nonwriters, and so on. In the meantime, there was a growing interest in the specialized languages of the mass media, along with a strong critique of their manipulative role in advanced capitalist societies. Thus the study of new languages and technologies was always accompanied during this period by an interest in their political and sociological context and by an uncompromisingly critical view of their function, an approach highly influenced by the Frankfurt School in all its ramifications.

This expansion of German Studies toward new horizons was favored by the general cultural climate. The great increase in the number of politically and socially active people among students and in society at large had created a new reading public whose interest went beyond specialist publications: German students were no longer interested solely in reading their assignments and passing their exams, but wished to widen their perspectives beyond that of received knowledge and develop a sense of general political and humanistic culture. In this desire to pursue their studies and education independently, outside the canons and requirements of academic authorities, there was an element of revolt against the fathers. Also, the new fields of research and methods were popularized thanks to publishers (Athenäum, Fischer, Hanser, Metzler, Rowohlt, Suhrkamp) who had the foresight to target their products at the younger generations, offering economical editions that were purchased by an ever increasing public of young and less affluent readers interested in new themes and forms of knowledge.

These favorable circumstances helped develop a new communicative circuit—partly in opposition to and partly complementary to traditional German Studies—that was not directly addressed to the professional community and avoided academic forms and modes while maintaining very high standards of scholarship and analytical power. Many cultural and literary journals were involved in this process, fostering wider debate in the humanities and the social sciences: foremost amongst them *Akzente, Alternative, Das Argument, Ästhetik und Kommunikation, Berliner Hefte, Konkret, Kursbuch, Kürbiskern,* and *Merkur.* This new communicative circuit also had the merit of encouraging an open and unprejudiced interdisciplinary exchange in which German Studies was treated as a form of knowledge like any other, on the same level as the study of other national cultures and literatures. This exchange with other disciplines, less burdened by ideology and tradition, led to a partial disappearance of the rigid philological paradigm and to a more open attitude toward the outside world in German Studies. The discipline—though not all its members—began looking around, slowly abandoning its self-referential nature and its self-preserving mechanisms.

On the other hand, the time was ripe for a careful reflection on German Studies in the context of a more general critique of German ideology. A series of studies was published on the history of German Studies, in which, in different ways, the ideology of the discipline was put on trial.[4] The first works developed a critique of the discipline's ideology, while later ones focused on the history of German Studies, studying its institutionalization and development in the German universities. The critical-ideological approach was not abandoned, but its focus was shifted to more complex and less obvious aspects of the reproduction of false consciousness, such as the meaning and function of the interaction of state apparatuses, bureaucracy and administration, teaching methodologies and canons, research and its privileged fields and methods, the organization of schools and educational policies in Germany, and the role of specific individuals and personalities. Thus the period of the great themes was followed by more empirical and circumscribed studies that were also of great interest in terms of the way they teased out and analyzed from the inside the articulations of this formidable apparatus for the production, reproduction, and legitimation of consensus. This was the beginning of an accurate, extensive, and in-depth self-examination of the discipline, which obviously aroused different and opposite reactions within the community, but nevertheless resulted, in the following twenty years, in a series of works that served to precisely reconstruct the crucial themes and the decisive moments in the history of the discipline.[5]

The Return to Subjectivity

In the meantime, the conflict between the terrorists of the Rote Armee Fraktion (Red Army Party) and the German state was becoming increasingly harsh. Terrorism had a negative effect on the overall political climate, bringing about a limitation of freedom within universities and in society at large, reducing the interest in active politics and limiting it to a defense of democracy. On 28 January 1972 the presidents of the *Länder* made a joint statement called the *Extremisten-Beschluß* (extremism act, also known as the *Radikalen-Erlaß,* or ordinance on Radicals), later assented to by Prime Minister Willy Brandt. They declared that only those individuals who could prove that their behavior was consistent with the liberal and democratic principles on which the German Federal Republic was founded could be allowed to serve in public offices. Consequently, the authorities of the individual *Länder* had a right to preventively make inquiries about and proceed against all those whom they suspected of being hostile to the constitution. The result of this procedure was the so-called *Berufsverbot* (prohibition of work), as the political Left defined it, whereby those who were declared guilty of political extremism were prevented from holding jobs in the public administration. A witch hunt was mounted by the more conservative media and political parties: any civil servant who criticized the establishment was liable to be accused of being a sympathizer with terrorism. Only a few hundred persons were actually dismissed from their positions by reason of the *Berufsverbot,* but some thousands were subjected to inquiries, and the general climate of repression and intimidation affected all levels of society and culture. Many authors had to revise their theoretical and political stances; other intellectuals gave up their teaching positions or their jobs as civil servants.[6]

The conflict between the state and terrorism was violent, confused, and often incomprehensible from the outside. The price the new student generation had to pay to the arbitrary violence of the terrorists was the right to a political role, which was denied them by the new situation. At the same time, however, political authorities were able to offer a reformist response to the students' demands: while the number of university students increased constantly, new universities were founded both in Social Democratic *Länder* and in Christian Democratic ones, along with exciting new courses and programs. New disciplines, revolving mostly around communications and media in their various forms, appeared to offer new life perspectives and brilliant job opportunities, beyond the university or school market, in institutions such as publishing houses, ministries, radio and television, and wherever there was a need for experts in new communication technologies and languages. Thus thanks to this modernization process, which excluded any form of political activism by making it superfluous, the students were offered original and fascinating jobs as an alternative to the traditional outlets that German Studies could no longer guarantee.

In the meantime, conservative professors who had taken a backseat in the years of the protest while preserving their academic power almost intact now spoke up again, setting down the future methodological guidelines of the discipline. Benno von Wiese again took up the slogan "Methodological pluralism" as an antidote to intolerance (i.e., to the radical political critique of the status quo), while others called for a rapid burn-out of the latest cultural fashions and a return of the discipline to its traditional statute and mechanisms, against the politicization and sectarian dogmatism of the Left.[7] Of course von Wiese's views were representative of a large group that was still dominant in the upper hierarchies. In general, forces within the field of German Studies clustered around different poles corresponding to different and sometimes opposite strategies: thus, while some were calling for radical transformations, there was also a strong resistance within the discipline, firmly rooted in the habitus of the majority of its members.

In the context of this backlash, from the mid-1970s, in both East and West Germany, a symmetrical phenomenon developed under the name of "*Neue Subjektivität*" (new subjectivity), consisting basically of a return to the private sphere. While the term originally was applied to literature, it can be usefully employed to designate certain tendencies within *Literaturwissenschaft.*

The New Subjectivity in the Federal Republic

The post-1968 period was marked by reactions to the general politicization and hyperpoliticization of the discipline. The slogan "Politicize German Studies" had originally been an instrument used to demystify the status quo, indicating the desire to force the discipline to confront historical and political reality, but in practice the action it advocated had often turned into an end unto itself. Both the efforts to politically subvert the system and the effects of its actual reform (the increased number of collegial organisms and bureaucratic layers and the participation of students, administrative staff, and subaltern teachers as a response to the demand for democracy, accompanied by an abnormal development of the administrative apparatus as a modernizing rationalization of the system) had resulted in the thwarting of individual subjectivity in terms of both study choices and study approaches. The paradigm shift that to many had seemed almost compulsory and the standardization of university activities, accompanied by the inevitable disappointment when achievements fell short of expectations, had eroded the margins for the pleasure of the text and for an individual approach to it. Under the new subjectivity, sensibility, aesthetic tastes, and personal inclinations as to the choice of a work or an author were once again acceptable. However, this was not simply a return to a pre-1968 individualism but rather a search for a new postpolitical sensibility emerging from the ashes of the great collective passions of the past. If in 1968 the world had been read in terms of classes, movements, and groups, the achievement of any collective utopia was now perceived as impossible, and the emphasis turned to individual emancipation and liberty. Writers and critics focused anew on a series of often heterogeneous aspects that had been ignored by the rigid pan-political approach of 1968. A commonplace of the movement of 1968 had been that individual needs would be provided for after the revolution; up to then, militants would have to focus exclusively on achieving power. For example, any problems concerning the relations between the sexes were deferred to the future, while at the time the situation was allowed to remain virtually unchanged. New aspects of individuality (sexual preferences, eroticism, desire) aroused contradictory responses: while there was a marked interest in such issues in certain areas of the movement (the followers of Wilhelm Reich, of psychoanalysis, of new psychiatry, etc.), in general there was the idea that these questions, like all aspects of the private sphere, had to be subordinated to political priorities.

But now a subordination of the individual needs to the common cause seemed pointless, given that there was no longer a cause or a community, and what had been repressed surfaced in all its variety of forms. In literature, along with the rediscovery of individuality there was a rediscovery of dream, myth, fable, and in general of neoromantic themes. In scholarship, there was a renewed interest in studies on romanticism and on related authors. At the same time, there was a new attention to repressed and marginalized social groups and their specific subjectivity and expression, and a desire to affirm the rights of all those who had been persecuted for sexual, racial, or religious reasons, not simply on a political level but also on a critical-literary one. While exploring newly discovered authors, critics rediscovered from new angles those traditional ones who were better suited, due to their individual sensibilities and biographical or literary characteristics, to a reading emphasizing their marginality: Hölderlin, Kleist, E. T. A. Hoffmann, and women writers such as Bettina von Arnim and Karoline von Günterode. In the meantime, starting with Hans Mayer's penetrating book *Die Außenseiter* (1975), the taboo of homosexuality was broken for the first time. The question of homosexuality began to be freely debated, and a generally tolerant attitude toward homosexual authors developed. However, I would subscribe in passing to Hermand's observation that while the literary production of German Jews has definitely come out of the ghetto and has been largely canonized as German literature *tout court,* studied by Jewish and non-Jewish critics alike, homosexual literature and themes still tend to be studied only by homosexual critics, thus perpetuating a subtle form of discrimination.[8]

The other area of German Studies to develop extensively was feminist criticism, to some extent a spin-off of the movement of 1968.[9] Feminist German Studies, as part of German feminism at large, began exploring the universe of women's literature from romantic writers to the present day. An initial phase characterized by a harsh criticism of the phallocentrism of the discipline was followed by one of institutionalization and consolidation. Attention then turned to more complex and mature questions, such as the representation of women in male literature, women's writing and autobiography, feminine desire, and all that could serve to articulate a new feminine identity.[10] *Feministische Literaturwissenschaft* appropriated and responded to the theories of German (Nietzsche and Heidegger) and French (Derrida, Foucault, Lacan, and Lyotard) thinkers and their reelaboration by French and Anglo-American feminism.

This opening of the field to new thinkers and traditions was prepared for by the feminist scholars' attack on the establishment of their own discipline: feminist Germanists partially or completely rejected the patriarchal and phallocentric nature of German Studies in Germany. This patriarchal nature, I think, has unquestionably been inscribed in the discipline's tradition and apparatus as I have outlined them so far: from Lachmann to the present day, German Studies has remained patriarchal not only on account of the patrilineal hereditary system that has governed the assignment of chairs and the succession to the role of invested and acknowledged master, but also in terms of its constitutive obsession with the correct transmission of texts, which has always occurred through exclusively patrilineal and sacralized modes. In discussing Lachmann's method, which was later transferred to modern philology, Bernard Cerquiglini writes: "Philology is a bourgeois, paternalist and hygienist discourse of the family, which cherishes filiation, condemns adultery, is afraid of contamination. A discourse of guilt (the variant is a deviant conduct), which founds a positive methodology."[11] The variant (the mistake) is due to moral irresponsibility and is therefore a form of sin against the God-father-master.

The feminist critique of the patriarchal nature of German Studies makes it, to my mind, a particularly radical development. What we had here was a compact group that sought to break all chains, including the hereditary one, to eradicate all patriarchal structures. Certainly the specific object of feminist criticism was literature and the production of literary works, and its general field was the history of literature: in that it seems no different from traditional literary criticism, which aspires to objectivity and neutrality and supposedly has no gender connotations. But the feminist awareness of the difference between the sexes—both on a practical level and on the level of the production of symbolic forms and images, which is the basis of modern society—has entailed important consequences. The awareness that sexual difference is asymmetric and continuously engenders new asymmetries—that is, the systematic prevalence of one element over the other—has led feminist criticism to confront the general question of power and of gender politics, both in the material structures of the discipline and in the representations it produces. The strategy of German feminist criticism (I am forced here to briefly summarize an extremely complex and articulated position) was thus aimed at revealing the partiality of *Literaturwissenschaft,* which has traditionally presented itself as objective and neutral in regard to gender difference (as well as political and racial issues, as we have seen).[12] From this strategy derived the need to unveil all the aspects of literary history that the male perspective had obfuscated, a perspective that coincided with male interests but was presented as universal and necessary. Feminist criticism highlighted the contradictions of male discourse on various levels: in terms of methods, concepts, contents, retrieval and interpretation of relevant data, and so on. This was achieved by focusing on the way literature has represented women and the position of women in relation to literature and writing. Since the field of literature is a system of social relations and communications structured in a specific fashion, it was the responsibility of feminist criticism to show the way gender differences function in this context. Did men and women have the same possibilities of accessing the literary field and the field of the scientific study of literature? Furthermore, to what extent did literature and criticism contribute to perpetuating a symbolic system based on asymmetrical differences between genders?

Thus feminist criticism had a unique impact in demystifying the alleged neutrality of German Studies. Its working hypotheses soon diversified into many specific areas, also thanks to the capacity of feminist scholars to appropriate the theoretical results of other countries. Particular attention was given to nonfictional writing that immediately reflected women's experiences in private form: diaries, letters, and autobiographical writing in general. In time this type of research, which was prominent in the 1970s, lost some of its importance, and nowadays it is mostly valued as a source for reconstructing the history of women. Other areas of research were the genesis and consolidation of women's subjectivity and especially aspects such as desire, imagination and eroticism, and the activity of writing, not as an immediate self-healing activity, but as a privileged and at times inevitable path toward the construction of women's identity. If literature is part of a system of symbolic representations that constructs and maintains gender differences, then by operating with the necessary subversive awareness, it is possible to produce images of women that do not correspond to the dominant social-cultural order and that can affect it in turn. More recently there has been an effort to go beyond specific themes and engage instead in the reconstruction of a literary history of women that would simultaneously be a social and a cultural history.[13] The goal has been to integrate different approaches in order to reconstruct the extraliterary institutional context (the development of the literature market, the social structure of cultural life, the characters of literary criticism) and the more specifically literary one (analysis of taste and aesthetic preferences, codes, theoretical programs, canons, and social norms) to which women have—or do not have—access as writers.

As one can easily imagine, feminism found many enemies within German Studies. It questioned disciplinary paradigms using categories and languages that the academic discursive police could not and would not acknowledge. There were continuous clashes and determined efforts to prevent feminist German Studies from being institutionalized. On the other hand, part of the women's movement enacted various strategies of collaboration with academic authorities that led to an academic consolidation of *feministische Literaturwissenschaft,* which, starting from the stronghold of Hamburg, gradually extended to other cities (Berlin, Göttingen, Bielefeld).[14]

The Need for New Literary Histories

At the end of the 1970s a need for new literary histories arose. The term used to express this paradigmatic change is *Sozialgeschichte,* social history. According to Maria Zens:

> Social history is a concept that embraces the majority of the developments that took place after the scientific turn. Within this perspective, literature is seen as the result of human action throughout history. The production and reception of literary texts as well as of all other related elements and interactions take place within the framework of social conditions. Literature is social praxis. This does not mean that one can derive literary and artistic phenomena from the context of all periods according to the same model: social history

> is not based on the principle that literature is mechanically determined. The interaction of literary activities with other fields of social activity never predetermines the specific imprint of aesthetic-literary discourse, let alone that of a specific text. The relative autonomy of art remains unquestioned.[15]

The production and reception of literary texts, like any other element interacting with them, occurs in a context of relationships that involve society in its historical materiality. This does not mean that literary phenomena can be interpreted as a simple reflection of the society in which they are produced: the *Sozialgeschichte* does not subscribe to a deterministic view of literature; on the contrary, it arises precisely from an awareness of the need to overcome all mechanistic forms of Marxism, along with the forms of spiritualism or crude positivism dominant in traditional literary histories. The new conception of literary history does not try to deny the autonomy of the work of art. Rather, it considers literature as the expression of the cultural and social structure and of the very texture of a civilization.[16] Purely interpretative approaches based on identification (of the critic-reader with the work of art) are replaced by an approach that, while not denying the validity of hermeneutics, uses different methodologies aimed at describing and clarifying, from an unprejudiced intellectual and critical perspective, the position and function of literary texts in the context in which they are produced. This entails an extension of the traditional concept of literature (as exemplified by the interest in *Trivialliteratur,* that is, literature written for entertainment and immediate consumption), as well as an accurate reconstruction of the material conditions and even minute daily activities through which literature is produced, of the literary market, and of all those elements and institutions that interact with literature (academies, literary prizes, the tastes of the public, newspapers and journals).

As one can easily imagine, the interdisciplinary character of this approach was a direct consequence of its view of history as a social science dealing with the transformations in social structures. Following the example of the *Annales* School, this approach considered sociology, economics, political science, and all the social sciences equally important for the study of culture in all its dimensions. Of course many have found fault with this approach, and sometimes their criticism has been on target: for example, notwithstanding the rejection of reductive materialist approaches, at times the relation between society and literary production as described in the works of this school still appears too mechanical to be convincing.[17]

In order to establish the *Sozialgeschichte* and its theoretical and methodological foundations, in 1976 the journal *Internationales Archiv für Sozialgeschichte der deutschen Literatur* was founded. The program is already evident in the title: the term *Sozialgeschichte* indicates a desire to overcome the isolation of philology in favor of an interdisciplinary approach, the term *Archiv* indicates the interest in material evidence, while the adjective *International* stresses the importance of going beyond the confines of the national debate on German literature. The new theories produced a number of interesting publishing ventures dedicated to the history of literature by prestigious houses such as Athenäum, Fischer, Hanser, Metzler, and Rowohlt. This proliferation of social histories of literature is proof of the fact that there was an increasing awareness of the irreversible changes that had taken place in culture and society and of the widespread need for studies, including manuals, addressed to a public whose interest in literature went beyond the specificity of literary phenomena and their purely aesthetic value. The new literary histories, while reflecting the different approaches of the individual editors, shared the idea of literature as system and institution, endowed with a substantial degree of autonomy yet part of a network of political, social, and economic relations that variously interact with it. This new conception opened up new research perspectives along with new fields and methodologies, all based on the idea of literature as a form of social communication and action and, as such, part of a large historical and cultural formation.

The Emergence of Subjectivity in the German Democratic Republic

During the 1970s new areas of study emerged in East Germany, also related to an interest in subjectivity and individuality in literature and in the study of literature. A crucial political change that helped this new trend was the replacement of State Secretary Walter Ulbricht with Erich Honecker in 1971. A new political trend arose that took a more tolerant stance toward the free manifestation of subjectivity and private feelings in cultural and literary productions and in the academic study of the same. Critical parameters quickly adapted, and it became legitimate to provide subjective and individual interpretations of the contradictions of a given historical period as evidenced in literary texts. It was no longer necessary, as it had been in the past, to adopt as the only legitimate critical paradigm the theory of reflection, which affirmed the universal value of a given work of art by showing how it reflected, through the mediation of the individual artist, the structural features and the totality of a given period and specifically the necessary clash between progressive and reactionary forces. Critics were allowed to focus on the individual development of men and women in the context of historical processes. It was the quality of this interaction between individuality and history as manifested in contents, themes, language, or style that attracted the critics' attention. It was no longer mandatory to outline the great political or ideological coordinates of a literary text. Within a general process characterized by the gradual development of a sense of the relative autonomy of the cultural sphere, criticism moved toward a greater subjective liberty in understanding the functioning of literary texts and interpreting them.

An interesting and lively dialectic developed between wide-ranging and even ponderous works, such as the *Geschichte der deutschen Literatur* (the "official" literary history of the German Democratic Republic, whose long and difficult gestation I have already mentioned), and other more specific works focusing on, along with the more canonical aspects of national literature (Enlightenment literature, classicism, realism, socialist literature, etc.), authors and movements where the conflict between the individual and society appeared more irresolvable and more unsuitable to being ideologically appropriated for the construction of socialist society. Thus there was a resurgence of interest in Kleist, a rediscovery of women romantic writers, a modern and modernizing reinterpretation of the classics.[18] Cultivating these interests was also, to some extent, a political statement: the subjectivity of the artist could easily be identified with private individual liberty and therefore could, sooner or later, find itself in contrast with the collective good.

This trend, of course, was a novelty. In a society that aspires to socialism, all efforts have to focus on the realization of the common goal, according to the guidelines set out by the purported political incarnation of working-class conscience, namely the party, in this case the *Sozialistische Einheitspartei Deutschlands.* Focusing on private issues irrelevant to the collective goal was dangerous and could even lead to an accusation of boycotting the construction of the socialist system. From this perspective one can understand the insistence of East German critics on constantly examining and legitimating their positions on the theoretical and ideological plane by outlining their continuity with previous ones.[19] In any case, though the political and cultural situation was different from that of West Germany, here, too, at the end of the 1970s there was a marked effort to revise and reform German Studies. As Rainer Rosenberg notes, this effort had a double function: on the one hand, it was aimed at emphasizing past positions that could help stabilize the national identity of East Germany; on the other hand, it was meant to demonstrate that historical disciplines, and specifically German Studies, were capable of addressing, thanks to their critical conscience, all those questionable aspects of the history of the discipline that had been concealed or repressed after 1945.[20] In other words, there was an awareness that the tradition of German Studies could not be simply dismissed as nationalist or fascist. It was necessary to reexamine and reelaborate the history of the discipline, burdened as it was by thick ideological stratifications, using more diversified and less dogmatic analytical tools and approaches.

As a consequence, during the 1980s important studies were published on institutional, regional, and other specific sectors of the discipline, as well as, of course, its overall political and ideological function. One must also keep in mind the difficult and also contradictory situation of East German scholars. The official goal of the Socialist Party was the construction of a socialist society based on the democratic and humanist values of the past. The humanities were to serve this goal by helping in the creation of a *Kulturstaat* (culture state). This meant that a constant and almost obsessive pressure was applied to academics to continuously reelaborate and expand the nation's cultural heritage. This is not the place to discuss the legitimacy of this project, its theoretical limitations, and the ways in which it was carried out. What I wish to draw attention to are the consequences that this particular situation had for German Studies in East Germany. On the one hand, the regime acknowledged the discipline's important, and indeed crucial, role in the construction of the *Kulturstaat:* German Studies was given full legitimacy, great responsibilities in the construction of future society, and a prestigious status in the eyes of the German people. On the other hand, this meant that control over the discipline was more intense and that political restrictions were imposed on the discipline, though their severity and direction varied constantly according to contingent political events and the general internal and international situation. All intellectuals involved in study related to the humanities and culture had to be careful. In general, scholars quickly learned the hidden rules of the system and were permitted to navigate it with a certain self-censorial ease, so long as they avoided questioning the fundamental tenets of the socialist system. When necessary, it was very easy for political authorities to put pressure on scholars or even to directly blackmail them, whether they worked in universities or in other academic institutions. As a result, censorship and self-censorship often merged in a single inextricable reality.

The 1980s

While previous periods had been marked by the effort to transform German Studies from an institutional, methodological, and content perspective, during the 1980s there was a growing disaffection for historical master narratives and all those philosophical systems where the presence of a telos suggested utopian or metaphysical implications. Advanced industrial society as a whole was defined as postmodern to indicate the radical break with modernity and the ideology that had characterized it from the French Revolution to the recent past. The break was a break in the relation between culture, art, and literature, on the one hand, and the ideology of modernity as a whole. Specifically, postmodernity was seen as marked by a rejection of teleological interpretations of human history and of the subject that realizes it. Their place was taken by an uncontrollable plurality of interpretations and perspectives.

Among the new approaches to literary criticism was deconstruction, originally developed in the works of Jacques Derrida and Paul de Man. Deconstruction emerged as a critique of Western thought, which is polemically defined as logocentric. Deconstructionists viewed the intellectual constructions of the West as aimed at perpetuating power relations by founding philosophical norms and systems; they associated these constructions with current interpretative approaches characterized by a search for a single overall meaning and guided by metaphysical criteria (because they transcend the object of the interpretation and postulate the existence of truth or presence). The critical term *deconstruction,* combining the words "destruction" and "construction," indicated the possibility of avoiding the complete destruction of thought, the possibility of instead taking it apart and then putting it together again. The next step was that of rejecting any form of codified thought on which there was a generalized consensus, focusing instead on all that is hypothetical, ambiguous, stratified, transgressive, playful: anything, in other words, that was not open to univocal interpretations.

Obviously such a critical approach could have different outcomes. On the one hand, it could mean embracing antitotalitarian discourses, the plurality and freedom of meanings, the emancipation of reason from the repressive constraints of modern Enlightenment or post-Enlightenment society. On the other hand, it could mean abandoning meaning *tout court,* replacing history with "posthistory," reducing critical work to an endless, and ultimately cynical, avant-garde game. The final result, at the end of the 1980s, was a sort of renewed "methodological pluralism" characterized by constantly changing interpretative paradigms. This continuous emergence of new theories and reformulation of old ones produced a postmodern carousel where scientific discourse (or any discourse, for that matter) ended up losing validity and meaning.[21]

The Reunification and the Rebirth of History

In a cultural climate where there appeared to be no room for the great events of history and theories of posthistory were all the rage, an extraordinary event occurred: the fall of the Berlin Wall in 1989 and the reunification of Germany in 1990.[22] The reunification created yet another rupture in German history. It felt as if one had just finished furnishing his family house and finally making it comfortable when suddenly a long-lost brother had shown up, with family, furniture, pets, and a deed saying he had a right to half the house. Everything had to be rearranged; rooms had to be reassigned and redesigned according to the needs of the newcomers. Something similar happened, and is still happening, in the German humanities. Since the nineteenth century the humanities, and particularly German Studies, had been concerned with creating a strong national identity. The German literary heritage was constantly being adapted throughout the years to the historical context, modifying canons and paradigms and, when necessary, the theoretical and methodological premises of the discipline. German Studies had thus evolved into a powerful instrument that could be used for the analysis and restructuring of the new unified German conscience and identity. It is significant that after the reunification slogans such as "Umorientierung," "Vergangenheitsbewältigung," and "Aufarbeitung der Vergangenheit" (Reorientation, Overcoming the past, and Working through the past) have kept recurring, all indicating a process of reappropriation and critical reelaboration of the past and the need to rethink one's future. This difficult rethinking of national identity that Germany had to undergo yet another time involved a number of problems that need to be briefly examined.

As is well known, the "reunification" meant in practice the integration of the eastern territory into the Federal Republic. This was the quickest solution and perhaps the only one possible given the unsustainable economic and social situation of the German Democratic Republic. But the final outcome was to some extent a postwar one, with winners and losers.[23] In all academic fields, ad hoc committees were instituted to evaluate and certify the scientific credentials of the scholars and staff who worked in the highest cultural institutions of the Democratic Republic (universities, the Academy of Science, and other institutes). I do not wish to discuss the decisions of these committees, which were perfectly legitimate within the juridical and institutional context of the Federal Republic. I would like to examine instead the characteristics of these examination procedures.

The positions of all university staff were evaluated, and in some cases people were fired or forced to retire.[24] The less defendable positions were those of professors whose careers were based on political and ideological merits and who had collaborated at times with the *Stasi* (the secret service of the German Democratic Republic), subordinating the academic code of behavior and their own consciences to the requirements of the party. However, there were other less obvious cases, related, for example, to the question of Marxism. The Marxist-Leninist doctrine, or a variety of it, had been the official doctrine of the ruling party in East Germany. Therefore, in West Germany Marxism was declared "incompatible" with the freedom of teaching and with the liberal and democratic principles of Western society in general. But by condemning Marxism as the Weltanschauung of the totalitarian regime one ended up activating mechanisms that could be used to delegitimate any critical stance based on a theoretical approach even remotely related to Marxism.[25] The result was a dismantling and reorganization of East German structures and institutions according to the unwritten rule that all humanistic disciplines had to mold themselves to their Western counterparts. The latter ended up exercising a "hegemonic cultural function" legitimated by external paradigms and mechanisms foreign to those disciplines and dictated by ideological goals.[26]

The situation was made more complicated by the fact that in West Germany at the end of the 1980s German Studies had suffered a "loss of function."[27] As Bollenbeck notes, the discipline had responded to the cultural innovations of the 1980s by subjecting its interpretative paradigms to continuous revision. This, in turn, had produced a postmodern plurality entailing the loss of a clear-cut and well-defined identity, and hence of an overall cultural function. A lucid awareness of this loss of function of German Studies within German society marked the opening speech of sociologist Wolf Lepenies at the 1991 Congress of Germanists, the first in united Germany.[28] Lepenies expressed the hope that since the humanities, and especially German Studies, had ceased to serve as a paradigmatic model, they could be subjected to a correct and competent overall critical reexamination. The situation was ripe for abandoning old attitudes and contrasts between the German Studies of the two former states: two formidable apparatuses for cultural production and reproduction, hitherto opposed, could finally collaborate and develop a common ground.

Yet the impression of some of those present was that the corporation of Germanists was in fact completely sealed off from external stimuli.[29] What seemed common to German Studies in both East and West Germany was precisely a stubborn defense of their shared grounding value: an arbitrary and rigid "scientific" approach lacking any real substance or justification. For Seiler the situation was in fact worse than before: "The famous scientific character is now reduced to a pure listing of notes where citations with their correct indications replace the thought of the author."[30] Rolf Spinnler, after a brief survey carried out among students of German Studies, adopted a similar position, ironically observing that these students excelled at one and only one skill: "the art of making bibliographies."[31] Spinnler also raised the issue of the extremely expensive critical editions, which would be "an ideal work therapy for all those who, for fear of not being scientific, are no longer capable of putting their thoughts on paper."[32] While these statements were undoubtedly meant as provocations, the fact remains that extreme specialization and an exasperated quest for completeness (in the sense of the accumulation of data) end up concealing any original thought of the scholar. The emphasis on the philological paradigm, always a safe haven for the discipline in times of crisis, had been adopted as a scientific response, derived from the original statute of the discipline elaborated by the founding fathers and therefore necessarily serious and legitimate, to the difficult situation in which unified German Studies found itself.

Paradoxically, German Studies in East Germany had not suffered from any loss of function, that is, it had not felt delegitimated as a discipline, having always played an important role in the definition of the nation's culture and identity. As noted earlier, in the Democratic Republic the state had presented itself as the legitimate heir of the great national philosophical and literary tradition, as suggested by the formula *"Kulturstaat"*: literature and the study of literature had therefore been awarded special consideration. In a further paradoxical twist, from a different point of view, literature had been the only medium available to writers, and to critics and scholars of literature, to represent and discuss in transfigured or cryptic fashion the conflicts found in socialist society. The combined impact of both these valorizing factors explains why contemporary literature, along with the accompanying criticism, reviews, and the publication of new editions of classic authors, had been treated as great cultural events, capable at times of having a positive influence on the political system, which, while rejecting all explicit criticism, was respectful of artistic and cultural production. The unification of Germany put an end to this situation and to the communicative circuit it had produced, and East German literary criticism lost its prestige, its legitimization, and also any illusion of having a say in the real world.

Summarizing, one can say that while the West German Germanists had been faced for years with the problem of an increasingly meaningless and ill-defined role, after the reunification the East German Germanists were faced with the sudden loss of their socially and institutionally acknowledged function and the degree of social prestige it entailed. Yet the first became the model to which the second, after having undergone the previously mentioned scrutiny, had to conform. The situation was certainly complicated, and it was not easy for the two groups of Germanists to join forces and work peacefully side by side; nor was it easy, in the new *Länder,* for those from the East to modify on such short notice the established mentality, working systems, canons, and paradigms, automatically adapting them to those proposed by the Western "colonizers." Yet all East German scholars were forced to submit without question to these external impositions. In some cases East German universities were treated as virgin land that could be assigned to unemployed members of the Western intellectual work force. In other cases subaltern teachers who had been previously discriminated against for political reasons were able to take advantage of the new political climate. In other cases still local scholars adapted with difficulty to the suddenly changed qualification criteria (for example, when evaluating curricula, any research experience in American universities and the knowledge of English had become suddenly more valuable than similar experiences in the Soviet Union and a knowledge of Russian).[33] In any case, this process, which some have defined as one of "creative destruction," is now definitely over.[34] In some distant future, historians will be able to reconstruct it more in detail once they have access to documents now protected by privacy laws.

Nine

Beyond the Year 2000: German Studies between New Approaches and the Resurgence of Philology

German Studies has been in a state of crisis for more than thirty years, or rather it seems to go from one crisis to the next: the Congress of Munich; the movement of 1968; the self-criticism of the 1970s; the expansion and revision of the national literary canon, the emergence of new subjects; the renewed interest in literary history as social history; the 1980s and the end of master narratives; the critique of logocentrism, phallocentrism, and Eurocentrism; and, finally, 1989 and the fall of the German Democratic Republic with all its consequences. At present, German Studies seems to be still in a state of flux: the disintegration of linear thought has liberated a multiplicity of heterogeneous elements, decentered perspectives, unstable meanings, heterotopias, ruptures, and discontinuities, which has forced modern intellectuals, including Germanists, to elaborate new survival strategies. Hartmut Böhme has identified two main tendencies: the first is characterized by "an expansion of literary studies, the second by their restriction."[1]

Restriction means, of course, the readoption of the philological paradigm and its paraphernalia: critical editions, lexicons, corpora, bibliographies, biographies, sources *(Quellen)*, manuals, anthologies, and introductions, preferably on CD-ROMs. But all this immense and unquestionably qualified work, argues Jost Hermand, is a disciplinary activity reserved "solely for the so-called corporation."[2] Furthermore, according to Böhme, this type of work—which takes up at least half of the funding available for research—is carried out without any public debate.[3] The other approach, on the other hand, is openly debated on all levels.[4] It calls for an expansion of disciplinary borders and is aimed at developing German Studies as *Kulturwissenschaft,* following the model of Anglo-American cultural studies. These two basic approaches leave room, of course, for many variants, interactions, and influences; however, for the sake of clarity I shall reduce the wide range of potential articulations to a few basic types.

The Revival of Philology

In the first place, I shall examine the tendency in literary studies to restrict its field, most notably to the production of critical editions and similar editorial activities. Certainly one of the goals of national literary studies is to pass on the heritage of the nation's writers and language. It is also important for editions to be reliable and to enable readers to understand the genesis of a work, to the extent that it is possible to reconstruct it. Critical editions can also "age," and canons may change, making new editions of a canonical author or a first edition of a previously neglected author necessary. Editions, in short, are always tied to the perception that a given historical period and a given generation has of its literature, its culture, its values. Indeed one could argue that most critical editions age very rapidly and should be revised every thirty or forty years in order to take into account new philological discoveries, but also the transformations in the historical and social context in which those editions are produced.[5] Therefore, philology is, or should be, the "secular" job of scholars gathering and ordering texts according to the most objective criteria and the ones that best conform to the historical views of a given period.

Yet for reasons I have abundantly discussed in the previous chapters, in practice this was not always the case. Starting with the "original sin" of the discipline's filiation from Lachmann and proceeding through its various transformations, this sector of German Studies has always been considered the most serious, the one with the greater educational value. Dedication, asceticism, priestly devotion, sublimation of the ego, defense of the text from the attacks of time and the threat posed by outsiders, absolute submission to the master's interpretation, along with accusations of moral indignity and then excommunication and censure for those who do not comply—these were its apparatus.

From this apparatus arose, as already noted, the fear of errors and variants, which were seen as blasphemy against the sacred character of the text and as transgression of patrilineal norms.

One could claim that all this belongs to the prehistory of the discipline since, at least in theory, things have changed very much in this regard.[6] Yet there are those who argue that a hidden but widespread "Angst" characterizes German Studies as a consequence of the excessive and uncontrollable expansion and diversification of its field.[7] Given the sense of loss of direction that pervades literary studies, which is subject to continuous centrifugal forces, the return to the text still represents a comfortable ivory tower. Those who work on critical editions often have to dedicate themselves completely to their work, even though editorial work itself is no longer that of the past: "Without question, editors today are no longer unworldly celibate priests, at the service of the most sacred thing, writing."[8] However, philological work still constitutes a sort of privileged refuge vis-à-vis the rapid evolution of historical-hermeneutical disciplines over the last thirty years. Furthermore, editorial work provides prestige, power, and fame. Critical or historical-critical editions are incredibly demanding in terms of both time and financial resources: they involve a long-time investment in organizational as well as financial terms, of which the editor is the manager. Also, as the embodiment of "serious" work in German Studies, new editions are usually reviewed in major national newspapers besides specialized journals, and the editor reaps the advantages of all this attention.[9]

However, if one takes a closer look at the process of creating a critical edition, one realizes that the emphasis on philological work is even now not a harmless one. First of all, the editor who takes all the credit in fact relies on a series of assistants working under his or her guidance. Notwithstanding their help, editorial work still takes a long time and often runs far beyond the set schedule: to cite one extreme example, the national edition of Schiller *(Schiller-Nationalausgabe)* was planned by Julius Petersen in 1939, then continued by Gerhard Fricke, Benno von Wiese, and, from 1980 on, Norbert Oellers, and it is still not finished.[10] Thus the production of critical editions involves, for years and even decades, groups of people who dedicate themselves completely to the work (dedication, as we know, is the primary philological virtue). For a precariously low stipend, each assistant works night and day without ever exceeding the narrow confines of his field, with a kind of ascetic heroism that also entails social isolation. After many years of hard work, the reward is having one's name cited along with those of the other collaborators. The scholar, it is true, can find consolation in the fact that his work is "a milestone in the path toward eternity" and in the belief that "interpretations pass, editions stay."[11] From a career perspective, however, the situation is problematic. This type of editorial work is not grounds for habilitation, but for a given number of years it prevents scholars from engaging in the type of work that would make habilitation possible. Thus the cost of editions is not solely financial, but also "human."

Let us now consider the actual products. Most existing editions are marked by their editors' almost megalomaniac desire for completeness, bordering on the impossible. This desire is of course part of the DNA of the philologist, whose ambition is to rediscover the written word in its entirety. The moral integrity of the editor has always been measured by his or her capacity to correctly add up, through sacrifice and dedication, the "correct" choices of the past as well as all other newly discovered elements, creating a true fetishism for exhaustive documentation. As Hans Zeller notes, "The notion of completeness, one of the implicit values of historical-critical editions of complete works" can go as far as "the printing of rent receipts."[12] These traditional motivations have been compounded by more recent ones, such as the rejection of the notion of closed texts and the emergence of theories of open-ended textuality, which argue in favor of accepting all existing variants, in contrast with the previous fetishistic obsession with authentic lections and correct choices. But the somewhat paradoxical result of this poststructuralist critique of the text as a closed, autonomous, and self-sufficient entity has been the appearance of critical editions where everything is treated as important: the pre-text, the para-text, the peri-text, and whatnot. Each fragment, each phase of the writing, can be seen as important now that philology is no longer hierarchically organized, but on the contrary decentered or polycentric. This liberates an almost infinite series of possible discourses. Thanks to this new theoretical framework, the editor can freely move from one text to another, from one stage of the text to another, and so on, in the name of intertextuality.

The result of all this work—in many ways laudable and fascinating—is the production of incredibly expensive editions that few can afford to purchase (including German libraries and institutions, which are currently facing budget cuts and the increasing costs of continuous technological modernization). One cannot help wondering whether it would not be a good idea to plan the distribution of resources on a national level and set a limit on the drive for completeness. In any case, once the price hurdle has been jumped the reader finds himself lost in a labyrinth. As Böhme notes: "The ratio of the pre-text, commentary and documentation to the main text is absurdly high. The amplitude of the pre-texts makes the editions illegible. The interpretative part has taken over. The commentary is too specialized. Intertextual connections turn into inscrutable rhizomes. Selection has been replaced by maximum extension. Editions are increasingly subordinated to theories of textual criticism that are imposed on the textual material. Theoretical extremism reigns, giving the impression that the editor's goal is to create a monument not to the author but to himself."[13]

To these considerations I would add the following. Whoever opens a critical edition is immediately confronted with a jungle of at first incomprehensible signs. These are the diacritical signs: consistent with philology's tradition as a "society of discourse," they arguably represent the secret language of the initiates of philology. Critical editions are sometimes accompanied by many pages that should serve to help the reader correctly interpret the signs. Furthermore, it often happens that, since there has been more than one generation of editors, diacritical signs have been modified in the process and new ones have been introduced. But since volumes are almost never published in the order of their numbering, the new criteria adopted for volume 2 may not be valid for volume 3, which had been published earlier.[14] The situation is so extreme that even some prestigious philologists have (rhetorically) raised the question of whether other editions are indeed necessary.[15] The response—coming from a somewhat biased source, since most of those who have participated in the debate have been publishers—has been that new editions are indeed necessary.[16] Yet the simple fact that the question was asked is an indication of the extent of the problem. There is a generalized demand for a new approach to editing based on greater planning, a decrease in the sizes of editions, a unification of the system of diacritical signs, and, most important, a change in the structure and organization of editorial work. Editions should no longer be the "private feudal property of full professors . . . who employ a multitude of subordinates."[17]

The problem, though, is that precisely the patronage system governing editorial and research activities is the basis of academic power and of the strategies for acquiring and preserving the same. In the field of German Studies, working on critical editions carries great prestige and the possibility of accumulating a substantial scientific and cultural capital. The capacity of top scholars to accumulate cultural capital (by participating in commissions, editorial and scientific committees, and research groups) in order to be able to arbitrarily redistribute it is closely linked to the existence of a consistent and valid group of followers, of *clientes*. It is important to keep in mind that this kind of academic power can be exercised only as long as the would-be professors are willing to accept the principle of co-optation, that is, the principle according to which the reproduction of the academic body occurs through a series of consecrations in the field of cultural production that are never clearly and explicitly institutionalized. Among the prerogatives of academic power is also that of establishing relations of authority and dependence that endure for long periods of time, at least as long as subordinates trust in the final reward awaiting them and are therefore willing to accept their destined trajectory. Those who have what Bourdieu calls the "institutional charisma" (meaning a form of cultural authority that is created wherever there is power within an institution charged with cultural production and reproduction) have the capacity to make their "clients" wait, arousing, encouraging, or cooling, when necessary, their expectations and desires.[18] This ability to act on the desires of their pupils, who in turn are willing to play and invest in a game that is generally uncertain (one never knows for certain whether one is actually going to make it to professor, though some can be confident their chances are very good), is one of the distinctive features of academic charisma; those who have academic power must rely on this charisma to impose and legitimate their choices in the eyes of those who depend on their strategies.[19]

In this context, it is worthwhile recalling the already mentioned procedures necessary for the acquisition of the habitus of the professor. In the case of German Studies, obviously the long process of cultural inculcation necessary to produce an effective and lasting interiorization of the cultural arbitrary is accomplished to a large degree by having pupils work on critical editions. These are still among the best disciplinary training grounds: on the one hand, since they have a high symbolic value in terms of the philological heritage, they allow the young scholars to feel themselves worthy of being part of the group on the strength of their co-optation into the enterprise (an act they rightly perceive as significant); on the other hand, they serve to discipline the would-be professors by containing and deferring their expectations in a dialectic of anticipation, frustration, and gratification extending over an unpredictable length of time.

The Perspectives for Research

The other and opposite strategy pursued in German Studies has been the expansion of its field through the adoption of a series of magic keywords such as *Kulturwissenschaft,* multiculturalism, interculturalism, interdisciplinarity, internationalization, comparative literature, and so on. These new approaches have their roots in the self-critique that German Studies, along with other disciplines, carried out in the early 1990s. The collective work of a number of well-known scholars provided the basis for a series of directives that were set down by the Federal Ministry of Research and Technology and that were consistently applied by the ministry in supervising research during the years that followed.[20] One of the main criteria was that research should be collective, involving various scholars, universities, and extra-academic institutions and also interdisciplinary work. The explicit goal of this directive was that of doing away with the tendency toward individual research, still dominant in the humanities, in favor of the collective research model habitually used in the natural sciences. I would add that collective work, by bringing together scholars from universities in West and East Germany, also had a socializing function, allowing East German Germanists—probably more used to collective work in the first place—to learn the approaches followed by their Western colleagues. Collective work was therefore a modernizing tool but also one that served to control and guide the transmission of new paradigms and values. In any case, whatever its explicit and implicit goals, this managerial model of research is now dominant: the product is no longer the result of individual qualities (seriousness, application, soundness, etc.), as in traditional German Studies, but of an efficient organizational model. Research is increasingly planned, carried out, and consecrated in assemblies of literary societies, congresses, and conferences financed by public and private sponsors. One could go as far as to say that the rhythm of research is nowadays "external," that is, determined by external exigencies (a particular congress, the need to publish a given article at a given moment in a given journal). Also, modern research projects require a great number of methodologically homogeneous participants, increasingly complex and expensive technological equipment, and an ability to accurately predict the timing and modalities of each project. This tendency is considered "irreversible and inevitable."[21]

The first result of this new approach to research has been an increase in specialization resulting from the extreme diversification of the field and the pressure toward production at all costs, given that in the current system, marked by extreme competition, this has become synonymous with quality. This leads "not only to the banalization of the objects of inquiry, but also to a (partial) infantilization of the intelligence of researchers."[22] Thus in the guise of modernization and the efficient use of resources one witnesses a reemergence of the old positivism, with its desire for secure, controllable, and predictable results and its aptitude to rest content with a fragmented, mechanical, and purely quantitative type of knowledge. Another consequence of the new research model is homogenization: since research is organized by groups of scholars and carried out collectively, in time scholars tend to become increasingly similar in their methods and beliefs. After all, they share the same activity, use the same structures, communicate through the same scientific network (journals, reviews, congresses, conferences, and seminars), and publish in collective works edited, in turn, by one or the other of them. Thus, whether they realize it or not, they quickly end up constituting a "society of discourse" characterized by its own language and internal norms. Within these groups there is little room for disagreement. Any controversy is firmly rejected, and the impression one has from the outside is that of a group of friends sharing the same opinions and communicating in a secret language of their own: "Each current creates its own circle with its own circuit of publishing opportunities, which gives them the possibility to find, along with 'a citations syndicate, a circle of friends sharing the same orientation' who cultivate their own specialized, or indeed secret, language."[23]

The others, those who do not belong to the group, have no way of entering the communication circuit on account of its hyperspecialization. However, they too belong to other circuits and groups where they share the same exclusive rights. Thus a series of subdiscourses is created within the discipline, sealed off from one another and tending inevitably to forms of repetitive "scholastic" knowledge.[24]

Having surveyed the general tendencies in the organization of research in German Studies, let us now consider those governing the choice of content. As I mentioned above, there is a general tendency to expand the field in almost all directions. In the absence of a privileged axis on which to build a homogeneous project, the strategy is to emphasize decentered processes. For Böhme: "Against all homologation of history, the idea is to affirm the multiplicity of histories and cultures, to safeguard the contradictory and heterogeneous elements of cultures and the richness of history, whose faithful co-reproducers in some of its most significant manifestations, that is, languages and literatures, should be the experts in the sciences of literature."[25]

Thus conceived, German Studies should function as a gathering place for all the stimuli coming from philosophical, social, and ethnological disciplines, which up to now have not been considered pertinent to the study of literature. This notion of *Kulturwissenschaft* represents, in my view, a return of sorts to Jacob Grimm's proposal of a "wild and untamable philology," which lost out to Lachmann's philological paradigm. It offers the methodological advantage of superseding the historical contradiction between scientific and historical-hermeneutic culture in favor of a new notion of culture that does not fear the violation of its borders: "Alternative proposals"—writes Böhme—"range from Lepenies' 'three cultures,' to 'trans-' and 'interculturalism,' all the way to the 'liquidization' of the concept of culture."[26]

This expansion of the field of literary studies, officially supported since the reunification of Germany, has had the effect of reducing the importance of the concept of national philology, which was still hegemonic in the Democratic Republic with only a few exceptions. Involving Germanists from East Germany (after their "evaluation") in the research work of West Germany, less rigidly tied to the old disciplinary paradigms, helped make them part of an international context characterized by different methodologies and interests. In fact, precisely for the purpose of further expanding the field of inquiry, the methods, and the number of researchers involved in the subject, there has been talk about the need to "internationalize" German Studies and to exploit its great "intercultural" potential.[27]

There is a growing exchange between the German Studies of all nations and especially an important dialectical relation between German Studies in Germany and in the United States. Ever since its foundation (with the major contribution of Jewish and antifascist intellectuals in the 1930s), German Studies in the United States has been characterized by a more free and original approach to the study of German literature than in Germany, and also by the adoption of a critical stance vis-à-vis some of the basic tenets of traditional German Studies. A case in point has to do with the polemics created by the publication in the United States of *Die Klassik-Legende* in 1972. The book developed out of the annual workshop at the University of Wisconsin, organized by Jost Hermand and Reinhold Grimm, who have played a leading role in the reinterpretation of German literature. It attacked the traditional interpretation of German classicism as humanistic, pedagogic, and basically apolitical, and therefore vulnerable to National Socialism, an interpretation also present at the time in North American German Studies. At the same time, it drew attention to those authors and literary movements (Jacobins, democratic authors of the *Vormärz,* naturalists, and expressionists) who represented a militant alternative to this quietist conception of literature.[28]

In recent times North American Germanists have expanded the field of German Studies, traditionally identified with the national values of German culture, toward other areas, adopting the theories of the Frankfurt School and of nonorthodox Marxist currents: from this perspective, an important role has been played by militant journals such as *New German Critique,* founded in 1973 by David Bathrick, Anson Rabinbach, and Jack Zipes. The result has been a particularly dynamic approach to German literature on various levels, calling for the revision of the literary canon in the two German states (and in the present Federal Republic) and an open discussion of the status of the discipline, and characterized by an insistence on the need to compare the theoretical paradigms of German Studies with those of other disciplines and currents present in North American academia, such as, for example, deconstruction, feminist theories of literature, gender studies, queer theory, linguistics, psychoanalysis, structuralism, Marxism, new historicism, and anthropology. The theoretical liveliness of German Studies in the United States has been further stimulated by the contributions of a number of French thinkers (Foucault, Derrida, Lacan, and Lyotard), often appropriated in new and original ways. The decisive factor, in any case, as Hohendahl notes, has been the rejection of the philological paradigm thanks to the "*German-Studies-Modell.*"[29] This does not mean, adds Hohendahl, that there should no longer be any "*philologische Tätigkeit*" (philological work), but rather that philology has lost its leading role. Cultural Studies (or *Kulturwissenschaft*) may represent an authentically interdisciplinary and open arena for theoretical debate.[30]

German Studies in the United States has been liberated, so to speak, from the need to pursue a philological approach to literature tied to notions of *Bildung, Kultur,* and so on, which are particularly problematic in present society. It is also free to take advantage of the many new theoretical stimuli that have developed and are constantly developing in the North American academic culture.[31] It no longer needs to define its identity by resorting to filiations and genealogies and can address, instead, the increasingly multicultural characteristics of North American society, academia, and students, operating in multiple directions.[32] According to Hohendahl, while North American German Studies as an institution is moving very slowly, on a theoretical and programmatic level the innovation process is very rapid. It is on this level that new tendencies emerge, tied to a particular sensitivity to ethnic and gender issues and to colonial and postcolonial cultures. In this context an obvious priority is that of rethinking the identity of German culture without insisting on becoming, qua Germanists, its official representatives and apologists. And this operation is obviously easier for someone working, as the North American Germanists programmatically do, in a condition of freedom from the heavy burden of traditional heritage.

Germanists in Germany, on the other hand, having for a long time been enclosed within insurmountable disciplinary walls, have, now that the Berlin Wall has fallen, seized the occasion to open the discipline to the many stimuli coming from the outside. This has required renouncing, at least on a theoretical level, the notion of a hegemonic cultural identity and of a single discipline that has the authority to correctly interpret it. It has meant accepting difference, otherness, the syncretic manifestation of various cultures; discourses on gender; and the aesthetic modes in which minorities of all times and places have expressed themselves. Written artifacts of high culture are no longer the only legitimate subject of Germanists. Clearly this new approach has opened infinite new possibilities for research in regard both to the past (archive work and interpretations of past social and cultural practices) and to the present (for example, mass media and the new ways of perceiving the world that they engender).

The Resistance of the Discipline

For Böhme the expansion of the field of the discipline in all directions obviously does entail the risk of favoring superficial and "amateurish" approaches.[33] As always in these cases, it is difficult to find a solution to the problem other than for the discipline to control discourse production. It seems to me that official German Studies has displayed a striking degree of resiliency, accepting its new statute and the expansion of its field of inquiry. In fact, the present situation is allowing it to rethink itself as the general discipline that studies culture in all its articulations and manifestations in the present and in the past; thus in some ways it marks a return to the hegemonic tendency of the past as a way to overcome the legitimation crisis that the discipline has been undergoing from 1965 to the present day through the various phases I have previously illustrated. In the present situation—thanks to the discipline's ability to expand and assimilate theories and procedures from neighboring fields—German Studies seems to Böhme "more efficient and productive than ever."[34]

But this willingness to be part of the processes of the transformation of society and of its culture (or cultures), repeatedly affirmed and accepted virtually with no reservations on a theoretical level, contrasts with the structure of the discipline, still characterized by an institutional apparatus that, as stated in the important collective document "Hilfreich und gut: 7 Thesen zur wissenschaftlichen Qualifikation," perpetuates "traditional models of socialization."[35] Let us consider thesis number 2: "The classical idea of the full professor who combines the role of researcher, teacher, and manager-administrator is kept alive as a general competence although a division of labor has long been established. The diversification of the sectors of activity requires a new professional figure and a new qualification."[36]

As witness this document (produced by a number of younger German scholars), at the end of a long path and after a number of extraordinary historical events, German Studies has remained basically the same in terms of the structure of the discipline, even while showing a surprising aptitude for adaptation and assimilation on other levels. Universities continue to be the universities of full professors, notwithstanding "the renowned millenarian mold under the academic robes," to use a favorite and still current expression of the movement of 1968. Full professors continue to dominate the places where research and teaching should be freely carried out. The increased teaching load (due to the rising number of students of German Studies), the growing extent of integrated research (requiring further coordination efforts as well as participation in preparatory meetings, conferences, seminars, etc.), and the heavier administrative load have not led to an increase in the number of chairs, which would be unthinkable in the present economic situation. This increase in workload directly affects the juridical figure of the assistant (whose institutional role is that of helping the professor) and has a number of negative consequences that are worth recalling. A graduate student who wishes to obtain a habilitation in German Studies needs 9.5 years to write his or her habilitation thesis (compared to the eight years of other disciplines) and usually obtains the habilitation at the age of 40.5 (in other disciplines at 39).[37]

Such a student is therefore subjected, as I have argued in previous chapters, to a longer and more intense process of disciplinary socialization, which provides him or her with the right habitus—and the length of time during which the power of inculcating the habitus is exerted is certainly an indicator of the importance attributed, whether arbitrarily or not, to a given academic discipline. At the end of this long period of training, the scholar has turned into a perfect example of what Bourdieu calls "*academica mediocritas*"[38]: "Furthermore, the current procedure for recruiting new professors prevents innovations rather than promoting them, because it favors the establishment of relations of dependence that can last for decades, with an enormous workload (as assistant = he who assists, who helps the professors burdened by work) and stress, which leads to an academic type who rises in his career smoothly and almost without risks, diligent and well-trained, and preserves the normal functioning, without however distinguishing himself in the production of new subjects for investigation or theoretical innovations."[39]

The profound transformation of German Studies as regards contents and approaches has not corresponded to a transformation on the plane of academic power and its articulations. Today, as in the past, the entrance to the realm of professorship occurs through what is increasingly perceived as an initiation rite, namely the habilitation. As a consequence of the hyperspecialization of all sectors of German Studies, the first rule of those who aspire to habilitation is to play it safe, gaining a complete knowledge of sources and bibliography. Their final thesis must be monumental, rich in references and bearing witness to the amount of knowledge the corporation has produced on the subject:

> This is also the scientific limitation of habilitation: it carries on what has already been established in the disciplinary field; in general, habilitation does not produce any innovative impulse. As a procedure, habilitation is conceived in order to contribute to the personal and objective consolidation of research in its institutional dimension. The promotion of originality and innovation is not among its goals. It is rather an instrument for integrating scholars through the interiorization of forms of behavior. At the same time, the latter serve to stabilize the discipline through the perpetuation of methodological conventions, usually on the basis of new materials. The forfeiting of originality is certainly not a failure of habilitation as an institution, but its true purpose.[40]

Habilitation can therefore be defined as a process of socialization or social control on the part of the institution, which would otherwise have no other formal rules to govern entrance into the corporation. The norms that must be respected are the general ones prescribed for the disciplining of the candidate and the formation of the habitus: "adaptability, the ability to avoid conflict, lack of aggressiveness, respect for authority, punctuality, respect of the existing rules of the game."[41] Furthermore, such a well-planned and well-oiled mechanism has the function of producing and reproducing a body of professors according to norms and rhythms that are controlled by the body itself. The exasperating length of the habilitation process extends the amount of time that the candidate who aspires to the position of father-master must wait.[42] The candidates are forced into an almost childish position of complete submission that excludes dissension and criticism, and their future is entirely dependent on dutifully following the path their master has established for them. Such a procedure eliminates any competition between generations and guarantees the reproduction of the academic body under the control of the same.

Indeed the thematic openness of recent German Studies has to some extent affected habilitation as well: as far as the topics of habilitation theses are concerned, there has been a slight change toward less traditional themes. However, it is still preferable to choose themes that are ipso facto considered more acceptable and more habilitating than others. It is true that, since habilitation is first and foremost a procedure of intellectual socialization, the what is not so important as the how. But even so, smart candidates favor subjects that allow them to demonstrate their qualifications while avoiding conflict and innovation. Since their work deals with an accumulated cultural patrimony, it is subject to the strategies and movements of cultural capital: some subjects are more easily invested than others in terms of values acknowledged by the corporation, making it possible to create monopolies, cartels, and so on. This helps explain why, in general, the situation has not changed much: in fact, the drive toward specialization has further reduced the possibility of innovation, favoring instead accumulative approaches.

Given that habilitation continues to be the necessary condition for being co-opted into the body of academics, one might as well—as the authors of the "7 Thesen" suggest—accept as grounds for habilitation the work done by candidates on critical editions for institutes, academies, national research projects, and specialized archives dealing with the history of literature and culture, eliminating the current anachronistic procedure: "The present favor accorded to qualification obtained through habilitation falls behind the development of science and does not take into account different attitudes and needs."[43] In light of the growing complexity of research that has resulted from the enormous expansion of the field of German Studies, it would be appropriate to introduce a *"prozessuale Qualifikation"* (procedural qualification) whereby research carried out on important projects or for qualified institutions would be considered sufficient grounds for habilitation (196). From this perspective, new research projects could be activated, planned, and carried out by groups of scholars working in libraries or archives chosen on the basis of their specialties: for example, Wolfenbüttel for the baroque period, Halle for the *Aufklärung*, Weimar for classicism, Marbach for modern and contemporary literature and for the history of German Studies, and so on.

To this list I would add the many archives of the former Democratic Republic, which are slowly being ordered and being made available for study. They certainly contain documents of great importance for reconstructing the institutional context of literature and German Studies both in the post-war period and in the years before 1945, since, as is well known, a lot of post-1871 documentation on German history was kept in what became the Soviet zone after World War II. For various reasons, the documents were often kept secret: some because they could be used to blackmail people in the context of the Cold War, some because it was simply impossible to catalog existing materials due to their sheer mass. After the reunification, however, all existing documents are being reordered and cataloged. Those interested in the capacity of political power to orient the discourses on literature and to control the institutions where such discourses are elaborated (universities, academies, archives, organizations that award literary prizes, literary societies, etc.), will surely find important elements in the documents that are being made available for study. As one can easily imagine, many of the crucial moments in the literary and cultural history of Germany may have to be revised in light of new discoveries.

But any project of reorganization of the discipline must deal with the present academic career system, centered, as noted in the "7 Thesen," on "habilitation and nomination" (205).[44] It is true that in March 2002 a new juridical rank of professorship was created: the *Juniorprofessur,* or junior professorship. This status can be achieved without habilitation, and that might seem a partial step toward the transformation of the recruiting system. However, the junior professors do not have the status of *Beamte,* that is, state functionaries who cannot be discharged from their offices: they have contracts that can be renewed for a given period, but are not tenured. This innovation, then, does not structurally alter the hegemony of full professors over the academic institution; rather, as many habilitated candidates for professorship and many candidates for habilitation have noted, it multiplies the categories of subaltern academic figures, increases competition, and makes it more difficult for each individual candidate to achieve full professorship in the future.

The obverse of the candidates' precariousness and subordination is, of course, the safe and untouchable status of those who have been habilitated and nominated. Once they achieve these goals, professors often act like "submarines"; they disappear, and no one knows when or where they will surface again (200).[45] This is possible because there is no transparent evaluation process, either for professors or for non-habilitated scholars. Furthermore, at present there is a marked unbalance between research and teaching. Often an excessive teaching load prevents scholars from engaging in research; and teaching, even though everybody formally subscribes to Humboldt's notion of the close interdependence of research and teaching, continues not to be taken into account when "evaluating" a candidate or establishing his or her qualifications (205).[46] According to the authors of the "7 Thesen," a "criteria catalog" should be designed providing an overall evaluation of a professor's activities, taking into account research, teaching, and administrative activities performed by a professor (206).[47] The adoption of the same criteria, with a few modifications, for the *Nachwuchs,* that is, nonhabilitated scholars, would provide a transparent, symmetrical, and reliable evaluation system, since it would take into account *all* the activities carried out by scholars, whatever their ranks.

As one can see from the "Thesen" I have abundantly referred to, there is still widespread dissatisfaction (though obviously not all would agree) in regard to the organization of research, the importance of teaching, the organization of the universities, and academic hierarchies. One of the most pressing demands is the possibility of doing research autonomously, outside the traditional places of discipline, thus avoiding, to some extent at least, the present mechanism for selection and co-optation. Yet it seems to me that, because of its very nature, academia cannot and will not accept the demands of those who disagree with the present system. It falls to them to find new solutions, keeping in mind that every innovation carries dangers and the risk of failure, along with potential advantages.

The fact is that German Studies is currently a field marked by contrasting forces and individual trajectories, whose result is no longer predictable. At least since 1968, much worthwhile criticism has been leveled against the institutional apparatus and its mechanisms. This does not mean that the latter are on the verge of being destroyed or superseded, but it does mean that they are losing some of their legitimacy. When society at large is in a state of crisis, the correspondence between the subjective structures governing the acceptance of practices that are acknowledged as valid, on the one hand, and the objective structures governing the reproduction of the established system can fail. The habitus is not a destiny: as Bourdieu keeps reminding us in all his work, the habitus is the acquisition of social practices that become ingrained. The endurance of the idea that people must accept the habitus, that they should inherit it against their will, that they should undergo initiation rites of which they no longer accept the consecrating validity, has created divergent positions within the field. Strategies of domination and power preservation are based on the aptitude and willingness of subjects to play according to the rules.

At present, many players in the "game" of German Studies are taking a different attitude: they no longer accept the validity of the rules, yet they insist on playing according to new ones. In other words, they wish to be part of the game, modifying the power relations between the dominant and the dominated within the field.

Notes

Introduction

1. Klaus Weimar, *Geschichte der deutschen Literaturwissenschaft bis zum Ende des neunzehnten Jahrhunderts* (Munich: Fink, 1989); Jürgen Fohrmann and Wilhelm Vosskamp, eds., *Wissenschaftsgeschichte der Germanistik im 19. Jahrhundert* (Stuttgart and Weimar: Meztler, 1994); Jost Hermand, *Geschichte der Germanistik* (Reinbek: Rowohlt, 1994); Christoph König, Hans-Harald Müller, and Werner Röcke, eds., *Wissenschaftsgeschichte der Germanistik in Porträts* (Berlin and New York: de Gruyter, 2000). *Internationales Germanistenlexikon 1800–1950*, in three volumes, edited by Christoph König, is also forthcoming from de Gruyter.

2. Jürgen Fohrmann, "Organisation, Wissen, Leistung: Konzeptuelle Überlegungen zu einer Wissenschaftsgeschichte der Germanistik," *Internationales Archiv für Sozialgeschichte der deutschen Literatur*, 16: 1 (1991): 110–25.

3. Peter Uwe Hohendahl, "Probleme der Wissenschaftsgeschichte am Beispiel der Untersuchungen von Jürgen Fohrmann und Klaus Weimar," *Internationales Archiv für Sozialgeschichte der deutsche Literatur*, 16: 1 (1991): 126–38, 138.

4. See Heinz Ickstadt, "A Letter from Berlin," *Critical Inquiry*, 17 (Spring 1991): 650–54.

5. For an analysis of the evaluation procedure see Eberhard Lämmert, "Der lange Anlauf: Von der Evaluierung zur Chanchengleichheit der Wissenschaftler in Ost und West," *Merkur: Zeitschrift für europäisches Denken*, 47: 1 (1993): 30–45.

6. Michel Foucault, "Nietzsche, Genealogy, History" (1971), in *Language, Counter-Memory, Practice: Selected Essays and Interviews*, ed. by and with an introduction by Donald F. Bouchard, trans. Donald F. Bouchard and Sherry Simon (Ithaca, N.Y.: Cornell University Press, 1977): 138–64; quote on 143. Page numbers of this work will henceforth be included parenthetically in the text.

7. The more pronounced internal dialectics present in German Romance Studies

as compared with German Studies as early as the 1920s has been documented by Peter Jehle, *Werner Krauss und die Romanistik im NS-Staat* (Hamburg-Berlin: Argument Verlag, 1996).

8. About German Studies in the U.S.A. see in particular Frank Trommler, ed., *Germanistik in den USA: Neue Entwicklungen und Methoden* (Opladen: Westdeutscher Verlag, 1989); Robert Bledsoe, Bernd Estabrook, J. Courtney Federle, et al., eds., *Rethinking Germanistik: Canon and Culture* (New York: Peter Lang, 1991); John A. McCarthy and Karin Schneider, eds., *The Future of Germanistik in the USA: Changing Our Prospects* (Nashville, Tenn.: Vanderbilt University Press, 1996); Peter Uwe Hohendahl, "Germanistik in den Vereinigten Staaten: Eine Disziplin im Umbruch," *Zeitschrift für Germanistik,* new series, 6: 3 (1996): 526–35.

9. See Jost Hermand, "Zur Situation der Germanistik in den USA: Eine Historische Bilanz," *Zeitschrift für Germanistik,* new series, 11: 3 (2001): 578–89.

10. "Erstens ist Deutschland seit dem Jahr 1989, d.h. seit dem Zusammenbruch des Ostblocks, dem Fall der Berliner Mauer und damit dem Ende der unmittelbaren Konfrontation mir der UdSSR, außenpolitisch und militärstrategisch für die USA ein relativ unwichtiges Land geworden." Hermand, "Zur Situation der Germanistik in den USA," 585.

11. On the individual German Studies schools in Eastern Europe see Christoph König, ed., *Germanistik in Mittel- und Osteuropa 1945–1992* (Berlin and New York: de Gruyter, 1995).

12. See *Fachdienst Germanistik: Sprache und Literatur in der Kritik deutschsprachiger Zeitungen,* 6 (June 2002): 8.

13. See Jost Hermand's comments on the cultural inadequacy revealed in Bill Clinton's complacent remarks on the spread of Chicago Bulls T-shirts as a welcome sign of the presence of American culture in China and in Al Gore's choice of the Internet as an ideal to be cultivated in American youth "because it is the soul of capitalism": Hermand, "Zur Situation der Germanistik in den USA," 588.

1. The Origins of Modern German Studies

1. A current definition of *Germanistik* and its present branches can be found in Dieter Gutzen and Friederike Schomaker, *Germanistik in Deutschland* (Bonn: Deutscher Akademischer Austauschdienst, n.d.).

2. See Ludwig Börne, *Menzel der Franzosenfresser* (1837), in *Menzel der Franzosenfresser und andere Schriften,* ed. Walter Hinderer (Frankfurt: Insel Verlag, 1969).

3. Wolfgang Menzel, *Die deutsche Literatur* (Stuttgart: 1828; reprinted, with an afterword by Eva Becker, Hildesheim: Gerstenberg Verlag, 1981), 249–51. (Die neue Partei macht im Gegensatz gegen die Wissenschaft das Gewissen zum Prinzip, im Gegensatz gegen die Abgeschlossenheit der Kaste die republikanische Öffentlichkeit zur Form des Rechts. . . . Wir dürfen diese Partei im Gegensatz gegen die Romanisten die Germanisten nennen. Sofern die Germanisten das Gewissen zum Rechtsprinzip erheben, und die Öffentlichkeit zur Rechtsform, neigen sie zur Demokratie. Sie betrachten die Beurtheilung eines Rechtsfalls als etwas natürliches und allen Menschen gemeinsames. Nicht eine Aristokratie von Gelehrten, sondern das gemeine Volk richtet. Mithin autorisiert sich das Volk auch selbst dazu und die Rechtsgewalt fällt mit der Souveranität des Volkes zusammen. . . . Die Demokratie kann sich nicht nach dem Ausspruch eines einzigen richten. . . . Die Monarchie kann sich nicht nach dem Ausspruch vieler richten. . . . Mithin muß das römische Recht nothwendig zur Autokratie, das deutsche Recht nothwendig zur Republik führen. . . . Die Rechtsfragen sind also politische. Der

Streit über Rechtsprinip und Rechtsform fällt genau mit dem über Staatsprincip und Staatsform zusammen.)

4. Maria Carolina Foi summarizes and lucidly analyzes the internal debate of German jurists in her essay *Heine e la vecchia Germania: Le radici della questione tedesca tra poesia e diritto* (Milan: Garzanti, 1990).

5. *Verhandlungen der Germanisten zu Frankfurt am Main am 24., 25. und 26. September 1846* (Frankfurt: 1847), 5, quoted in Jörg Jochen Müller, "Germanistik—eine Form bürgerliche Opposition," in *Germanistik und deutsche Nation 1806–1848: Zur Konstitution bürgerlichen Bewußtseins*, ed. Jörg Jochen Müller (Stuttgart: Metzler, 1974), 5–112; quote on 5. (. . . die sich der Pflege des deutschen Rechts, deutscher Geschichte und Sprache ergeben.)

6. The term *Literaturwissenschaft* is commonly used in German Studies to indicate the "science" of literature. No exactly equivalent term is used in either French- or English-speaking countries: the first usually adopt a lexical area that approximately includes *histoire littéraire, critique littéraire,* and *philologie,* while the latter often resort to periphrases and additions. For example, in his brilliant *Allegories of History: Literary Historiography after Hegel* (Baltimore and London: Johns Hopkins University Press, 1992), Timothy Bahti uses the expression "scientific study and scholarship" to translate the term "science" used in conjunction with history *(Geschichtswissenschaft)* and translates the adjective *wissenschaftlich* "scholarly and scientific," as the author explains in a note (295). The enduring fortune of the term *Literaturwissenschaft* in Germany may be understood within the context of the transition from nondisciplinary and nondisciplined knowledges to science, as I argue in this chapter. When knowledges are disciplined—as, for example, with the foundation of the University of Berlin—the object and the collection of constraints we call science is born. Philosophy loses its role as intermediary between knowledges and is replaced by classic philology *(Altertumswissenschaft),* the discipline that aspires to be the general science of antiquity. From this discipline philology was born later on, also claiming for itself the status of a science. Later on as well, the study, analysis, and criticism of literature were transformed into university disciplines, but only when they acquired the status of sciences, that is, when they proved to be capable of organizing knowledge as global fields around given axioms and using criteria of selection, normalization, hierarchy, and centralization. The insistence on the term *Literaturwissenschaft* betrays, in my opinion, the desire to affirm the superiority of organized and normalized knowledge over nonknowledge and over forms of knowledge beyond the control of the corporation of specialists. On *Literaturgeschichtsschreibung* see Jürgen Fohrmann, "Geschichte der deutschen Literaturgeschichtsschreibung zwischen Aufklärung und Kaiserreich," in *Wissenschaftsgeschichte der Germanistik,* ed. Jürgen Fohrmann and Wilhelm Voßkamp (Stuttgart and Weimar: Metzler, 1994), 576–604.

7. On the political and ideological implications of the definition *deutsche Wissenschaft* from Jacob Grimm up to 1945, see Eberhard Lämmert's essay "Germanistik—eine deutsche Wissenschaft," in *Germanistik—eine deutsche Wissenschaft,* ed. Eberhard Lämmert, Walther Killy, Karl Otto Conrady, and Peter von Polenz (Frankfurt: Suhrkamp Verlag, 1967), 9–69. Modern and contemporary literature, because of its insistence on individual freedom and its middle-class and antifeudal ethos, was difficult to adopt within institutional contexts. See note 31.

8. Lämmert, for example, seems inclined to see Grimm's stance as nonpolitical. See Lämmert, "Germanistik—eine deutsche Wissenschaft," 28.

9. Jacob Grimm, "Über die wechselseitige Beziehungen und die Verbindung der drei in der Versammlung vertretenen Wissenschaften," in Jacob Grimm, *Kleinere Schriften,*

ed. Eduard Ippel (Berlin: Dümmler, 1884), vol. 7, 556–63; quote on 562. (Was die eigentliche politik betrifft, so bleibe sie unseren zusammenkünften, die nichts darüber zu beschließen haben, fremd.)

10. Grimm, *Kleinere Schriften,* vol. 7, 562. (Was die eigentliche politik betrifft, so bleibe sie unseren zusammenkünften, die nichts darüber zu beschließen haben, fremd, so natürlich und unvermeidlich es sein wird, auf dem boden der geschichte, des rechts und selbst der sprache aufsteigende fragen, die an das politische gebiet streifen, mit wissenschaftlicher strenge aufzunehmen und zu verhandeln. mitten auf solcher grenze auszuweichen, in lebendiger, alle herzen bewegender gegenwart, würde einzelner männer unwerth scheinen, geschweige einer versammlung, deren glieder nach allen seiten hin aufzuschauen gewohnt sind und in freier rede nicht jedes ihrer worte vorher auf die wage zu legen brauchen.)

11. On the symbolic significance of the choice of place and city, see Jörg Jochen Müller, "Die ersten Germanistentage," in Müller, *Germanistik und deutsche Nation 1806–1848,* 297–318; citation on 299.

12. Karl August Varnhagen von Ense, *Tagebücher* (Leipzig: Brockhaus,1862), vol. 3, 447. (Eine Merkwürdigkeit erster Art ist die Versammlung der Germanisten in Frankfurt am Main; deutsche Gelehrte—und die größten Namen—verhandeln öffentlich die schleswig-holsteinische Frage und gegen den König von Dänemark! Metternich muß darob die Hände über den Kopf zusammenschlagen! Die Sache machte sich wie von selbst, und die Schüchternheit von Grimm und Pertz, welche alle alles Politische ausschließen, nur das wissenschaftliche zulassen wollten, konnte die Verhandlung nicht hindern, eine politische Demonstration zu werden.)

13. See the interesting overview of this debate in Müller, "Die ersten Germanistentage."

14. Grimm had published the essay *Von der Poesie im Recht* in 1816 and *Deutsche Rechtsaltertümer* in 1828. His attention to the relevance of the legal system to the overall cultural identity of the nation, however, was keen throughout his work.

15. Grimm, "Über die wechselseitige Beziehungen und die Verbindung der drei in der Versammlung vertretenen Wissenschaften," 557. (. . . ein volk ist der inbegriff von menschen, welche dieselbe sprache reden.)

16. See Jacob Grimm, "Über den Namen der Germanisten," in Grimm, *Kleinere Schriften,* vol. 7, 568–69; citation on 569 (it was Grimm's third report at the Frankfurt Conference).

17. Grimm, *Kleinere Schriften,* vol. 7, 563–66; quote on 565. (Die genauen wissenschaften reichen über die ganze erde und kommen auch den auswärtigen gelehrten zugute, sie ergreifen aber nicht die herzen.)

18. Ulrich Wyss, who wrote some of the most intelligent and stimulating things on Jacob Grimm—see his monograph *Die wilde Philologie: Jacob Grimm und der Historismus* (Munich: Beck, 1979)—has also argued for the nonracist character of Grimm's effort to found a German philology. Wyss stressed Grimm's interest in France, in the Serbian language, in Slavic studies, and in Spanish in the context of a dialectic between what is domestic and what is foreign, founded on the unity of supernational reality. On this see also Ulrich Wyss, "Jacob Grimm et la France," in *Philologiques, I: Contribution à l'histoire des disciplines littéraires en France et en Allemagne au XIX siècle,* ed. Michel Espagne and Michel Werner (Paris: Editions de la Maison des Sciences de l'Homme, 1990), 57–67.

19. "Why should not the father pick a couple of words and in the evening test the children's language abilities and brush up his own? Mother, too, would gladly listen." Jacob and Wilhelm Grimm, *Deutsches Wörterbuch von Jacob und Wilhelm Grimm* (Leipzig: Hirzel, 1854–1961), vol. 1, column 13. (Warum sollte sich nicht der vater ein

paar wörter ausheben und sie abends mit den knaben durchgehend zugleich ihre sprachgabe prüfen und die eigne auffrischen? die mutter würde gern zuhören.) All words are holy, as Grimm stated in his preface to the dictionary, and none can be ignored. This explains the folly of his enterprise: the effort to gather the infinite richness of the German language within a single text, an enterprise that was accomplished only after 98 years and that, even then, was not exempt from defects, from a strictly scientific perspective. As Wilhelm Scherer noted, "The dictionary is not quite scientific in its form." In *Jacob Grimm,* reprinted from the second edition, ed. Sigrid v.d. Schulenbarg (Berlin: Dom, 1921), 252. (Das Wörterbuch ist strenggenommen keine wissenschaftliche Form.)

20. Pedantry was for Grimm the quintessence of the violence exercised on language, to be avoided at all costs. See his essay "Über das Pedantische in der deutschen Sprache" (speech presented at the Akademie der Wissenschaften on 21 October 1847), now in Jacob Grimm, *Selbstbiographie: Ausgewählte Schriften: Reden und Abhandlungen,* ed. Ulrich Wyss (Munich: Deutscher Taschenbuch Verlag, 1984), 125–53. His attitude was not exempt from criticism. On 22 December 1864, Karl Müllenhof wrote to Scherer: "The old man, in recent years, in fact since he came to Berlin, has been increasingly prone to a senseless collectionist fixation and has concerned himself with things that he should never have touched, lacking any method whatsoever, indeed any form of coherent thought: he thinks in leaps and jumps. It is incredible the stupid things he has collected and noted. . . . The certainty of his genius has made him quite mad." In *Briefwechsel zwischen Karl Müllenhof und Wilhelm Scherer,* ed. Albert Leitzmann (Berlin and Leipzig: de Gruyter, 1937), 100. (Der Alte ist in den letzten Jahren, eigentlich seit er in Berlin ist, immer mehr in eine ganz sinnlose Sammelwuth und auf Dinge geraten, die er lieber nicht hätte anrühren sollen, da ihm jede strenge Methode abgieng, ja jedes zusammenhaengende Denken: er dachte in Sprüngen und Sätzen. Es ist unglaublich was fuer dummes Zeug er gesammelt und sich notiert hat. . . . Das Bewusstsein seiner Genialität hat ihn zuletzt wild gemacht.)

21. "He cannot certainly be an authority and master for us. Jacob Grimm has had above all else the luck—and this is the most salient trait of his greatness—of not becoming a true authority in the scientific field." Wilhelm Scherer, *Kleine Schriften,* ed. Karl Burdach and Erich Schmidt (Berlin: Weidmannsche Buchandlung, 1893), vol. 1, 396. (Autorität und Muster kann er uns gewiss nicht sein. Jacob Grimm hat ja überhaupt das Glück gehabt—und das ist einer der hervorstechendsten Züge seiner Grösse—thatsächlich in der Wissenschaft nicht Autorität zu werden.)

22. Wyss offers an interesting analysis of the eulogies prepared at Grimm's death and of the reception strategies adopted by his contemporaries, which shows a general conviction of his methodological unreliability. In the opinion of these eulogists and contemporaries, in his later years Grimm had been left behind by the great advances of philology. In this regard see the opinion of Moriz Haupt, "Gedächtnisrede auf Jacob Grimm," in Haupt, *Mauricii Hauptii opuscula* (Leipzig: Hirzel, 1876), vol. 3, 164–200, and its discussion by Wyss in *Die wilde Philologie,* 23 ff.

23. As Barthes noted, Martianus Capella, the pagan African scholar, codified the hierarchy of liberal arts during the fifth and sixth centuries through the allegory that represents the marriage of Mercury and Philology (here seen as all-encompassing knowledge). Philology is the sage virgin whose dowry consists of the seven liberal arts, among which Grammatica, an old woman who carries in an ivory casket a knife and file with which to correct the mistakes of children. Roland Barthes, "L'ancienne rhétorique: aide-mémoire," *Communications,* 16 (December 1970).

24. In his eulogy Georg Waitz cited a letter written to him by Jacob Grimm (no longer extant) in which the latter confessed: "How often is one forced to go back in

his mind to the sad fate of our fatherland and feel his heart leap and his life become embittered. There is absolutely no salvation one can think of, except through great dangers and upheavals. . . . It can be solved only through merciless violence. The more I grow old, the more democratic do I become." Waitz, *Zum Gedächtnis an Jacob Grimm* (Göttingen: Dieterich 1863), 23. (Wie oft muss einem das traurige Schicksal unsers Vaterlandes in den Sinn kommen und auf das Herz fallen und das Leben verbittern. Es ist an gar keine Rettung zu denken, wenn sie nicht durch grosse Gefahren und Umwälzungen herbeigeführt wird. . . . Es kann nur durch rücksichtslose Gewalt geholfen werden. Je älter ich werde, desto demokratischer gesinnt bin ich.)

25. We must bear in mind that the Grimm brothers, especially Jacob, had been invited to Berlin to the Akademie der Wissenschaften (Academy of Sciences) to work on the *Deutsches Wörterbuch* with the possibility of also holding lectures at the university (therefore they were not members of the professional academic community). According to Bettina von Arnim, an eyewitness to the events and negotiations that preceded the invitation to the two brothers, Lachmann opposed the decision. Friedrich Wilhelm himself, at the time the crown prince, confessed in a letter to Bettina that he was in no position to demand the appointment of the Grimm brothers on account of the principle of the independence of the university. See *Der Briefwechsel Bettine von Arnims mit den Brüdern Grimm 1838–1841,* ed. H. Schultz (Frankfurt: Insel Verlag, 1984). For Bettina's observations on Lachmann see especially the letter to Wilhelm Grimm of 10 March 1839 (85–89) and the "Bericht über Lachmann," attached to the letter to Wilhelm of 2 June 1839, but bearing the date May 1839 (94–99). Prince Friedrich Wilhelm's confession of his impotence—"I have in no way already failed, they simply still have not let me finish" (Ich bin durchaus nicht gescheitert, nur hat man mich noch nicht landen lassen)—dates to 15 May 1840 (207–8). Lachmann instead wrote to Dorothea Grimm: "Our crown prince already knows and is particularly acting on behalf of Jacob and Wilhelm . . . , but if he cannot do anything . . . , what can one hope for?" *Briefwechsel der Brüder Jacob und Wilhelm Grimm mit Karl Lachmann,* ed. Albert Leitzmann, 2 vols. (Jena: Frommann, 1927), vol. 2, 893. In light of the above, it is difficult to understand what exactly happened and how the various people involved truly acted. (Unser Kronprinz weiss es freilich und ausserdem interessiert er sich speziell für Jacob und Wilhelm . . . , aber wenn er nichts vermag . . . , was kann man da hoffen?)

26. The scholars in the field of German Studies expressed a definite intention to overcome the territorial and political fragmentation of Germany through parliamentary representation of the whole German nation. See Müller, "Die ersten Germanistentage," 315 ff.

27. Grimm's speech, entitled "De desiderio patriae" (1830), now in Grimm, *Kleinere Schriften,* vol. 6: *Rezensionen und Vermischte Aufsätze,* 411–17, though presented in Latin following tradition, mentioned among other things the pernicious effects of using Latin instead of German.

28. On the complex negotiations for von der Hagen's appointment, see Müller, "Germanistik—eine Form bürgerlicher Opposition," in *Germanistik und deutsche Nation,* 83 ff.

29. Friedrich von der Hagen, "Vorwort" to *Das Nibelungenlied* (Berlin: Unger, 1807). (So ist . . . jetzt, mitten unter den zerreißenden Stürmen, in Deutschland die Liebe zu der Sprache und den Werken unserer ehrenfesten Altvorden rege und thätig, und es scheint, als suche man in der Vergangenheit und Dichtung, was in der Gegenwart schmerzlich untergeht. Es ist aber dies tröstliche Streben noch allein die lebendige Urkunde des unvertilgbaren Deutschen Karakters, der über alle Dienstbarkeit erhaben, jede fremde Feßel über kurz oder lang immer wieder zerbricht, und dadurch nur belehrt

und geläutert, seine angestammte Natur und Freiheit wieder ergreift. . . . Kein anderes Lied mag ein vaterländisches Herz so rühren und ergreifen, so ergötzen und stärken, als dieses.) On the patriotic function of *Das Nibelungenlied* in the years of the establishment of German Studies, see Hinrich C. Seeba, "Nationalbücher: Zur Kanonisierung nationaler Bildungsmuster in der frühen Germanistik," in *Wissenschaft und deutsche Nation: Zur Entstehungsgeschichte der deutschen Literaturwissenschaft,* ed. Jürgen Fohrmann and Wilhelm Voßkamp (Munich: Fink, 1991), 57–71. Seeba also recalls the "battlefield" edition of the work, edited by August Zeune and published in 1815, as a "Feld- und Zeltausgabe" for the soldiers preparing to fight against Napoleon.

30. It is worthwhile to briefly note the countless persecutions suffered by Germanists. The most blatant episode was that of the seven professors from Göttingen (the Grimm brothers, the historian Dahlmann, the historian Gervinus, the jurist Eduard Albrecht, the orientalist Heinrich Ewald, and the physicist Wilhelm Weber) who were removed from their posts and some of them exiled (the two Grimms, Dahlmann, and Gervinus) for having written a protest on 18 November 1837 against the abolition of the constitution in the kingdom of Hannover by the new king, Ernst August II. The notion of the apolitical character of early German Studies is contradicted by the great number of Germanists who were prosecuted for political crimes: according to a biographical study by Müller (*Germanistik und deutsche Nation,* 22ff.), one-fourth of the Germanists in the period from 1806 to 1848 were sentenced or tried or at least persecuted for political reasons. This is an important piece of evidence that contradicts the common notion of an apolitical German Studies and helps reestablish the category of German professors, who have been traditionally considered subservient to the state.

31. Since the *Aufklärung,* the German Enlightenment, German literature had been strongly marked by nationalist and antifeudal themes. For this reason it had been boycotted by those who disliked the libertarian drive and the middle-class self-awareness it expressed. Specifically, the discourse on the history of national literature called for the realization of national political unity as the coronation of the unity of language and literature. When national unity was established, it sufficed to claim that the Second Reich was the ultimate goal of all past national literature to ensure its retrospective legitimation.

32. In this regard see the accurate overview of the birth and consolidation of philology by Holger Dainat and Rainer Kolk, "'Geselliges Arbeiten': Bedingungen und Strukturen der Kommunikation in den Anfängen der deutschen Philologie," in *Von der gelehrten zur disziplinären Gemeinschaft,* ed. Jürgen Fohrmann and Wilhelm Voßkamp (Stuttgart: Metzler, 1987), 7–41 (published in a special issue of *Deutsche Vierteljahrsschrift für Literaturwissenschaft und Geistesgeschichte,* 1987).

33. Jacob Grimm wrote: "How does it happen that these display so much philological arrogance, which has better grounds than the one of the noblemen, but still resembles it? None among all the sciences is more arrogant, aristocratic, quarrelsome than philology and so unforgiving of mistakes." Grimm, "Über Schule, Universität, Akademie" (1849), in Grimm, *Kleinere Schriften,* vol. 1: *Reden und Abhandlungen,* 236. (Wie geschieht es, dasz sie so gern einen philologischen stolz zeigen, der bessern grund hat als adelstolz, aber ihm doch vergleichbar ist? keine unter allen wissenschaften ist hochmütiger, vornehmer, streitsüchtiger als die philologie und gegen fehler unbarmherziger.)

34. Karl Müllenhof, "Die deutsche Philologie, die Schule und die klassische Philologie" (1854), now in *Eine Wissenschaft etabliert sich 1810–1870,* ed. Johannes Janota (Tübingen: Max Niemeyer Verlag, 1980), 277–303; quote on 303. (. . . ist nicht für Dilettanten und wohlmeinende Freunde da, es giebt in der That nur eine Philologie.)

35. Important contributions on this issue are Michel Werner, "A propos de la notion

de philologie moderne: Problèmes de définition dans l'espace franco-allemand," and Pierre Judet de la Combe, "Philologie classique et Légitimité: Quelques questions sur un 'modèle,'" *Philologiques I,* ed. Espagne and Werner, 11–21 and 23–42.

36. In this regard see Werner, "A propos de la notion de philologie moderne," 19–20.

37. Pierre Bourdieu, *Language and Symbolic Power,* ed. John B. Thompson, trans. Gino Raymond and Matthew Adamson (Cambridge, Mass.: Harvard University Press, 1991), 122. Bourdieu believed that one of the main activities within the social process of institutionalization is the "inculcation of durable dispositions" (122–23) in individuals who undergo that process.

38. Bourdieu, *Language and Symbolic Power,* 123.

39. Bourdieu, *Language and Symbolic Power,* 119.

40. In this regard see Janota, introduction to *Eine Wissenschaft etabliert sich,* 48 ff.

41. On the qualities that allowed philology to become the pedagogical discipline par excellence within the reformed Prussian university, see Detlev Kopp and Nikolaus Wegmann, "Die deutsche Philologie, die Schule und die Klassische Philologie: Zur Karriere einer Wissenschaft um 1800," in *Von der gelehrten zur disziplinären Gemeinschaft,* ed. Fohrmann and Voßkamp, 123–51.

42. To understand the ideological consequences of that process—that is, the extent to which *Philologisierung* made corporate interests coincide with the general interests of the ruling class—the reader can usefully refer to Rainer Rosenberg, *Zehn Kapitel zur Geschichte der Germanistik* (Berlin: Akademie Verlag, 1981), 41–61.

43. There is naturally a massive bibliography on Lachmann: I would recommend especially Nikolaus Wegmann, "Was heisst einen 'klassischen Text' lesen? Philologische Selbstreflexion zwischen Wissenschaft und Bildung," in *Wissenschaftsgeschichte der Germanistik im 19. Jahrhundert,* ed. Fohrmann and Voßkamp, 334–450, especially 399 ff. For further indications on Lachmann, written in a lucid and discursive style, I would recommend also Dieter Liewerscheidt, *Schlüssel zur Literatur* (Düsseldorf, Vienna, and New York: Econ Verlag, 1987), 180 ff.

44. On the contrast on meter, see Jacob Grimm, "Rede auf Lachmann" (1851), reprinted in Grimm, *Selbstbiographie,* 78–92.

45. Nowadays philology as textual criticism prefers to outline for the reader the process through which it has reconstructed the text in order to allow the possibility of a nonnormative reading of the text. This approach is a consequence of various methodological influences, including Foucault's, bent on avoiding teleological reconstructions founded on the authority of author and publisher, and preferring instead contingent readings based on decentering, negation, and a pluralistic philosophy. See Espagne, "La référence allemande dans la fondation d'une philologie française," in *Philologiques I,* ed. Espagne and Werner, 157 ff.

46. See Foi, *Heine e la vecchia Germania,* 73.

47. Eulogies can be regarded as institutional acts, that is, acts that represent, express, and symbolize the authority of an institution through the ideal conditions of their performance (place, occasion, audience attending) and the qualities of the persons performing these acts, a person legitimized and acknowledged by the community addressed. Institutional acts share a codified rhetoric and the "stylistic features which characterize the language of priests, teachers and, more generally, all institutions, like routinization, stereotyping and neutralization" (Bourdieu, *Language and Symbolic Power,* 109) and that must normally be respected. Grimm, again, did not obey the discursive rules of the institution and trespassed the boundaries of official, orthodox, and legitimate discourse, thus opening a conflict that implicitly threatened the institutional order. The words he spoke on this occasion with reference to his own criticism

of the deceased—"Warum soll es hier nicht gesagt werden?" (Why shouldn't we say so here?)—clearly display his awareness of the rules of funeral oration as an institutional act and his simultaneous decision to break them in order to defend his own idea of what philology should be. See Grimm, "Rede auf Lachmann," 87–88.

48. Grimm, "Rede auf Lachmann," 82. (Man kann alle philologen, die es zu etwas gebracht haben, in solche theilen, welche die worte um der sachen, oder die sachen um der worte treiben.)

49. Grimm, "Rede auf Lachmann," 84 ff.

50. The definition is in Wyss, *Die wilde Philologie,* 282.

51. In this context it is significant that for many years both Lachmann and Haupt were professors of both classical philology and German philology.

52. Michel Foucault, *"Il faut défendre la société": Cours au Collège de France (1975–1976),* ed. Mauro Bertani and Alessandro Fontana, general eds. François Ewald and Alessandro Fontana (Paris: Seuil and Gallimard, 1997), 161–62 (my translation).

53. Foucault, *"Il faut défendre la société,"* 163 (my translation). As Foucault writes elsewhere: "Literature is the contestation of philology (of which it is nevertheless the twin figure): it leads language back from grammar to the naked power of speech, and there it encounters the untamed, imperious being of words." Michel Foucault, *The Order of Things: An Archaeology of the Human Sciences,* trans. Alan Sheridan (New York: Vintage, 1994), 300.

54. Foucault, *"Il faut défendre la société,"* 164 (my translation).

55. As Janota notes (in his introduction to *Eine Wissenschaft etabliert sich,* 34, n. 74), Lachmann's entire work is characterized by "an unquestionable fixation on high literature, and artistic poetry" *(eindeutige Fixierung auf die hohe Literatur, auf die Kunstpoesie).*

56. The term "apparatus" is the technical term used by Foucault as an alternative to *episteme* because it includes both discursive and nondiscursive practices. It is a heterogeneous category that includes discourses, institutions, systematizations, and regulations of spaces, laws, administrative norms, cultural practices, and scientific statements. The apparatus is made up of practices that act coherently as instruments whose purpose is to construct subjects and organize them according to the interaction of power and knowledge.

57. In his complex introduction to his *Eine Wissenschaft etabliert sich,* Janota reminds us (42) that going counter to Lachmann's rules and popularizing texts that should have been preserved from such profanation could mean being ostracized from the philological community. Rainer Kolk provides further examples of marginalizing strategies in "Wahrheit-Methode-Charakter: Zur wissenschaftlichen Ethik der Germanistik im 19. Jahrhundert," *Internationales Archiv für Sozialgeschichte der deutschen Literatur,* 14: 1 (1989): 50–73, particularly 54 ff.

58. M. Foucault, "The Order of Discourse," trans. Ian McLeod, in *Untying the Text: A Post-Structuralist Reader,* ed. Robert Young (Boston and London: Routledge and Kegan Paul, 1981), 61.

59. Foucault, "The Order of Discourse," 62–63.

60. Foucault, "The Order of Discourse," 63–64.

61. Bourdieu, *Language and Symbolic Power,* 145. Those who are outside the society of institutionalized discourse belong to the *"Laienstand"* (layman status) (Franz Pfeiffer, "Rezension: Des Minnesangs Fruehling" [1858], now in *Eine Wissenschaft etabliert sich,* ed. Janota, 224). Elsewhere Pfeiffer ("Zum Erek: Anhang" [1859], in *Eine Wissenschaft etabliert sich,* 227 ff.) calls *"Laien"* those who are in a layman (profane) position in regard to the philological community.

62. One could apply to this the terms of Foucault's analysis of the birth of medical power and of the related practices of exclusion and interdiction, and in particular his comments on the criterion of moral authority that Quakers and French rationalists established when investing doctors with the power to decide which patients should be admitted into or released from asylums: "However, and this is the essential point, the doctor's intervention is not made by virtue of a medical skill or power that he possesses in himself and that would be justified by a body of objective knowledge. It is not as a scientist that *homo medicus* has authority in the asylum, but as a wise man." Michel Foucault, *Madness and Civilization: A History of Insanity in the Age of Reason,* trans. Richard Howard (New York: Vintage, 1988), 270.

63. Franz Schultz, "Die Entwicklung der Literaturwissenschaft von Herder bis Wilhelm Scherer," in *Philosophie und Literaturwissenschaft,* ed. Emil Ermatinger (Berlin: Junker und Dünnhaupt, 1930), 1–42; quote on 37. (Philologisches Ethos: Die zurückhaltende Selbstverantwortlichkeit, Treue im Kleinen, Andacht zum Unbedeutenden, eingezogene Lebensführung, Scheu vor subjektivistischen Vorläufigkeiten und bloßen Impressionen, der Verzicht in jeder Hinsicht, die Idiosynkrasie vor dem "Journalismus" und "Feuilletonismus," das stolze Sichabgrenzen.)

64. The rules of the mandarins prohibited the communication of the secrets on which the group's power was based.

65. Karl Lachmann, *Kleinere Schriften zur deutschen Philologie,* ed. Karl Müllenhof (Berlin: Reimer, 1876), 279. (Monens Werk ist . . . ein abschreckendes Beyspiel davon, was man im Jahre 1821 Ausgabe, Kritik und gelehrte Deutung zu nennen gewagt habe. Wir sehen auf diesem Felde nicht eine große Zahl ehrwührdige Muster vor uns, deren bloße Betrachtung den Verirrten heimleiten könnten. Darum ist Pflicht der Redlichen, jedem Unfuge zu steuern. . . . Glimpfliche Sanftmuth wäre hier pflichtwidrig, weil unser Mann schon gezeigt hat, dass sie ohne Erfolg an ihn verschwendet wird.)

66. Lachmann, *Kleinere Schriften zur deutschen Philologie,* 140, 153, and 155. (. . . die ungründliche Bemühungen eines Liebhabers; . . . Anzahl von Willkürlichkeiten; . . . Schnitzer der gröbsten Art; Auch thut es Noth, die jüngeren Freunde unseres Studiums zu warnen vor solchen eiteln und trägen Leichtfertigkeiten, vor der nur ein ernster wissenschaftlicher Sinn der redlich-strebend bewahrt.) On this subject see Kolk, "Wahrheit-Methode-Charakter," 53–54.

67. On Lachmann's superior moral stance, see Rainer Kolk, "Liebhaber, Gelehrte, Experten: Das Sozialsystem der Germanistik bis zum Beginn des 20. Jahrhunderts," in *Wissenschaftsgeschichte der Germanistik im 19. Jahrhundert,* ed. Fohrmann and Voßkamp, 48–114, particularly 59 ff.; on the polemics against "amateurs," see Kolk, "Wahrheit-Methode-Charakter," 54, and Müllenhof, "Die deutsche Philologie, die Schule und die klassische Philologie" (1854), now in *Eine Wissenschaft etabliert sich,* ed. Janota, 291. Müllenhof explicitly attacked self-taught scholars and supported the increase in the teaching of classical languages against those who favored an increase in the study of German philology. Access to medieval culture, according to Müllenhof, was guaranteed by philological training in Latin and Greek and in German grammar.

68. An utterance can be regarded as "serious" only once a community of scholars or experts has established the procedures necessary for its validation. Lachmann's main contribution to the establishment of German Studies was exactly his formal institutionalization of an authority, or caste, endowed with the prerogative of acknowledging and legitimizing individual utterances as serious discourse.

69. On the establishment of the first German Studies seminars, see Janota's introduction to *Eine Wissenschaft etabliert sich,* 51 ff.

70. The definitive introduction of German language as a subject in high schools

and classical lyceums was marked by Wilhelm II's speech of 1890: "We must adopt German as the foundation of the Gymnasium; we should educate young nationalist Germans and not young Greeks or Romans. . . . We must make German our basis." Quoted in Janota's introduction to *Eine Wissenschaft etabliert sich,* 53–54. (Wir müssen als Grundlage für das Gymnasium das Deutsche nehmen; wir sollen nationale junge Deutsche erziehen und nicht junge Griechen und Römer. . . . Wir müssen das Deutsche zur Basis machen.) The fight for the German Gymnasium, "der Kampf um das deutsche Gymnasium," was thus won by German Studies against classical philology, of which it was, however, the legitimate heir.

71. See chapter 3 of the present work dedicated to Scherer.

72. Pierangelo Schiera, *Il Laboratorio borghese: Scienza e politica nella Germania dell'Ottocento* (Bologna: Il Mulino, 1987), 256–57; my translation.

73. Wilhelm Scherer, memo to Minister of Culture Von Gossler, 9 August 1884, quoted in Uwe Mewes, "Die Gründung germanistischer Seminare an den preussischen Universitäten (1875–1895)," in *Von der gelehrten zur disziplinären Gemeinschaft,* ed. Fohrmann and Voßkamp, 69–122; quote on 99. (Mit Bibliotheken ausgestattete Seminare, in denen die vom Direktor aufgenommenen Mitglieder von Morgens bis Abends ungestört arbeiten können, in denen auch die vom Direktor geleiteten Übungen stattfinden, haben einen ähnlichen Vortheil für die philogischen und historischen Wissenschaften wie die Laboratorien für die Naturwissenschaften. Den Lernenden wird das Arbeitsmaterial selbst in die Hand gegeben. Es giebt wohl keine wissenschaftliche Untersuchung auf dem Gebiet der Philologie und Geschichte, die mit einem oder wenigen Büchern geführt werden kann In wissenschaftlicher Untersuchung sollen wir Universitätslehrer aber unsere Schüler unterweisen: das wissenschaftliche Lernen können sie mit Hilfe der Vorlesungen für sich allein abmachen. Und untersuchen lernt man nur, indem man sich in der selbständigen Forschung unter Anleitung des Lehrers versucht. Zur Durchführung einer Untersuchung aber ist der unbehinderte, sofortige und gleichzeitige Gebrauch vieler Bücher nothwendig. Schon um ältere Behauptungen und Ansichten über den Gegenstand der Untersuchung zu prüfen, ist es nothwendig, eine große Masse von Citaten nachzuschlagen; denn die Grundlagen einer Untersuchung dürfen nie aus zweiter Hand, sie müssen stets aus den Quellen selbst geschöpft werden.)

74. Mewes, "Die Gründung germanistischer Seminare an den preussischen Universitäten," 100. (Es ist ein großer Unterschied, ob der Direktor einfach das richtige *sagt* oder ob es der Schüler in Gegenwart des Direktors durch eigene Bemühungen ermittelt.)

75. Michel Foucault, *Discipline and Punish: The Birth of the Prison,* trans. Alan Sheridan (New York: Vintage, 1995), 138.

76. Foucault, *Madness and Civilization,* 251.

77. Julius Zacher, "Eröffnungsrede," in Zacher, *Verhandlungen der Versammlungen deutscher Philologen und Schulmänner 1867* (Leipzig: 1868), 145–49; quote on 146. (Wodurch aber ist dieser grosse und rasche Erfolg erreicht worden? Die wahre Ursache ist keine andere als die consequente straffe preussische Zucht, das wohlüberlegte methodische, aber nicht pedantische, sonder energisch Handeln. Straffe Zucht, richtige, energisch gehandhabte Methode, das ist also das Geheimnis, durch welches Preussen die Begründung der Einheit Deutschlands bewirkt hat; und dasselbe ist es, durch welches Grimm und Lachmann die Begründung der deutschen Philologie erreicht haben.)

78. Julius Petersen, "Der Ausbau des Seminars," in Petersen, *Das Germanistische Seminar der Universität Berlin: Festschrift zu seinem 50. järigen Bestehen* (Berlin and Leipzig: de Gruyter, 1937), 31. (. . . erzieherisch sehr heilsame Glossenarbeit.)

79. See the testimony of a direct witness, Adalbert von Hanstein, *Das jüngste*

Deutschland: Zwei Jahrzehnte miterlebte Literaturgeschichte, 3rd edition (Leipzig: R. Voigtländers Verlag, 1905), 5 ff.

80. See note 31.

81. Bourdieu, *Language and Symbolic Power,* 124, 125.

82. Bourdieu, *Language and Symbolic Power,* 124.

83. Foucault, *Madness and Civilization,* 253. Foucault draws attention to the fact that even in modern therapeutic centers (those established after the French Revolution) the human group had to be reduced to its original and simplest forms. The goal was to re-create elementary social relations based on absolutely rigorous moral principles. Families seemed the ideal place for returning people to the moment before society departed from nature. This place—the asylum, the community, the family—was ideal for cleansing the spirit from all the attachments and disorderly factors that society had imbued it with, re-creating moral and social uniformity. A similar function belongs to the seminar: that of establishing a moral order and peacefully recruiting members using disciplinary technologies applied to body and mind.

84. Within this general ascetic and repressive framework it is worthwhile to note what Wyss said about Jacob Grimm: "Throughout his life Jacob Grimm refused to be a father or a son, nor was he husband to any woman" (In seinem eigenen Leben weigerte sich Jakob Grimm, Vater und Sohn zu sein—er wurde aber auch nicht der Mann einer Frau). And: "He must not have experienced his single existence as a tragedy of loneliness" (*Einleitung* to Grimm, *Selbstbiographie,* 9 and 10). Grimm, in turn, wrote about Lachmann: "The fact he was not married was painfully experienced during his last major sickness, when there was no soft and delicate hand of a loving wife to assist him, and even his friends could not once approach him, with the exception of Moriz Haupt, who had arrived from Leipzig, and stayed up day and night till the end of his master" (Grimm, *Rede auf Lachmann,* 92). (Dasz er unverheiratet geblieben war, wurde in seiner letzten schweren krankheit wehmütig empfunden, wo ihn keine weichen, sanften hände einer liebenden frau pflegen konnten, nicht einmal seine freunde ihm nahen durften, auszer dem von Leipzig herüber gefahrnen Moriz Haupt, der nacht und tag seiner bis ans ende wartete.)

85. The prestige of patriarchy is rejuvenated by the bourgeois family. The patriarchal order experienced in university seminars of the early nineteenth century (but also later) employed a myth of Western culture that made it into the destiny of modern civilization. This meant that the world of academia was enveloped in an Oedipal fog that proved difficult to dispel. Master-pupil relations took on the form of an ambivalent father-son relation, but also, as Wyss notes in his *Die wilde Philologie,* 90, of a master-servant relation. This meant that disagreements and conflicts were interpreted as profanation, rebellion, blasphemy agaist the father, as the impossibility of breaking the Oedipal chain. On this see Foucault, *Madness and Civilization,* 253 ff.

86. Pierre Bourdieu, *Homo Academicus,* trans. Peter Collier (Stanford, Calif.: Stanford University Press, 1988), 90.

87. Bourdieu, *Language and Symbolic Power,* 131.

88. On primogeniture see Bourdieu's crucial observations in *Homo Academicus,* 153–54.

89. This was the opinion of classical philologist Friedrich Wilhelm Ritschl, "Zur Methode des philologischen Studiums," *Opuscula philologica,* 5 (Leipzig: 1879), 31. (Besser methodisch irren, als zufällig das Wahre finden.) Ritschl's biographer, Otto Ribbeck, stressed the extraordinary success of Ritschl's school, which by 1872 had created 36 university professors and 38 lyceum professors. Ribbeck, *Friedrich Wilhelm*

Ritschl: Ein Beitrag zur Geschichte der Philologie, 2 vols. (Leipzig: Teubner, 1879–81). See also Kolk, "Wahrheit-Methode-Charakter," 56 ff.

90. Martin Hertz, *Karl Lachmann: Eine Biographie* (Berlin: Wilhelm Herz, 1851), 82–84. (Diesen Erfolg erzielte er durch strenge, methodische Zucht. . . . Denn Klarheit vor Allem forderte Lachmann, sicheres Bewußtsein von den Grenzen des eigenen Wissens. Jedes Rathen, Tasten, Raisonnieren über halbgewusste Facta war ihm verhasst. . . . Er trug daher auch kein Bedenken gelegentlich sein Nichtwissen auszusprechen, einen Irrthum anzuerkennen, von einem Seminaristen Belehrung anzunehmen. Aber Faselei und vorlauten und naseweisen Dünkel wies er mit eben der Unbarmherzigkeit zurück, als umhertappendes Halbwissen: "solche Bursche," meinte er, "muss man kappen.") I draw attention to the verb *"kappen,"* which means to cut, prune, castrate. See Grimm and Grimm, *Deutsches Wörterbuch von Jakob Grimm und Wilhelm Grimm* (Leipzig: Hirzel, 1873), vol. 5, columns 197–98. Seminar learning, monastic lifestyle, patriarchal discipline, and castration fears: this general apparatus controlling the socialization of students needs little comment. Lachmann had the merit of having made explicit one of the institutional goals in the training of philologists and, in general, of academic power: that of controlling the possibility of the body of potential academics to reproduce.

91. *Statute* is used here to refer to the body of rules and laws that determine the functioning of the discipline.

92. On the rules governing academic succession, see Bourdieu, *Homo Academicus,* 84 ff. and 143 ff. The law of primogeniture works, according to Bourdieu, as a "veritable *lex insita,* as Leibnitz says, an immanent law of the social body which, having become immanent in the biological bodies, causes the individual agents to realize the law of the social body without intentionally or consciously obeying it: in the absence even of any express regulation or any explicit warning, aspirations tend to adjust themselves to the modal *trajectory,* that is the normal trajectory for a given category at a given moment" (143).

93. According to Bourdieu, it is very difficult for university disciplines to experience such crises as put into question their very structure. Even at times of acute social and political turmoil, the external crisis makes the university appear by contrast as the domain of objective and scientific certainties, where only minor adjustments are needed, not changes to its structure and functioning (Bourdieu, *Homo Academicus,* 159 ff.).

94. Kolk ("Wahrheit-Methode-Charakter," 72) seems to me to use this expression to indicate a sort of turmoil, an internal upheaval within the discipline that remains, however, within established paradigms.

95. See note 84.

96. Wilhelm Scherer, "Moriz Haupt," in *Allgemeine Deutsche Biographie,* Auf Veranlassung Seiner Majestät des Königs von Bayern hrsg. durch die historische Kommission bei der Königl. Akademie der Wissenschaften (Leipzig: Verlag von Duncker und Humblot, 1880), vol. 11, 72–80; quote on 74. (Für die Philologie ist es ein unberechenbarer Vorteil gewesen, daß Lachmann gleichsam zweimal erschien, daß ihm in Haupt eine so verwandte Natur, eine so ebenbürtige Kraft erstand, welche volle Befriedigung darin empfand, die Art des Freundes sich anzueignen und in Schrift und Lehre fortzusetzen, fortzupflanzen.)

97. *Zeitschrift für deutsches Altertum,* 1: 1 (1841), now in *Eine Wissenschaft etabliert sich,* ed. Janota, 212–16; quote on 212. (Die gräber die man zu hunderten aufgedeckt hat sind doch fast stumm geblieben über die alte zeit deren sprache verhallt ist.)

98. *Zeitschrift für deutsches Altertum,* 1: 1, 213. (Ich werde dafür sorge tragen daß hier nur würklich merkwürdiges gedruckt wird.)

99. *Zeitschrift für deutsches Altertum,* 1: 1, 214. (. . . den rost zu tilgen der alte kunstwerke überzieht.)

100. *Zeitschrift für deutsches Altertum,* 1: 1, 215. (. . . erforschung des einzelnen; . . . das letzte ziel aller dieser bestrebungen.)

101. *Zeitschrift für deutsches Altertum,* 1: 1, 216. (. . . das bleibendere; . . . in der form von nachträgen und berichtigungen.)

102. Jan-Dirk Müller, "Moriz Haupt und die Anfänge der 'Zeitschrift für deutsches Altertum,'" in *Wissenschaft und deutsche Nation,* ed. Fohrmann and Voßkamp, 147.

103. Scherer recalls how young Haupt developed as a philologist in a rigidly controlled fashion, constantly obsessed by the fear of making mistakes (Scherer, "Moriz Haupt," 74). His political choices were quite different.

104. Bourdieu, *Language and Symbolic Power,* 75.

105. Bourdieu, *Language and Symbolic Power,* 122.

106. On controversies within the discipline, see the excellent Rainer Kolk, *Berlin oder Leipzig? Eine Studie zur sozialen Organisation der Germanistik im "Nibelungenstreit"* (Tübingen: Niemeyer, 1990).

107. "Insults, like naming, belong to a class of more or less socially based acts of institution and destitution through which an individual, acting in his own name or in the name of a group that is more or less important in terms of its size and social significance, indicates to someone that he possesses such and such property, and indicates to him at the time that he must conduct himself in accordance with the social essence which is thereby assigned to him." Bourdieu, *Language and Symbolic Power,* 105–6. Insults express a claim to symbolic authority, the intention of imposing a socially acknowledged power from which the legitimacy of the scientific statement descends. In his review of Pfeiffer's *Walther von der Vogelweide,* where Pfeiffer criticizes Lachmann, although he had been his pupil, Julius Zacher accused him of having kicked the old dead lion ("dem totden Löwen einen Fusztritt"), lacking the guts to do so when he was alive. See Zacher, "Franz Pfeiffer (hrsg. von), Walther von der Vogelweide," in *Neue Jahrbücher für Philologie und Pädagogik,* 11 (1865): 451. See also Kolk, "Wahrheit-Methode-Charakter," 67. Pfeiffer returned the favor as follows: "They [Lachmann and his followers] have been impotent for quite a while now, only in insolence can they currently achieve results." Pfeiffer, letter to Bartsch, 9 June 1862, in *Franz Pfeiffer-Karl Bartsch, Briefwechsel,* ed. H.-J. Koppitz (Cologne: Greven Verlag, 1969), 112. (Impotent sind sie ja laengst, nur in der Insolenz leisten sie noch erkleckliches.)

108. *Franz Pfeiffer-Karl Bartsch, Briefwechsel,* ed. Koppitz, 112.

109. See note 107.

110. See Janota's introduction to *Eine Wissenschaft etabliert sich,* 44ff.

111. F. Pfeiffer, "Prospekt" to *Germania* (1856), now in *Eine Wissenschaft etabliert sich,* ed. Janota, 320–23; quote on 321. (Es ist also das ganze deutsche Alterthum, das ganze deutsche Leben in allen seinen Äusserungen, was Gegenstand unserer Forschung werden soll.)

112. Pfeiffer, "Prospekt," 322. (. . . Geist und Ton der Behandlung; . . . den Kreis der Mitforschenden.)

113. Ibid. (Aber es ist nicht zu läugnen, dass auf dem Gebiete der deutschen Philologie, wie auf keinem anderen Felde der Gelehrsamkeit, die Herrschaft der Autorität, das Ansehen der Schule eine Höhe erreicht hat, die nicht mehr fördernd, sondern hemmend wirkt, und mit freier Forschung und rücksicktlosem Bekenntnis der Wahrheit unerträglich ist.)

114. Pfeiffer, letter to Bartsch, 9 June 1862, in *Franz Pfeiffer-Karl Bartsch, Briefwechsel,* ed. Koppitz, 112. (Dieser Clique gilt die Wissenschaft und die Wahrheit nichts.

Alles dagegen ihr Ruhm und ihr Ansehen. Um dies aufrecht zu erhalten, ist ihnen kein Mittel zu schlecht und zu erbärmlich. . . . Wer aber kann in Zweifel sein, wo, auf welcher Seite reges geistiges Leben und Fortschritt ist? und wo Faulheit, Indolenz und Versumpfung?)

115. Pfeiffer, letter to Bartsch, 7 November 1858, 50. (Dieser Glaube muß zerstört werden, sonst ist kein Fortschritt möglich.)

116. Bourdieu, *Homo Academicus,* 56.

117. Bourdieu, *Homo Academicus,* 83.

118. Bourdieu, *Homo Academicus,* 95. The French original has a stronger expression: "horreur de la liberté et du risque intellectuel." Pierre Bourdieu, *Homo academicus* (Paris: Editions de Minuit, 1984), 127.

119. On the fear of mistakes, see Scherer's remarks on Haupt, mentioned in note 103.

120. See Michel Foucault, "The Subject and Power," afterword to Hubert L. Dreyfus and Paul Rabinow, *Michel Foucault: Beyond Structuralism and Hermeneutics,* 2nd edition, with an afterword by and an interview with Michel Foucault (Chicago: University of Chicago Press, 1983), 221.

2. Under the Aegis of Goethe

1. For a definition of the expression *Oppositionswissenschaft* see Rainer Rosenberg, *Zehn Kapitel zur Geschichte der Germanistik* (Berlin: Akademie-Verlag, 1981), 22. I attempted a political and ideological interpretation of literary historiography in the years 1830–70 in my "Dilthey e la Literaturwissenschaft liberale in Germania (Gervinus e Danzel)," in *Nazione, storia e scienze sociali tra Otto e Novecento,* ed. Gustavo Corni (Pescara, Italy: Editrice Itinerari, 1992), 149–68.

2. By *Vormärz* I refer to the decade preceding 1848.

3. On the discursive elaboration of the notion of *Literaturgeschichte* see Jürgen Fohrmann's important study *Das Projekt der deutschen Literaturgeschichte: Entstehung und Scheitern einer nationalen Poesiegeschichtsschreibung zwischen Humanismus und Kaiserreich* (Stuttgart: Metzler, 1989).

4. Gervinus was the founder in Germany of a "history of literature" based on scientific premises and integrated into a national education project. See in this regard Hans Mayer, "Literaturwissenschaft in Deutschland," in *Fischer-Lexikon Literatur,* ed. W. H. Friedrich und Walther Killy (Frankfurt: Fischer, 1965), vol. 2: 1, 317–33; citation on 322. On Gervinus and the birth of the *Literaturgeschichte* in Germany see also Vittorio Santoli, "Deutsche Literaturgeschichte und Literaturkritik" and "An den Anfängen der nationalen Literaturgeschichte: G. G. Gervinus und J. Grimm," in *Philologie und Kritik: Forschungen und Aufsätze* (Bern and Munich: Francke, 1971), 102–14, 114–32.

5. See Gervinus's autobiography, *G. G. Gervinus' Leben: Von ihm selbst (1860),* ed. J. Keller (Leipzig: Engelmann, 1893), 297.

6. G. G. Gervinus, "Einleitung," in *Geschichte der poetischen National-Literatur der Deutschen,* 5 vols. (Leipzig: Engelmann, 1835–42), vol. 1, 1–18; now in G. G. Gervinus, *Schriften zur Literatur,* ed. Gotthard Erler (Berlin: Aufbau Verlag, 1962), 145–64; quote on 152. (Unter uns scheint es doch endlich einmal Zeit zu sein, der Nation ihren *gegenwärtigen* Wert begreiflich zu machen, ihr das verkümmerte Vertrauen auf sich selbst zu erfrischen, ihr neben dem Stolz auf ihre ältesten Zeiten Freudigkeit an dem jetzigen Augenblick und den gewissesten Mut auf die Zukunft einzuflößen.)

7. Gervinus, "Einleitung," 156. (Ich habe mit der ästhetischen Beurteilung der Sachen nichts zu tun, ich bin kein Poet und kein belletristischer Kritiker.)

8. Gervinus, "Einleitung," 159. (. . . für die Bearbeiter und gelehrten Kenner dieser Literatur, . . . nicht für eine besondere Klasse von Lesern, sondern . . . für die Nation.)

9. The concept of "Zeitgeist" had a key role for the *Vormärz* generation and for Gervinus, who turned it from a neutral concept into one that emphasized the tendency in history toward progress and liberty. See in this regard Bernd Hüppauf, especially his complex and stimulating "Einleitung" to *Literaturgeschichte zwischen Revolution und Reaktion: Aus den Anfängen der Germanistik, 1830–1870,* ed. Bernd Hüppauf (Frankfurt: Athenäum Verlag, 1972), 14–15.

10. Gervinus, *Geschichte der poetischen National-Literatur der Deutschen,* vol. 4, 270.

11. See Heinrich Heine, "The Romantic School," in *The Romantic School and Other Essays,* ed. Jost Hermand and Robert C. Holub (New York: Continuum, 1985).

12. Heinrich Heine, "Concerning the History of Religion and Philosophy in Germany," in *The Romantic School and Other Essays,* ed. Hermand and Holub.

13. Gervinus, *Geschichte der poetischen National-Literatur der Deutschen,* vol. 5, 735. (Der Wettkampf der Kunst ist vollendet; jetzt sollten wir uns das andere Ziel stecken, das noch kein Schütze getroffen hat, ob uns auch da Apollon den Ruhm gewährt, den er uns dort nicht versagte.)

14. See Gotthard Erler's introduction to G. G. Gervinus, *Schriften zur Literatur,* 62 ff.

15. Gervinus, *Geschichte der poetischen National-Literatur der Deutschen,* vol. 5, 507.

16. Gervinus, *Geschichte der poetischen National-Literatur der Deutschen,* vol. 5, 509, 516, 582 ff., 637 ff., 706 ff.

17. Gervinus, *Geschichte der poetischen National-Literatur der Deutschen,* vol. 5, 638. (Grillen des Alters.)

18. See Viktor Žmegač: "For the science of literature outside *Germanistik* and outside Germany the notion of 'Weimar Classicism' is only a construction of German Studies and has no binding value beyond the national context." "Zur Klassik-Diskussion: Terminologische Fragen und kein Ende," *Jahrbuch der deutschen Schillergesellschaft,* 33 (1989): 400–408; citation on 407.

19. Gervinus's opinion of the romantic movement was obviously negative. See especially *Geschichte der poetischen National-Literatur der Deutschen,* vol. 5, 582, 637 ff.

20. Hermann Hettner, *Literaturgeschichte des 18. Jahrhunderts* (Braunschweig: Vieweg, 1856–70); Wilhelm Scherer, *Geschichte der deutschen Literatur* (Berlin: Weidmannsche Buchhandlung, 1883). In 1927 Scherer's history ran up to the sixteenth edition.

21. For a general interpretation of Danzel's work see the introductory essay by Hans Mayer, "Danzel als Literaturhistoriker," in Theodor Wilhelm Danzel, *Zur Literatur und Philosophie der Goethezeit: Gesammelte Aufsätze,* ed. H. Mayer (Stuttgart: Metzler 1962), 5–42.

22. Theodor Wilhelm Danzel, "Über die Behandlung der Geschichte der neueren deutschen Literatur," in T. W. Danzel, *Zur Literatur und Philosophie der Goethezeit: Gesammelte Aufsätze,* 286–94; now also in *Deutsche Literaturkritik im 19. Jahrhundert,* ed. Hans Mayer (Frankfurt: Goverts, 1976), 317–27. All quotations are from this last edition; page numbers of this work will henceforth be included in the text, while the original text of the quotations will be provided in the notes.

23. "Ein wechselseitiger Austausch zwischen den verschiedenen Nationalliteraturen und ein gemeinsamer Boden, auf welchem sie alle miteinander standen."

24. ". . . nach 20–30 Jahren."

25. "Geschichte der Literatur ist sonst im allgemeinen wie eine Art von Kunstgeschichte zu betrachten: das heißt, ihre Aufgabe ist, ohne links und rechts zu sehen, die Metamorphosen der poetischen Produktion rein aus dieser selbst aufzustellen."

26. The historian Leopold Ranke had founded the *Historisch-politische Zeitschrift* in 1832, at the request of the Prussian Ministry of Foreign Affairs, for the purpose of representing Prussian conservative views for the German middle class. See in this regard Sibylle Obenaus, *Literarische und politische Zeitschriften 1830–1848* (Stuttgart: Metzler, 1986), 78–79.

27. See also Leopold Ranke, "Über die Epochen der neueren Geschichte," in L. Ranke, *Aus Werk und Nachlaß* (Munich and Vienna: Oldenbourg 1971), vol. 2, 59–60.

28. Theodor Wilhelm Danzel, "Über Goethes Spinozismus," in Danzel, *Zur Literatur und Philosophie der Goethezeit*, 24–126.

29. See Mayer, "Danzel als Literaturhistoriker," 17 ff.

30. Danzel, "Uber Goethes Spinozismus," 53, 59. (Selbsterhaltung des Individuums.)

31. Danzel, "Uber Goethes Spinozismus," 58 (den endlichen Zweck kleinlicher Interessen, die losgelassen und sich bestialisch austummelnde Endlichkeit), 59 (ein Kampf um die Erhaltung eines besseren Selbst). In Hegel *"das Selbst"* is a general name for the Spirit in its purest form of self-moving subject. It thus corresponds to pure concept, pure thought, self-representation, and so on.

32. Danzel, "Uber Goethes Spinozismus," 60 (zu einer höheren Totalität), 63 (zugleich die Methode der Erkenntnis), 81 (eine ruhige Anschauung der Dinge in ihrer ewigen Wesenheit), 87 (in sich selbst zum Ewigen).

33. See Bernd Peschken's penetrating essay "Gervinus und Danzel als Vertreter entgegengesetzter Richtungen der Literaturauslegung," *Monatshefte,* 63: 3 (1971): 209–19.

34. See Stefan Breuer, *Ästhetischer Fundamentalismus* (Darmstadt: Wissenschaftliche Buchgesellschaft, 1995). For a more general discussion see also Pierre Bourdieu's seminal work *Distinction: A Social Critique of the Judgement of Taste,* trans. Richard Nice (Cambridge, Mass.: Harvard University Press, 1984), in particular the "Postscript: Towards a 'Vulgar' Critique of 'Pure' Critiques," 485 ff.

35. Gervinus, *Leben: Von ihm selbst,* 59–61.

36. Danzel, "Über Goethes Spinozismus," 87. (. . . absolute Anschauung.)

37. See Gunter Reiß's lucid observations in his "Einführung" to *Materialien zur Ideologiegeschichte der deutschen Literaturwissenschaft,* ed. G. Reiß, 2 vols. (Tübingen: Niemeyer, 1973), vol. 1, vii–xli.

38. On the institutionalization of *Literaturwissenschaft,* of literary historiography, and of German Studies there are many studies—mostly written during the 1970s—that focus on the ideological aspects of that process, and other more recent ones that, taking those previous studies as a point of departure, have achieved important results by focusing instead on the very structure of German Studies, seeking to identify and reconstruct the history of its constitutive elements. In the first group, I would especially recommend *Germanistik und deutsche Nation 1806–1840,* ed. Jörg Jochen Müller (Stuttgart: Metzler, 1974); Johannes Janota, "Einleitung," in *Eine Wissenschaft etabliert sich 1810–1870* (Tübingen: Niemeyer, 1980), 1–60; Rainer Rosenberg, *Zehn Kapitel zur Geschichte der Germanistik* (Berlin: Akademie Verlag, 1981); Rainer Rosenberg, *Literaturwissenschaftliche Germanistik* (Berlin: Akademie Verlag, 1989); in the second group, Jürgen Fohrmann, *Das Projekt der deutschen Literaturgeschichte: Entstehung und Scheitern einer nationalen Poesiebeschreibung zwischen Humanismus und Deutschem Kaiserreich* (Stuttgart: Metzler, 1989) and Klaus Weimar, *Geschichte der deutschen Literaturwissenschaft bis zum Ende des 19. Jahrhunderts* (Munich: Fink, 1989). Peter Uwe Hohendahl's work deserves a separate discussion. In *Literarische Kultur im Zeitalter des Liberalismus 1830–1870* (Munich: Beck, 1985) Hohendahl—without losing sight of the ideological import of the subject matter—seeks to reconstruct, on the basis of the category of "literature as institution," the relationship between literary history

and economic, political, and social history. For an extended overview of the present debate see Jürgen Fohrmann and Wilhelm Voßkamp, eds., *Wissenschaft und Nation: Zur Entstehungsgeschichte der deutschen Literaturwissenschaft* (Munich: Fink, 1991); Michel Espagne and Michel Werner, eds., *Philologiques I: Contribution à l'histoire des disciplines littéraires en France et en Allemagne au XIX siècle* (Paris: Editions de la Maison des sciences de l'homme, 1990).

39. Rudolf Haym (1821–1901) was one of the few intellectuals who did not give up his liberal-democratic beliefs after 1848. He wrote, among other things, the monograph *Hegel und seine Zeit: Vorlesungen über Entstehung und Entwicklung, Wesen und Werth der Hegel'schen Philosophie* (Berlin: Gaertner, 1857) and an influential essay on German romanticism: *Die romantische Schule: Ein Beitrag zur Geschichte des deutschen Geistes* (Berlin: Gaertner, 1870). Robert Prutz (1816–72) was one of the most active figures during those years as poet, journalist, historian, and literary critic. A selection of his works has been reprinted as *Zur Theorie und Geschichte der Literatur,* ed. Ingrid Popperle (Berlin: Akademie Verlag, 1981).

40. See Hohendahl, *Literarische Kultur im Zeitalter des Liberalismus,* 225 ff.

41. See Hüppauf, "Einführung" to *Literaturgeschichte zwischen Revolution und Reaktion,* 35.

42. The years 1862–66 witnessed a series of conflicts within the Prussian parliament, opposing the German Progressive Party (*Deutsche Fortschrittspartei,* of liberal-democratic tendencies) and Bismarck's government, about funding the reform of the Prussian army and consequently the state expenditure. Throughout that period, Bismarck governed the country without a parliamentary vote on the state budget. The conflict was solved thanks to the great Prussian victory over Austria (at Königgraz on 3 July 1866), which practically marked the success of the program of national unification under Prussian hegemony, to the exclusion of Austria. On 14 September of the same year, a war reparation act passed by the majority of parliament retrospectively healed the conflict between the Bismarck government and the Prussian Parliament. The same period also witnessed the decline of the German Progressive Party and the success of the new National Liberal Party (the *Nationalliberale Partei,* founded on 12 June 1867), which was more conservative and ready to accept compromises with Bismarck's government about freedom and constitutional rights in the name of national unity.

43. Wilhelm Scherer, "An Karl Müllenhof" (1868), in *Materialien zur Ideologiegeschichte der deutschen Literaturwissenschaft,* vol. 1, 1–2 (System der nationalen Ethik); Wilhelm Dilthey, "Wilhelm Scherer zum persönlichen Gedächtnis" (1886), in *Materialien zur Ideologiegeschichte der deutschen Literaturwissenschaft,* vol. 1, 11–30, citation on 30, also in Wilhelm Dilthey, *Gesammelte Schriften,* vol. 11: *Jugendaufsätze und Erinnerungen,* 2nd ed. (Stuttgart and Göttingen: Teubner 1960), 236–53 (. . . inmitten der materiellen und politischen Interessen unserer Tage).

44. Writing in the liberal-democratic tradition, Hermann Hettner (1821–82) published a successful literary history of the eighteenth century, cited in note 20. Julian Schmidt (1818–86), a professional journalist and literary critic, was the author of a fairly popular *Geschichte der deutschen Literatur seit Lessing's Tod* (Leipzig: Herbig, 1866–69). Dilthey's essay is in Dilthey, *Gesammelte Schriften,* vol. 11, 195–205.

45. Journal entry of 22 February 1865, in Wilhelm Dilthey, *Der junge Dilthey: Ein Lebensbild in Briefen und Tagebüchern 1852–1870,* ed. Clara Misch (Stuttgart: Teubner, 1960), 190. (Das Wesen der Geschichte ist die geschichtliche Bewegung selber, wenn man dieses Wesen Zweck nennen will, so ist sie allein Zweck der Geschichte.)

46. Wilhelm Dilthey, *Das Erlebnis und die Dichtung,* ed. Rainer Rosenberg (Leipzig: Verlag Philipp Reclam jun., 1988).

47. Wilhelm Dilthey, "Die dichterische und philosophische Bewegung in Deutschland 1770–1800" (opening lesson presented at the University of Basel, 1867), in Dilthey, *Gesammelte Schriften,* vol. 5, 12–27, quotes on 13 (geistige Bewegung; in einem geschlossenen und kontinuierlichen Gange), 14 (eines fertigen Nationalgeistes; ein zersplittertes Land).

48. Dilthey, "Die dichterische und philosophische Bewegung in Deutschland," 13. (. . . eine Lebens- und Weltansicht . . . , in welcher der deutsche Geist seine Befriedigung finde.)

49. Dilthey, "Die dichterische und philosophische Bewegung in Deutschland," 17.

50. Dilthey, "Die dichterische und philosophische Bewegung in Deutschland," 15. (. . . persönliche Bildung, geistige Auszeichnung.)

51. On the ideological implications of Dilthey's work in relation to German Studies in Germany see Bernd Peschken, *Versuch einer germanistischen Ideologiekritik: Goethe, Lessing, Novalis, Tieck, Hölderlin, Heine in Wilhelm Diltheys und Julian Schmidts Vorstellungen* (Stuttgart: Metzler 1972), especially 117–71.

52. See Dilthey, *Gesammelte Schriften,* vol. 15, 225 ff.

53. The different role taken on by the history of national literature in the post-1848 political, ideological, and institutional context is lucidly illustrated by Peter Uwe Hohendahl, "Von der politischen Kritik zur Literaturwissenschaft: Zum institutionellen Status der Literaturgeschichte nach 1848," in *Zum Funktionswandel der Literatur,* ed. Peter Bürger (Frankfurt: Suhrkamp, 1983), 194–217.

54. For a definition of *Bildungsbürgertum* see chapter 4, note 9.

55. See Peschken, *Gervinus und Danzel als Vertreter entegegesetzter Richtungen der Literaturauslegung,* 11 ff. See also Hans-Martin Kruckis, "'Ein potenziertes Abbild der Menschheit': Idolatrie und Wissenschaft der Goethe-Biographik bis Gundolf," dissertation, Bielefeld, 1989, and "Goethe-Philologie als Paradigma neuphilologischer Wissenschaft im 19. Jahrhundert," in *Wissenschaftsgeschichte der Germanistik im 19. Jahrhundert,* ed. Jürgen Fohrmann and Wilhelm Voßkamp (Stuttgart: Metzler: 1994), 451–93.

3. The Science of Literature and the Steam Engine

1. Wilhelm Scherer, *Briefwechsel zwischen Karl Müllenhof und Wilhelm Scherer,* ed. Albert Leitzmann (Berlin: de Gruyter, 1937), 160. (. . . kein Staat mehr, sondern eine bloße Polizeianstalt.)

2. Wilhelm Scherer, *Vorträge und Aufsätze zur Geschichte des geistigen Lebens in Deutschland und Österreich* (Berlin: Weidmannsche Buchhandlung, 1874), 300. (. . . beten und erwerben, häusliche und Privattugenden entwickeln.)

3. Scherer, *Briefwechsel zwischen Karl Müllenhof und Wilhelm Scherer,* 174. (. . . die Zeit des Kampfes um die Garantien der Freiheit.)

4. Short typed account of the debate at the Reichstag, session of 20 May 1871; quoted in Franz Greß, *Germanistik und Politik: Kritische Beiträge zur Geschichte einer nationalen Wissenschaft* (Stuttgart: Verlag Frommann-Holzboog, 1971), 60. (. . . durch die Macht der deutschen Waffen, . . . durch die Macht des deutschen Geistes.)

5. Ibid. (. . . Pioniere des deutschen Geistes.)

6. Scherer, *Kleine Schriften,* ed. Konrad Burdach and Erich Schmidt (Berlin: Weidmannsche Buchhandlung, 1893), vol. 2, 22. (. . . Colonistenarbeit.)

7. See Wolfgang Höppner, *Das "Ererbte, Erlebte und Erlernte" im Werk Wilhelm Scherers* (Cologne: Böhlau, 1993), 152. (. . . auch vom politischen Standpunkte besonderen Werth.)

8. By *socialization* I mean the acquisition of lasting norms and behaviors that serve to stabilize society as a whole.

9. I refer especially to *Weimarer Goethe-Ausgabe,* ed. E. Schmidt, H. Grimm, B. Seuffert, and B. Suphan (1887–1919), to *Schiller-Ausgabe,* ed. Karl Goedeke (1867–76), to the editions of Herder by Bernhard Suphan, of Klopstock by Franz Muncker, of Grillparzer and Stifter by August Sauer, and of Kleist by Erich Schmidt. As for biographies, see the biographies of Lessing by E. Schmidt, of Klopstock by F. Muncker, of Schiller by Jakob Minor, and of Goethe by K. Goedeke, Richard M. Meyer, and Albert Bielschowsky.

10. See the interesting introduction by Gunter Reiß in Wilhelm Scherer, *Poetik: Mit einer Einleitung und Materialien zur Rezeption,* ed. G. Reiß (Tübingen: Niemeyer, 1977), ix–xlii. Scherer's works were published posthumously in 1888.

11. Wilhelm Scherer, "An Karl Müllenhof," in *Materialien zur Ideologiegeschichte der deutschen Literaturwissenschaft,* ed. Gunter Reiß, 2 vols. (Tübingen: Niemeyer, 1973), vol. 1, 1–3. (Was jeder für sich wünschen und in bescheidener, aber gründlicher Überlegung zu seiner und zu des Ganzen Wohlfahrt anstreben darf, das wünschen und erstreben wir noch in viel höheren Masse für den menschlichen Verein, dem wir alles Größte und Beste danken, was wir besitzen und unseren echtesten Werth ausmacht: für unsere Nation.)

12. Scherer, "An Karl Müllenhof," vol. 1, 1–2. (. . . ein System der nationalen Ethik; . . . was wir sind und bedeuten.)

13. Scherer, *Kleine Schriften,* vol. 1, 389. (Gegenüber Kosmopolitismus die Nationalität, gegenüber der künstlichen Bildung die Kraft der Natur, gegenüber Centralisation die autonomen Gewalten, gegenüber der Beglückung von oben die Selbstregierung, gegenüber der Allmacht des Staates die individuelle Freiheit, gegenüber dem construirten Ideal die Hoheit der Geschichte, gegenüber der Jagd nach Neuem die Ehrfurcht vor dem Alten, gegenüber dem gemachten Entwickelung, gegenüber Verstand und Schlußverfahren Gemüth und Anschauung, gegenüber der mathematischen Form die organische, gegenüber dem Abstracten das Sinnliche, gegenüber dem Mechanischen das Lebendige.)

14. Scherer, *Kleine Schriften,* vol. 1, 389.

15. Scherer, *Kleine Schriften,* vol. 2, 66. (Die historische Grundkategorie ist die Causalität.)

16. Scherer, "An Karl Müllenhof," 3. (Wir glauben . . . , daß der Determinismus, das demokratische Dogma vom unfreien Willen, diese Centrallehre des Protestantismus, der Eckstein aller wahren Erfassung der Geschichte sei.)

17. Wilhelm Scherer, "Die neue Generation," in Scherer, *Vorträge und Aufsätze zur Geschichte des geistigen Lebens in Deutschland und Österreich,* 408–14; quote on 411. (Dieselbe Macht, welche Eisenbahnen und Telegraphen zum Leben erweckte, dieselbe Macht, welche eine unerhörte Blüte der Industrie hervorrief, die Bequemlichkeit des Lebens vermehrte, die Kriege abkürzte, mit einem Wort die Herrschaft des Menschen über die Natur um einen gewaltigen Schritt vorwärts brachte-dieselbe Macht regiert auch unser geistiges Leben: Sie räumt mit den Dogmen auf, sie gestaltet die Wissenschaften um, sie drückt der Poesie ihren Stempel auf. Die Naturwissenschaft zieht als Triumphator auf dem Siegeswagen einher, an den wir alle gefesselt sind.)

18. It is well known that the relationship between Nietzsche and philology was extremely controversial, although Nietzsche, as a full professor of classic philology, was himself a member of the professional community. Nietzsche never had any followers or anything resembling a "school," and, unlike writers and philosophers, German philologists virtually ignored his work as the product of an *Außenseiter.* Nietzsche dismissed the functionaries of modern culture among whom philologists had an im-

portant position as a "generation of eunuchs," capable only of passively reproducing the values of the dominant class: "Isn't the past great enough to find something in it that doesn't make you appear so ridiculously arbitrary? But as I said, they are a generation of eunuchs." Friedrich Wilhelm Nietzsche, *Unmodern Observations,* general editor William Arrowsmith (New Haven, Conn.: Yale University Press, 1990), 111. Nowadays, when studies in France and the United States have "rephilologized" the philosopher, the histories of German Studies have begun to discuss Nietzsche. See for example the important remarks by Nikolaus Wegmann, "Was heißt einen 'klassischen Text' lesen? Philologische Selbstreflexion zwischen Wissenschaft und Bildung," in *Wissenschaftgeschichte der Germanistik im 19. Jahrhundert,* ed. Jürgen Fohrmann and Wilhelm Voßkamp (Stuttgart: Metzler, 1994), 334–450, in particular 419–41.

19. Quoted in Franz Greß, *Germanistik und Politik,* 43 (. . . Produktionsmittel . . . wie eine Dampfmaschine").

20. Helmut Böhme, *Prolegomena zu einer Sozial- und Wirtschaftsgeschichte Deutschlands im 19. und 20. Jahrhundert* (Frankfurt: Suhrkamp, 1969), 80 (. . . entscheidende prägende Kraft der Entwicklung.)

21. Pietro Rossi, introduction to *Positivismo e società industriale* (Turin: Loescher, 1973), 31.

22. Klaus Laermann, "Was ist literaturwissenschaftlicher Positivismus?" in *Zur Kritik literaturwissenschaftlicher Methodologie,* ed. Viktor Žmegač and Zdenko Škreb (Frankfurt: Athenäum Verlag, 1973), 51–74; quote on 58. (. . . Objektivationen des Geistes der Nation.)

23. Jost Hermand and Evelyn Torton Beck, "The Rise and Fall of Positivism," in *Interpretive Synthesis: The Task of Literary Scholarship* (New York: F. Ungar, 1975), 11–25; quote on 16.

24. Wrote Scherer: "We need particular research projects, where manifest appearance, once it has been recognized with certainty, is traced back to the creative power that called it forth into being" (Wir verlangen Einzeluntersuchungen, in denen die sicher erkannte Erscheinung auf die wirkende Kraft zurückgeführt wird, die sie ins Dasein riefen). Scherer, "Die neue Generation," 411.

25. Hermand and Beck, "The Rise and Fall of Positivism," 16.

26. Wilhelm Scherer, *Aufsätze über Goethe,* ed. Erich Schmidt (Berlin: Weidmannsche Buchhandlung, 1886), 15. On the subtle but crucial differences between Taine's and Scherer's formulas see R. Wellek, *A History of Modern Criticism: 1750–1950,* vol. 4: *The Later Nineteenth Century* (New Haven, Conn.: Yale University Press, 1991), 27–57, 82–86.

27. Laermann, "Was ist literaturwissenschaftlicher Positivismus?" 64. (. . . die Einheit von Leben und Werk.)

28. The *Geschichte der deutschen Literatur* had an extraordinary success: in 1927 it reached the sixteenth edition. Since Scherer's history went only as far as the death of Goethe, it was integrated after 1918 by Oskar Walzel with a section titled *Deutsche Literatur seit Goethes Tod.*

29. Wilhelm Scherer, *Geschichte der deutschen Literatur,* 15th ed. (Berlin: Weidmannsche Buchhandlung, 1922), 20. (. . . drei große Wellen, Berg und Tal in regelmäßiger Abfolge.)

30. Scherer, *Geschichte der deutschen Literatur,* 19. (Um das Jahr 1800 besitzt Deutschland seinen Goethe, seinen Schiller, deren dichterische und gelehrte Genossen und Nachfolger, welche die Bildungszuflüsse aus französischen, englischen, antiken und älteren einheimischen Quellen in sich vereinigen, läutern und dem nationalen Leben zuführen. Und wieder stehen die alten Heldenlieder auf; die Nibelungen erlangen neuen

Ruhm; neue Poeten ergreifen den Stoff; und die Brüder Grimm werden die Führer einer neuen Wissenschaft, welche die entschwundenen Schöpfungen der Vorzeit mit sorglicher Hand für die Gegenwart zu retten sucht.)

31. On Frederick the Great see the long chapter entitled "Das Zeitalter Friedrichs des Großen," 394–525. Scherer's pro-Prussian attitude led him to retrospectively emphasize the role of Frederick the Great and of his state in the development of national literature. The remarks on the future function of national literature are on p. 719.

32. In the *Geschichte der deutschen Literatur* he curtly dismissed him on p. 644. In another essay his dislike for the author of *Hyperion* was clarified: Hölderlin was a negative and contagious example to the nation. He had fallen victim to a "spiritual epidemy" *(geistige Epidemie)* that after the eighteenth century attacked and destroyed weaker souls. Wrote Scherer: "Nein, unter uns ist kein Raum mehr für den Weltschmerz. Was will da Schopenhauer? Was will da Hölderlin?" Wilhelm Scherer, "Friedrich Hölderlin," in Scherer, *Vorträge und Aufsätze,* 346–55 quote on 353. In this case Scherer dismissed the poet using the same accusations he used against philologists, namely the absence of an ethos and of a positive attitude toward the external world: "The will power was not strong in him" (355). (Die Kraft des Willens war nicht stark in ihm.)

33. Scherer, *Geschichte der deutschen Literatur,* 720. (. . . eine Periode der nationalen Expansion und des wirtschaftlichen Aufschwunges.)

34. Scherer, *Geschichte der deutschen Literatur,* 719. (. . . handeln und wirken.)

35. Scherer, *Geschichte der deutschen Literatur,* 720.

36. Scherer, *Geschichte der deutschen Literatur,* 719.

37. On Scherer as literary critic see Höppner, *Das "Ererbte, Erlebte und Erlernte" im Werk Wilhelm Scherers,* 149 ff.

38. Originally published in the October 1878 issue of the *Deutsche Rundschau,* then in Scherer, *Aufsätze über Goethe,* 47–71.

39. See Adalbert von Hanstein, *Das jüngste Deutschland: Zwei Jahrzehnte miterlebter Literaturgeschichte,* 3rd ed. (Leipzig: R. Voigtländers Verlag, 1905), 6.

40. Scherer, *Kleine Schriften,* vol. 1, 250. (Die Deutschen, die es mit der ästhetischen Bildung ihres Volkes gut meinen, sind aus der Schule der Griechen. In Athen ist ihre geistige Heimat, nicht in der trüben Tiefe des Rheins.)

41. Wilhelm Scherer, *Deutsche Bildnisse: Dichter- und Gelehrenporträts,* ed. Alexander Eggers (Berlin: Deutsche Bibliothek, 1919), 165, 166. (. . . nationales Selbstgefühl der Deutschen; . . . Überhebung.)

42. See the precise overview of these events in Höppner, *Das "Ererbte, Erlebte und Erlernte" im Werk Wilhelm Scherers,* 241 ff.

43. Letter from Scherer to Elias von Steinmeyer, 10 November 1880, now in Wilhelm Scherer and Elias von Steinmeyer, *Briefwechsel 1872–1886,* ed. Horst Brunner, Joachim Helbig, and Ulrich Pretzel (Göppingen: Kümmerle Verlag, 1982), 195. (Gegen unangenehme Briefe Müllenhofs kann wohl weder Ihnen noch irgend einem Sterblichem eine Garantie gegeben werden. Dickfelligkeit ist das einzige Mittel, welches dagegen möglich. Ich selbst habe nicht mehr den geringsten Einfluß auf ihn. Er hat mir übel genommen, daß ich die Ansicht ausgesprochen habe, es sei der deutschen Nation unwürdig, neue Judenverfolgungen einzuleiten. Und seitdem bin ich ihm ein Majestätsverbrecher an den Heiligthümern der deutschen Nation.)

44. Wilhelm Dilthey, "Wilhelm Scherer zum persönlichen Gedächtnis," in *Materialien zur Ideologiegeschichte der deutschen Literaturwissenschaft,* ed. Gunter Reiß, 2 vols. (Tübingen: Niemeyer, 1973), vol. 1, 11–30; quote on 17. (. . . Pietätsverhältnis; . . . in alt deutscher Weise ein Gefolgschaftsverhältnis.)

45. Scherer, *Kleine Schriften,* vol. 1, 59. (. . . Hingabe, Unterordnung, Ehrfurcht, Bescheidenheit, Treue, Festigkeit, Reinheit.)

46. See Wilhelm Scherer, "Wissenschaftliche Pflichten: Aus einer Vorlesung Wilhelm Scherers," in *Materialien zur Ideologiegeschichte der deutschen Literaturwissenschaft,* ed. Reiß, vol. 1, 47–50; quote on 48. These are notes he used for his lessons that were edited by his pupil Erich Schmidt. (. . . Codex philologischer Pflichten.)

47. Scherer, *Kleine Schriften,* vol. 1, 93. (. . . sichere stolze Art; . . . ohne Angaben von Gründen; Man fürchtet ihn, auch wenn man ihn liebt. Ein philologischer Nachwüchsling kann vor ihm einen Schrecken bekommen, wie ein sündiger Enkel, der sich plötzlich vor dem Bilde eines tugendhaften gestrengen Ahnen sieht.)

48. Ernst Elster, "Über den Betrieb der deutschen Philologie an unseren Universitäten" (keynote speech delivered at the Versammlung deutscher Philologen und Schulmänner of 1909), in *Materialien zur Ideologiegeschichte der deutschen Literaturwissenschaft,* ed. Reiß, vol. 1, 72–74; quote on 74. (. . . nicht nur ein Wissen, sondern auch ein Können.)

49. See Konrad Burdach, "Über deutsche Erziehung" (1886), in *Materialien zur Ideologiegeschichte der deutschen Literaturwissenschaft,* ed. Reiß, vol. 1, 3–11.

50. Friedrich Panzer, "Grundsätze und Ziele des deutschen Germanisten-Verbandes," in *Materialien zur Ideologiegeschichte der deutschen Literaturwissenschaft,* vol. 1, 83–91; quote on 87. (. . . ein bequemes Mittel scharfer geistiger Zucht . . . , wie etwa das Üben der Gewehrgriffe oder des Paradeschritts, als ein Mittel militärischer Disziplin.)

51. Jost Hermand, *Literaturwissenschaft und Kunstwissenschaft,* 2nd ed. (Stuttgart: Metzler, 1971), 28. (. . . eine absolute Autonomie des Spirituellen, die sich im Bereich ahistorischer oder phänomenologischer Typologie bewegt.)

4. Wilhelm Dilthey and *Geistesgeschichte*

1. There is an extensive bibliography on the concept of *Geistesgeschichte.* A useful starting point is the collection of essays edited by Christoph König and Eberhard Lämmert, *Literaturwissenschaft und Geistesgeschichte 1910–1925* (Frankfurt: Fischer, 1993). This collection provides a valuable survey of this decisive moment in the history of German Studies, also taking into account the institutional and ideological context.

2. See for example Erik Lunding's entry under *Literaturwissenschaft,* in *Reallexikon der deutschen Literaturgeschichte,* ed. Paul Merker and Wolfgang Stammler, 4 vols. (Berlin: de Gruyter, 1965), vol. 2, 199.

3. György Lukács, *Skizze einer Geschichte der neueren deutschen Literatur* (Berlin: Aufbau Verlag, 1955).

4. Wilhelm Dilthey, *Das Erlebnis und die Dichtung,* ed. Rainer Rosenberg (Leipzig: Verlag Philipp Reclam jun., 1988).

5. Dilthey, *Das Erlebnis und die Dichtung,* 163. (. . . bis zum Dämonischen des Übermenschentums.)

6. Dilthey, *Das Erlebnis und die Dichtung,* 156. (. . . das Gemüt ist der Lebensgrund aller Poesie.)

7. This expression is found in the context of the studies on the establishment of hermeneutics, "Die Entstehung der Hermeneutik" (1900); now in Wilhelm Dilthey, *Gesammelte Schriften,* vol. 5: *Die geistige Welt: Einleitung in die Philosophie des Lebens* (Stuttgart and Göttingen: Teubner, 1964), 317–38; quote on 320. (. . . in der persönlichen genialen Virtuosität des Philologen.)

8. On Dilthey's method see the classic René Wellek, *A History of Modern Criticism: 1750–1950,* vol. 4: *The Later Nineteenth Century* (New Haven, Conn., and London:

Yale University Press,1965), 320–35. See also the penetrating discussion of Dilthey's doctrine in Rainer Rosenberg, "Wilhelm Diltheys 'Verstehenslehre' und das Problem einer wissenschaftlichen Hermeneutik," in Rainer Rosenberg, *Zehn Kapitel zur Geschichte der Germanistik* (Berlin: Akademie Verlag 1981), 139–81.

9. For the *Bildungsbürgertum* I would adopt as a working definition the one provided by cultural sociologist Stefan Breuer: it is a heterogeneous group of the German middle class that began developing in the eighteenth century as a sort of spiritual aristocracy based on the humanistic values of German classicism. It arose from an opposition to feudal society and with the advent of mass society it concentrated its energies on opposing the diffusion of modern mass-culture: see Breuer's entry *Bildungsbürgertum,* in *Anatomie der konservativen Revolution* (Darmstadt: Wissenschaftliche Buchgesellschaft, 1993). Those who wish to further explore the theme of *Bildungsbürgertum* might usefully consult *Bildungsbürgertum im 19. Jahrhundert,* vol. 1, ed. Werner Conze and Jürgen Kocka (Stuttgart: Klett-Cotta, 1985), vol. 2, ed. Reinhart Kosellek (Stuttgart: Klett-Cotta, 1990).

10. See Paul Gorceix's observations in his concise and penetrating study *Les grandes étapes de l'histoire littéraire allemande* (Paris: Presses Universitaires de France, 1977), 59.

11. Rudolf Unger, "Philosophische Probleme in der neueren Literaturwissenschaft," in *Gesammelte Studien,* vol. 1: *Aufsätze zur Prinzipienlehre der Literaturgeschichte* (lecture presented in 1907, published in 1908; reprint Darmstadt: Wissenschaftliche Buchgesellschaft, 1966), 1–32; quote on 1. (. . . die Methode der klassischen Philologie in die Germanistik; . . . in vollem Umfange und voller Strenge.) Page numbers of this work will henceforth be included parenthetically in the text, original language in the notes.

12. (. . . prinzipienlose Willkür.)

13. (Einmal wurde dadurch in der Tat der organische Zusammenhang der neueren deutschen Literaturgeschichte mit der Wissenschaft von den älteren Perioden der deutschen Literatur und mit der Sprachwissenschaft hergestellt oder enger gestaltet. Daß darin ein entschiedener Fortschritt lag, bedarf keiner besonderen Begründung. Wohl aber ist darauf hinzuweisen, daß durch diese Verbindung mit der älteren und längst als vollbürtige Wissenschaft anerkannten Germanistik die neuere Literaturgeschichte auch in jenen Kreisen zu wissenschaftlicher Geltung gelangte, denen sie bisher mehr oder minder als schöngeistiger Dilettantismus gegolten hatte. In engem Zusammenhang damit stand es, daß nun auch an den Universitäten die Vertretung dieser Disziplin, die bisher meist Philosophen, Ästhetikern oder Kunsthistorikern als Nebenfunktion überlassen worden war oder ganz gefehlt hatte, in die Hände geschulter Germanisten kam. Auch die germanistischen Fachzeitschriften öffneten nun nach und nach ihre Spalten den Forschungen über die literarische Entwicklung der Neuzeit, und bald begannen diese sich auch periodische Organe zu schaffen. Durch all dies schien tatsächlich der Dilettantismus, der sich bisher auf diesem Gebiet breit gemacht hatte, entschieden zurückgedrängt werden zu sollen. Ferner wuchs durch Verwertung jener genannten methodischen Gesichtspunkte der jungen Wissenschaft eine Fülle neuer Anregungen und Probleme zugleich mit den Mitteln und Wegen zu ihrer Bearbeitung zu, wovon alsbald die rege Tätigkeit zeugte, die insbesondere auf dem Gebiet der Textkritik (Goethe, Schiller, Herder, Lessing, usw.), der Entstehungsgeschichte einzelner Dichtungen, der Quellen-, Motiv- und Typenforschung, dann auch der internationalen Literaturbeziehungen, der biographischen und bibliographischen Studien, der Theatergeschichte usw. einsetzte. Ein reicher Quell von fruchtbaren Anregungen und belebender Kraft ging so aus von dieser "philologischen" Bewegung, wie ich Scherers Richtung in Analogie zur psychologistischen in der Philosophie, mit der sie ja die empiristische Grundtendenz teilt, nennen möchte.)

14. (Allen tieferen und schwierigeren Problemen der Literaturwissenschaft gegenüber hat die philologistische Methode im Grunde versagt.)

15. (. . . Irrtum.)

16. Rosenberg, *Zehn Kapitel zur Geschichte der Germanistik*, 187. (Hypertrophie der Einfluß-Forschung.) The German for the terms quoted from Unger are "wechselseitige Erhellung der Künste," "Jagd," and "eine Art wissenschaftlichen Sports."

17. (. . . individuelle Eigenart des einzelnen; . . . organisch gewachsene innere Besonderheit; . . . der äußeren Erscheinung und Daseinsform.)

18. (Je mehr man von den elementaren Aufgaben der Textbehandlung zu den umfassenderen und tieferen Problemen fortschritt, desto dringlicher sah man sich genötigt, aus der philologischen Abschließung herauszutreten und sich mit Psychologie, Ästhetik und noch manchen anderen nichtphilologischen Wissenszweigen zu befreunden.)

19. (. . . Welt- und Lebensauffassung.)

20. (. . . in rein stofflicher Hinsicht.)

21. (Das innere Leben des Individuums wie der Gemeinschaften kompliziert und vertieft sich immer mehr; die Bedingungen geistiger Beeinflußung, geistiger Verarbeitung und geistigen Schaffens werden immer mannigfaltigere und verwickeltere: alles dies natürlich in um so höherem Maße, je bedeutender, umfassender, genialer eine Persönlichkeit ist. Damit vervielfachen, komplizieren und vertiefen sich auch die Aufgaben der Literaturwissenschaft in wachsendem Maße, und zwar speziell in psychologischer Hinsicht. Jetzt gilt es, in erster Linie vom Buche zum Menschen durchzudringen, alle Literatur als Ausdruck inneren, seelischen Lebens zu verstehen. Der organische Zusammenhang zwischen dem äußeren und namentlich dem inneren Leben und dessen schriftstellerischen Äußerungen muß erforscht, die Eigenart und Entwicklung dieses inneren Lebens, die Entfaltung der individuellen Anlagen wie die unmittelbaren und mittelbaren Einwirkungen, die diese durch Erziehung, Umwelt, Leben, Lektüre, Zeitgeist erfahren, müssen ergründet werden. Nur durch die Einsicht in diese subjektiven, persönlichen Grundlagen der schriftstellerischen Produktion wird ein wirklich eindringendes Verständnis der Früchte dieser Produktion gewonnen, der literarischen Werke. Denn diese Werke tragen, entsprechend dem ganzem geistigen Charakter der Neuzeit, im Gegensatz zu denen der älteren Perioden im allgemeinen ein ausgesprochen persönliches Gepräge. Stoff und Formgebung erscheinen hier, und zwar durchschnittlich in um so höheren Grade, je bedeutender ihre Schöpfer sind, ungleich individueller durchgebildet, so daß das objektive Interesse an ihnen als solchen weit zurücktritt gegenüber der Frage nach ihrer subjektiven Gestaltung im Einzelfalle und nach dem individuellen Innenleben und der schriftstellerischen Persönlichkeit, als deren Ausdruck diese Gestaltung kundgibt.)

22. Unger's work had the significant subtitle "Zur Frage geisteshistorischer Synthese, mit besonderer Beziehung zu Wilhelm Dilthey." It is now in Unger, *Gesammelte Studien*, vol. 1, 137–70.

23. (. . . etwas Fremdes.)

24. Unger, "Literaturgeschichte als Problemgeschichte," in Unger, *Gesammelte Studien*, vol. 1, 159 ff.

25. With the term "aesthetic fundamentalism" Breuer is referring, in my opinion, to a rejection of the modern rationalization of the world in favor of an absolute aesthetic existence, a rejection of which George and his circle are an excellent example. See Stefan Breuer, *Ästhetischer Fundamentalismus: Stefan George und der deutsche Antimodernismus* (Darmstadt: Wissenschaftliche Buchgesellschaft, 1995).

26. Friedrich Gundolf, *Goethe* (Berlin: Georg Bondi, 1916), 27. (. . . das religiöse, das titanische oder das erotische; . . . sein Erlebnis deutscher Vorwelt, Shakespeares, des klassischen Altertums, Italiens, des Orients, selbst sein Erlebnis der deutschen

Gesellschaft.) Page numbers of this work will henceforth be included parenthetically in the text, original language in the notes.

27. (. . . auf die Darstellung von Goethes gesamter Gestalt, der größten Einheit worin deutscher Geist sich verkörpert hat.)

28. (. . . ein Vorher und ein Nachher.)

29. (. . . der Künstler existiert nur insofern er sich im Kunstwerk ausdrückt.)

30. (. . . das Leben eines Künstlers, oder neuerdings das Erleben, ist bereits von vornherein eingetaucht in seine Kunst, ist derselbe Trieb und dieselbe Kraft wie sein Werk.)

31. (Der nichtkünstlerische Mensch glaubt, der Künstler, der Dichter erlebe ungefähr dasselbe wie er und auf dieselbe Art, vielleicht ein bißchen abenteuerlicher oder fremdartiger, nur habe er außerdem als ein zufälliges Akzidens die Gabe diese Erlebnisse in Bildern, Gedichten, Musikstücken herausstellen zu können: das sogenannte "Talent." Das gilt auch für die überwältigende Mehrzahl der Hersteller von Bildern, Gedichten, Musikstücken—es gilt nicht für den wirklichen Künstler, den wirklichen Dichter, der alle hundert Jahre einmal auftritt. Dieser erlebt schon in einer so völlig anderen Sphäre und in einer so völlig anderen Form als der unkünstlerische Mensch (in unserer Welt also, als der Bürger aller Stände) daß sein Erleben und der Ausdruck seines Erlebens (beides ist wesentlich eines) von diesem nie verstanden werden kann, auch wo es ihn überwältigt und beherrscht durch seine größere Wirklichkeit. Es ist einer der Unterschiede zwischen Dichtkunst und Literatur, daß jene Ausdruck einer eigenen, von der fertigen Welt unabhängigen Wirklichkeit, diese Abbild, Nachbild einer fertigen Wirklichkeit ist, einerlei ob ein naturalistisches, romantisches oder idealisierendes Abbild. Da der Banause nur eine Wirklichkeit, seine eigene kennt, so meint er überall wo er Wirklichkeit spürt seine eigene wiederzufinden, auch wenn es eine völlig andere ist. So hält er zum Beispiel Shakespeare für einen guten Schilderer der Wirklichkeit. Darauf beruht auch die ganze Theorie von der Kunst als Nachahmung oder die neuere der Einfühlung. Kunst ist weder die Nachahmung eines Lebens noch die Einfühlung in ein Leben, sondern sie ist eine primäre Form des Lebens, die daher ihre Gesetze weder von Religion, noch Moral, noch Wissenschaft, noch Staat, anderen primären oder sekundären Lebensformen, empfängt: keinen anderen Sinn hat der Satz *l'art pour l'art.*)

32. Friedrich Gundolf, *Dichter und Helden* (Heidelberg: Weiss'che Universitätsbuchhandlung, 1921), 49.

33. René Wellek, *A History of Modern Criticism: 1750–1950,* vol. 7: *German, Russian, and Eastern European Criticism, 1900–1950* (New Haven, Conn.: Yale University Press, 1991), 16–17.

34. (. . . eine eigene Gestalt und ein Eigenes Werk; . . . ein eigenes Schicksal; . . . der gewöhnliche Mensch hat bloße Eigenschaften, Meinungen, Beschäftigungen und Erfahrungen die von außen bedingt, nicht von innen erbildet sind. Ebenso hat der gewöhnliche Mensch nur Zufälle, Ereignisse, Begebenheiten von denen er sich treiben oder beeinflußen läßt.)

35. (. . . Kräftekugel; . . . Jahresringe an Bäumen.)

36. (. . . der geheimnisvolle Zeus; . . . sein dämonisches Wissen; . . . ein Evangelium, die Stimme einer heiligen Gestalt.) For Wellek's remarks see Wellek, *A History of Modern Criticism,* vol. 7, 19–20.

37. (. . . mit der keuschsten und bescheidensten Ehrfurcht.)

38. (Goethe ist der einzige Deutsche der jene Harmonie völlig erreicht hat, er ist deshalb unser vorzugsweise klassischer Mensch.)

39. Gundolf, *Dichter und Helden,* 44. (Die erste Aufgabe und Folge aller Bildung [ist] die Ehrfurcht wachzuhalten: den Sinn für Würde und Größe des Menschen.)

40. See in this regard Rainer Kolk, "Reflexionformel und Ethikangebot," in *Literaturwissenschaft und Geistesgeschichte,* ed. König and Lämmert, 38–45.

41. *Literaturwissenschaft und Geistesgeschichte,* ed. König and Lämmert, 39.

42. *Euphorion* 1: 1 (1894): 1–4. Now in *Materialien zur deutschen Ideologiegeschichte der deutschen Literaturwissenschaft,* ed. Gunter Reiß, 2 vols. (Tübingen: Niemeyer, 1973), vol. 1, 47–50; quote on 48. (. . . niederen Pflichten.)

43. *Euphorion* 1: 1 (1894): 48.

44. August Sauer, "Literaturgeschichte und Volkskunde," rectorate speech presented at Karl-Ferdinand-Universität in Prague on 18 November 1907, 4. (. . . die eigentlich nationale Seite unserer Literaturgeschichte.)

45. Sauer, "Literaturgeschichte und Volkskunde," 4. (. . . der einzelnen deutschen Stämmen, Landschaften, Provinzen und Länder.)

46. Sauer, "Literaturgeschichte und Volkskunde," 5. (. . . des Bodens, . . . des Volksstammes.)

47. Sauer, "Literaturgeschichte und Volkskunde," 8. (. . . Blutmischung.)

48. Sauer, "Literaturgeschichte und Volkskunde," 14–15. (. . . Hyperkultur, Ästhetentum, Spekulation, Künstelei, Spielerei, Virtuosentum.)

49. Josef Nadler, quoted in F. Greß, *Germanistik und Politik: Kritische Beiträge zur Geschichte einer nationalen Wissenschaft* (Stuttgart: Frommen Holzboog Verlag, 1971), 134. (. . . Programm und Kommentar einer umfassenden Kulturpolitik. Literaturgeschichte soll keine Kathederangelegenheit sein, sondern kulturpädagogische Einsicht und kulturpolitische Handweisung werden.)

50. On this issue see Greß, *Germanistik und Politik,* 133.

51. See, for example, Viktor Suchy, "Josef Nadler und die österreichische Literaturgeschichte," *Wort in der Zeit,* 9 (1963), 3rd series, 19–30.

52. Josef Nadler, *Literaturgeschichte der deutschen Stämmen und Landschaften,* vol. 1 (Regensburg: Habbel, 1912), vii. (. . . Blut und Erde.)

53. Nadler, *Literaturgeschichte der deutschen Stämmen und Landschaften,* 6. (Das wirtschaftliche Problem steht im innigsten Zusammenhange mit den einzelnen Landschaften, mit dem Boden und seinen Gaben und den Stämmen, die von ihrer Heimat erzogen wurden. Literatur und Kunst, als ein Überschuß wirtschaftlicher Kräfte, mitbewegt von den Bedingungen und Erträgnissen materieller Arbeit, können dort erklärt und begriffen werden, wo der Mensch mit tausend Fasern an einem bestimmten Erdfleck festgewachsen ist, wieder nur aus der Gesamtheit aller Wirkungen, die zwischen Heimat und Abkunft spielen.)

54. Nadler, *Literaturgeschichte der deutschen Stämmen und Landschaften,* vol. 2, 5. (. . . Blutgemeinschaften.)

55. On Nadler's racism and anti-Semitism see the numerous instances cited by Greß and the accompanying commentary (Greß, *Germanistik und Politik,* 147).

56. Nadler, *Literaturgeschichte der deutschen Stämmen und Landschaften,* vol. 3, 9. (Romantik ist die Krönung des ostdeutschen Siedelwerkes, als das gemischte Blut langsam zur Ruhe gekommen war, die Verdeutschung der Seele nach der Verdeutschung der Erde und des Blutes. Und wenn man die Augen in die weiteste erkennbare Ferne kreisen läßt: Romantik war das Umschalten der einstmals slawischen Völker zwischen Elbe und Memel von Ostrom auf Westrom, vom griechischen zum lateinischen Wesen, vom Morgenland zum Abendland.)

57. Nadler, *Literaturgeschichte der deutschen Stämmen und Landschaften,* vol. 3, 9. (. . . mit der Stunde, da die Neustämme geboren wurden: Sie war das Erwachsen des deutschen Blutes in den eingedeutschten Völkern. . . . Deutsch wurde der Osten erst in der Romantik.)

58. Unger, for example, had criticized Nadler's positions as a mixture of "popular Romanticism and sociological positivism." See Rudolf Unger, "Die Vorbereitung der Romantik in der ostpreußischen Literatur des 18. Jahrhunderts: Betrachtungen zur stammeskundlichen Literaturgeschichte," in Unger, *Gesammelte Studien,* vol. 1, 176. (. . . volkhafter Romantik und soziologischem Positivismus.)

59. "Erklärung der Hochschullehrer des deutschen Reiches," now in Klaus Röther, *Die Germanistenverbände und ihre Tagungen* (Cologne: Pahl-Rugenstein Verlag, 1980), 156. (Im deutschen Heere ist kein anderer Geist als in dem deutschen Volke, denn beide sind eins und wir gehören auch dazu.)

60. Only after Roethe's death (1926) were the procedures for this second chair resumed. After they came to power, the National Socialists assigned it to their specialists (Gerhard Fricke first, then Franz Koch). The controversy—reconstructed on the basis of unpublished documents by Wolfgang Höppner in "Eine Institution wehrt sich: Das Berliner Germanische Seminar und die deutsche Geistesgeschichte," in *Literaturwissenschaft und Geistesgeschichte 1910–1925,* 362–80—constitutes an extraordinary combination of academic stupidity, individual narcissism and arrogance, political and cultural conservatism, corporate defense of one's school, anti-Semitism, and whatnot.

61. *Zeitschrift für Deutsche Bildung,* 1 (1925): 1. (Es ist die Bildung des Deutschen zum Deutschen, die Verwurzelung der deutschen Einzelseele in der deutschen Volksseele. Es handelt sich heute nicht nur um die Erziehung zum Gemeinschaftsmenschen, es geht um die Erziehung zum bewußten deutschen Staatsbürger. Und der Weg der Erziehung zum deutschen Staatsbewußtsein führt über die Erziehung zum deutschen Volksbewußtsein, und die Erziehung zum Volksbewußtsein geht über die Erziehung zum deutschen Heimatbewußtsein. In der Heimat liegt das Geheimnis aller Urkräfte völkischen Staatslebens beschloßen. Von der engeren Heimat zum deutschen Volk und vom deutschen Volk zum deutschen Staat, das ist der Weg, den unsere Jugend gehen soll.)

62. Julius Petersen, "Literaturwissenschaft und Deutschkunde," now in *Materialien zur Ideologiegeschichte der deutschen Literaturwissenschaft,* vol. 2, 19–34; quote on 20. (. . . Kanäle vaterländischer Wissenschaft . . . zu einem großen Strom.)

63. Petersen, "Literaturwissenschaft und Deutschkunde," 33. (. . . verloren in materialistischem Chaos; die nationalpädagogischen Aufgaben.)

64. Petersen, "Literaturwissenschaft und Deutschkunde," 33. (Wo können führerlos wir besser leitende Kräfte hernehmen als aus der vaterländischen Geschichte und aus dem Nacherleben großer Persönlichkeiten unserer Vergangenheit?)

65. Petersen, "Literaturwissenschaft und Deutschkunde," 33. (. . . Selbsterkenntnis, . . . Selbstgefühl, . . . Selbstbewußtein, . . . Selbsterziehung.)

66. Hermann Nohl, "Deutsche Bewegung und die idealistischen Systeme," originally published in 1912; now in Hermann Nohl, *Die deutsche Bewegung: Vorlesungen und Aufsätze zur Geistesgeschichte von 1770–1830* (Göttingen: Vandenhoeck und Ruprecht, 1970).

5. German Studies in the Years of National Socialism

1. On National Socialist cultural policy and on its apparent contradictions see Jan-Peter Barbian, *Literaturpolitik im "Dritten Reich," Institutionen, Kompetenzen, Betätigungsfelder* (Frankfurt: Buchhändler-Vereinigung, 1993). On the situation in German Studies see Gerd Simon's *Einleitung* to *Germanistik in den Planspielen des Sicherheitsdienstes der SS,* ed. Gerd Simon, *Teil I: Einleitung und Text* (Tübingen: Verlag der Gesellschaft für interdisziplinäre Forschung, 1998), ix–lxvi. I wish to thank

Gerd Simon for allowing me to benefit from the results of his research, then not yet published, at an early stage of my work.

2. The *Gutachten* are written statements by experts (university professors, political officials, or police commissars) on the scientific, personal, or political qualifications of candidates to a post. Obviously when civil liberties were being curtailed, more weight was given to political evaluations of candidates, whereas in more democratic political climates the criteria established by the discipline have been the determining ones.

3. See also Holger Dainat, "Anpassungsprobleme einer nationalen Wissenschaft," in *Atta Troll tanzt noch: Selbstbesichtigungen der Literaturwissenschaftlichen Germanistik im 20. Jahrhundert,* ed. Petra Boden and Holger Dainat (Berlin: Akademie Verlag, 1997), 103–26.

4. Walter Dietze, *Georg Witkowski (1863–1939)* (Leipzig: Karl Marx Universität, 1973), 41.

5. See Peter Sturm's important work *Literaturwissenschaft im Dritten Reich: Germanistische Wissensformationen und politisches System* (Vienna: Edition Praesens, 1995), 226–29.

6. Klaus Weimar, "Deutsche Deutsche," in *Atta Troll tanzt noch,* ed. Boden and Dainat, 127–37; citation on 131.

7. See Gudrun Schnabel, "Gerhard Fricke: Karriereverlauf eines Literaturwissenschaftlers nach 1945," in *Deutsche Literaturwissenschaft 1945–1965: Fallstudien zu Institutionen, Diskursen, Personen,* ed. Petra Boden and Rainer Rosenberg (Berlin: Akademie Verlag, 1997), 61–84.

8. See Barbian *(Literaturpolitik im "Dritten Reich"),* who, along with giving examples of sheer repression, also describes the intense cultural and literary life, not devoid of internal contrasts, that was characteristic of National Socialist culture in its various components.

9. Hans-Ulrich Thamer, "Das Dritte Reich: Interpretationen, Kontroversen und Probleme des aktuellen Forschungsstandes," in *Deutschland 1933–1945: Neue Studien zur nationalsozialistischen Herrschaft,* ed. Karl Dietrich Bracher, Manfred Funke, and Hans Adolf Jacobsen (Düsseldorf: Droste, 1992), 507–41; citation on 513.

10. Karl Viëtor, letter to Erich Rothacker, July 1934, quoted in Dainat, "Anpassungsprobleme einer nationalen Wissenschaft," 106. (. . . parteimässige[r] Gleichschaltung.)

11. Viëtor, letter to Erich Rothacker, 114. (. . . in politischer Hinsicht . . . keine Bedenken, . . . untragbar . . . , weil der Einsatz derart eindeutig weltanschaulich katholisch bestimmter Persönlichkeiten für die Partei unmöglich ist.)

12. Viëtor, letter to Erich Rothacker, 119.

13. Simon, *Germanistik in den Planspielen des Sicherheitsdienstes der SS,* 64. (Die Zusammenarbeit zwischen Rassenkunde und Germanistik ist eines der vordringlichsten Probleme beider Wissenschaften. Die bisherigen Versuche auf beiden Seiten sind lediglich Ansätze und *zum Teil* noch unbefriedigend. In diesem Zusammenhang ist für die Germanistik wichtig eine Auseinandersetzung mit der stammeskundlichen Literaturgeschichte von Prof. Josef Nadler, Literaturhistoriker an der Universität Wien.)

14. Dainat cites other cases in which, because of contrasting *Gutachten,* certain scholars had to renounce their ambitions. See Dainat, "Anpassungsprobleme einer nationalen Wissenschaft," 119–21.

15. In Reichsstelle zur Förderung des deutschen Schrifttums, *Lektorenbrief der Reichsstelle zur Förderung des deutschen Schrifftums,* 1 (1938), 3rd series, 1. (Es muss aber bei klarer und nüchterner Betrachtung gesagt werden, dass die nationalsozialistische Weltanschauung auf dem Boden der Geisteswissenschaften nur langsam Neuland

gewinnt, bzw. gewonnen hat. Das kann auch nicht anders sein, angesichts der Tatsache, dass gerade hier einseitiger Intellektualismus und bindungslose Geistigkeit, sowie eine hoffnungslose Aufspaltung und Zerfahrenheit der Methoden und Standpunkte sowie ein ausgesprochener Alexandrismus [sic], wie man wohl sagen kann, am ungehemmtessten sich entfaltet hat. Eine andere Ursache hierfür ist darin zu suchen, dass in der wissenschaftlichen Forschung noch die ältere Generation überwiegt und die jüngere erst allmählich das Feld besetzt.)

16. Rössner, an intelligent Germanist and author of penetrating works on the *George-Kreis* (the George circle, an influential group of writers and intellectuals during the Weimar period), enrolled in 1933 in the SA and then pursued his career in the SS and in the Security Service, becoming in 1940 the director of the Ableitung III C 3 "Kunst und Volkskultur" of the SS Security Service. In 1948 he was sentenced to a fine of 2,000 marks for "belonging to an organization declared as criminal," but in 1950 he was "denazified" and inserted in group IV, that of the *Mitläufer* ("sympathizers") of National Socialism. He later worked as a reader for the Piper publishing house in Munich. On his life see Simon, introduction to *Germanistik in den Planspielen des Sicherheitsdienstes der SS,* xx–xxii. Page numbers of this work will henceforth be included parenthetically in the text, original language in the notes.

17. (Im Rahmen der weltanschaulichen Neuordnung und Kulturpolitik des nationalsozialistischen Staates fällt allen Wissenschaften, die die Geschichte und das Wesen des germanisch-deutschen Menschen und seiner kulturellen Leistungen erarbeiten, erhöhte und lebenswichtige Bedeutung zu. Auch die Germanistik als Wissenschaft von der Geschichte und vom Wesen der germanisch-deutschen Sprache und Dichtung erhält dabei eine entscheidende Aufgabe, die weit über die Grenzen eines nur fachlichen Wissenschaftsbetriebes hinausreicht. . . . Sie hat das geschichtliche Material wissenschaftlich zu erfassen und für den kulturpolitischen Einsatz aufzuarbeiten. Insbesondere muss sie in der sprachlichen und dichterischen Überlieferung des germanisch-deutschen Volkstums die germanischen Grundwerte so aufzeigen, dass sie zum geistigen Besitz aller Volksgenossen, insbesondere des sogenannten akademischen Nachwuchses, und das heißt vor allem der kommenden deutschen Lehrerschaft, werden.)

18. (Es ist auch heute noch festzustellen, dass die Germanistik als Wissenschaft vom germanisch-deutschen Wesen und Menschentum, wie es in der Sprache Ausdruck und Gestalt gefunden hat, ihre große Aufgabe und Chance, die ihr durch die nationalsozialistische Revolution geboten wurde, noch in keiner Weise voll erkannt hat. Im Gegenteil ist festzustellen, dass gerade auf dem kulturpolitisch lebenswichtigen Gebiet der Germanistik noch ein ausgesprochen liberaler Wissenschaftsbetrieb herrscht, in dem eine Menge von gegnerischen oder zumindest reaktionären und liberalen Kräften noch immer am Werk ist.)

19. (Große einheitliche Gesamtplanung.) By "aesthetic vision" the report refers to a self-referential art that does not look for inspiration to the reality of the nation or the people.

20. The accusation of spiritualism was directed especially at the members of the *George-Kreis,* to which Rössner, also on account of the Jewish origins of some of its members, ascribed the tendency to see the poet as a "great aristocratic and creative figure in a free 'New *Reich*' of the pure spirit" (grosse, aristokratische, schöpferische Gestalt in einem freien 'Neuen Reich' des reinen Geistes) (8).

21. (. . . als nicht ernst zu nehmende Sonderlinge und Halbwissenschaftler.)

22. (. . . Literaturpapst; . . . der erzieherische Ansatz und die kulturpolitische Aufgabe der Germanistik.)

23. (. . . gegen die zunehmende bolschewistische Zersetzung unseres deutschen Literaturbetriebs und der sprachlichen Ausdrucksformen.)

24. (. . . fachwissenschaftlich im strengen Sinn.)

25. The actual title of the journal was *Deutsche Vierteljahrsschrift für Literaturwissenschaft und Geistesgeschichte.*

26. Heinz Kindermann, full professor at Münster university, was evaluated in the following terms: "The evaluation is positive, he has unclear ties with Catholicism" (Wird positiv beurteilt, katholische Bindungen unklar) (12). On the following page of the report he was listed among the "Positive Wissenschaftler," that is, those who could be regarded as "impeccable or at least ready for action" from the scientific, ideological, and political point of view (einwandfrei oder zumindest als besonders einsatzbereit) (13).

27. (Ihr kulturpolitischer und erzieherischer Einsatz beschränkt sich weder auf den Rahmen der Hochschule und wissenschaftlichen Forschungsrichtungen, noch erschöpft er sich in der fachlichen Ausbildung des akademischen Nachwuchses. Er liegt vielmehr wesentlich darin, die Grundwerte der neuen Weltanschauung aus der sprachlichen Überlieferung des gesamten Volkstums rein herauszuarbeiten, sie überhaupt wieder voll sichtbar uns zum geistigen Besitz aller Volksgenossen zu machen. Die Germanistik hat darüber hinaus ein wissenschaftliches einwandfreies Bild zu erarbeiten von der Verbreitung, dem Einfluss und der Wirkung des germanisch-deutschen Erbstromes, soweit er in der Sprache und Dichtung greifbar wird, im europäischen und aussereuropäischen Kulturraum und seinen rassisch und politisch anders geformten Volktümern.)

28. (. . . Germanenkunde, Rassenkunde, Vorgeschichte, Kunstgeschichte, Geschichte, Volkskunde.)

29. (. . . von den persönlichen Wünschen des Ordinarius.)

30. There was an explicit mention of "certain specialist sectors of Oriental Studies, Classic Philology, etc." (gewisse Spezialgebiete der Orientalistik, der Altphilologie usw) (68).

31. (. . . einen gesunden Ausgleich.)

32. (. . . gerade liberale Germanisten suchten sich . . . eine weltanschauliche und politiche Deckung zu verschaffen.)

33. On the definition of "cultural arbitrary" see the opening chapter of Pierre Bourdieu and Jean-Claude Passeron, *Reproduction in Education, Society and Culture,* trans. Richard Nice, with a foreword by Tom Bottomore (London, Thousand Oaks, Calif., and New Delhi: Sage, 1990). Page numbers of this work will henceforth be included parenthetically in the text.

34. See also Wolfgang Keim, *Erziehung unter der Nazi-Diktatur,* 2 vols. (Darmstadt: Wissenschaftliche Buchgesellschaft, 1995).

35. Petersen had even titled one of his works *Die Sehnsucht nach dem Dritten Reich in deutscher Sage und Dichtung* (The yearning for the Third Reich in German legends and poetry) (Stuttgart: Metzler, 1934), manifesting all his enthusiasm for the new Reich and for the Führer.

36. Simon, *Germanistik in den Planspielen des Sicherheitsdienstes der SS,* 13.

37. Simon, *Germanistik in den Planspielen des Sicherheitsdienstes der SS,* 68. (. . . liberale Führung.)

38. Jost Hermand, *Geschichte der Germanistik* (Reinbek: Rowohlt, 1994), 100.

39. See Klaus Weimar's penetrating "Deutsche Deutsche," in *Atta Troll tanzt noch,* ed. Boden and Dainat, 127–37.

40. On the political and ideological implications of Celtic studies see Joachim Lerchenmüller's illuminating study *"Keltischer Sprengstoff": Eine wissenschaftgeschichtliche Studie über die deutsche Keltologie von 1900 bis 1945* (Tübingen: Niemeyer, 1997).

41. The research on romanticism between 1933 and the years after 1945 is the subject of an interesting chapter in Markus Gärtner, *Kontinuität und Wandel in der*

neueren deutschen Literaturwissenschaft nach 1945 (Bielefeld: Aisthesis Verlag, 1997), 188–282.

42. Hellmuth Langenbucher, *Deutsche Dichtung in Vergangenheit und Gegenwart* (Berlin: Bong, 1937); Walther Linden, *Geschichte der deutschen Literatur von den Anfängen bis zur Gegenwart* (Leipzig: Reclam, 1937); Heinz Kindermann, *Die deutsche Gegenwartsdichtung im Aufbau der Nation* (Berlin: Junge Generation, 1936); Franz Koch, *Geschichte der deutschen Dichtung* (Hamburg: Hanseatische Verlagsanstalt, 1937); Karl Justus Obenauer, *Volkhafte und politische Dichtung* (Leipzig: Armanen, 1936); Adolf Bartels, *Geschichte der deutschen Literatur,* 16th ed. (Braunschweig: Westermanns, 1937); Benno von Wiese, *Dichtung und Volkstum* (Frankfurt: Klostermann, 1933).

43. One of the merits of Barbian's *Literaturpolitik im "Dritten Reich"* is that of reconstructing the complex network of relations and mediations between National Socialist writers (and their various associations) and the institutions of the Third Reich, designed to stimulate and propagate the new literature throughout the nation.

44. See Dainat, "Anpassungsprobleme einer nationalen Wissenschaft," 116.

45. My expression "philological capital" is meant as a reference to the broader notion of "cultural capital": by "cultural capital," analogous to economic capital, Bourdieu designates what is accumulated through investments (study, training), what is transmitted through inheritance (the chair, commanding positions in research institutes), and the possibility of making profits (on an economic and cultural level, both on the plane of social relations, thus increasing one's social capital, and on the symbolic plane, thus increasing one's symbolic capital). For a definition of the various types of capital see Pierre Bourdieu, *Distinction: A Social Critique of the Judgement of Taste,* trans. Richard Nice (Cambridge, Mass: Harvard University Press, 1984). Most of Bourdieu's sociology of culture, to which I refer in this book, revolves around these categories.

46. Franz Koch and Gerhard Fricke, "Einladung an die Hochschulgermanisten zur Beteiligung am 'Kriegseinsatz der Germanistik'" (1940), now in *Im Vorfeld des Massenmords: Germanistik im 2. Weltkrieg,* ed. Joachim Lerchenmüller and Gerd Simon (Tübingen: Verlag der Gesellschaft für interdisziplinäre Forschung, 1997), 70. (Der gegenwärtige Krieg ist in besonderem Masse nicht nur eine militärische sondern zugleich eine geistig-kulturelle Auseinandersetzung, in der auch über die geistige Ordnung Europas entschieden wird. Daher gilt es gerade auch für die deutsche Geisteswissenschaft, in dieser entscheidenden geschichtlichen Stunde aktiv zu sein, die geistespolitische Lage mit weiter Sicht zu durchdringen und die Ideen vorzubereiten und zu klären, auf denen ein neues Europa politisch-kulturell errichtet werden kann. Neben den Naturwissenschaften, deren praktischer Einsatz unmittelbar einleuchtet und in breitester Grundlage im Gang ist, hat die Geisteswissenschaft in diesem Entscheidungkampf um die deutsche und europäische Zukunft ihre eigene wichtige Ausgabe. Indem auch sie sich entschlossen einreiht in die geistige Front des alle Deutschen fordernden Krieges, kämpft sie zugleich für ihre eigene, noch keineswegs unangefochtenene Rechtfertigung und Neubegründung.)

47. Lugowski belonged to the new generation of National Socialist scholars. He worked at Königsberg University, one of those positively mentioned in the report, and had still not been accepted among professors (he was still only "Dr." Lugowski), but the sum designated for the publication of the volumes was deposited to his bank account.

48. Franz Koch, *Von deutscher Art in Sprache und Dichtung,* 5 vols. (Stuttgart and Berlin: Kohlhammer 1941), vol. 1, v. (Der totale Krieg, wie wir ihn erleben, ist nicht nur eine militärische, sondern zugleich auch eine geistig kulturelle Auseinandersetzung größten Maßes.)

49. Heinz Otto Burger, "Die deutsche Sendung im Bekenntnis der Dichter," in *Von deutscher Art in Sprache und Dichtung,* vol. 5, 305. (Durch die nationalsozialistische Revolution und den Krieg hat sich das deutsche Volk nicht allein seine gleichberechtigte Stellung unter den europäischen Völkern wieder erobert, es kann sich vielmehr bereits anschicken, den ganzen Erdteil zu erobern.)

6. The Break in Political Continuity and the Continuity of the Disciplinary Apparatus, 1945–1968

1. See Wilhelm Voßkamp, "Literaturwissenschaft als Geisteswissenschaft: Thesen zur Geschichte der deutschen Literaturwissenschaft nach dem Zweiten Weltkrieg," in *Die sogenannten Geisteswissenschaften: Einleitende Bemerkungen,* ed. Wolfgang Prinz and Peter Weingart (Frankfurt: Suhrkamp, 1990), 240–47.

2. Information on this issue is often contradictory: see Marcus Gärtner, *Kontinuität und Wandel in der neueren deutschen Literaturwissenschaft nach 1945* (Bielefeld: Aisthesis Verlag, 1997), 42–52.

3. The Munich Conference witnessed a hard conflict between the highest ranks of the corporation (Benno von Wiese) and some representatives of the younger generation (Karl Otto Conrady, Eberhard Lämmert, Peter Wapnewski) about the theme of the conference. Finally the two sides compromised, settling on "*Nationalismus in Germanistik und Dichtung*" instead of "*Nationalsozialismus und Germanistik.*" See Karl Otto Conrady, "Miterlebte Germanistik: Ein Rückblick auf die Zeit vor und nach dem Münchner Germanistentag von 1966," in *Diskussion Deutsch,* 100 (1988): 126–43.

4. Klaus R. Scherpe, "Die Renovierung eines alten Gebäudes. Westdeutsche Literaturwissenschaft nach 1945," in *Wissenschaft im geteilten Deutschland,* ed. Walter H. Pehle and Peter Sillem (Frankfurt: Fischer, 1992), 149–63.

5. The emphatic and uncritical celebration of the new was an effective strategy of repression very common during the first postwar years.

6. In Heidelberg, for example, five days after the arrival of the Americans some professors met with Karl Jaspers to establish a committee for the reopening of the university. In September the University of Göttingen also reopened, and many others quickly followed its example.

7. See Gärtner, *Kontinuität und Wandel in der neueren deutschen Literaturwissenschaft nach 1945,* 37.

8. Karl Otto Conrady, "Reminiszenzen und Reflexionen," in *Wie, warum und zu welchem Ende wurde ich Literaturhistoriker?* ed. Siegfried Unseld (Frankfurt: Suhrkamp, 1972), 68. (. . . weg[zu]treten, aus[zu]scheren, [zu] flüchten aus den Qualen der Gegenwart, aus der Not, das Geschehene begreifen zu müssen, hin zum Fernen, Fremden, zum vermeintlich Unpolitischen, ins Reich der Innerlichkeit.) See also Conrady's observations in Karl Otto Conrady, "Spuren einer Erinnerung an die Zeit um 1945 und an den Weg der Germanistik," in *Zeitenwechsel: Germanistische Literaturwissenschaft vor und nach 1945,* ed. Wilfried Barner and Christoph König (Frankfurt: Fischer, 1996), 404–10.

9. See, for example, Adorno's studies.

10. On the strategy of cultural reconstruction in the four occupied zones see Bernard Genton, *Les Alliés et la culture: Berlin, 1945–1949* (Paris: Presses Universitaires de France, 1998).

11. See Gärtner's overview in *Kontinuität und Wandel in der neueren deutschen Literaturwissenschaft nach 1945,* 303.

12. Written to the mayor of Berlin to protest against his removal from his university

post. On this subject see Wolfgang Höppner's observations, supported by many previously unpublished documents, in Wolfgang Höppner, "Franz Koch und die deutsche Literaturwissenschaft der Nachkriegszeit," in *Atta Troll tanzt noch,* ed. Boden and Dainat, 175–92; quote on 180. (. . . das Feld kampflos dem Parteidilettantismus.)

13. Pyritz was already "denazified" in November 1946 and began his slow march toward Hamburg University (in the British zone). In January 1950 he became a full professor at the university and immediately thereafter head of the faculty and a member of the academic senate. The transfer of the *berliner Schule* to its safe haven was thus successfully achieved. See also Christa Hempel-Küter and Hans-Harald Müller, "Zur Neukonstituierung der neueren deutschen Literaturwissenschaft an der Universität Hamburg nach 1945," in *Zeitenwechsel,* ed. Barner and König, 19–34.

14. The letter is partially quoted in Höppner, "Franz Koch und die deutsche Literaturwissenschaft der Nachkriegszeit," 187–88.

15. See the proceedings in Gudrun Schnabel, "Gerhard Fricke: Karriereverlauf eines Literaturwissenschaftlers nach 1945," in *Deutsche Literaturwissenschaft 1945–1965: Fallstudien zu Institutionen, Diskursen, Personen,* ed. Petra Boden and Rainer Rosenberg (Berlin: Akademie Verlag, 1997), 61–95; quote on 73. (. . . Mitläufer.)

16. Schnabel, "Gerhard Fricke," 77.

17. The speech may be found at the Deutsches Literaturarchiv of Marbach am Neckar and has been published as an appendix to Schnabel, "Gerhard Fricke," 85–95; quote on 90. (. . . die unleugbaren positiven Impulse.)

18. Schnabel, "Gerhard Fricke," 92–93. (. . . einen Neubeginn, . . . eine wirkliche Zukunft, . . . eine Gemeinsamkeit, . . . einen sinnvollen Dienst am Ganzen.)

19. *Schiller: Briefe* (1955); *Goethe: Sämtliche Werke* (1958); *Friedrich Hebbel: Werke,* 5 vols. (1963).

20. See the accurate reconstruction of the strategy in Christa Hempel-Küter, "Die Wissenschaft, der Alltag und die Politik: Materialien zur Fachgeschichte der Hamburger Germanistik," in *Deutsche Literaturwissenschaft 1945–1965,* ed. Boden and Rosenberg, 1–33.

21. See the accurate overview by Peter Sturm in *Literaturwissenschaft im Dritten Reich: Germanistische Wissensformationen und politisches System* (Vienna: Edition Praesens, 1995). See also Gärtner, *Kontinuität und Wandel in der neueren Literaturwissenschaft nach 1945,* 45.

22. Ludwig Jäger, *Seitenwechsel: Der Fall Schneider/Schwerte und die Diskretion der Germanistik* (Munich: Fink Verlag, 1998), 11. (. . . Raum, Geist, Tat und Erbe des nordrassischen Indogermanentums.) On the Schneider/Schwerte case see Joachim Lerchenmüller and Gerd Simon, *Masken-Wechsel: Wie der SS-Hauptsturmführer Schneider zum BRD-Hochschulrektor Schwerte wurde und andere Geschichten über die Wendigkeit deutscher Wissenschaft im 20. Jahrhundert, mit zahlreichen Dokumenten und einem bisher ungedruckten Text von Hans Schwerte aus neuester Zeit* (Tübingen: Verlag der Gesellschaft für interdisziplinäre Forschung, 1999).

23. See the list of members of the *Ahnenerbe* in *Im Vorfeld des Massenmords: Germanistik im 2. Weltkrieg,* ed. Joachim Lerchenmüller and Gerd Simon (Tübingen: Verlag der Gesellschaft für interdisziplinäre Forschung, 1997), 88. The membership list of the *Wissenschaftseinsatz* is on p. 90. Schneider was also charged with having commandeered from scientific labs of occupied countries the equipment that was to be used in Dachau for experiments on the prisoners. See Claus Leggewie, *Von Schneider zu Schwerte: Das ungewöhnliche leben eines Mannes, der aus der Geschichte lernen wollte* (Munich: Hanser, 1998), 133–40.

24. Jäger, *Seitenwechsel,* 281–94. Among the candidates, to mention a few names,

were Walter Müller-Seidel, Jost Hermand, and Peter Szondi. In the case of Hermand, for example, there was open speculation on his commitment sometimes voiced "mit sozialistischem Akzent" (with a socialist emphasis) (288). The series of events that led to Schwerte's hiring suggests the existence of a network of solidarity among Germanists compromised by the past regime. It is also true, as Leggewie notes (*Von Schneider zu Schwerte,* 245), that in 1964 Schwerte was considered a left-wing liberal and thus potentially at odds with the conservative commission whose members eventually nominated him full professor at Aachen. On the other hand, one cannot exclude the possibility of a skillful setup by a former Nazi applicant and a commission made up of former Nazis and conservatives, with the former Nazi applicant taking on the role of the liberal intellectual and the commission showing its scientific impartiality by choosing him. All this is highly speculative, of course, and it is impossible to reach any positive conclusion.

25. See Leggewie, *Von Schneider zu Schwerte,* 278 (. . . Aachener Modell).

26. *AstA-Info,* 12 (1991), quoted in Leggewie, *Von Schneider zu Schwerte,* 279–80. (Obwohl er . . . oft dem Druck der Professoren . . . nachgeben mußte, versuchte er immer, die anstehenden Probleme rational und objektiv zu lösen. Er bemühte sich auch, die Interessen derjenigen Gruppen . . . geltend zu machen, die bisher zum Schaden der Hochschule nicht ausreichend in ihren Gremien vertreten sind.)

27. The expression is repeatedly used in lecture XI, "An Alternative Way out of the Philosophy of the Subject: Communicative versus Subject-Centered Reason," in Jürgen Habermas, *The Philosophical Discourse of Modernity: Twelve Lectures,* trans. Frederick Lawrence (Cambridge, Mass.: MIT Press, 1987), 294–326.

28. Simon goes as far as to speculate that Schneider/Schwerte might have had a third identity due to his membership in the Security Service. See Gerd Simon, "'Ihr Mann ist tot und läßt sie grüßen': Hans Ernst Schneider alias Schwerte im 3. Reich," *Sprache und Literatur,* 77 (1996): 82–119.

29. It is interesting to note that a whole chapter of Leggewie's book was eliminated by the publisher because some Germanists at the University of Aachen felt directly alluded to in some passages where Leggewie mentioned the *"Aachener Sumpf"* (Aachen's swamp) with reference to German Studies at that university. On the polemics see also Ulrich Greiner, "Der Mann mit allzu vielen Eigenschaften," *Die Zeit,* 39 (17 September 1998): 56. The whole episode is certainly open to surmise of all sorts. It should be noted that the well-documented and already quoted book *Seitenwechsel* by Jäger (one of the Germanists who felt their loyalties had been called into question as a dweller in the "Aachen swamp"), stops "at the threshold of the present age as if in fear of its consequences" (such is Greiner's view). One should not forget, in any case, that most recent data about the institutional life of universities are protected under the privacy act: this makes it difficult to reconstruct, say, a professor's recent academic career without the formal consent of the same.

30. On the "Berendsohn case" see Christa Hempel-Küter, "Die Wissenschaft, der Alltag und die Politik," 20–1. The previously cited letter, dated 23 October 1947 and addressed to Berendsohn by the Staff Office of the Hamburg Senate, is on p. 20. (In Ihrem Fall wird ein Anrecht auf Wiedergutmachung hier in Hamburg dem Grund nach anerkannt. Mangels gesetzlicher Handhabe erfolgt die Wiedergutmachung hier in Hamburg bisher in und an derselben Stelle. Das würde bedingen, daß Sie hierher zurückkehren müßten, und einen Ihrer früheren Tätigkeiten entsprechenden Arbeitsplatz einnehmen müßten. Sie wollen zunächst mitteilen, ob Sie hierzu bereit sind. Alsdann würden von hier die entsprechenden Schritte zur Freimachung eines solchen Arbeitsplatzes unternommen werden. Es wird vorausgesetzt, daß Sie über die hier herrschenden materiellen Nöte unterrichtet sind. Insbesondere wird bei der sich immer noch verschärfenden Raumnot

die angemessene Unterbringung einer Familie selbst mit behördlichen Förderung große Schwierigkeiten bereiten.)

31. Hempel-Küter, "Die Wissenschaft, der Alltag und die Politik," 21. (. . . nach Auffassung der Fakultät darf mit einer an Gewißheit grenzenden Wahrscheinlichkeit vermutet werden, daß Herr Professor Berendsohn auch ohne den Umsturz von 1933 und dessen Folgen nicht zu einem planm. ao. [oder gar ordentl.] Lehrstuhl gelangt wäre.)

32. See Gärtner, *Kontinuität und Wandel in der neueren deutschen Literaturwissenschaft nach 1945*, 37–61.

33. Richard Alewyn, "Goethe als Alibi," speech presented in 1949 during ceremonies celebrating the bicentenary of Goethe's birth, *Hamburger Akademische Rundschau,* 3: 8–10 (1948–49): 685–87. The issue was entirely dedicated to Goethe, with various articles (among them one by Hans Pyritz, "*Goethes Verwandlungen,*" 589–601) and with extensive reviews of the publications issued for the celebration—and it was indeed a celebration—of Goethe and, in the same tones, *mutatis mutandis,* of the years of National Socialism.

34. "The Universities in the British Zone; Bericht der Delegation des britischen Hochschullehrerverbandes," *Göttinger Universitäts-Zeitung* [hereafter GUZ], 3: 1 (1947–48): 15. (Seit der allierten Besetzung sind neue politische, wirtschaftliche und soziale Kräfte zum Zuge gekommen, gleichzeitig streben frühere Traditionen, die unter der Nazi-Herrschaft teilweise oder ganz unterdrückt oder in Schach gehalten waren, danach, sich wieder geltend zu machen. Wir meinen, daß wir in unserem Bericht in erster Linie unseren starken und einhelligen Eindruck davon vermerken müssen, daß keine durchgreifende und dauerhafte Reform der Universitäten, die wir besuchten, allein auf Grund der Initiative der Universitäten selber wahrscheinlich ist.) On the function of the *Göttinger Universitäts-Zeitung* and the *Hamburger Akademische Rundschau,* two students' journals that, however, were addressed to a larger public, see P. C. Bontempelli, "Die Rolle der *Göttinger Universitäts-Zeitung* und der *Hamburger Akademischen Rundschau* in der Erneuerung der Universität, im literarischen Leben und im Selbstverständnis der deutschen Literaturwissenschaft der ersten Nachkriegsjahre," *Igitur,* 7: 2 (1995): 57–71.

35. "The Universities in the British Zone," 15. (. . . professorale Tyrannei.)

36. "The Universities in the British Zone," 15. (. . . servile Haltung.)

37. Klaus Ziegler, "Gegenwärtigkeit," GUZ, 2: 4 (1946–47): 1–4; citation on 1. Page numbers of this work will henceforth be included parenthetically in the text, original language in the notes.

38. (. . . mit nüchterner Demut, . . . des Sachlich-Wirklichen.)

39. (. . . Synthese von wissenschaftlicher Sachlichkeit und lebendiger Gegenwärtigkeit.)

40. (. . . Arbeiterhochschulen.)

41. (Es gilt demnach stets das gleiche: es geht nicht so sehr um die Formen des wissenschaftlichen Betriebes als vielmehr um den Geist, der sie erfüllt, um den menschlichen Habitus der Hochschulehrer.)

42. (. . . die innere Lebendigkeit.)

43. Karl Barth, "Verlorene Generation?" GUZ, 2: 12 (1946–47): 1–2.

44. Barth, "Verlorene Generation?" 2.

45. Barth, "Verlorene Generation?" 2. (Es ist fatal, daß so viele deutsche Studenten dem Unterricht, der Erziehung, dem Vorbild gerade dieses Professorentypus ausgeliefert sind. In dieser Schule werden sie keine freien Menschen werden.)

46. Erich von Holst, "Universitätslehrer—eine Gefahr?" GUZ, 2: 15 (1946–47): 3–6, quote on 5. (Ich hatte sie—und meine meisten Lehrer und Freunde ebenfalls—in der wissenschaftlichen Arbeit.)

47. Von Holst, "Universitätslehrer?" 6. (Ich erlaube mir, ihn, welches auch seine persönlichen Vorzüge und wissenschaftlichen Meriten sein mögen, für eines der Hindernisse auf dem Weg des heutigen deutschen Studenten anzusehen.)

48. Kurt May, "Eigengesetzlichkeit deutscher Literaturwissenschaft," GUZ, 2: 22 (1946–47): 2–3; quote on 3. (Heute, da sie vor ihrem Wiederaufbau steht, konzentriert sie sich nach einer langjährigen uferlosen Expansion und vielfältigen Selbstentfremdung auf die innere Linie ihrer Wesensbestimmtheit von den ihr eigenen Gegenständen her. Lebensvolle Sachlichkeit sei die Parole ihrer Jünger!) Page numbers of this work will henceforth be included parenthetically in the text, original language in the notes.

49. (Wer sich also zum Studium der Literatur geeigneter erweisen soll als andere, muß die Anlage mindestens zu dem eigentümlichen synthetischen Verhalten mitbringen, in dem die Interpretation des Dichtwerks gründet: dem Vermögen, sich selbst in einer Art von mystischer Union den geformten seelisch-geistigen Lebensgehalten der Werke sympathetisch zu verschmelzen.)

50. (. . . nacherleben; . . . selbsterleben; . . . Einfühlungsvermögen und starke Einbildungskraft.)

51. (. . . zur dilettantischen Selbstaussprache.)

52. (. . . Lebensdeutung.)

53. (. . . rechter Philologe; Jeder Germanist betrete sein Studiengebiet in der Gewißheit von der unerschütterlichen idealen Einheit einer Wissenschaft von Geschichte der deutschen Literatur und deutscher Sprache von den frühesten Anfängen bis in die Gegenwart.)

54. Josef Peter Stern, "Freiheit des Lernens: Die Stimme eines Ausländers," GUZ, 2: 24 (1946–47): 3–4; quote on 3. (. . . intellektuelle Unmündigkeit; . . . Identifizierung der professoralen Kunstauffassung mit Kunstauffassung schlechthin.)

55. Stern, "Freiheit des Lernens," 3. (. . . entweder der professorale Dogmatismus wird anerkannt, gelernt, bei Prüfungen vorgezeigt und vielleicht an neue Generationen weitergegeben, oder es kommt zu einer Katastrophe, die einen ganzen Lebeslauf beeinflußt.)

56. Bourdieu offers a number of particularly acute observations on the notion of *Eigengesetzlichkeit* in the scientific field and within the academia. See Pierre Bourdieu, *Practical Reason: On the Theory of Action* (Stanford, Calif.: Stanford University Press, 1998), 127–45.

57. I am not suggesting that May's students were forced or blackmailed into siding with their master. They probably acted in complete autonomy, perhaps out of genuine affection and respect. In fact, one of the effects of the "symbolical violence" exerted over the servant-student is to transform the power relationship into a personal one and power into charisma. In Bourdieu's analysis of master-servant, boss-secretary, teacher-student relationships he found that "symbolic violence is the violence which extorts submission, which is not perceived as such, based on 'collective expectations' or socially inculcated beliefs." Bourdieu, *Practical Reason,* 103. The result—or rather, one of the results of this long work of incorporation—is immediate adherence, a doxical submission to the current dogmas. May's unanimous defense by his pupils was therefore wholly to be expected. See also Gärtner, *Kontinuität und Wandel in der neueren deutschen Literaturwissenschaft nach 1945,* 39.

58. Wolfgang Gruncke, "Meinungsstreit um die deutsche Philologie: Verursacht professoraler Dogmatismus studentische Unmündigkeit?" GUZ, 3: 2 (1947–48): 7–8. (. . . Die deutsche Art des Studierens wie des Dozierens.) See also the other articles in favor of May on pp. 8 ff., as well as Walter Matthias, "Hüterin der Sprache: Freiheit und Bindung in der germanistischen Wissenschaft," GUZ, 3: 4 (1947–48), 6 ff., to whom Stern specifically addressed his reply.

59. Josef Peter Stern, "Windmühlen deutsche Philologie: 'Freiheit des Lernens' Schlußwort des Verfassers," GUZ, 3: 6 (1947–48): 11–12; citation on 11.

60. Jost Hermand, "Neuere Entwicklungen zwischen 1945 und 1980, " in *Literaturwissenschaft: Ein Grundkurs,* ed. Helmut Brackert and Jörn Stückrat (Reinbek: Rowohlt, 1992), 564–78; quote on 564. (. . . eine Germanistik des Vertuschens, Verschweigens, ja der Maskenhaftigkeit.)

61. See Terry Eagleton, *The Significance of Theory* (Oxford: Basil Blackwell, 1990), 30.

62. See Adorno's first impressions, upon his return to Frankfurt after the war, of the complete absence of innovation in German culture and of the compensatory and consolatory function of postwar conservatism in Theodor W. Adorno, "Die auferstandene Kultur?" *Frankfurter Hefte,* 5 (1950), now in T. W. Adorno, *Gesammelte Schriften,* ed. Rolf Tiedemann, vol. 20, book 2 (Frankfurt: Suhrkamp, 1986), 453–64.

63. Jost Hermand, *Geschichte der Germanistik* (Reinbek: Rowohlt, 1994), 121. (. . . Könige.)

64. Kurt May, "Über die gegenwärtige Situation einer deutschen Literaturwissenschaft," *Trivium,* 5 (1947): 293–303; quote on 303. (. . . Diätkur.)

65. Hermand, *Geschichte der Germanistik,* 121–40.

66. In this regard see the accurate reconstruction of the slow acceptance of expressionist poetry by Germanists before and after 1945 in Gärtner, *Kontinuität und Wandel in der neueren deutschen Literaturwissenschaft nach 1945,* 64–187.

67. Precisely for his Jewishness, Kafka was often treated as a representative of a rootless cosmopolitan humanity and, to some extent, as a symbol of the modern intellectual. At the same time, however, any reference to the Jewish question in Germany was carefully avoided. On this subject see Konrad Feilchenfeld, "Die Wiederentdeckung des 'Juden' in der Neueren deutschen Literaturwissenschaft nach 1945," in *Zeitenwechsel,* ed. Barner and König, 231–44.

68. On the discussion within the faculty of Korff's nomination at Leipzig see Marion Marquardt, "Zur Geschichte des Germanistischen Instituts an der Leipziger Universität von seiner Gründung 1873 bis 1945," in *Zeitschrift für Germanistik,* 9: 6 (1988): 681–87; citation on 686.

69. The reunification of Germany has opened to scholars the archives of the former Democratic Republic. This has allowed scholars to reconstruct the history of German Studies, first in the Soviet zone and later in the Democratic Republic, both in terms of its internal (structural and institutional) aspects and in terms of its relation with the political and ideological guidelines that political power sought to impose. These complex issues require a specific study of their own, so I refer the reader to the following chapters in *Deutsche Literaturwissenschaft 1945–1965,* ed. Boden and Rosenberg: Peter Jehle, "Werner Krauss: 'Deutschland ist nur in einem Zustand des Projekts erträglich': Zur Reorganisation der literaturwissenschaftlichen Romanistik zwischen Ost und West," 97–118; Petra Boden, "Universitätsgermanistik in der SBZ/DDR: Personalpolitik und Struktureller Wandel 1945–1958," 119–59; Peter Th. Walther, "Denkraster- und Kaderpolitik der SED in der Deutschen Akademie der Wissenschaften zu[Ost]Berlin," 161–71; Dorothea Dornhof, "Von der 'Gelehrtenrepublik' zur marxistischen Forschungsgemeinschaft an der Deutschen Akademie der Wissenschaften: Das Institut für deutsche Sprache und Literatur," 173–201; Rainer Rosenberg, "Zur Begründung der marxistischen Literaturwissenschaft der DDR," 203–40; Gunter Schandera, Hiedrun Bomke, Dagmar Ende, Dieter Schade, and Heike Steinhorst, "Die 'Weimarer Beiträge' zwischen 1955 und 1961: Eine Zeitschrift auf dem Weg zum 'zentralen Organ der marxistischen Literaturwissenschaft in der DDR'?" 261–332;

Simone Barck, "Literaturkritik zwischen Parteiauftrag und Professionalität in der DDR der sechziger Jahre," 333–43.

70. The original planning of this colossal work dates back to 1955. For years its general "guidelines" *(Hauptrichtungen)* were openly discussed at various institutional locations. The work was entrusted to various specialists: Klaus Gysi, Kurt Böttcher, and others. The result was a history of literature in twelve volumes, sometimes divided into subvolumes, which were published over a period of twenty-three years. See the following chapters of *Deutsche Literaturwissenschaft 1945–1965*, ed. Boden and Rosenberg: D. Dornhof, "Von der 'Gelehrtenrepublik' zur marxistischen Forschungsgemeinschaft," 184–201, and R. Rosenberg, "Zur Begründung der marxistischen Literaturwissenschaft der DDR," 226–40.

7. The Dialectics of Rebellion

1. Having started in 1812, when it was introduced in the statutes of the University of Berlin, *Habilitation* is a procedure aimed at ascertaining the scientific qualifications of the candidate. After passing the *Habilitation* exam the candidate belongs to the faculty even though he (or, only more recently, she) has no tenured post. The habilitation process, therefore, plays a crucial role in enlarging the faculty, and decisions about it belong exclusively to full professors. When hiring a professor for a new post, the faculty proposes to the Ministry of Education a list of candidates with an indication of the priorities and preferences of the university, and the ministry makes a decision on the basis of this list. As can be seen, professorial autonomy (or arbitrariness) plays a crucial role in the habilitation process. For a history of the *Habilitation* process and its implications in Germany see Peter J. Brenner, "Habilitation als Sozialisation," in *Geist, Geld und Wissenschaft: Arbeits- und Darstellungsformen von Literaturwissenschaft*, ed. Peter J. Brenner (Frankfurt: Suhrkamp, 1993), 318–56.

2. Now in *Universität und Widerstand: Versuch einer politischen Universität in Frankfurt*, ed. Detlev Claussen and Regine Dermitzel (Frankfurt: Europäische Verlagsanstalt, 1968), 157–65. On 1968 and the changes in German Studies and in the universities see Rainer Rosenberg, Inge Münz-Koenen, and Petra Boden, eds., *Der Geist der Unruhe: 1968 im Vergleich: Wissenschaft-Literatur-Medien* (Berlin: Akademie Verlag, 2000).

3. On the long negotiations on the agenda see the testimony of Benno von Wiese, at the time president of the Association of German Germanists, in his memoirs, *Ich erzähle mein Leben: Erinnerungen* (Frankfurt: Insel Verlag, 1982), 350–56.

4. Now republished with slight changes in Eberhard Lämmert,Walter Killy, Karl Otto Conrady, and Peter von Polenz, eds., *Germanistik: Eine deutsche Wissenschaft* (Frankfurt: Suhrkamp Verlag, 1967).

5. Jost Hermand, *Geschichte der Germanistik* (Reinbek: Rowohlt, 1994), 146. (. . . plötzlich aus einem unkritischen zu einem kritischen Bewußtsein erwachten.)

6. The expression *Paradigmawechsel* indicates a paradigm shift, that is, a change of perspective that widened the field of the authors and works deemed worthy of critical attention to include other authors and literary movements besides the canonical classical-romantic constellation.

7. "Aus der Debatte der Germanisten-Vollversammlung" (7 July 1967), in *Alternative*, 55 (1967), special issue: *Heft: Germanistik*, 147. (Was nach 1945 zunächst in existenziellen Beschwörungsformeln, dann in ästhetisierender Werkimmanenz weiterlebte, ist heute durch die integrierende Aufnahme scheinmarxistischer, soziologisierender Elemente gegen jeden Angriff von außen immun geworden.) The issue includes a series

of papers and documents on the theme of the *Politisierung der Germanistik* (the politicization of German Studies).

8. As Benno von Wiese reports: "There was a general agreement that I would make a statement in favor of structural changes in German Studies as a discipline." Von Wiese, *Ich erzähle mein Leben: Erinnerungen,* 354. (Man war wohl damit einverstanden, daß ich für Strukturveränderungen im Fach der Germanistik eintrat.)

9. Both Conrady and Lämmert, for example, were at one time presidents of the association of German Germanists. According to von Wiese (*Ich erzähle mein Leben,* 355), both sought to prevent personal attacks on the previous generation. Von Wiese also notes, with a hint of pride, that among the Munich rebels there were many of his former students, who had already achieved or were about to achieve high-level academic positions (354 and 356). He adds that none of his pupils ever actively participated in left-wing extraparliamentary political organizations (356). As one can see, the control mechanisms of the discipline worked perfectly.

10. The story of the habilitation denied to Benjamin at Frankfurt University is reconstructed in detail in Burkhardt Lindner, "Habilitationsakte Benjamin: Über ein 'akademisches Trauerspiel' und über ein Vorkapitel der 'Frankfurter Schule' (Horkheimer, Adorno)," *Zeitschrift für Literaturwissenschaft und Linguistik,* 14: 53–54 (1984): 147–65.

11. See "Resolution zur Politisierung der Germanistik," *Alternative,* 55 (1967), special issue: *Heft: Germanistik,* 145 ff.

12. The idea of a "critical university," where knowledge, its structure, and its forms of reproduction would be subject to rational and radical analysis, was one of the most interesting if short-lived proposals of the student movement. On this see Oskar Negt, "Über die Idee einer kritischen und antiautoritären Universität," in *Universität und Widerstand,* ed. Claussen and Dermitzel, 166–95.

13. H. Lethen, "Aus der Debatte der Germanistenversammlung," *Alternative,* 55 (1967), special issue: *Heft: Germanistik,* 146.

14. "Zur 'Methoden-Toleranz' einer Massendisziplin," *Alternative,* 55 (1967), special issue: *Heft: Germanistik,* 166 ff.

15. "Zur 'Methoden-Toleranz' einer Massendisziplin," 145. (Politisierung der Germanistik bedeutet demnach Demokratisierung des Verhältnisses von Professoren, Assistenten und Studenten. Mitbestimmung der Studenten bei der Lehrplangestaltung, der Etatverteilung, und der Besetzung von Lehrstühlen ist Voraussetzung und Konsequenz einer solchen Demokratisierung.)

16. "Schafft die Germanistik ab!" in *Universität und Widerstand,* ed. Claussen and Dermitzel, 162. (Der desolate Zustand dieser Wissenschaft reproduziert sich in ihrer Praxis, in den Institutionen. . . . Wissenschaftliche Positionen reduzieren sich auf apodiktisch vertretene Meinung der Ordinarien, die um sich akklamierende Assistenten und konsumierende Studenten sammeln. Kritik an der Wissenschaft, die nicht zugleich Organisationskritik ist, wird von der autoritären Praxis absorbiert, sei's als Narrenfreiheit, sei's als Beitrag zum Methodenpluralismus.)

17. Pierre Bourdieu, *The Rules of Art: Genesis and Structure of the Literary Field,* trans. Susan Emanuel (Stanford, Calif.: Stanford University Press, 1996), 33.

18. Pierre Bourdieu, *Homo Academicus,* 172.

19. See H.-D. Kittsteiner, "Demonstration als Aufklärung," in *Alternative,* 55 (1967), special issue: *Heft: Germanistik,* 141. The difficulty of dealing with these provocation tactics is clearly exemplified by the contrasts that arose when Adorno was invited on 7 July 1967 to the Seminar of German Studies of the Berlin Freie Universität to give a talk titled "Zum Klassizismus von Goethes 'Iphigenie.'" The students asked him to

transform his conference into a political debate. Without getting into the detail of the discussion that arose, let me just stress how Adorno's professorial habitus proved to be incompatible with the new verbal and nonverbal language of the Berlin students. Adorno left Berlin, and shortly thereafter Marcuse arrived, with an entirely different attitude. See the account of this episode in Rolf Wiggershaus, *The Frankfurt School: Its History, Theories, and Political Significance,* trans. Michael Robertson (Cambridge, Mass.: MIT Press, 1994), 619–22.

20. See Hermand, *Geschichte der Germanistik,* 155–64.

21. Bourdieu defines it as follows: "that combination of dispositions and interests associated with a particular class of social position which inclines agents to strive to reproduce at a constant or an increasing rate the properties constituting their social identity, without even needing to do this deliberately or consciously." Bourdieu, *Homo Academicus,* 176.

22. See the testimony of political expert Wilhelm Hennis, "Studentenbewegung und Hochschulreform," in *Hochschulreform—und was nun?* ed. Horst Albert Glaser (Frankfurt, Berlin, and Vienna: Ullstein, 1982), 51.

23. The issue of *Alternative* dedicated to the reform of German Studies ends with the "Thesen zur deutschen Germanistik" (182–83; citation on 183).

24. See especially the papers by Eberhard Lämmert ("Germanistik—eine deutsche Wissenschaft"), Walter Killy ("Zur Geschichte des deutschen Lesebuchs"), Karl Otto Conrady ("Deutsche Literaturwissenschaft und Drittes Reich"), and Peter von Polenz ("Sprachpurismus und Nationalsozialismus") in *Germanistik: Eine deutsche Wissenschaft,* ed. Lämmert, Killy, Conrady, and von Polenz.

25. "Thesen zur deutschen Germanistik," 183.

26. Bourdieu, *The Rules of Art,* 11 (italics in the original).

27. See Bourdieu's penetrating observations in his essay "The contradictions of inheritance," in Pierre Bourdieu et al., *The Weight of the World: Social Suffering in Contemporary Society,* trans. Priscilla Parkhurst Ferguson et al. (Stanford, Calif.: Stanford University Press, 1999), 507.

28. Ibid.

29. For Bourdieu, "Families are *corporate bodies* animated by a kind of *conatus,* in Spinoza's sense, that is, a tendency to perpetuate their social being, with all its powers and privileges, which is at the basis of *reproduction strategies:* fertility strategies, matrimonial strategies, successional strategies, economic strategies, and last but not least, educational strategies." Pierre Bourdieu, *Practical Reason: On the Theory of Action* (Stanford, Calif.: Stanford University Press, 1998), 19. The *conatus* is therefore the impulse—found in any group with a corporate spirit—to perpetuate its unity and reject divisive elements.

8. After 1968

1. (Die Philosophen haben die Welt nur verschieden interpretiert; Es kommt aber darauf an sie zu verändern.) "Marx: Eleventh Thesis on Feuerbach," in Karl Marx and Friedrich Engels, *Basic Writings on Politics and Philosophy,* ed. Lewis S. Feuer (London: Collins, 1969), 286. Marx's eleventh thesis on Feuerbach was inscribed in golden letters on a red marble plaque and set in the atrium of Humboldt University in Berlin. After the reunification, starting in 1991, there was a proposal to remove the plaque, seen as a symbol of dogmatic and intolerant ideology. A lively and highly significant debate took place involving philosophers, historians, politicians, art historians, professors, and so

on. See *Eine angeschlagene These: Die 11. Feuerbach-These im Foyer der Humboldt-Universität zu Berlin,* ed. Volker Gerhardt (Berlin: Akademie Verlag, 1996).

2. See Jost Hermand's account of the whole episode in his interesting autobiography *Zuhause und anderswo: Erfahrungen im Kalten Krieg* (Cologne, Weimar, and Vienna: Böhlau Verlag, 2001), 154–58.

3. The notion of "cultural capital," modeled on the Marxist category of capital and applied to the field of intangible symbolic goods, is a central and recurrent one in all of Bourdieu's works. See in particular Bourdieu, *Distinction.* For a brilliant exploration of these issues in the context of American studies and academia, see John Guillory, *Cultural Capital: The Problem of Literary Canon Formation* (Chicago and London: University of Chicago Press, 1993).

4. Critical analyses of the ideology of German Studies are found in Marieluise Gansberg and Paul Gerhard Völker, *Methodenkritik der Germanistik: Materialistische Literaturtheorie und bürgerliche Praxis* (Stuttgart: Metzler, 1970); Franz Greß, *Germanistik und Politik* (Stuttgart: Verlag Frommann-Holzboog, 1971); Bernd Hüppauf, ed., *Literaturgeschichte zwischen Revolution und Restauration: Aus den Anfängen der Germanistik 1830–1870* (Frankfurt: Athenäum Verlag, 1972); Gunter Reiß, ed., *Materialien zur Ideologiegeschichte der deutschen Literaturwissenschaft,* 2 vols. (Tübingen: Niemeyer, 1973); Jörg Jochen Müller, ed., *Germanistik und deutsche Nation 1806–1848* (Stuttgart: Metzler, 1974).

5. It is very difficult to select the most significant studies on the history of German Studies and its institutions, given the immense quantity of works published in the last two decades. I limit myself to the following: Johannes Janota, ed., *Eine Wissensschaft etabliert sich 1810–1870* (Tübingen: Niemeyer, 1980); Rainer Rosenberg, *Zehn Kapitel zur Geschichte der Germanistik* (Berlin [DDR]: Akademie Verlag, 1981); Rainer Rosenberg, *Literaturwissenschaftliche Germanistik* (Berlin [GDR]: Akademie Verlag, 1989); Jürgen Fohrmann, *Das Projekt der deutschen Literaturgeschichte: Entstehung und Scheitern einer nationalen Poesiebeschreibung zwischen Humanismus und Deutschem Kaiserreich* (Stuttgart: Metzler, 1989); Klaus Weimar, *Geschichte der deutschen Literaturwissenschaft bis zum Ende des 19. Jahrhunderts* (Munich: Fink, 1989); Jürgen Fohrmann and Wilhelm Voßkamp, eds., *Wissenschaft und Nation: Zur Entstehungsgeschichte der deutschen Literaturwissenschaft* (Stuttgart: Metzler, 1991); Jürgen Fohrmann and Wilhelm Voßkamp, eds., *Wissenschaftsgeschichte der Germanistik im 19. Jahrhundert* (Stuttgart: Metzler, 1994); Jost Hermand, *Geschichte der Germanistik* (Reinbek: Rowohlt, 1994).

6. On the *Extremisten-Beschluß,* its circumstances, and its consequences see Karl Dietrich Bracher, Wolfgang Jäger, and Werner Link, *Republik im Wandel: 1969–1974: Die Ära Brandt* (Stuttgart: Deutsche Verlags-Anstalt, and Mannheim: Brockhaus, 1986), 77–86, and Gregg O. Kvistad, "Radicals and the State: The Political Demands on West German Civil Servants," *Comparative Political Studies,* 21 (1988): 95–125.

7. Benno von Wiese, "Ist die Literaturwissenschaft am Ende?" *Frankfurter Allgemeine Zeitung* (23 October 1973). On the positions of the conservative side, obviously not always identifiable with Nazism, see Hermand, *Geschichte der Germanistik,* 166–72.

8. Hermand, *Geschichte der Germanistik,* 206.

9. From a purely chronological perspective, the feminist movement was born in Germany in the *Sozialistischer Deutscher Studentenbund* (SDS). In January 1968, in West Berlin, seven of its members founded the *Aktionsrat zur Befreiung der Frau* (Action Council for the Liberation of Women) in open polemic against male fellow members. The organization demanded an immediate modification of gender relations inside the revolutionary socialist movement. Later, having decided that it was impossible to alter

the male chauvinist nature of the SDS, the women began establishing grassroots groups called *Weiberräte* (women's committees). Groups of women interested in studying and fighting to improve the condition of women eventually arose in all of West Germany. On the history of the women's movement see Jutta Osinski, *Einführung in die feministische Literaturwissenschaft* (Berlin: Erich Schmidt Verlag, 1998).

10. See, for example, Silvia Bovenschen, *Die imaginierte Weiblichkeit: Exemplarische Untersuchungen zu kulturgeschichtlichen und literarischen Präsentationsformen des Weiblichen* (Frankfurt: Suhrkamp, 1979); Sigrid Weigel, *Die Stimme der Medusa: Schreibweisen in der Gegenwartsliteratur von Frauen* (Reinbek: Rowohlt, 1989).

11. (La philologie est une pensée bourgeoise, paternaliste et hygiéniste de la famille, chérit la filiation, pourchasse l'adultère, s'effraie de la contamination. Pensée de la faute [la variante est une conduite déviante], fonde une méthodologie positive.) Bernard Cerquiglini, *Eloge de la variante: Histoire critique de la philologie* (Paris: Editions du Seuil, 1989), 76–77.

12. See Maria Zens's lucid overview, "Feministische Literaturwissenschaft," in Rainer Baasner, ed., *Methoden und Modelle der Literaturwissenschaft: Eine Einführung* (Berlin: Erich Schmidt Verlag, 1996), 151–70.

13. See Hiltrud Gnüg and Renate Möhrmann, eds., *Frauen Literatur Geschichte: Schreibende Fraue vom Mittelalter bis zur Gegenwart* (Stuttgart: Metzler, 1985); Gisela Brinker-Gabler, ed., *Deutsche Literatur von Frauen,* 2 vols. (Munich: Beck, 1988).

14. See Osinski, *Einführung in die feministische Literaturwissenschaft,* 88.

15. Zens, "Sozialgeschichte der Literatur," 183–208; quote on 183. (Sozialgeschichte ist ein Sammelbegriff, der weite Teile der Entwicklung seit dem scientific turn zusammenspannt. Aus dieser Perspektive ist Literatur ein Ergebnis menschlichen Handelns im Laufe der Geschichte. Produktion und Rezeption von literarischen Texten sowie alle anderen mit ihnen verbundenen Interaktionen und Ereignisse geschehen unter sozialen Rahmenbedingungen. Literatur ist soziale Praxis. Dabei wird nicht behauptet, aus den Handlungszusammenhängen verschiedenster Zeitalter ließen sich die jeweiligen literarisch-künstlerischen Phänomene nach einem immer gleichen Muster ableiten: Sozialgeschichte geht nicht von einer Determiertheit der Literatur aus. Die Verknüpfung literarischen Handelns mit anderen sozialen Handlungsräumen präformiert nicht die je spezifische Ausprägung des ästhetischen-literarischen Diskurses oder gar des einzelnen Textes: die relative Autonomie der Literatur bleibt unbestritten.) The "scientific turn" mentioned by the author refers to the changes in German Studies after 1966.

16. An extraordinary example of an overall analysis of a civilization from a literary perspective that takes full advantage of the tools of *Sozialgeschichte* is Peter Uwe Hohendahl's *Literarische Kultur im Zeitalter des Liberalismus 1830–1870* (Munich: Beck, 1985).

17. On the contradictions of the *Sozialgeschichte der Literatur* see Hans Peter Herrmann, "Sozialgeschichte oder Kunstautonomie? Zur Problematik neuerer Geschichten der deutschen Literatur," in *Kritik der Sozialgeschichtsschreibung,* ed. Rüdiger Scholz (Hamburg: Argument Verlag, 1990, 173–214).

18. The best-known example is the story by Ulrich Plenzdorf, *Die neue Leiden des jungen W.* (1972).

19. The journals *Sinn und Form, Neue Deutsche Literatur,* and *Weimarer Beiträge* played a leading role in studying and identifying new and more complex contradictions in societies that were moving toward socialism.

20. Rainer Rosenberg offers an accurate reconstruction of the birth of German Studies in East Germany in "Zur Geschichte der literaturwissenschaftlichen Germanistik in der DDR," in *Wissenschaft und Nation: Zur Entstehungsgeschichte der deutschen*

Literaturwissenschaft, ed. Jürgen Fohrmann and Wilhelm Voßkamp (Munich: Fink Verlag, 1991), 29–41. Rosenberg's study was finished in August 1989, before the fall of the Berlin Wall. He returned to the subject in "Zur Begründung einer marxistischen Literaturwissenschaft in der DDR," in *Deutsche Literaturwissenschaft 1945–1965,* ed. Boden and Rosenberg, 202–40.

21. See Georg Bollenbeck's response to a *Weimarer Beiträge* survey in "Zur Situation der Literatur-, Kunst- und Kulturwissenschaften," *Weimarer Beiträge,* 1(1991): 13–21.

22. See Pier Carlo Bontempelli, "La caduta del Muro e la filologia: note e osservazioni sulla germanistica tedesca," *Igitur,* 4: 2 (1992): 43–64.

23. On the extensive restructuring of scientific research and universities in the new *Länder* see Hans Joachim Meyer, "Science et établissements d'enseignement supérieur," in *Les conséquences de l'unification allemande,* ed. Dieter Gutzen (Paris: Presses Universitaires de France, 1997), 235–59.

24. This process has been problematically analyzed by Eberhard Lämmert (one of the "judges") in "Der lange Anlauf: Von der Evaluierung zur Chancengleichheit der Wissenschaftler in Ost und West," *Merkur,* 47: 1 (1993): 30–45.

25. Helmut Peitsch, in the *Weimarer Beiträge* survey (see note 21), voiced his reservations on the dismissive attitude toward any form of critical thought even remotedly related to Marxism and to the Marxism=GDR assumption (32–44).

26. Bollenbeck, "Zur Situation der Literatur-, Kunst-, und Kulturwissenschaften," 15.

27. Bollenbeck, "Zur Situation der Literatur-, Kunst-, und Kulturwissenschaften," 16. (. . . Funktionsverlust.)

28. Wolf Lepenies, "Deutsche Zustände zwei Jahre nach der Revolution: Grenzen der Gemeinschaft," *Mitteilungen des deutschen Germanistenverbandes,* 4 (1991): 4–16.

29. Manfred Seiler, "Die Angst vor dem Urteil: Germanistentag in Ausburg: Anmerkungen zum Zustand einer Wissenschaft," *Die Zeit,* 44 (25 October 1991): 78.

30. Ibid. (Weil die hochgerühmte Wissenschaftlichkeit zu einer reinen Fußnotenzählerei verkommen ist, wo das Zitat mit seinen korrekten Angaben den eigenen Gedanken ersetzt.)

31. Rolf Spinnler, "Die Meister der Fußnoten: Über die Beschädigung der Literatur in der Literaturwissenschaft," *Süddeutsche Zeitung,* 16 (19–20 January 1991): 210. (. . . Die Kunst des Bibliographierens.)

32. Spinnler, "Die Meister der Fußnoten," 210. (. . . die ideale Beschäftigungstherapie für Leute . . . die—aus Angst unwissenschaftlich zu sein—keine eigenen Gedanken mehr zu Papier bringen können.)

33. See Cornelius Weiss, "Erneuern und bewahren? Die Umgestaltung der ostdeutschen Universitäten aus der Sicht eines Handelnden und Betroffenen," in *Les conséquences de l'unification allemande,* ed. Dieter Gutzen, 270–75; citation on 273.

34. Bollenbeck, "Zur Situation der Literatur-, Kunst- und Kulturwissenschaften," 15.

9. Beyond the Year 2000

1. Hartmut Böhme, "Die Literaturwissenschaft zwischen Editionsphilologie und Kulturwissenschaft," in *Perspektiven der Germanistik: Neueste Ansichten zu einem alten Problem,* ed. Anne Bentfeld and Walter Delabar (Opladen: Westdeutscher Verlag, 1997), 32–46; quote on 32. (. . . in einer Engführung der Literaturwissenschaft, die andere in deren Erweiterung.)

2. Hermand, *Geschichte der Germanistik,* 231. (. . . nur für die sogenannte Zunft.)

3. Böhme, "Die Literaturwissenschaft zwischen Editionsphilologie und Kulturwissenschaft," 32.

4. For example, there was a research project financed by the Federal Ministry for Research and Technology on the nature and type of research found in the humanities. The project was carried out between 1987 and 1990 and resulted in a series of *Empfehlungen* (recommendations) that were adopted by the ministry. On the activity and results of the research group see Wolfgang Früwald, Hans Robert Jauß, Reinhart Kosellek, Jürgen Mittelstraß, and Burkhart Steinwachs, *Geisteswissenschaften heute: Eine Denkschrift* (Frankfurt: Suhrkamp, 1991).

5. A lively debate on similar themes has taken place, for example, in contemporary North American literary studies in the context of the publication of the first great literary histories in the United States since World War II. See the *Columbia Literary History of the United States,* edited by Emory Elliot (1988), and the still partially unpublished multivolume *Cambridge History of American Literature,* edited by Sacvan Bercovitch for Cambridge University Press, of which the first volume came out in 1994 after a decade of planning and widespread debate.

6. See Gunter Martens and Hans Zeller, eds., *Texte und Varianten: Probleme ihrer Edition und Interpretation* (Munich: Beck, 1971); Herbert Kraft, *Editionsphilologie,* with an introduction by Jürgen Gregolin, Wilhelm Ott, and Gerd Vonhoff (Darmstadt: Wissenschaftliche Buchgesellschaft, 1990); Norbert Oellers, "Editionswissenschaft um 1945," in *Zeitenwechsel: Germanistische Literaturwissenschaft vor und nach 1945,* ed. Wilfried Barner and Christoph König (Frankfurt: Fischer, 1996), 103–18. The journal *Text: Kritische Beiträge* began publication in 1995, carrying special issues on the most recent and controversial tendencies in textual philology.

7. Böhme, "Die Literaturwissenschaft zwischen Editionsphilologie und Kulturwissenschaft," 33.

8. Böhme, "Die Literaturwissenschaft zwischen Editionsphilologie und Kulturwissenschaft," 35. (Und mitnichten sind Editoren heute noch weltfremde Zölibatäre im Dienst am Allerheiligsten der Handschrift.)

9. I cite here some of the many editions currently being published: *C. F. Meyer-Ausgabe,* ed. Hans Zeller and Alfred Zach (1959–1996), an edition in many ways exemplary in terms of innovative perspectives; *Mörike-Ausgabe* (1967 ff.); *Heine-Sekuläirausgabe* (1970 ff.); *Düsseldorfer Heine-Ausgabe* (1973 ff.); *Annette-von-Droste-Hülshoff-Ausgabe* (1973 ff.); *Hamburger Klopstock-Ausgabe* (1974 ff.); *Brentano-Ausgabe* (1975 ff.); *Hofmannsthal-Ausgabe* (1975 ff.); *Frankfurter Hölderlin-Ausgabe* (1976 ff.); *Kafka-Ausgabe* (1982 ff.); *Berliner* (later *Brandenburger*) *Kleist-Ausgabe* (1988 ff.); *Lenau-Ausgabe* (1989 ff.); *Celan-Ausgabe* (1990 ff.).

10. On the incredible story of the *Schiller-Nationalausgabe* see Norbert Oellers, *Fünfzig Jahre Schiller-Nationalausgabe—und kein Ende?* (Marbach am Neckar: Deutsche Schillergesellschaft, 1991).

11. Böhme, "Die Literaturwissenschaft zwischen Editionsphilologie und Kulturwissenschaft," 36. (. . . ein Markstein an der Straße der Ewigkeit"; . . . Interpretationen vergehen, Editionen bestehen.)

12. Hans Zeller, "Befund und Deutung," in *Texte und Varianten,* ed. Martens and Hans Zeller, 88, n. 86. (Die Vollständigkeit, die im Anspruch einer historisch-kritischen Gesamtausgabe enthalten ist; . . . bis zum Abdruck von Mietquittungen). Zeller is referring to the *Historisch-kritische Gesamtausgabe der Werke von Karl Marx und Friedrich Engels* (MEGA), planned in 120 volumes and co-edited by the Institute for Marxism-Leninism of the Central Committee of the Communist Party of the Soviet Union and the Institute for Marxism-Leninism of the Central Committee of the Unified Socialist Party of the German Democratic Republic.

13. Böhme, "Die Literaturwissenschaft zwischen Editionsphilologie und Kulturwissenschaft," 38. (Das Verhältnis vom Haupttext zu den avant-textes und zu den Kommentaren und Dokumenten läuft aus dem Ruder. Der Aufwand mit den avant-textes macht Editionen unleserlich. Die interpretativen Teile nehmen überhand. Die Kommentare sind zu spezialistisch. Die intertextuellen Verwebungen werden zu unübersichtlichen Rhizomen. An die Stelle von Selektion tritt die maximale Ausdehnung. Zunehmend werden Editionen gelenkt von texttheoretischen Positionen, die dem Material übergestülpt werden. Es herrscht ein Maximalismus, bei welchem man den Eindruck gewinnt, daß Editoren nicht dem Autor, sondern sich selbst ein Denkmal setzen.)

14. The contradictions found in the edition, begun in 1927 and finished in 1996, are highlighted in Walter Morgenthaler, "Johann Heinrich Pestalozzi: Sämtliche Werke: Kritische Notizen zum Abschluß einer kritischen Ausgabe," *Text,* Heft IV: *Datum* 2 (1998): 119–38. As for this, even in the acclaimed edition of the works of C. F. Meyer, finished in 1996, there are a number of discrepancies, meticulously noted by Roland Reuß in his "Kritisches Selbstgespräch: Zum Abschluß der historisch-kritischen C. F. Meyer-Ausgabe," *Text,* Heft IV: *Datum* 2 (1998): 161–74.

15. Ulrich Ott, "Dichterwerkstatt oder Ehrengrab? Zum Problem der historisch-kritischen Ausgaben," *Jahrbuch der Deutschen Schillergesellschaft,* 33 (1989): 3–6.

16. Günter Martens, Norbert Oellers, Siegfried Scheibe, Hartwig Schultz, Gert Vonhoff, and Hans Zeller asserted, with various motivations, the importance of critical editions. For the debate see *Jahrbuch der Deutschen Schillergesellschaft,* 34 (1990): 398–428.

17. Böhme, "Die Literaturwissenschaft zwischen Editionsphilologie und Kulturwissenschaft," 39–40. (. . . private Rittergüter von Ordinarien . . . die eine Schar von Abhängigen beschäftigen.)

18. Bourdieu, *Homo Academicus,* 303, n. 35.

19. For a lucid outline of the whole process see chapter 3, "Types of Capital and Forms of Power," in Bourdieu, *Homo Academicus.*

20. See note 4.

21. Peter J. Brenner, "Das Verschwinden des Eigensinns: Der Strukturwandel der Geisteswissenschaften in der modernen Gesellschaft," in *Geist, Geld und Wissenschaft. Arbeits-und Darstellungsformen von Literaturwissenschaft,* ed. Peter J. Brenner (Frankfurt: Suhrkamp, 1993), 21–65; quote on 44. (. . . irreversibel und unvermeidbar.)

22. Karl Markus Michel, "Wozu Geisteswissenschaften?" *Kursbuch,* 91 (1988): 30–31. (. . . nicht nur zur Banalisierung der Forschungsgegenstände, sondern auch zur [partiellen] Infantilisierung der Forscherintelligenz.)

23. Brenner, "Das Verschwinden des Eigensinns," 48. (Jede Richtung bildet ihre eigenen Zirkel mit einem eigenen Umkreis von Publikationsmöglichkeiten, der die Gelegenheit bietet, neben einem "Zitatenkartell auch einen freundlichen Kreis von Gleichgesinnten zu finden," die ihre je eigene Fach-, wenn nicht ihre Geheimsprache pflegen.)

24. Brenner, "Das Verschwinden des Eigensinns," 64, n. 108.

25. Böhme, "Die Literaturwissenschaft zwischen Editionsphilologie und Kulturwissenschaft," 41. (Gegen lineare Homogenisierung der Geschichte gilt es, die Vielfalt von Geschichten und Kulturen zu verteidigen, das Widersprüchliche und Heterogene der Kulturen und den Reichtum der Geschichte zu wahren, deren getreue Korepetitoren in einigen ihrer wertvollsten Momente, den Sprachen und den Literaturen, Literaturwissenschaftler sein sollten.)

26. Böhme, "Die Literaturwissenschaft zwischen Editionsphilologie und Kulturwissenschaft," 42. (Die Alternativvorschläge reichen von 'drei Kulturen' [Lepenies], über 'Trans-' und 'Interkulturalität' bis hin zu 'Verflüssigung' des Kulturbegriffs.)

27. For a study of the themes related to the notion of intercultural German Studies see Alois Wierlacher, "Internationalität und Interkulturalität: Der kulturelle Pluralismus als Herausforderung der Literaturwissenschaft: Zur Theorie interkultureller Germanistik," in *Wie international ist die Literaturwissenschaft?* ed. Lutz Danneberg and Friedrich Vollhardt (Stuttgart and Weimar: Metzler, 1996), 550–90.

28. On this subject see Frank Trommler, "Introduction," in *Germanistik in den USA: Neue Entwicklugen und Methoden,* ed. Frank Trommler (Opladen: Westdeutscher Verlag, 1989), 7–43.

29. Peter Uwe Hohendahl, "Germanistik in den Vereinigten Staaten: Eine Disziplin im Umbruch," *Zeitschrift für Germanistik,* new series, 6: 3 (1996): 527–35; citation on 529.

30. See David Bathrick, "Cultural Studies im Lichte der Massenmedien," in *Zeitschrift für Germanistik,* new series, 6: 3 (1996): 536–44.

31. From this perspective an exemplary work is Robert Bledsoe et al., eds., *Rethinking Germanistik: Canon and Culture* (New York: Peter Lang, 1991).

32. See Arlene A. Teraoka, "Deutsche Kultur, Multikultur: Für eine Germanistik im multikulturellen Sinn," in *Zeitschrift für Germanistik,* new series, 6: 3 (1996): 545–60.

33. Böhme, "Die Literaturwissenschaft zwischen Editionsphilologie und Kulturwissenschaft," 43.

34. Böhme, "Die Literaturwissenschaft zwischen Editionsphilologie und Kulturwissenschaft," 46. (. . . so leistungsstark wie niemals zuvor.)

35. Ansel et al., "Hilfreich und gut: 7 Thesen zur wissenschaftlichen Qualifikation," in *Perspektiven der Germanistik,* ed. Bentfeld and Delabar, 195–207; quote on 195. (. . . überkommene Sozialisationsmuster.)

36. Ansel et al., "7 Thesen zur wissenschaftlichen Qualifikation," 196. (Die klassische Vorstellung vom Ordinarius, der in seiner Person die Rolle des Forschers, Lehrers und Wissenschaftsverwalters/Managers vereinigt, wird im Sinne einer Generalkompetenz aufrechterhalten, obwohl längst eine Arbeitsteilung eingesetzt hat. Die Differenzierung der Tätigkeitsbereiche verlangt ein neues Berufs- und Qualifikationsbild.)

37. Brenner, "Habilitation als Sozialisation," 352, n. 73.

38. See the definition in Bourdieu, *Homo Academicus,* 94.

39. Ansel et al., "7 Thesen zur wissenschaftliche Qualifikation," 200. (Zudem verhindert das derzeitige Verfahren der Nachwuchsrekrutierung eher Innovationen, als daß es sie fördert, da jahr(zehnt)elange Abhängigkeitsverhältnisse unter z. T. enormer Arbeitsbelastung (als Assistent = Beisteher, Helfer überlasteter Professoren) und Zeitdruck einen Akademikertypus begünstigen, der ohne Umwege und mit geringem Risiko Karriere macht, der fleißig und kenntnisreich vor allem den Betrieb aufrechterhält, jedoch kaum durch neue produktive Problemstellungen und aufregende Erkenntnisse auffällt.)

40. Brenner, "Habilitation als Sozialisation," 344. (Hier liegt aber auch schon die Grenze des wissenschaftlichen Ertrags der Habilitation: Sie führt fort, was im Fach schon angelegt ist; in aller Regel gehen innovative Impulse von ihr nicht aus. Die Habilitation als Verfahren ist so konzipiert, daß sie zur personellen wie sachlichen Konsolidierung etablierter Forschung beiträgt; die Förderung von Originalität und Innovation gehört nicht zu ihren Aufgaben. Sie ist vielmehr Instrument der Integration von Wissenschaftlern durch Internalisierung von Verhaltensformen. Zugleich dienen sie der Stabilisierung einer Disziplin durch Fortschreibung von methodischen Konventionen anhand von in der Regel neuen Materialien. Der Verzicht auf Originalität freilich ist kein Versagen der Institution Habilitation, sondern ihr Ziel.)

41. Hans Werner Prahl, "Gesellschaftliche Funktionen von akademischen Abschlußprüfungen und Graden," dissertation, University of Kiel, 1977, 462. (. . . Anpassung, Konfliktvermeidung, Verzicht auf Aggressivität, Anerkennung der Autorität, Pünktlichkeit, Anerkennung vorgegebener Spielregeln.)

42. Bourdieu notes that the term *Doktorvater,* used to designate the supervisor, is an indication of the relation established between professor and pupil. Bourdieu, *Homo Academicus,* 88.

43. Ansel et al., "7 Thesen zur wissenschaftlichen Qualifikation," 201. (Die bisherige Privilegierung des Qualifikationweges über die Habilitation ist von der Wissenschaftsentwicklung überholt und trägt den verschiedenen Begabungen und Erfordernissen nicht Rechnung.) Page numbers of this work will henceforth be included parenthetically in the text, original language in the notes.

44. (. . . Habilitation und Berufung.)

45. (. . . U-Boote.)

46. (. . . Evaluierung.)

47. (. . . Kriterienkatalog.)

Index

While undoubtedly a useful appendage for such a work as the present one, a final bibliography would have been of inordinate length. To obviate its lack, included in the index, along with the key concepts and main authors discussed in the text, are the names of all critics mentioned in the notes, providing references for the first mention of each of their works (unless previously discussed or referred to in the text). The works discussed are indexed under the author's name. All titles are in German, excepting the few cases where standard English translations exist.

PIER CARLO BONTEMPELLI is associate professor of German Studies at the University of Cassino, Italy. He is the author of *La Germania Federale* and several essays on nineteenth- and twentieth-century German culture.

GABRIELE POOLE teaches English language at the University of Cassino, Italy. He has published essays on English and American poetry and theater, and he works regularly as a translator.